D1207168

THE HANK WILLIAMS READER

Readers on American Musicians
Scott DeVeaux, Series Editor

The Hank Williams Reader

Edited by Patrick Huber, Steve Goodson,
and David M. Anderson

OXFORD
UNIVERSITY PRESS

OXFORD
UNIVERSITY PRESS

Oxford University Press is a department of the
University of Oxford. It furthers the University's objective
of excellence in research, scholarship, and education
by publishing worldwide.

Oxford   New York
Auckland   Cape Town   Dar es Salaam   Hong Kong   Karachi
Kuala Lumpur   Madrid   Melbourne   Mexico City   Nairobi
New Delhi   Shanghai   Taipei   Toronto

With offices in
Argentina   Austria   Brazil   Chile   Czech Republic   France   Greece
Guatemala   Hungary   Italy   Japan   Poland   Portugal   Singapore
South Korea   Switzerland   Thailand   Turkey   Ukraine   Vietnam

Oxford is a registered trademark of Oxford University Press in the UK and
certain other countries.

Published in the United States of America by
Oxford University Press
198 Madison Avenue, New York, NY 10016

© Oxford University Press 2014

All rights reserved. No part of this publication may be reproduced,
stored in a retrieval system, or transmitted, in any form or by any means,
without the prior permission in writing of Oxford University Press,
or as expressly permitted by law, by license, or under terms agreed with
the appropriate reproduction rights organization. Inquiries concerning
reproduction outside the scope of the above should be sent to the
Rights Department, Oxford University Press, at the address above.

You must not circulate this work in any other form,
and you must impose this same condition on any acquirer.

Library of Congress Cataloging-in-Publication Data
The Hank Williams reader / edited by Patrick Huber,
Steve Goodson, and David M. Anderson.
pages   cm
Includes bibliographical references and index.
ISBN 978-0-19-974319-3 (hardcover : alk. paper)
1. Williams, Hank, 1923–1953—Criticism and interpretation.
2. Country music—History and criticism.
3. Country musicians—United States.
I. Huber, Patrick.   II. Goodson, Steve.
III. Anderson, David M. (David Myrwin)
ML420.W55H36   2014
782.421642092—dc23   2013018074

9 8 7 6 5 4 3 2 1
Printed in the United States of America
on acid-free paper

For Katie, Genevieve, and William,
whose love and many sacrifices made this book possible

—PH

In memory of my father, Howard Goodson (1927–2003),
who saw him perform, stood outside at the funeral, and introduced me
to the music

—SG

For my dear friend and teacher, Jay Coughtry,
thank you for changing my life

—DMA

Contents

PART V

*Scenes from the Lost Highway: Shedding Light on the Dark Side
(1975–1984)* 165

PART VI

*"Gone But Not Forgotten Blues": Entering the American Mainstream
(1985–1994)* 205

PART VII

Our Hank Williams: Becoming an American Icon (1995–2013) 241

A Note about Editorial Policies

The Hank Williams Reader compiles selected writings that originally appeared in a diverse array of sources over the course of more than sixty years. In transcribing and editing these pieces, we have attempted to balance the practices of historical scholarship with the demands of general accessibility. In cases of obvious typographical errors and occasional minor misspellings, punctuation errors, and grammatical mistakes, we have corrected them without comment. We have, however, retained meaningful misspellings (such as "Grand Old Opry" or those of persons' names) and incorrect song titles, as well as idiosyncratic spellings, grammar, and capitalization, in order to convey something of the character and quality of the original work. We have inserted the correct spelling of names in brackets following their initial appearance within a selection, the two exceptions being Lillie Williams's first name, which is sometimes alternatively spelled "Lilly," and Rufus Payne's nickname, which is usually rendered as "Tee-Tot" but has been spelled in various ways. Readers should be aware that although most of the original pieces enclosed song titles within quotation marks, others presented them in italics or in all capital letters, and, in these cases, we have retained the original formatting. Likewise, we have reprinted the titles of books, magazines, newspapers, and radio programs as they appeared in the original sources. Occasionally, in order to improve clarity, we have inserted emendations in brackets, but we have limited our use of the intrusive "[sic]" to only the most substantive factual errors, misspellings, and grammatical mistakes.

Many of the selections, particularly the earliest ones, contain factual errors, and we have attempted to point out the most significant of these inaccuracies, but usually only at the first appearance of such an error in this anthology. Readers should also bear in mind that the sheer number of errors and questionable historical claims has prevented us from addressing all of them, but we trust that our introductions and headnotes will provide readers with the information they need to evaluate the documents. Annotations, whether to note factual errors or identify unfamiliar persons and terms, are indicated with symbols and can be found in the footnotes at the bottom of the page. Where chapter endnotes appear, they represent the work of the author(s) of the selection and are indicated by Arabic numerals. Finally, in the interest of brevity and to eliminate repetitive material, we have abridged many of the longer articles, indicating our editorial omissions with the use of bracketed ellipses ([...]). All other ellipses appear in the original sources.

THE HANK WILLIAMS READER

Studio portrait of Hank Williams, ca. 1948. Courtesy of the Alabama Department of Archives and History, Montgomery, Alabama.

Introduction

For all we seem to know about Hank, we know very little. He left almost no inter-
views—everything that he said that was reported would barely fill a page. There's
very little footage of him, maybe 20 or 30 minutes total. It became very difficult to
separate Hank from the myth. In a sense, Hank became a blank screen onto which
people projected their vision of him. In some way, he is unknowable; he said so little,
except in his songs.

—Colin Escott, quoted in the *Washington Post*, 1999

In the predawn hours of New Year's Day 1953, country music star Hank
Williams, numbed by a lethal combination of alcohol and narcotics, died in
the backseat of his chauffeured Cadillac en route to a scheduled performance
in Canton, Ohio. Over the next few weeks, the newspapers in his adopted
hometowns of Montgomery, Alabama, and Nashville, Tennessee, devoted considerable space to his death and funeral, and featured retrospectives of his life
and career. The *New York Times*, in contrast, marked his passing with only a
brief, mistake-marred Associated Press obituary headlined "'King of Hillbillies' Dies in Sleep in Auto." "The 29-year-old one-time shoe shine boy [and]
composer of 'Jambalaya,'" the newspaper reported in its January 2, page-four
story, " . . . sang doleful mountain ballads in a nasal voice, accompanying himself on a guitar, which he began playing at the age of 6 years." It also noted that
Williams's recording of "Lovesick Blues"—misidentified as one of his original
compositions—"was said to have sold more than a million copies" and mentioned a handful of his other hit songs. Over the next nine days, the *Times* ran
three follow-up stories, each of them equally cursory and buried progressively
deeper within the newspaper: a January 5 article titled "20,000 at Williams
Rites" commented on the throngs of mourners who attended the singer's funeral in Montgomery, while two other items, one on January 3, "Singer's Death
Still Mystery," and the other on January 11, "Williams Died of Heart Ail-
ment," reported the progress and then the official findings of the coroner's

jury investigating his untimely death. With these four articles, together totaling fewer than four hundred words, the New York Times opened, and presumably closed, its coverage of Hank Williams.

Forty-five years later, the November 8, 1998, Sunday edition of the New York Times featured a lengthy essay about Williams, titled "Still Standing Tall over Country," by music critic Tom Piazza. In his nearly two-thousand-word review of Mercury Records' new boxed set The Complete Hank Williams, Piazza extolled the now-legendary singer-songwriter as a decisive figure in the development of twentieth-century American music. "If there has been a gravitational center to country music since World War II," Piazza began, "Hank Williams occupies it. As a performer he had few peers; as a songwriter he had none." Piazza asserted that "it is impossible to understand contemporary country music, or popular music for that matter, without addressing Hank Williams' legacy." Williams's influence far transcended his own genre, Piazza argued, citing as an example the artist's "almost universal appeal among rock-and-rollers." "As Bob Dylan did for the folk music world just over a decade later," he concluded, "Williams introduced a new, edgy element, a different attitude that…made him matter, and endure, beyond many of his contemporaries."

Clearly, a great deal had changed in four-and-a-half decades. "Hillbilly" music had become "country" music, now an acceptable topic of respectful analysis in the pages of the nation's leading newspaper. Indeed, an entire cottage industry, encompassing magazines, newspapers, books, radio, television, and the Internet, had developed, devoted to the serious discussion and evaluation of all aspects of American popular culture, with one result being that Hank Williams, who in 1953 had been something of a puzzling footnote for the New York Times, now ranked as a seminal figure in twentieth-century American music. In this new cultural context, the Times understandably paid far more attention to the release of The Complete Hank Williams than it had to the artist's shockingly sudden death nearly half a century earlier.

The ascension of Hank Williams to the status of an American icon forms the principal subject of this book. The story of this cultural transfiguration ranges far beyond the pages of the New York Times, however, and reflects broader changes that have occurred in American culture since World War II. Williams's death at the age of twenty-nine seemed, at the time, a sad ending to a poignant but largely regional and class-bound saga of rags-to-riches success and anguished self-destruction. As it would turn out, his demise was only the beginning of an equally gripping story, as the succeeding decades saw him evolve from a popular hillbilly singer and songwriter into a celebrated American legend. Over the years, dozens of his songs have been recorded by an impressive roster of artists from across the popular music spectrum, including Louis

Armstrong, Dean Martin, Ray Charles, James Brown, Bob Dylan, the Grateful Dead, Elvis Presley, the Carpenters, the Red Hot Chili Peppers, and Norah Jones. Today, Hank Williams is widely considered to be the greatest singer and songwriter in the history of country music, and his preeminence has been officially sanctioned by the nation's cultural authorities, ranging from the U.S. Postal Service to the Smithsonian Institution to the Pulitzer Prize Board.

Recognition from such institutions would have been unimaginable during Williams's lifetime, but even then there was no denying his accomplishments. Although his recording career spanned a mere six years, during his lifetime he placed thirty singles on the *Billboard* Top Ten country-and-western charts, seven of which reached No. 1; following his death, seven more of his records reached the Top Ten, one as recently as 1989 ("There's a Tear in My Beer," his electronically enhanced "duet" with his son, Hank Williams, Jr.). Within the songwriting field, Williams's rare gift for expressing complicated emotions in plainspoken language earned him acclaim during his lifetime as the "Hillbilly Shakespeare," or, in more contemporaneous comparisons, the "Irving Berlin of the straw stack" and the "Hillbilly Hammerstein." In the early 1950s, he broke through the wall that separated country music from the nation's musical mainstream when Tony Bennett, Rosemary Clooney, and numerous other vocalists climbed the popular music charts with "cover" versions of his compositions. An electrifying stage performer, Williams toured throughout the United States and Canada, played military bases in Germany and Austria, and made network television appearances on *The Perry Como Show* and *The Kate Smith Evening Hour.*

Still, Williams was not the only country music star of his day. Nor, despite all his extraordinary singing and songwriting skills, was he necessarily the nation's most popular country act. Eddy Arnold and Hank Snow, for instance, consistently outpolled him in *Country Song Roundup*'s national surveys of its readers' favorite country singers. Arnold also sold more records than Williams between 1949 and 1952, while Snow, Ernest Tubb, Red Foley, and Lefty Frizzell sold as least as many. And by mid-1952, although Williams's singles continued to dominate the country-and-western charts, his life outside the recording studio was careening out of control, as his chronic drunkenness, abuse of prescription drugs, and increasingly erratic behavior led to his August firing from country music's premier radio program, WSM's *Grand Ole Opry*, and to frequent stays in hospitals and sanitariums.

In the months that followed his dismissal from the *Opry*, Williams's personal decline continued. In October, he married his second wife, Billie Jean (Jones) Eshliman, following a whirlwind courtship and then relocated to her hometown of Bossier City, Louisiana. He made—but sometimes missed—

scheduled appearances in nearby Shreveport on KWKH's *Louisiana Hayride*, the second-tier radio barn-dance program that had launched him to stardom three years earlier. As his physical and mental health deteriorated, bookings, at least in larger venues, became difficult to attain. At the time, it might have been easy to dismiss Williams as a soon-to-be has-been intent on wrecking his own dazzling career. Nevertheless, as 1952 came to an end, Williams remained a major hillbilly star with a remarkable string of hit records and an impressive catalog of songs to his credit. While New Year's Day brought a definitive end to his melancholy life and tumultuous career, his legacy remained uncertain. Would he be remembered in the months and years that followed, or would he, like so many one-time celebrities, fade into obscurity?

A preliminary answer to this question came just days later in Montgomery, where as a teenager Williams had begun his professional career. There, his sudden death triggered a spectacular outpouring of public grief on an unprecedented scale. "Reporters answering telephone queries concerning Williams's death," noted the *Montgomery Advertiser* on January 2, 1953, "said many of the callers cried when informed that the reports were true." According to the *Advertiser*, the Williams family received some fifteen thousand sympathy cards and letters from all over the United States in the week after his death. An estimated 15,000 to 20,000 mourners attended his funeral service on January 4 at the Montgomery City Auditorium, and in the days that followed his burial in Oakwood Cemetery Annex, thousands more visited his gravesite to pay their last respects. "Never in the history of this town," declared an *Advertiser* editorial, "have so many thronged the funeral of a citizen as they did in the case of Hank Williams. Bankers, jurists, physicians, writers, governors and philanthropists have been returned unto dust in Montgomery, but the coffin of none was followed as was that of the dead singer."

Equally dramatic was the immediate surge in sales of Williams's records and song folios. His label, MGM Records, kept its pressing plant working overtime to meet the overwhelming demand for his discs, and his publisher, Acuff-Rose, reported that by January 24 sales of his two song collections had increased sevenfold. "Within four months of his death," reported *Variety* magazine in April 1953, "Hank Williams has already assumed the mantle of an immortal to his hillbilly colleagues and fans.... Williams, in fact, is enjoying greater popularity dead than alive." By the close of 1953, Williams had racked up four posthumous No. 1 country hits, including the classics "Kaw-Liga" and "Your Cheatin' Heart," and at least twenty tribute songs to the late singer had blared from the nation's radios and jukeboxes.

Few observers during Williams's lifetime would have questioned his popularity, but only with his death and funeral did it become strikingly clear that there had been something different, something truly phenomenal, about his stardom. His magnetic public persona, emotionally vulnerable lyrics, and captivating performing and singing styles inspired a level of fan devotion enjoyed by few other country artists, even those whose records often outsold his. "We have listened to Hank Williams on disc jockey shows so often that we felt he was a friend of ours; someone we had known for a long time," wrote a Wisconsin woman to the *Montgomery Advertiser* in the days after his death. Likewise, a grieving Alabama fan explained, "Those of us who like and enjoy hillbilly-folk music...have lost a great friend....So many of his songs so aptly expressed the loneliness, disappointment and hardship so many of us at one time endure." Like all great popular artists, Williams provided his fans with a powerful means of personal and collective identification, and his success seemed to validate their emotional investment in his music. They loved and revered him perhaps even more after he was gone—a fact that startled commentators who knew little about Williams's music and could never have anticipated the mass public anguish engendered by his passing.

Throughout his career, Williams had repeatedly surprised those who underestimated or dismissed him. He continued to confound skeptics from the grave. Caught completely off guard by the tremendous demand for his records and song folios, New York and Nashville music executives rushed to capitalize on their unexpected windfall. The industry's promotional machinery shifted into overdrive, beginning the process of transforming the now-safely dead hillbilly singer from, as sociologist Richard A. Peterson has written, a "fading earthly star" into an "icon of country music," the "model of the authentic country music entertainer."

Williams's enhanced posthumous reputation was the result of more than music industry machinations, however. In the years following his death, a handful of other country music stars, including Patsy Cline, Jim Reeves, and Johnny Horton, also died relatively young, under equally tragic circumstances, and at the peak of their commercial success. But none of them has attracted the sustained fascination or achieved the cultural status that Williams has attained. Williams's extraordinary musical achievements, his remarkable bond with his fans, his turbulent personal life, and his tragic and still-mysterious death combined to make him a uniquely compelling figure.

Williams has lent himself to an almost endless variety of interpretations. As his sister, Irene Williams Smith, once observed, he was "many things to many people," and so, for more than sixty years now, an ever-lengthening parade of writers—including such notables as David Halberstam, Garrison Keillor, Lee Smith, Ralph J. Gleason, Greil Marcus, Chet Flippo, Rick Bragg, Nick Tosches, Elizabeth Gilbert, and Nat Hentoff—have attempted to define and explain the man, the artist, and the legend. Yet, for all the literary attention he has received, Williams remains something of a paradox, familiar and accessible, yet at the same time indefinable and maddeningly elusive. The same artist who is celebrated by many observers as personifying "authentic" country music is heralded by others as an originator of rock 'n' roll. The man whom some liken to a lay preacher is hailed by others as the archetypal country "Outlaw." Scholars, for their part, have found in Williams and his music a revealing window onto larger historical issues: the cult of celebrity, the American Dream, the transformations of the modern South, the cultural dimensions of social class—the list goes on. Defined and redefined, he has been invested with all manner of competing and often conflicting meanings by different groups and individuals for varying purposes. But after all this time and all these efforts to capture the essence of the man and his music, much about Hank Williams remains interpretively up for grabs.

GOALS AND PURPOSES

The year 2013 marked the ninetieth anniversary of Hank Williams's birth and the sixtieth anniversary of his death, making it an excellent vantage point from which to survey the impressive body of literature that has been produced about him over the decades. The onetime "King of Hillbillies" has inspired more writing than all but a few American musical artists of the twentieth century. He has been the subject of at least fifteen biographies, more than seventeen hundred articles in newspapers, magazines, and scholarly journals, and scores of essays, encyclopedia entries, album reviews, liner notes, poems, plays, novels, and short stories. Yet only a small sampling of this vast and growing body of literature has ever been critically appraised. This anthology thus represents two important milestones: it is both the first reader and the first book-length historiographical study devoted exclusively to this internationally acclaimed figure of American popular music.

Obviously, no single anthology can compile all the worthy Williams-related writings or fully capture him and his meaning for American history and culture. Out of the nearly two thousand writings we identified, however, we have selected seventy-nine that we believe to be the most representative, revealing, insightful, well-crafted, or historically significant, ranging from those published as early as 1947 to those appearing as recently as 2011. Collectively, these selections provide a multidimensional portrait of Williams that is by turns compelling and clarifying, clouded and contradictory, much like the man himself. Moreover, in tracing the various literary representations of Williams, this anthology simultaneously traces broader changes in American culture, illuminating important social, intellectual, and commercial developments that have transpired since the end of World War II.

In selecting the documents for *The Hank Williams Reader*, we were guided by five main criteria. First, we wanted to offer examples of the principal interpretations of Hank Williams's life and legacy. As in the cases of other twentieth-century icons who died young, such as James Dean and Marilyn Monroe, the amount of writing about Williams that has appeared since his death far exceeds that published during his lifetime, and through this body of literature we can track chronologically the wide range of understandings that writers have advanced about him and his place in American popular culture. For convenience, we have labeled the most significant of these interpretations: the "Organization Man," "Populist Poet," "Tragic Hero," "Model Family Man," "Tabloid Celebrity," "Ordinary Guy," "Rock 'n' Roll Pioneer," "Original Outlaw," "Lay Preacher," and "American Icon."

Second, we wished to collect those early foundational writings about Williams, several of them hard-to-find and never before republished, that laid the groundwork for many of the published accounts that followed. Frequently, these pioneering pieces were the first to relate memorable anecdotes or make claims that later became standard elements of his biography. These early selections provide readers with a context for understanding and evaluating the choices that subsequent writers made when crafting their own portrayals of Williams's life.

Third, we wished to showcase a wide range of voices. The earliest writings about Williams, from the mid-1940s to the early 1950s, were produced chiefly by newspaper and music industry journalists. Over the ensuing decades, family members, friends and bandmates, music critics, biographers, industry insiders, musicians, and ordinary fans contributed their own portraits of Williams, while scholars came to embrace him as a legitimate focus of academic study and novelists, poets, playwrights, screenwriters, and songwriters found in him inspiration for their own work. By including selections from such a broad assortment of authors, we hope to underscore that with each passing decade the number and variety of writers drawn to Williams's life and music have expanded.

Fourth, we wanted to include writings that raise fundamental questions about the deeper meanings of Williams's life and work, as well as about his place within the broader context of American history and culture. Whether identifying him as an embodiment of postwar Nashville commercialism, a godfather of rock 'n' roll, a voice of the southern white working class, a humble exponent of Christian evangelicalism, or the personification of country music authenticity, numerous writers have conceived of him as representing momentous themes that transcend the narrow confines of country music or even music itself. Their approaches have produced some of the most insightful and thought-provoking writing about Williams. Finally, we sought out those pieces that merit recognition due to the extraordinary quality of their writing. Here pieces by David Halberstam, Rick Bragg, and Brian Alcorn, to name a few, stand out as particularly eloquent and well-crafted tributes to Williams's life.

ORGANIZATION

The Hank Williams Reader consists of seven parts. Each opens with a brief introduction that provides an overview of the selected writings, highlights their major themes, and situates them within both the broader historical setting and the Hank Williams literary canon. Within each part, the selections are, with only a few exceptions, organized chronologically, so that the reader can follow the unfolding development of Williams's career and his legacy. A brief headnote explains each selection's context and discusses its significance. Many of the writings collected in this anthology were created in dialogue with other accounts, and as much as is practicable, our headnotes include cross-references to selections with related interpretations.

Each of the seven parts of the anthology corresponds to a discrete historical period and reflects key interpretative shifts that occurred within the expanding body of Hank Williams literature. Covering the period between 1947 and 1953, Part I collects several of the earliest and most important writings published during his lifetime, the bulk of which consist of newspaper and trade journal articles. The authors took Williams seriously as a vital force in the booming postwar Nashville country music industry, and, in so doing, they established the first major interpretative theme in the Hank Williams canon, one that we term the "Organization Man," which depicts him as a consummate professional, a star in the country music field who had discovered a successful formula for manufacturing hit songs. Typically, such writers noted Williams's upward mobility ("Hillbilly Hits the Jackpot after Lean Years in Youth," reads a typical headline), his six-figure income, his accumulation of lavish material possessions, and his overall impact on American popular music (one writer dubbed him "The Prairie Sinatra")—elements that, when taken together, made him appear more like a suburban businessman than a honky-tonk singer. While these journalists readily acknowledged his remarkable commercial success, virtually none of them yet conceived of Williams as possessing any greater cultural significance.

Part II presents writings published in January and February 1953, in the immediate aftermath of Williams's death. These selections represent the first concerted attempt to assess the late star's larger contribution to American culture. The impassioned public reaction to his passing, the spectacle of his funeral, and his staggering posthumous record sales compelled newspaper editors and columnists and music industry journalists across the nation to come to grips with Williams's extraordinary appeal. Together, they developed a second interpretation in the Hank Williams literary canon, that of the "Populist Poet," which portrays him as a "voice of the common man" whose songs expressed the beliefs and values of his chiefly southern white working-class audience. Williams's death and funeral also prompted writing that introduced another new interpretation, that of the "Tragic Hero," which depicts him in darker, almost Shakespearian terms as an admirable but deeply flawed star who, despite great popularity and commercial success, never managed to overcome his personal demons. No country singer, not even Jimmie Rodgers, the so-called Father of Country Music, had ever been the subject of such widespread commentary. Yet at the time, there was still no guarantee that his memory would linger past the original shock of his sudden death or that he would attain anything approaching the lofty status he has since achieved.

Part III features selections originally published between 1953 and 1964 that helped establish Williams's legendary status and introduced three more enduring interpretations. The first, the "Model Family Man," portrays him as a dutiful son, faithful husband, and doting father, the epitome of an upright, pious, and decent southern gentleman. This sentimental, almost Victorian image of him originally emerged, not surprisingly, in the recollections of his own family members, most notably in his mother Lillie Stone's booklet, *Our Hank Williams, "The Drifting Cowboy," as Told by His Mother to Allen Rankin* (1953), the first published biography of the singer and one of his family's initial attempts to shape his posthumous image in deliberate ways. A second, equally romantic interpretation to emerge at this time, that of the "Lay Preacher," also first found expression in the writings of Williams's mother and particularly those of his older sister, Irene Williams Smith. A religious variant of the "Populist Poet," this particular portrayal establishes Williams as a devout evangelical Christian, a folk preacher who spread the Gospel through his music—an interpretation reinforced by the many sacred songs he wrote and recorded, as well as by the fourteen moralizing recitations he cut under the pseudonym "Luke the Drifter." In contrast, the final and most disturbing interpretation to appear during this period is one that we call the "Tabloid Celebrity," which casts Williams as a self-destructive hedonist. This dark portrait of Williams received its fullest treatment in a half-dozen or so articles published between the mid-1950s and the early 1960s in celebrity scandal sheets and men's adventure magazines. Although it is easy to dismiss such accounts as salacious rumormongering or outright fabrication, several of Williams's later biographers would accept as fact many of the pulp magazines' unsubstantiated accusations, and incorporate them wholesale into their books. This pivotal phase in the literature culminated with the 1964 release of MGM Studios' cinematic version of the late singer's life, *Your Cheatin' Heart*, which combined elements of all the existing major interpretations of Williams—both the positive and the negative—with decidedly mixed results.

Meanwhile, Nashville music insiders within the fledgling trade group the Country Music Association (CMA), came to embrace Williams as a potent symbol in their campaign to shift their industry from the margins to the mainstream of American entertainment. Determined to combat pernicious stereotypes of country music as a crassly commercial and culturally backward genre, the CMA recast the music as a genuine American art form and positioned Williams—now depicted as a wholesome, country-boy composer of classic songs of "Americana"—as its most authentic practitioner. The CMA confirmed Williams's exalted status in 1961 by inducting him into its newly formed Country Music Hall of Fame as part of its inaugural class.

Part IV covers the important writings that appeared between 1965 and 1974 during a period of escalating interest in Hank Williams. During these years, two new interpretations emerged. One of these, the "Ordinary Guy," figured prominently in published recollections of family members, friends, and former bandmates, and highlighted the commonplace aspects of Williams's personality and everyday life, in marked contrast to the legendary aura that had begun to envelop him. At the same time that these writers were attesting to his ordinariness, seminal works appeared by the first group of journalists and academic scholars to view Williams as a subject worthy of serious intellectual analysis. In *Sing a Sad Song: The Life of Hank Williams* (1970), the first full-length interpretative biography of the country star, author Roger M. Williams (no relation) articulated this period's second new interpretation, that of the "American Icon," which would become perhaps the most popular and durable of all. Roger Williams advanced the notion that the late Alabama singer-songwriter was "one of the most remarkable figures in the history of American show business," and that, thanks to his enduring popularity and pronounced influence, his life and music would continue to "live on in a manner unparalleled in American popular culture."

Part V surveys writings published between 1975 and 1984, particularly those by a cohort of young music critics who, deeply influenced by the sixties counterculture, approached rock 'n' roll as serious art. These "new rock critics," determined to establish the genre's legitimacy in the history of American music, devoted considerable effort to tracing its genealogy. In attempting to pinpoint

Hank Williams's place within that lineage, they established a new interpretation in the canon, one that we term the "Rock 'n' Roll Pioneer," which celebrates him as a precursor—or sometimes even an exponent—of rock music. Interest in Williams among rock critics and fans heightened in 1978, when PolyGram, which had six years earlier acquired MGM Records, began releasing Williams's catalog, in its original form, in a series of attractively packaged albums and double-LP sets on the Polydor label. In addition, a variety of rock and country-rock artists recorded cover versions of Williams's songs during this period, enhancing his standing as an architect of rock 'n' roll and paving the way for his 1987 induction into the Rock and Roll Hall of Fame and Museum in its Early Influence category.

During the 1970s, Hank Williams also proved a powerful inspiration for dissident singer-songwriters such as Waylon Jennings and Kris Kristofferson, who chafed under corporate Nashville's domination of the country music industry. For these self-styled "Outlaws," Williams reigned as a model of artistic integrity, and his simple, heartfelt songs provided the measure of how much the stranglehold of the major record labels had corrupted contemporary country music. Equally important, these nonconformists also sought to emulate the late star's debauched life and what they viewed as his rebellion against entrenched Nashville music interests. Mirroring this musical trend was a new crop of music critics and journalists who recast the older "Tabloid Celebrity" version of Williams into Williams the "Original Outlaw," a defiant antihero who unabashedly consumed drugs and alcohol, resented the men and women who tried to control his life, and thumbed his nose at the Nashville country music establishment. Meanwhile, the "Lay Preacher" and the "Tragic Hero" interpretations—both of which had emerged in the weeks and months following Williams's death—achieved their fullest expressions in book-length biographies: *I Saw the Light: The Gospel Life of Hank Williams* (1977), by Al Bock, and *Hank Williams: Country Music's Tragic King* (1979), by Jay Caress.

Part VI offers selections published between 1985 and 1994, a decade that witnessed the first sustained wave of scholarly writings about Hank Williams. The growing interest in the now-legendary country star among historians and cultural studies scholars reflected larger academic trends, including the broadening of humanities disciplines and the emergence of new methods and approaches, particularly in the fields of American Studies and the "new" social history, both of which used the analysis of popular culture to probe the consciousness and values of ordinary Americans. Generally, these scholars rejected the "Original Outlaw" interpretation in favor of a more nuanced version of the earlier "Populist Poet" reading, depicting Williams as a representative figure whose life and music embodied the regional and class experiences shared by his core audience of white working-class southerners. This period in the literature concluded with the publication of Colin Escott's critically acclaimed *Hank Williams: The Biography* (1994), written with the assistance of George Merritt and William MacEwen. Escott's exhaustive research supported his self-described goal of reclaiming "the real Hank Williams from the myth," and his measured, documentary-style narrative produced what critics have hailed as the "definitive" biography, one that helped elevate Williams into the pantheon of American musical giants.

Part VII contains selected writings from the latest phase of the literature, which marks the final ascension of Hank Williams to iconic status. During the period between 1995 and 2013, the revered country legend garnered significant attention from U.S. cultural institutions, the national media, and the music industry that solidified his position as one of the nation's cultural treasures. In addition to the 1998 release of Mercury Records' meticulously annotated ten-CD boxed set *The Complete Hank Williams*, he was the subject of a 2001 coffee-table book of photographs and documents, *Hank Williams: Snapshots from the Lost Highway*, and a 2004 PBS American Masters series documentary, *Hank Williams: Honky Tonk Blues*. Of all the accolades Williams received, however, perhaps none was more prestigious than the posthumous 2010 Special Citation that the Pulitzer Prize Board awarded him for lifetime achievement. Confident that his status as a national icon was beyond question, commentators and critics celebrated, or routinely referred to, Williams as a transcendent cultural figure, often equating him with the qualities of sincerity, authenticity, and artistic integrity, and citing him as a founding father of both rock 'n' roll and the American "roots" music now grouped under the catch-all term "Americana." Today, Hank Williams belongs in the company of only a select handful of immortals in the history of American popular music.

CODA

Hank Williams was a remarkably complex man, and in spite of all that has been written about him, as Colin Escott has remarked, in many ways he remains "unknowable." As we trust this anthology shows, a tremendous amount of insightful and stimulating writing has appeared since those ever-receding days when Williams ruled auditorium stages, record charts, and radio airwaves. As we assembled this reader, we struggled to narrow our selections to the ones included here. The original manuscript, in fact, was well over twice the length of this book. However, space limitations, along with copyright restrictions, prevented us from including literally dozens of other worthwhile pieces. But we are confident that from the rich lode of available books, articles, and other writings we have selected the most significant, representative, and essential pieces available to us. And there is cause for excitement in the knowledge that so much about Hank Williams remains to be learned and shared. We hope that this book will provide a useful resource for those committed to further examination of this hauntingly enigmatic American icon.

Cover of *Pathfinder* magazine, June 4, 1952. Authors' collection.

Part I

~~~~~~

"King of the Hillbillies"
Chronicling Hank Williams During His Lifetime (1947–1953)

The first published writings about Hank Williams, which traced his rise from modest acclaim as a local radio and stage performer to national success as a recording artist, radio entertainer, and songwriter, appeared during a period of significant change in the country music industry. During the mid-1930s, when the teenaged Williams first entered the business in Montgomery, Alabama, the still-embryonic "hillbilly" music industry was far from the multibillion-dollar international enterprise it is today. Professional singers and musicians earned their livelihood from radio performances and personal appearances rather than from phonograph records, which typically yielded little income for the artists. The onset of the Great Depression had devastated the nation's recording industry, and the market for hillbilly records was particularly dismal. Although a handful of top hillbilly acts made records that sold relatively well, and a few of them, particularly "singing cowboys" such as Gene Autry and Roy Rogers, appeared in Hollywood films and even became national celebrities, most performers operated within a limited geographical area, with little press attention beyond local newspapers. With thousands of professional and semiprofessional hillbilly singers and musicians toiling throughout much of the United States, national stardom in this field was exceedingly rare.

During World War II, however, bolstered by southern working-class migrations to Midwest and West Coast cities, hillbilly music soared to unprecedented popularity. Professional opportunities for singers and musicians multiplied, and record production expanded to accommodate rising demand from fans, jukebox owners, and, eventually, disc jockeys. Following the war, what was increasingly known as "folk" or "country-and-western" music flourished as it entered what many historians have described as a "Golden Era" of commercial and creative success.

By the mid-1940s, when Hank Williams committed himself to a career in country music, Nashville, Tennessee, home to both WSM's *Grand Ole Opry* and the Acuff-Rose publishing house, was just emerging as the national center for the industry. There, the country music business soon came to feature an interlocking system that combined radio programs, stage shows, phonograph records, print media, and, eventually, television shows, all of which dramatically increased the music's exposure and profitability. As several biographers have stressed, Williams arrived on the scene at a fortuitous time when the expanded popularity and enhanced marketing of country music could facilitate his rapid rise from the bottom rungs of the business to its highest echelon.

The first significant writings about Williams, which date to 1947 and 1948, appeared in the newspapers published in his hometown of Montgomery, Alabama, where he gained local fame as a radio and stage performer. Within a few years, though, his mounting success at the regional and national levels led to articles in larger newspapers, both within and outside of his native South, as well as in nationally circulated country music fan magazines (such as *Country Song Roundup* and *National Hillbilly News*) and major entertainment trade publications (such as *Billboard* and *Cash Box*). Such articles tended to be short, insubstantial puff pieces containing only the barest of biographical details, and their dominant theme was almost invariably his commercial achievements. Journalists routinely stressed Williams's "rags-to-riches" success story and frequently cited his views on topics such as his songwriting method, the postwar boom in hillbilly music, and his record-marketing strategies. In essence, contemporary writers depicted him as what we term the "Organization Man," a dedicated and knowledgeable expert in his chosen field. Although many writers and fans later came to consider Williams principally a creative artist who remained above crassly commercial considerations, in not one article published during his lifetime is there any mention of his artistic ambitions. Rather, he is presented, and he presents himself, as a consummate professional entertainer who measured success entirely in terms of chart standings and record sales. Almost no one yet wrote of him as anything more than a successful radio and recording artist and songwriter. Now-familiar interpretations of Williams—as the folksy populist poet or the tortured, self-destructive outlaw—emerged later, after he had drawn his last breath.

| I |

William E. Cleghorn: Hank Williams Rides on Down Trail of National Popularity on Air Records

This article represents the first feature story on Hank Williams to appear in a Montgomery, Alabama, newspaper and marks the beginning of his ascent from local radio and stage personality to nationally known recording artist. Just two years earlier, the aspiring singer-songwriter had been largely unknown outside of south Alabama. Banned in February 1945 from Montgomery's flagship radio station, the 5,000-watt WSFA, for drunkenness and unreliability, he lived at his mother's boardinghouse and played small-time engagements at schoolhouses, theaters, and dance halls, accompanied by his wife Audrey and his band, the Drifting Cowboys. But Williams's fortunes turned in January 1946 when WSFA rehired him and he began to attract a devoted radio following. Nine months later, in the most critical move of his career, he signed a songwriting contract with Acuff-Rose, the Nashville music publishing firm headed by former Tin Pan Alley songwriter Fred Rose, who would serve as Williams's mentor, producer, and, at times, de facto manager. Rose subsequently secured recording contracts for Williams, first with the small, New York–based Sterling Records, which released the singer's first four records in early 1947, and then, in March of that year, with a major label, MGM Records, for whom he recorded for the remainder of his career.

Despite Williams's growing popularity, it took a hit record, "Move It On Over," for him to garner a profile in a local newspaper, and even then, it appeared not in the city's leading paper, the *Montgomery Advertiser*, but in its upstart competitor,

SOURCE   William E. Cleghorn, "Hank Williams Rides on Down Trail of National Popularity on Air Records," *Montgomery Examiner*, August 21, 1947.

the *Montgomery Examiner*. In what would become typical of the press depictions of Williams during his lifetime, reporter William E. Cleghorn (1919–1968) portrays him as a carefree but upwardly mobile professional entertainer with a blissful family life. In the process, though, he makes one repeated mistake. Despite the fact that "Move It On Over" had recently climbed to No. 4 on *Billboard*'s hillbilly record charts, Cleghorn consistently refers to the song as "Move It Over."

Local scenes and local people are featured in many songs written by Hank Williams, Montgomery's happy, roving cowboy.

"Move It Over," [the] latest hit by Hank and his Drifting Cowboys, is now running fourth among the nation's most played juke box folk records, according to The Billboard.

Hank, popular music artist and long time favorite in his home town, has been airing cowboy ballads, love songs, plaintive hill ditties and sacred hymns over Montgomery radio stations since 1936.

The spur-jangling Sinatra of the Western ballad has written 23 songs published by Acuff and Rose, Nashville, but he never hit the jack pot until "Move It Over" moved him up.

That M.-G.-M. platter broke the 100,000 mark in less than two months.

Based on a couple's disagreement, the song winds its way through fusses and fights with the old man ending up in the doghouse.

WAITS FOR INSPIRATION

"Where the inspiration for that song came from, I couldn't say," Hank admitted. It wasn't his own married life. Mr. and Mrs. Hank Williams lead a model domestic life.

"Miss Audrey," his wife, is the featured vocalist with the band.

Hank taught her how to sing after their marriage. "Miss Audrey" is a native of Pike County [Alabama].

"I have been living in Montgomery so long that I call it home. We are building our home here," he said.

Large radio stations in other sections of the country have gone after Hank now that his popularity has become nation-wide, but he likes it here at WSFA and expects to stay.

GOOD MANAGER

Hank mentioned Bill Hamm, WSFA commercial manager, as one of his closest friends and one man who has helped him a great deal.

The Decca Company made Hank an offer recently, but he is loyal to M.-G.-M. and the Acuff-Rose publishing house.

Hank says that Roy Acuff, the Tennessee Troubadour, and Fred Rose, song writer, have done much for him. Rose is Hank's personal recording manager.

Home town folk are plugging Hank for the movies. They claim he would be a natural for Western shows. Slim, quiet and nice looking, he has a large following among the younger set in these parts.

WHITE SOMBRERO

Always seen with a white sombrero and with a white scarf knotted at the throat, Hank speaks and looks the part of a happy, roving cowboy.

Another big hit by Hank is "Pan American," written about the L&N train that leaves Montgomery each day headed for New Orleans. [...]

RELIGIOUS SONGS

Two of Hank's religious songs on records are "When Wealth Won't Save Your Soul" and "When God Comes and Gathers His Jewels."

Singing in a lusty backwoods style, with the fiddlers and guitars of his Drifting Cowboys, Hank sings his songs in spirited tempo.

Hank's next record release will be "Fly Trouble."

Hank writes all kinds of songs, but he says the juke songs go best. A juke song is—well, "Move It Over" is a juke song.

Hank, deeply religious himself, likes hymns and sings at least one on his daily 4 p.m. program.

TAKES 30 MINUTES

When it comes to writing songs, Hank whips them out in about 30 minutes if the idea is good. And if the idea is not good, Hank soon knows and discards it.

As for a song, Hank says you will never know how it will go until it has been released for about three months.

Hank and the Drifting Cowboys spend part of their week playing at school houses, dances, theaters, and shows.

The well-known theme song of the Cowboys, "Happy Roving Cowboy," is an indication of their cheerful nature.

| 2 |

Reverend A. S. Turnipseed: Pulpit Echoes

The only writer known to speculate about Hank Williams's broader cultural significance during the singer's brief lifetime was the Reverend Andrew Spencer Turnipseed, Sr. (1911–2002), an Alabama-born minister who presided over Montgomery's Dexter Avenue Methodist Church and wrote a regular column for the *Montgomery Examiner*. At the time he witnessed Williams's midnight concert in December 1947, Turnipseed and the city's other white liberals anticipated a bright future, buoyed by populist Democrat James E. "Big Jim" Folsom's victory in Alabama's 1946 gubernatorial election. Gazing out at Williams's audience of "common people," Turnipseed saw them as harbingers of modernization and progressive change. By suggesting that Williams was somehow representative of the masses of ordinary residents of his native city and state, Turnipseed anticipates an important theme in later writings that cast the hillbilly star as a "Populist Poet" who embodied and expressed the values of white working-class southerners.

The other night we saw and heard Hank Williams and The Drifting Cowboys. It was a midnight show but the bottom floor of the large auditorium was filled. Some people were in the balcony.

The people were of all ages with young people in the majority. None of them were dressed as to indicate any affluence. They were the common people.

The crowd was surprising in its restraint. Any preacher who has preached in the rural sections of the white counties of Alabama has observed the same restraint even when highly emotional preaching was going on. A few times, however, the crowd "broke over" and began to clap in time with the music. This was very much like the shouting that sometimes "breaks out" in the rural white church services.

About half the time of the program was devoted to "corny" jokes and "horse play." The people responded to all of this. The greatest response came when the comedian in the troupe said that something was "as good as snuff."

SOURCE   Rev. A. S. Turnipseed, "Pulpit Echoes," *Montgomery Examiner*, December 11, 1947.

MUSIC TOLD A STORY

The music was revealing. One religious number was played which pictured the joys of heaven. In some country revivals by actual count we have found that 95 percent of the songs sung in the services dealt with Heaven.

With real charm Hank introduced his numbers. When he played "Move It On Over" the reserve of the audience was completely broken. Apparently everybody there at one time or another had been in the "dog house." The number second in importance was "The Pan-American." In this song Montgomery was mentioned. Apparently everybody there knew the fascination of trains.

Hank Williams is not only a hillbilly musician—he is a phenomenon. In Tennessee it is Roy Acuff. In Louisiana it is [Jimmie] "You Are My Sunshine" Davis (now Governor of Louisiana). [...]

This music is popular with the common people because it furnishes a good means of escape from the hard reality of their lives. Like any folk music its themes are love, sorrow, religion, work, etc.

HANK WILLIAMS COMING

The Hank Williams audience the other night is symbolic of changes taking place rapidly in Montgomery and Alabama. Not many years ago Montgomery was a typical black belt town. Today many Hank Williamses have moved into the city from the sandy land counties to the south of us and the hill counties to the north of us. The change in the culture of Montgomery is reflected in the political life. People no longer have to belong to ante-bellum families to be elected to the legislature or to the city commission.

Hank Williamses are moving into all of the towns of Alabama. They are finding work in mills and factories. They are being organized into labor unions. Their children are going to the public schools of the towns. [...]

All of these Hank Williamses in town and in the country got the "feel" of political power in the last governor's race. The South is changing. The Poll Tax[*] and the lack of re-appointment[†] cannot hold back this rising tide. As Hank Williams plays, Rome is burning.

~~~~~~

---

[*] A "tax," or fee, required to vote, one of a series of suffrage restrictions passed by southern state legislatures between the 1890s and 1900s, that were designed to both consolidate the political power of the dominant conservative white Democrats and effectively disenfranchise African American voters.

[†] Reapportionment of legislative districts. Turnipseed appears to be referring to liberals' efforts to ban certain provisions of political redistricting in Alabama and other states that granted rural areas disproportionately more representatives in state legislatures than urban areas. The U.S. Supreme Court's 1964 decision in *Reynolds v. Sims*, which originated in Jefferson County, Alabama, struck down this practice.

| 3 |

Allen Rankin: 'Cause Hank Is Moving In, Move It Over, Big Time

When this column appeared in Montgomery's leading newspaper, Hank Williams had reached a critical point in his career. After two years of professional success and relative domestic stability, he had resumed his heavy drinking, which increased tensions with his wife Audrey and led to the couple's first divorce in May 1948. Williams's career had stalled as well. He had failed to produce a successful follow-up to "Move It On Over," and a nationwide strike by the American Federation of Musicians had suspended all commercial recording activities. Meanwhile, music publisher Fred Rose, "fed up" with Williams's "foolishness," had written to instruct the singer not to contact him again until he was "ready to straighten out."

None of Williams's problems, however, are evident in this piece by *Montgomery Advertiser* columnist Allen Rankin (1917–1991), who befriended the young singer-songwriter and, over the next four and a half years, vigorously promoted his career. Significantly, Rankin's article marks the first appearance in print of Williams's nickname "Shakespeare" (later modified to "The Hillbilly Shakespeare") as well as the first published acknowledgement of the crucial role that African American street singer Rufus "Tee-Tot" Payne played in Williams's musical development.

In the months after this column appeared, Williams pulled himself together, reconciling with Audrey and reviving his career, thanks, in part, to the success of "Honky Tonkin' " and its follow-up, "I'm a Long Gone Daddy," both of which were Top Twenty hits. More important, in August 1948, Fred Rose, convinced that Williams was back on the straight and narrow, secured the singer a regular spot on Shreveport's *Louisiana Hayride*, where he would establish himself as a major hillbilly star.

"Honky Tonkin'" is the latest Hank Williams hit, recorded by M-G-M. If you haven't heard it yet it's because it just hit the juke boxes and music stands yesterday.

SOURCE   Allen Rankin, "Rankin File: 'Cause Hank Is Moving In, Move It Over, Big Time," *Montgomery Advertiser–Alabama Journal*, April 4, 1948. Reprinted courtesy of the *Montgomery Advertiser*.

If it's anything like Hank's other 46 published tunes, it will shower Hank with more new $100 bills than a tapped jackpot* showers nickels. That is to say it will loose more ready money in Hank's only-too-willing hands than most sober-minded drudges who don't go honkytonkin' can make in a year.

Especially will it do so if it turns out to be anything like Hank's "Move It On Over," his No. 1[†] hillbilly hit which already has sold more than 108,000 records.

Which is also to say that hillbilly Hank, who three times a day sings, chirps, brays, or moans bouncy ditties over Station WSFA to the whangings of his guitar, is not getting any poorer. With three cents a copy pouring in from his sheet music, plus two cents a record for each recording, plus another "half cent a side" for writing the things, he bids fair to become Montgomery's most famous and successful composer. "If things go right" this year he may pick up a neat $15,000 or $20,000[‡] in addition to the rather golden chicken feed he scratches for his three daily commercial programs on WSFA.

This is why the boys around the studio—even avowed haters of hillbilly—get quiet and reverent when Hank looks like he might be even beginning to think of having another song idea.

"Shhh," they say, "That's Shakespeare. It used to be hillbilly. Now it's Shakespeare!"

"FANS? THERE'S A MOB OF 'EM!"

Hank was 13 when in 1936 he walked into WSFA and said, quote: "I think I'm good enough to play and sing." Auditioners heard the slight, dark kid who lugged a battered guitar slung on his neck with a yellow string. "You'll do," they said when he finished. Hank has done.

As he puts it modestly at 26[§]: "I got the popularist daytime program on this station."

And that is as if Harry James[¶] were to say: "I got the hottest little trumpet." When Hank Williams chirrups and plunks, the studio is usually pushing with admirers, who yesterday included four very pretty young ladies, indeed, and one hotel bellboy, drawn up from the lobby.

"Fans?" says Hank. "There's a mob of 'em up here every mornin' and every afternoon! Some come from 50 miles! A lady from Opelika wrote me just this

---

* A slot machine.

† "Move It On Over" actually peaked at No. 4 on the nation's hillbilly record charts.

‡ In *Hank Williams: The Biography* (1994), Colin Escott estimates that Williams earned only one-tenth of this figure at this point in his career.

§ Williams was twenty-four-and-a-half years old at the time.

¶ Henry "Harry" James (1916–1983), celebrated trumpeter and band leader during the "Swing Era" of the 1930s and 1940s.

mornin'—Here, read it. She says: 'Say, Hank. How much do it cost to come up and hear you sing? If it don't cost too much, we may came up there.'"

Love letters are nothing to Hank. This week's Billboard Magazine views him strictly as a musician, describes one of his new records as "drone folk blues with spry fiddlin'"; the other as "Nasal voiced chirp brays, bouncy ditty in fine style. Deft Ork‖ Beat." But many radio admirers take him for a male Dorothy Dix.** They assume Hank can patch up a busted love affair as readily as a busted string.

Complains Hank: "If anybody in my business knew as much about their business as the public did, they'd be all right!"

HANK'S KIND IS THEIR KIND

"Just lately," said Hank, "somebody got the idea nobody didn't listen to my kind 'a music. I told everybody on the radio that this was my last program. 'If anybody's enjoyed it,' I said, 'I'd like to hear from 'em.' I got 400 cards and letters that afternoon and the next mornin'...They decided they wanted to keep my kind of music."

Hank's kind of music began when he was six. "My mother played the organ in church at Georgiana, and I sat on the seat beside her. I'd raise up and you could hear me [singing] above everybody."

Between then and WSFA, things happened. The Williams' house burned down. They moved into a big vacant house "'til we were able to pay rent." Hank broke his left arm, but could still move his fingers. To let him move them to advantage, his mother, who worked as a nurse, bought him a guitar. Then came the only music lessons Hank ever had—the ones he got from an old Negro named Tee Tot. He left Tee Tot's teachings to start his own radio program. Last year he went to Nashville and played and sang his songs for Fred Rose, music publisher and folksong expert.

From that moment Hank was "in."

"JUST TALKIN' TO THE DOG"

His first big hit, "Move It On Over," moved up to No. 2 for the Nation on Hillbilly's hit parade. Only "Smoke" †† was hotter.

‖ *Billboard* slang for "orchestra."

** Pseudonym of American journalist Elizabeth Meriwether Gilmer (1861–1951), who pioneered the syndicated newspaper advice column.

†† Tex Williams and His Western Caravan's hit, "Smoke! Smoke! Smoke! (That Cigarette)."

How did he happen to move into this tune? "Well," says Hank, "I was just talkin' to the dog. There ain't a man livin' who hasn't talked to his dog. If he tells you he hasn't you bet [*sic*] not believe him anymore. I was just talkin' to the dog."

Came in last night at half past ten
That baby of mine wouldn't let me in
So move it on over (MOVE IT ON OVER)
Move it on over (MOVE IT ON OVER)
Move over little dog 'cause a big dog's movin' in!

There are various substitutions: Scoot it on over, drag it on over, shake it on over, sneak it on over. An old dog moves over for a new dog; a nice dog for a mad dog; a cold dog for a hot dog—but you get the general idea.

Only in his second year of composing such masterpieces, Hank already is buddy-buddy with barn dance's big names. He has recorded tunes like "Rootie Tootie" and "Fly Trouble" for Fred Rose. His own works have been recorded by such notables as Roy Acuff, Cowboy Copas, Jimmy and Leon Short, Grandpa Jones, Molly O'Day and Clyde Grubs [Grubbs].

MORE POETRY THAN TRUTH

Hank has written 500 songs. He knocks them out in 15 minutes. "And if it takes any longer than 15 minutes I know the idea's no good and throw it away."

So dashed off was "I'll Be a Bachelor Till I Die," another M-G-M recording which just popped out yesterday [as the B-side to "Honky Tonkin'"].

~~~~~~

| 4 |

Gene L. Roe: Got "Lovesick Blues"? No Sir, Not Hank Williams

Hank Williams's contemporary reputation as a musical artist of national renown rested primarily on three best-selling records: "Lovesick Blues" (1949), "Cold, Cold Heart" (1951), and "Jambalaya (On the Bayou)" (1952). While the latter two demonstrated his uncanny ability for writing country songs that became cross-over hits for popular singers, it was the phenomenal success of "Lovesick

SOURCE   Gene L. Roe, "Got 'Lovesick Blues'? No Sir, Not Hank Williams," *National Hillbilly News*, January–February 1950, pp. 51–52.

Blues," a Tin Pan Alley number first published in 1922, that initially indicated his ability to attract a mass audience of hillbilly music fans and that seemingly overnight placed him among the genre's biggest stars.

Released in February 1949, while he was still a member of the *Louisiana Hayride*, Williams's recording of "Lovesick Blues" spent sixteen weeks at No. 1 and earned him a long-coveted spot on the *Grand Ole Opry*, country music's premier radio program. Increased press coverage followed, beginning with feature stories in country music fan magazines, including the piece below from the Huntington, West Virginia–based bimonthly, *National Hillbilly News*. Hewing to the prevailing "Organization Man" interpretation, author Gene L. Roe (1933?–2004?) celebrates Williams's extraordinary success as a hillbilly entertainer, praises his remarkable songwriting talent, and takes pains to separate the domestic strife described in many of his songs from the marital harmony he reportedly enjoyed in real life. Although Roe's and similar fan magazine articles were often little more than unpolished puff pieces, the extensive coverage Williams received in such publications played a pivotal role in establishing him as a country music celebrity.

(Although we had a story on Hank Williams in our last issue, we have received so many requests for a picture and complete story on him that we decided to run a feature story. He is one of our favorite singers and it is always a pleasure to give our readers the stories they want.)

He's got the "Lovesick Blues" and sings those "Wedding Bells" will never ring for me, but of course all this is only about a fellow he sings about on his popular MGM recordings. The real Hank Williams is far from especially the love sick blues, for he is happily married to a beautiful girl and has two fine children, a girl eight years old* and a small son. Aside from this Hank is enjoying the success that comes from twelve years of radio work, in which he has known the ups and the downs that go with the life of an entertainer.

He started in radio work in 1936 over station WSFA in Montgomery, Alabama, with "The Drifting Cowboys" and has drifted to several stations over the country where his down-to-earth and heart songs have won him many faithful fans.

From KWKH in Shreveport, La., he came to WSM in Nashville and the Grand Ole Opry, where he made an immediate hit with the "Opry" listeners.

---

* Williams's stepdaughter, Lycrecia Ann Guy (b. 1941), who now goes by the surname Williams.

Not only does Hank have a beautiful singing voice, but he is a song writer with unusual talent for turning out religious and heart songs by the dozens. He says that he has written over five hundred songs in all, and it is odd that of all of the songs of his own [the one] that made him on the road to stardom is an old minstrel song, "Lovesick Blues."

Hank says that the song was first made famous some twenty years ago by a black face comedian by the name of Emmett Miller. Hank has sung the song for years but as he says, he never dreamed that it would make the big success that it is.

Among the many songs that are written by Hank are several of those recorded by Molly O'Day, such as "I Don't Care If Tomorrow Never Comes," "Six More Miles," "When God Gathers His Jewels" and others. Roy Acuff also has recorded several of his songs. His first hit recording of his own voice was "Move It On Over" which came out in 1946[†] on the MGM label.

The latest Hank Williams tunes to be released at the time of this writing are "You're Gonna Change" and "Lost Highway," a beautiful song written by the blind singer Leon Payne. Two other fine songs by Hank are "Loveless Mansion" and "I Just Told Mother Goodbye."

Appearing with Hank are his top-flight musicians known as "The Drifting Cowboys." The band consists of Hank on the guitar, backed up by Jerry Rivers on the fiddle, Don Helm [Helms] on electric [steel] guitar, Hillous Burtrum [Butrum] on bass.

This long tall Alabama boy has come a long way since he first won an amateur contest at the age of ten, [and] although he is only twenty-six now, he has the experience of a much older performer. Hank was born in Mt. Olive, Alabama, on September 17, 1923. It has been an uphill pull for him but if the fans of "Lovesick Blues" have anything to say about it, Hank Williams is here to stay!

| 5 |

Gold in Them Hillbillies

One of Hank Williams's more revealing interviews appeared several days after his 1951 performance at County Hall auditorium in Charleston, South Carolina.

SOURCE   "Gold in Them Hillbillies," unidentified newspaper, March 10, 1951, clipping from the private collection of George Merritt.
† "Move It On Over" was released in 1947.

Unfortunately, the source of this newspaper article remains unknown, but in it, Williams vigorously defends country music while providing seriocomic commentary on the behavior of his fans. Like many other mainstream journalists who wrote about hillbilly performers during this period, the unidentified author condescends to his subject, transcribing some of Williams's Alabama dialect phonetically ("cain't," "figger") and comically elevating his own writing style ("courting a backwoods muse") in implicit contrast to the singer's rough-hewn language.

A tall, hollow-cheeked hillbilly drew one lanky leg over the other in a comfortable position and drawled, "Sure, plenty people make fun of me, but I just ignore them. I figger they're ignorant and don't know any better."

Hank Williams, $100,000-a-year folk singer who says he began by playing every one-room schoolhouse and pig path in the state of Alabama, launched into an impassioned defense of his profession.

"The way I feel," he said, "is that if you don't like folk music stay away from my shows. Personally, I cain't stand classical stuff, but I don't tell the world about it. I just turn the radio off. Now, why cain't these folks who don't like my kind of music do the same?"

He shook his head.

"When they start making fun of me I don't even answer them. And when these wise guys come just to whoop and holler and cut up I tell them to get out. They're plain ignorant."

Folk songs, said Hank, who was interviewed in Charleston a few days ago while appearing at County Hall, date back to the old English ballads. They were brought to the hills by immigrants from Britain and have been handed down from father to son through the generations.

"Why, even 'Goodnight Irene' was the melody to an old English ballad," he said—and began to sing the song the mountaineers knew, a lachrymose ditty called "Pere Ellen." *

"I like to think," said Hank when the ballad was ended, "that folk songs express the dreams and prayers and hopes of the working people."

"That's why it makes me mad to hear these popular orchestras make a jazzed-up comedy of a religious song like 'Wreck on the Highway.' It isn't a funny song. Roy Acuff made the first recording of it and Roy can quote you as much of the Bible as a preacher."

---

* Probably the author's misunderstanding of "Fair Ellen," an old British ballad once widely known in southern Appalachia but entirely unrelated to "Goodnight, Irene."

Sincerity, Hank explained, is the prime requisite for success in both writing and singing folk music.

"I know a few singers," Hank said, "who have made over $100,000 a year singing this music. Roy Acuff has been doing it for the last 15 years. They have big homes right there outside of Nashville, but they're still sincere when they sing."

And what happens, I asked, should they lose the "common touch?"

"Well," he replied, "they lose them big homes 'fore long."

Hank lives up to every standard of looks for a genuine, sho'-nuff hillbilly. He has long legs, stooped shoulders, lazy eyes, and an accent right out of the country—Southern country, that is.

When he's not assailing the Philistines who won't appreciate his music, Hank decries pop bands who hold it in contempt until a hit like "Tennessee Waltz" or "Goodnight Irene" comes along and popular demand makes them "stoop" to play it.

"Yes, indeed! I have noticed," Hank laughed, "that these pop bands will play our hillbilly songs when they cain't eat any other way!"

Is it true, I asked, that a voice is not an absolute necessity for a folk singer's success? Hank's eyes flamed.

"Let me tell you," he began, "the fellows who really get me mad are the ones who couldn't make the grade in the pop field and move over into this racket because they figger any old dope can sing that corny stuff. So they put on a cowboy suit and a false accent and try it."

Hank gave an almost imperceptible smirk.

"And starve to death just as fast as anybody I know."

With an air of meekness and long-suffering Hank told about the price a humble man of the hills pays for successfully courting a backwoods muse.

"It's my fans," he confided. "You see, in this business if you're a success there's some folks who actually worship you. I have been to some places where it's impossible to walk across the stage without having the major portion of my outfit torn off for souvenirs."

"They even," he added, rubbing his thinning mass of crowning glory, "grab fistfuls of hair."

Those who don't carry Hank away in little pieces write letters.

"When you get to be a big success," Hank said, "folks have a habit of writing you and telling you their troubles—all kinds of troubles; if their husband dies and they're left with eight starving kids they write, and if their sweetheart done them wrong they write, and if they feel sort of blue they write. I dunno," Hank sighed and gave a puzzled shrug. "I reckon they think I'm something like the Red Cross."

The 27-year-old Alabamanian [*sic*] doesn't know how to write music. He has to record his tunes and then have someone write the score. To date he has published some [illegible] songs. When I asked Hank how he got the inspiration for that impressive stack of lyric writing, he meditated a bit.

"Well," he said finally, "I reckon it's just a gift you get from God."

~~~~~~

| 6 |

Golden Oatunes: H. Williams Clefs 22 Hillbilly Toppers

Until this article appeared in October 1951, the music industry's leading trade journal, *Billboard*, had paid scant attention to Hank Williams. To be sure, the magazine had noted his various career moves, concisely reviewed his new releases and traced their movement up the charts, and even featured a photograph of him on the cover of its March 25, 1950, issue. (The image showed music industry executives congratulating Williams on his second No. 1 hit, "Long Gone Lonesome Blues," at a national jukebox operators' convention in Chicago.) But what attracted the magazine's attention in late 1951 was Williams's emerging reputation as the first hillbilly songwriter to compose and record songs that also consistently became crossover hits for pop artists. Jerry Wexler (1917–2008), then a reporter at *Billboard* and later a successful producer at Atlantic Records, reportedly wrote this unsigned, "slanguage"-filled article, including its snappy headline. By noting Williams's commercial achievements and the material comforts that success had provided, Wexler succinctly encapsulates the "Organization Man" theme that so dominated the writings about Williams during his lifetime. From this point on, *Billboard* would treat the country star as a nationally prominent recording artist, performer, and songwriter, and would publish several additional features about him in the remaining year of his life and in the weeks immediately following his death.

CHICAGO, Oct. 20—Hank Williams, who's been the top h.b.[*] recording star with a string of 18 oatunes[†] on The Billboard h.b. and Western pop charts since his first "Lovesick Blues" hit on MGM in February, 1949, has blossomed out as a full-fledged pop writer.

SOURCE "Golden Oatunes: H. Williams Clefs 22 Hillbilly Toppers," *Billboard*, October 27, 1951, p. 15. Used by permission.
[*] *Billboard* abbreviation for "hillbilly."
[†] Slang for "country music songs," probably derived from "oaters," entertainment industry jargon for "westerns" or "cowboy films."

Not only is Williams the first h.b. writer to score big as a writer of country ditties that hit later the pop field, but the majority of his 22 hits to make the pop charts were songs which he either wrote or co-authored. Floyd Tillman, who had three songs that switched from country hits on Columbia to pop hits elsewhere on wax within a 16-month period two years ago, is the only one to approach Williams' record.

Currently, the ex-Birmingham [sic] warbler has "Cold, Cold Heart" by Tony Bennett on Columbia, along with "Hey, Good-Looking" by Frankie Laine and Jo Stafford on Columbia, and by Tennessee Ernie [Ford] and Helen O'Connell on Capitol, and the latest Guy Mitchell release on Columbia, "I Can't Help It." Previous to his current splurge, Kay Starr disked[‡] his "Lovesick Blues"[§] for Capitol, while Polly Bergen cut "Honky Tonkin'" for a Coast indie, and Theresa [Teresa] Brewer cut it for London. Don Cherry's Decca waxing of "I Can't Help It" is already out, while MGM has just released "Lonesome Whistle" by Blue Barron. In addition, his "Moanin' the Blues" was cut by two r.&b. diskeries.[¶]

In the 32 months that have elapsed since Williams hit with "Lovesick Blues," the WSM, Nashville, country star has penned 11 of the 18 songs that have hit big on the rustic retail and juke market. All of his songs have been published by Acuff-Rose, with the exception of "Lonesome Whistle," which he co-wrote with Jimmy [Jimmie] Davis and which is pubbed[||] by Davis' subsidiary firm in Southern Music.

Williams told The Billboard that he intends to take more time from his heavy schedule of bookings, set by Jim Denny, of the WSM Artists' Service, to concentrate on his tune-writing. He currently has a song scheduled to be cut by Frankie Laine and another by Der Bingle[**] on Decca.

Williams will soon branch out as a screen actor. He recently inked a four-year pact with MGM films, guaranteeing him one picture per year at $10,000 for a maximum of four weeks' work on each film. Pact is graduated to $5,000 per week if Williams hits as a featured player-singer. Joe Pasternak, of MGM, has planned parts in big films for Williams, with no horse opera[††] parts scheduled. Pasternak told Williams that he is considering him for a part in a forthcoming Esther Williams flicker, tentatively titled "Peg o' My Heart."

[‡] Slang for "recorded."

[§] Williams did not write "Lovesick Blues," as this article seems to suggest; originally titled "I've Got the Love-sick Blues," the song was a 1922 Tin Pan Alley collaboration by Irving Mills (1894–1985) and Cliff Friend (1893–1974).

[¶] Slang for "record companies."

[||] Slang for "published."

[**] Billboard nickname for Decca's star singer, Bing Crosby (1903–1977).

[††] Another slang term for "Hollywood westerns."

Williams and his frau, Audrey, who just inked a pact with MGM Records (she previously cut duets with Williams on MGM), operate a Western clothing shop in Nashville. In addition, they just bought a 500-acre farm outside of Nashville.

~~~~~~

| 7 |

Hank Has a Method: Williams Tells How and Why His Disks Click

In the years since his death, Hank Williams has acquired a romantic aura as a natural artist who prized personal expression and resented the high-pressure commercialism of the music business. While he might have complained privately to friends and family members about such matters, when interviewed by journalists the resulting articles typically portrayed him as a calculating, market-driven performer with one eye on the record charts and the other on the bottom line. The shrewd businessman highlighted in this *Billboard* piece contrasts sharply with Williams's later image as an artist who rebelled against a Nashville music establishment that placed profit above creativity.

NEW YORK, Nov. 17—Too many artists fail to realize the importance of limiting the number of records released for them by their diskeries, according to Hank Williams, currently one of the hottest country and Western artists in the business. Williams, the scripter of such country-derived pops* as "Cold, Cold Heart," "Hey, Good Lookin'," "I Can't Help It" and "Crazy Heart,"† said that he followed a specific pattern in having his own MGM disks released. He limits himself to 12 sides a year as Hank Williams, and 12 as Luke the Drifter, his nom de disk‡ on the same label.

According to Williams, record companies and artists both often fail to give a new release sufficient time to reach its full sales potential. By limiting the number of sides to be released, and spacing them properly, each disk, he claims, can get the full benefit of disk jockey exploitation and juke box play.

SOURCE "Hank Has a Method: Williams Tells How and Why His Disks Click," *Billboard*, November 24, 1951, p. 22. Used by permission.
* *Billboard* slang for "pop songs."
† Although often mistakenly attributed to Williams, as in this article, "Crazy Heart" was written by Fred Rose (1898–1954) and one of his Tin Pan Alley friends, Maurice Murray (born Maurice Fisher) (ca. 1906–1954).
‡ A pseudonym under which an artist's phonograph recordings are released.

Williams' pattern of releasing records also takes into account the type of material waxed. Warbler⁵ feels that jump tunes should be alternated with blues or ballad items, that a strong-selling ballad can be followed with other ballads or blues songs, but that a jump or rhythm type song should be followed by two consecutive slow numbers.

According to Williams, MGM Prexy¶ Frank Walker has been extremely co-operative in spacing disk releases properly. Both Williams and MGM have agreed not to record an album of eight new sides. The release of an album, they feel, would only spread jockey and juke plays too thinly instead of getting the concentrated push on a single record.

In New York for an appearance on the Perry Como video show, Williams left Friday [...] to return to Nashville and his newly purchased 570-acre farm. He is set for a TV appearance on Ed Sullivan's "Toast of the Town" in the near future. Williams said he turned down an offer to guest on the Milton Berle TV show. "The last time I worked with him, in St. Louis, there like to have been a killing," he said.‖

| 8 |

Rufus Jarman: Country Music Goes to Town

The following piece, originally published in *Nation's Business*, the magazine of the U.S. Chamber of Commerce, ranks as one of the most often-cited and re-printed articles in country music scholarship. In it, author Rufus Jarman (1911–1966) examines the growing popularity of country music, not only in the United States but also around the globe. He focuses mainly on Western Europe, where, during the early years of the Cold War, the United States established a series of military bases and operated the Armed Forces Network (AFN), whose most popular program at the time was *Hillbilly Gasthaus*. Jarman's article is best known for its concluding commentary by Hank Williams, who died the month before its publication. Jarman probably interviewed him for this piece sometime

SOURCE   Rufus Jarman, "Country Music Goes to Town," *Nation's Business*, February 1953, pp. 45, 46, 48, 51. © 1953 by U.S. Chamber of Commerce. Reprinted by permission, www.uschamber.com, June 2010.

⁵ Slang for "the singer," in this case, Williams.

¶ Slang for "president."

‖ Williams is apparently referring to an offstage confrontation he had with Berle when both were performing on the 1951 Hadacol Caravan tour. According to several of Williams's biographers, however, the incident occurred in Kansas City rather than in St. Louis, Missouri.

prior to Williams's August 1952 dismissal from the *Grand Ole Opry*, and to his credit, Jarman managed to elicit from the singer what have become his most widely quoted statements regarding the essential nature and appeal of country music.[*]

An interesting new development has been observed recently in the musical tastes of the peoples of Western Europe, who have given to the world Brahms, Beethoven, Bach, Mendelssohn, Chopin, Wagner, Verdi and the waltzes of Johann Strauss. Now, it appears that European musical culture has taken a surprising and ardent fancy to the works of a new school of composers and performers, who include [...] the late Hank Williams, a sort of "Irving Berlin of the straw stack," among whose compositions are "Lovesick Blues," "Hey, Good Lookin'," and "Honky-Tonkin'."

In short, Europe has been exposed to—and has taken to—hillbilly and western (American) music. Until comparatively recent times, this form of musical expression had been confined to the fiddling "hoedowns" in the cabins and one-room schoolhouses of the Tennessee-Kentucky-Ozark hill country, and to the nasal wailings of cowboys on the lone prairie who, in song at least, are generally solitary and always sad.

Nowadays this homely artistry has gone international. American armed service personnel and this country's expanding participation in world affairs have made American "country music" almost as prominent in Western Europe as the Marshall Plan.[†] [...] Perhaps the greatest foreign hillbilly fan movement is in western Germany and the Germanic countries, long renowned as music lovers. In the beamed-and-plastered Teutonic beer gardens and brew houses, which for generations have resounded to Viennese waltzes and the umpah-ing of German bands, the high-pitched, scrappy fiddling of hoedown music now rings out, almost like Arkansas. Native bands, in some cases, have abandoned Strauss, and have taken names for themselves such as "Hank Schmitz and his Goober Growlers" or "Red Schmucker and his Mountain Boys." [...]

What brought this homely music out of the back-roads and into great popularity nationally—and now internationally—was radio in general and in particular station WSM, owned by the National Life & Accident Insurance Company. Through country music, Nashville is now a phonograph-recording

---

[*] Williams did possess some firsthand knowledge of country music's growing international appeal, at least as it applied to American military personnel serving overseas. In November 1949, he participated in a two-week concert tour of U.S. military bases in Germany and Austria, as a member of a troupe of *Grand Ole Opry* stars.

[†] Officially known as the European Recovery Program, the Marshall Plan provided $15 billion of U.S. aid to Western Europe between 1948 and 1951 to help rebuild war-torn countries and prevent the spread of communism.

center comparable to New York and Hollywood. WSM has become the "big time" to country musicians, as the old Palace [Theatre in Manhattan] once was to vaudeville. The *Wall Street Journal* has estimated that country music in Nashville now amounts to a $25,000,000-a-year industry. [...]

[The] country music glamour boys [who perform on WSM's *Grand Ole Opry*] are as big—sometimes bigger—in record sales and juke box popularity as Bing Crosby or Frank Sinatra. These men make up to $300,000 a year. They live in mansions with swimming pools attached in Nashville's fashionable suburbs, drive immense automobiles bearing their initials in gold, and wear expensive western getups—loud suits costing $300 each, $50 hats and $75 boots. [...]

Besides their radio programs and records, the Opry stars constantly manifest themselves to their followers through personal appearances [....] Every night one or more troupes of Opry stars are appearing in some city about the land. They have crammed Carnegie Hall in New York and played before sellout audiences in white ties and tails in Constitution Hall in Washington. More often they appear on Sundays in picnic groves in Pennsylvania, Illinois or Ohio. Not long ago, one troupe played to 65,000 persons in four days in Texas.

To fill this schedule, the Opry stars live a hard life. They usually leave Nashville in their cars on Sundays, and drive hard from one engagement to another, heading back to Nashville in time for Saturday. Often they don't sleep in a bed for nights on end, but take turns driving. [...] The touring stars have simple living tastes. One observer who has traveled with them reports that some stars, making hundreds of thousands of dollars a year, will eat the same meal three times a day—fried potatoes, fried eggs and fried pork chops. For, in spite of their fancy clothes, big cars and abundant money, the Opry stars remain simple people who "were raised hard and live hard," as one of them has said. Some of them do not know a note of music, but their great appeal as entertainers is in the rawness of their emotions and their sincerity in conveying them.

Hank Williams was discussing that shortly before his death in January. Williams was a lank, erratic countryman who learned to play a guitar from an old Negro named Teetot in his home village of Georgiana, Ala.

"You ask what makes our kind of music successful," Williams was saying. "I'll tell you. It can be explained in just one word: sincerity. When a hillbilly sings a crazy song, he feels crazy. When he sings, 'I Laid My Mother Away,' he sees her a-laying right there in the coffin."

"He sings more sincere than most entertainers because the hillbilly was raised rougher than most entertainers. You got to know a lot about hard work. You got to have smelt a lot of mule manure before you can sing like a hillbilly. The people who has been raised something like the way the hillbilly has knows what he is singing about and appreciates it."

"For what he is singing is the hopes and prayers and dreams and experiences of what some call the 'common people.' I call them the 'best people,' because they are the ones that the world is made up most of. They're really the ones who make things tick, wherever they are in this country or in any country."

"They're the ones who understand what we're singing about, and that's why our kind of music is sweeping the world. There ain't nothing strange about our popularity these days. It's just that there are more people who are like us than there are the educated, cultured kind."

"There ain't nothing at all queer about them Europeans liking our kind of singing. It's liable to teach them more about what everyday Americans are really like than anything else."

~~~~~~

| 9 |

Audrey Mae Williams and Hank Williams: Excerpts from Divorce Complaint and Defendant's Answer and Cross-Bill in *Audrey Mae Williams vs. Hank Williams, Et Al.*

Hank Williams was an intensely private man, a fact that, when combined with the more discreet press coverage of his day, prevented fans from knowing much about his personal life, including his tumultuous marriage to his first wife, Audrey Mae (Sheppard) Williams (1923–1975), the most significant figure in his life. The couple met in her hometown of Banks, Alabama, probably around August 1943, and they were married on December 15, 1944, just ten days after Audrey was granted a divorce from her first husband.* Over the next seven years, she would relentlessly push her less-ambitious husband toward professional success, while also purportedly providing the inspiration for many of his now-classic songs. Unfortunately, Audrey believed that she, too, was a gifted vocalist, an opinion shared by almost no one who heard her sing. Still, Hank reluctantly allowed her to make occasional appearances on his shows, helped her obtain a recording contract, and even recorded a handful of duets with her.

Problems in their marriage abounded almost from the beginning. The couple separated on several occasions, and even divorced in May 1948, only to reconcile and have their divorce voided the following year. Their marital troubles soon

---

SOURCE   *Audrey Mae Williams vs. Hank Williams, Et Al.* (1952), Rule No. 71124, Office of Clerk and Master, Chancery Court of Davidson County, Nashville, Tennessee.

* Audrey's divorce decree stipulated a sixty-day waiting period before she could remarry, so, under Alabama law, theirs was a common-law marriage.

resumed, however. After a series of domestic disputes over the Christmas holidays in 1951, Audrey filed for another divorce, citing "cruel and inhuman treatment" and abandonment. In early March 1952, a bitter Hank brought a countersuit for divorce on his own grounds and requested custody of their two-year-old son, Randall (better known today as Hank Williams, Jr.).

The following selections, excerpted from the Williamses' 1952 divorce suit and countersuit, constitute the only heretofore unpublished items included in this anthology. Products of their times, these documents reflect many of the stereotypical gender expectations of mid-twentieth-century America, while also revealing the sad, sordid details of the couple's failed marriage. Oddly, while Hank charges that Audrey had numerous extramarital affairs and an illegal abortion (complications from which required her hospitalization), she never mentions her estranged husband's alcoholism or the December 30, 1951, shooting incident that finally convinced her to end the marriage. Under the terms of their May 29, 1952, divorce settlement, she received custody of their son and a sizeable amount of their property, including half of what turned out to be by far the most valuable asset: Hank's future earnings from recording and publishing royalties.

"THE BILL OF COMPLAINT OF AUDREY MAE WILLIAMS, COMPLAINANT, VS. HANK WILLIAMS, ET AL., DEFENDANTS," IN *AUDREY MAE WILLIAMS VS. HANK WILLIAMS, ET AL.* (1952), (FILED JANUARY 10, 1952)
During the very early years of their married life, before the defendant [Hank Williams] had become a successful artist, the parties were comparatively happy, having the differences of opinion normally to be expected early in the marriage of young people. The defendant's conduct just prior to the year 1947, however, and his mistreatment of the complainant [Audrey Williams] became such that the complainant was forced to separate from him. Upon the defendant's earnest, and apparently sincere, promises that he would change and improve his attitude toward the complainant, she did agree to return to him, and the parties were reunited. Complainant, however, had been so embarrassed and humiliated by his mistreatment of her in Montgomery, Alabama, that she insisted that they move their residence to some other place; whereupon, the parties removed to Shreveport, Louisiana, at which place the defendant first began to achieve [...] success in his profession [....] While the parties were not completely happy in their marital relationship in Shreveport because of the continued misconduct of the defendant, they did enjoy some degree of happiness. Finally, in 1949, the parties removed to Nashville, Tennessee, since which time the defendant's attitude toward complainant and toward his home has become progressively more unsatisfactory and more unreasonable, without any occasion for such change

in attitude. About nine months ago the defendant's conduct and attitude toward, and mistreatment of, the complainant became intolerable. While he had been inconsiderate, and even cruel at times before, he then became most abusive, cursing the complainant without provocation, and striking her on numerous occasions.

On the afternoon of Saturday, December 29, 1951, the defendant after berating, cursing and abusing her, in extreme anger struck her with such force and violence as that she would have been knocked to the floor had she not caught on a desk to prevent herself from falling. This cruel attack occurred in the presence of the complainant's two young children. In order to avoid a repetition of this scene before the children, complainant left the home, taking the children with her, and did not return until the following Sunday afternoon, that is the next day.

Defendant was at home on this Sunday, December 30th. Petitioner returned in the company of several of her friends, who are elderly ladies. She asked these people to go with her, since she feared that the defendant might inflict even greater violence upon her than had been done on the preceding day if she returned alone. When she did enter the home the defendant again became most abusive, cursing and threatening her, and was prevented from inflicting more violence upon her only by the hurried departure of complainant. She did not return to her home with the children until the defendant had left.

Upon her return to the home of the parties on Thursday, January 3, 1952, the complainant learned that the defendant had departed. He left no funds whatsoever for the complainant. She is now confronted with numerous bills to be paid, not only for household expenses, but for business matters.

The foregoing specific instances are but samples of the cruel and inhuman treatment which has been inflicted upon the complainant by [the] defendant at numerous times, and practically throughout their entire married life, the degree and extent thereof having become more intense within the past several months, to the point that even though complainant has every desire to maintain the home of the parties, and to preserve this marriage, she is not physically or mentally able further to endure this mistreatment. Defendant is a man of violent disposition when aroused, and this violence is particularly aggravated when the complainant, herself, is the object thereof. As has been demonstrated in the past, the defendant does not hesitate to make a physical attack upon the complainant. She is desperately afraid that when this bill is served upon him, he, if not prevented by the process of this Court, will inflict more grievous and serious bodily injury and harm upon her than ever heretofore.

The defendant, particularly within the past few months, has been engaging in the wildest extravagances, and wasting the funds which come into his hands.

At the same time defendant left her no funds with which to pay even living expenses. Complainant, therefore, is forced to appeal to this Court for the use of its extraordinary process, to the end that some reasonable part of the defendant's income may be sequestered and used by her for the necessary support of the child of the parties, the complainant, and their home [....]

"ANSWER AND CROSS-BILL OF THE DEFENDANT AND CROSS-COMPLAINT, HANK WILLIAMS," IN *AUDREY MAE WILLIAMS VS. HANK WILLIAMS, ET AL.* (1952) (FILED CA. MARCH 5, 1952)

The defendant [Hank Williams] positively denies that any misconduct on his part led to their separation in 1947 or 1948, but will show to the Court upon the hearing that that separation was brought about by the positive misconduct of the complainant [Audrey Williams], and that they became reconciled thereafter only upon the assurances of the complainant that she would desist from her course of misconduct and act in the manner in which a wife should act and maintain defendant's home properly, which she has positively refused to do since that time. [...]

Defendant positively denies that he has been guilty of any act of cruel and inhuman treatment or conduct towards the complainant as would render it unsafe and improper for them to live together, as alleged in the bill, and further positively denies that he has abandoned her or turned her out of doors and refused and neglected to provide for her. He further denies that he has given the complainant any cause which would entitle her to the relief sought in the prayer of this petition, but on the contrary, he will show to the Court upon the hearing that he has suffered every humiliation, abuse and mistreatment that a man could possibly take from a woman at the hands of the complainant in this cause, all of which will be shown to the Court upon the hearing. [...]

And now, having fully answered the allegations of the bill filed against him in this cause, your defendant, Hank Williams, asks leave of the Court to assume the character of cross-complainant and to file the following as his cross-bill in this cause against the cross-defendant, Audrey Mae Williams, and would show to the Court, as follows, in support of the same:

That he and the cross-defendant, Audrey Mae Williams, were married in Andalusia, Alabama, on December 15, 1944. [...] At this time your cross-complainant was an amateur singer around southern Alabama, earning from $25.00 to $40.00 per week. Neither he nor the cross-defendant had as much as $25.00 at the time of their marriage, and neither of them had ever been used to any money to any large amount. Cross-complainant will show to the Court that he worked hard and started attaining some degree of success as a hillbilly singer and entertainer. When he married the cross-defendant she brought her child by her former marriage[†] to live with them, and he has always taken care of and supported this child along with his own.

Cross-complainant would show to the Court that for several years of their marriage they lived in northern [*sic*] Alabama. The first years of their married life became trouble-some because of the inattention of the cross-defendant to her home and husband, and they started having trouble almost from the beginning. At that time the cross-defendant refused to appreciate the obligations of married life, denying her attentions and affections to her home and husband, insisting that she, too, was an entertainer and singer of ability, continuously insisting that the defendant include her on his programs and build her up as an entertainer, despite the fact that she had neither voice nor musical ability, with the result that she steadfastly refused to keep house or maintain the home as a mother and wife, but insisted on leaving the children with others and accompanying your cross-complainant on the road. As a matter of fact, she was so insistent in this direction that cross-complainant lost many jobs during the early part of his work in this field because the engagement refused to accept his wife as an entertainer on the bill with him. She complained, arguing that he was trying to keep her down and out of the business.

Even this far back, the cross-defendant, who has always been possessed of an ungovernable temper, would fly into fits and rages and curse and abuse, and condemn and castigate your cross-complainant, both privately and in the presence of others, because she could not share the program with him. She has done this to such an extent that she had on many occasions been evicted from studios and many other places of entertainment because of her fits and rages of this nature. However, your cross-complainant, while denied the comforts and assurances of a solid and substantial home life by reason of the cross-defendant's appetite for public appearances and her consequent neglect of their home and children, kept pushing and plugging ahead trying to better their conditions and exploit his abilities as much as possible.

Cross-complainant would show to the Court that during all this time the financial demands made upon him by the extravagant living and carousing of his wife were such as to keep his nose to the grindstone continuously in order to keep the bills paid. However, he would show that he loved his wife, despite her weaknesses, rages, flights and attacks upon him, and gave her everything that his income would allow, but instead of helping him to save part of their income, the cross-defendant indulged in every extravagance she could possibly

---

[†] Lycrecia Ann Guy (b. 1941), the only child from Audrey's first, short-lived marriage to James Erskine Guy.

stretch his income to cover. As a matter of fact, he will show to the Court upon the hearing by an abundance of proof that this extravagance on her part and insatiable thirst and hunger for clothes, jewelry, automobiles and luxuries far beyond their economic status in life has kept them drained dry financially. As a matter of fact, he will show upon the hearing of this cause that during last year, 1951, this cross-defendant, who has sworn to the allegation that your cross-complainant failed to provide for her, spent or caused to be spent from his income, or obligated your cross-complainant to spend, a total expenditure of approximately $50,000.00. Just at one store, to wit, Weinberger's, the cross-defendant spent $900.00 for evening gowns. She paid $350.00 for one dress.

Cross-complainant will show to the Court that all this same conduct back in 1947 and 1948 led to their separation and subsequent reconciliation. They then moved to Shreveport, Louisiana, where it was another chapter of the same type of living. As a matter of fact, cross-complainant would show that the cross-defendant has never kept her home as a mother and wife should, she has never shown any disposition or interest in staying at home, notwithstanding the fact that she was furnished with every convenience and luxury that money could buy, but she has always insisted upon traveling about, acting independent and free of all marital restraint and obligation, seeking and having everything she wanted and a good time all the time.

She hasn't spent one full day with their child since it was born, unless she was sick and confined to the house for that reason, or that she failed in her search to get someone to stay with the child. He would show to the Court that his child, as well as her child by another marriage, has spent three-fourths of its life in company of other people besides its mother. As a matter of fact, their only child refers to its nurse as "Mama."

By the time the parties moved to Nashville in 1949, your cross-complainant had, by hard work and application, traveling day and night, built up a reputation as a folk singer, music writer and radio entertainer. He would show to the Court by an abundance of proof upon the hearing to this cause that his application to this work, the hardships of continuous traveling in connection therewith, have reduced him in health until he is now a physical wreck, under the constant care of physicians, and spending much of his time in hospitals. In December, 1951, he underwent a serious spine operation at the Vanderbilt Hospital and was under the knife of Dr. George Carpenter and Dr. Benjamin Fowler. He has not been able to walk without the aid of crutches or a cane since that time. While he was in the hospital on this and other occasions, the cross-defendant showed no concern or interest in his welfare except to come to the hospital to condemn him and castigate him, curse him and call him the vilest and most vulgar of names.

Since they have been in Nashville, cross-complainant has furnished his wife and child with everything that money could buy, hoping that he could influence her to stay at home and maintain his home while he was away working. As stated above, he has invested over $70,000.00 in a beautiful, modern home on the Franklin Road, furnished with the most beautiful and modern furniture and appliances. Their home is a show place, one that would attract any woman and hold her interest as a mother and housekeeper. He has given the cross-defendant everything to wear that a woman could dream of, every type of jewelry, he has kept her riding in Cadillacs, wearing mink coats, and has given her all the other accessories and luxuries about which most women dream, but which few have.

Cross-complainant admits that he has sought to buy her interest. He admits he has, against his better judgment, spent thousands of dollars hoping that he could capture her interest and keep her in his home which she would maintain and preside over as a mother and wife. He would show that he could today be financially independent but for the fact that he insisted upon this course because he thought it was the only way he could hold her love and interest in their home. The cross-defendant has never shown the least bit of appreciation for this effort on his part. [...] In the presence of her ten-year-old daughter, whom your cross-complainant has always loved and taken care of, she has repeatedly, and on many, many occasions, referred to him as a "son-of-a-bitch," and many other names too vile and vulgar to incorporate in these premises. She has not confined this language about him to the family, but has referred to him in this manner before various friends and relatives. She has even called him a "son-of-a-bitch" to his own mother and other relatives. She has on innumerable occasions flown into rages of temper and fits, and cursed and abused him and struck him, scratched him, thrown furniture and articles at him, and inflicted violence upon him in almost every conceivable fashion. He has appeared in public appearances time after time with scratches and bruises upon his face and body as a result of altercations with his wife.

Since this trouble has come up, cross-complainant has learned that while he was pouring out his money and affections to the cross-defendant she was not only wrecking him financially, cursing and abusing him and doing him physical violence to his face, but to his back, while he would be away, she was engaging in practices in violation of her marital vows.

He would now show to the Court that the cross-defendant has continuously for the past fifteen months in particular, been going openly and notoriously with various other men. She has been carousing around both during the daytime and nighttime, both in Nashville and in Davidson County, and in other counties and states with other men. She has been infatuated with various men.

In particular, the cross-complainant would show that during the fall of 1951 she was going with a young man, who at that time worked for the Highway Patrol of Tennessee. She was visiting him in Bowling Green, Kentucky, and other places. She was having rendezvous with him at various places, both during the day and night in Davidson County and at Bowling Green, Kentucky, all of which will be shown to the Court upon the hearing of this cause.

He will show further that on the _____ [blank in the original] day of January, 1952, the cross-defendant was apprehended by police officers in an automobile on a side road in Davidson County, Tennessee, behind the Municipal Airport. The car was parked with the lights out, and under cover of darkness at a secluded spot on said road, she was in company with an automobile dealer whose name will be shown to the Court upon the hearing, and at the time they were apprehended she was in the arms of this man who was loving and kissing her in a character and manner which will be shown to the Court in detail upon the hearing of this cause.

During the summer of 1951, the complainant was going with another member of the Tennessee Highway Patrol, but who is not now working as a patrolman. She has been to various tourist courts and secluded places with this said patrolman, whose name will be shown to the Court upon the hearing. He [the cross-complainant] further alleges and will show that this patrolman has visited her on innumerable occasions in your cross-complainant's home. Cross-defendant has admitted this patrolman into her home on occasions when her own mother was in the house and it was necessary for her to slip him in the back door. On other occasions it was necessary for her to slip him in the house because the nurse was present at the time.

Cross-complainant will show to the Court that she has had dates with various other men whose names will be shown to the Court upon the hearing of this cause. She has accompanied them to various night clubs in and around Nashville and Davidson County, and other places. She is currently infatuated with a man here in Davidson County, and she has been going openly and notoriously with him, accompanying him to night spots and other places, he has been driving the Cadillac automobile which your cross-complainant furnished his wife, and as late as yesterday, March 4, 1952, he was driving her Cadillac automobile.

Notwithstanding the fact that the cross-defendant says he [the cross-complainant] has failed to provide for her, the cross-defendant has just returned from a trip to Miami, which she said was for the purpose of going to the races.

The cross-defendant has on innumerable occasions told him that she did not love him, that she hated him, and that she didn't expect to live with him.

She has not confined this to your cross-complainant, but she has told others that she hated his guts and had no respect for him and that she did not expect to live with him. She has always refused to have any association with your cross-complainant's mother, and has condemned and castigated him for showing any affection or love for her whatsoever. When he was carried to the hospital in December, after [which] he underwent this serious operation by Doctor Carpenter on the 13th, his mother came to the hospital on the 14th and was ordered away by the cross-defendant.

About eighteen months ago, the cross-defendant became pregnant and this made the cross-complainant very happy because he had one child and desired another. However, much to his humiliation and grief, he learned later that the cross-defendant had had an abortion performed on her in her home, and had become infected and had to be carried to St. Thomas Hospital.

Cross-complainant would now show to the Court that he has given the cross-defendant everything that a man could give to a woman, including everything he has made and his health. He would show that he has done this because he has loved her until he discovered she had been unfaithful to him, notwithstanding the mistreatment and abuse he has suffered at her hands all this time.

He would show to the Court that there is not now any chance for them to ever live together in peace and happiness. Together with the abuse which he has suffered from her, the humiliation she has caused him, when taken with the proof and evidence he now has that while he was away she was sharing her affections with other men, he is definite in his mind he could never live with her again. Cross-complainant loves his child and has every desire to see that this child is given every chance in life. However, he would show to the Court that it is not to the best interest of this young son that he remain in the custody and under the control of the cross-defendant. The cross-defendant has been guilty of such misconduct, all of which will be shown to the Court upon the hearing, that it is impossible to even think about her rearing the child. She is positively unfit to have the custody and control of her minor child. Cross-complainant stands ready and willing and able to see that the child is given a good home with his [Hank Williams's] mother, that it is raised under clean and Christian influences, and has a proper chance in life. He stands ready and willing to voluntarily provide for the child in any fashion or manner which the Court sees fit to direct.

Cross-complainant does not say to the Court that he has been perfect. He has perhaps been guilty of indiscretions which he will freely admit to the Court. However, he would show to the Court that the cross-defendant's conduct has made life so unbearable and miserable for him that it has been almost a continuous nightmare.

Cross-complainant therefore alleges that the cross-defendant, Audrey Mae Williams, has been guilty of such cruel and inhuman treatment and conduct towards him as renders it unsafe and improper for him to further cohabit with her.

~~~~~~

| 10 |

Edith Lindeman: Hank Williams Hillbilly Show Is Different

After a forced break in his performance schedule due to back surgery in mid-December 1951, Hank Williams hit the road again in early 1952. At a January 29 show at the Mosque Theater in Richmond, Virginia, he appeared on stage noticeably drunk and barely able to perform. Unfortunately for him, *Richmond Times-Dispatch* entertainment critic Edith Lindeman (1898–1984) was in attendance and reviewed the show for the newspaper.* Caustic and unsparing in her criticism, Lindeman produced the only known contemporary account of Williams on stage at his worst. At a second show the next night, according to Williams lore, the now-sober singer sarcastically dedicated his opening number—"Mind Your Own Business"—to "a gracious lady writer," drawing cheers from his audience. In the months following these Richmond appearances, Williams's tendency to miss or ruin shows would become more pronounced until, in August 1952, he was finally fired from the *Grand Ole Opry*.

Hank Williams, reported as the top hillbilly composer of the country, made quite an impression at the Mosque last night. Probably it was not the impression that he intended, but few of the 900 who attended the show will ever forget it. This is just about what happened:

The show opened with young Ray Price and four instrumentalists. They were Cedric Rainwater, bull-fiddler† and comic; Don Helms at the steel guitar; Lonnie Jones, guitarist; and Stan Cardinal, fiddler. Price sang well and the boys

---

SOURCE   Edith Lindeman, "Hank Williams Hillbilly Show Is Different," *Richmond (Va.) Times-Dispatch*, January 30, 1952. Reprinted by permission of the *Richmond Times-Dispatch*.

* Interestingly, Lindeman was a songwriter herself, penning the lyrics to both "Little Things Mean a Lot," a 1954 No. 1 hit for Kitty Kallen, and "The Red-Headed Stranger," which two decades later became the title song for a groundbreaking 1975 country album by Willie Nelson.

† One who plays the double bass (also known as a string or upright bass), which was often referred to in country music bands as a "bull fiddle."

filled in with hillbilly novelties. The audience was polite, but they were waiting for Hank Williams.

After about a half-hour, Price announced that Hank "had a serious operation on his spine nine weeks ago‡ but he made this engagement, so here he is." To a burst of applause, Hank came in. His spine most certainly was not holding him erect. He sang "Cold, Cold Heart," but did not get some of the words in the right places. Then he sang "Lonesome Blues," with a good deal of off-key yodeling.

POLICEMEN SHOW UP

Several couples got up and left the auditorium. Then Hank sang "I Hear That Lonesome Whistle Blow," and some more people got up. Hank walked off and intermission was called. It lasted 25 minutes, during which time between 50 and 75 people went to the box office to get their money back. No one there was authorized to refund admissions, and pretty soon 10 policemen appeared and the man in the box office went off with the receipts to take them to B. C. Gates, promoter of the show, who was reported to be ill at home.

After the intermission, Ray Price and his boys came back. They sang and played and ad-libbed and whipped up extra numbers. Half the audience applauded their stalwart efforts to keep the show going. The other half yelled for Hank to come back.

Presently Price was called offstage. When he came back, he said, "The situation seems a lot improved," and introduced Hank to the crowd again. This time his spine seemed to feel better. The audience greeted him with laughs and a few boos, to which he answered, "I wish I was in as good shape as you are." Then he looked around and said, "Hank Williams is a lot of things but he ain't a liar. If they's a doctor in the house, I'll show him I've been in the hospital for eight weeks and this is my first show since then. And if you ain't nice to me, I'll turn around and walk right off."

Price, who deserves some special place in hillbilly heaven after his stint last night, jumped in and said, "We all love you, Hank, don't we folks?" And the audience applauded and laughed.

Then Hank sang "Move It On Over," and it sounded pretty good—almost as good as one of his records after it has been played a few hundred times. He also introduced the instrumentalists all over again, and sang "I Can't Help It."

---

‡ Born with a spinal abnormality (probably the congenital disorder *spina bifida occulta*), Williams had undergone corrective back surgery at Vanderbilt Hospital in Nashville on December 13, 1951, a little more than a month and a half before this show. Contrary to what he claims later in this article, he remained hospitalized after the operation for only about eleven days; he was discharged early, at his insistence, on Christmas Eve, so that he could spend the holidays at home with his family.

As a finish he sang "Cold, Cold Heart" once more, remembering all the words. Then he walked out, and got in his big yellow automobile with a chauffeur to drive him home.

Another appearance of Hank Williams and the show is scheduled for the Mosque at 8:30 tonight. Whether or not his spine bothers him too much to allow him to appear, any audience will get a good show from that hard-working Ray Price and the rest of the crowd.

~~~~~~

| 11 |

Famous Song Composer Is Arrested Here

Hank Williams's posthumous appeal rests, in no small measure, on the public's endless fascination with his darker, self-destructive side: his turbulent marriages, his crippling alcoholism and drug abuse, his often-erratic behavior, and his occasional arrests. During his lifetime, however, few of the singer's failings were exposed publicly in the press. Even the article below, which appeared less than three weeks before his death, was buried several pages deep in the *Shreveport Times* and, except for the colorful description of his flamboyant attire, provides only minimal details in an unsensational manner.

Hank Williams, the singing cowboy, was arrested in downtown Shreveport yesterday afternoon on charges of being drunk and disorderly.

The arresting officer, H. H. Pittman, said he nabbed Williams in front of a downtown café at about 4:30 p.m. The arrest was made on the complaint of the café owner, who reported a "drunk in front of my place."

Pittman said Williams, who insisted that "I shouldn't have to go to jail," was dressed in a blue serge suit and a bright green hat with a big feather.

Pittman said that Williams was also carrying a. 38 caliber revolver when he was arrested. No weapons charge was filed against him.

Williams was released on bond at 9:45 p.m.

Williams is well known throughout the country for his hillbilly compositions, including "Lovesick Blues," which made him famous, "Jambalaya," currently popular, and several others.

SOURCE "Famous Song Composer Is Arrested Here," *Shreveport Times*, December 12, 1952. Reprinted by permission of the *Shreveport Times*.

LAST RITES FOR HANK WILLIAMS — Hank's funeral drew the largest crowd ever to attend any funeral in Montgomery. The funeral was held in the city auditorium in order that more people might attend but the crowd had to wait outside that cold January day.

Photograph of the crowd at Hank Williams's funeral service, published in an unidentified Alabama newspaper, ca. January 5, 1953. Courtesy of the Alabama Department of Archives and History, Montgomery, Alabama.

Part II

"Hank, It Will Never Be the Same without You"
Mourning the Death of Hank Williams (January–February 1953)

Hank Williams's sudden death on January 1, 1953, generated a tidal wave of published responses in the days and weeks that followed. These writings included not only editors' and journalists' attempts to make sense of the star's untimely passing, but also, significantly, the first efforts to determine his ultimate legacy. Their accounts signaled a noticeable shift in the writing about Williams, from a focus during his lifetime on the successful and supposedly contented "Organization Man" to a discussion of the more troubled elements of his life story. The earliest pieces consisted of rushed newspaper reports—often incomplete and littered with factual errors—that announced the shocking news that Williams, only twenty-nine years old, had been pronounced dead in Oak Hill, West Virginia. Subsequent articles added new details to the evolving story, covered his spectacular funeral in Montgomery, Alabama, and provided the results of his autopsy and the coroner's inquest. Williams had died, a coroner's jury concluded on January 10, of a "severe heart condition and hemorrhage[s]" in the heart and neck, adding that "No evidence was found of foul play." Although the autopsy revealed "alcohol in Williams's bloodstream," the Associated Press reported, "there was no indication of narcotics or other drugs." Despite the official determination that Williams had died of natural causes, a host of unanswered questions persist to this day, as it remains uncertain precisely when or where he died, and what exactly caused his death.

In these first days of January, editorials appeared in southern newspapers, particularly in the major city dailies in Montgomery and Nashville, which eulogized Williams and sought to explain his popularity. Reports of his massive January 4 funeral triggered another flurry of editorials, this time including newspapers based outside the South as well, that sought not so much to celebrate the late singer or his music as to account for the astonishing size of the crowd that had flocked to Montgomery's City Auditorium to attend his memorial service. In their attempts to comprehend the Williams phenomenon, editors and journalists grasped for comparisons with other deceased celebrities and public figures—Rudolph Valentino, Al Jolson, Jean Harlow, even President Franklin D. Roosevelt. Writers struggled, however, to identify those personal qualities that had enabled Williams to forge such a remarkable bond with fans throughout the United States. Some editorialists advanced the "Populist Poet" interpretation originally introduced by the Reverend A. S. Turnipseed in his 1947 newspaper column (no. 2), while others expressed skepticism about Williams's stardom and the rising popularity of country music. Still other commentators dwelt on the darker, Shakespearean dimensions of Williams's life and success that his death had exposed, depicting him as an admirable but deeply troubled "Tragic Hero" who, despite all his commercial achievements, never succeeded in overcoming his private demons.

By any measure, Williams's demise produced an unexpected windfall for the country music industry, as his fans, who seemed to multiply by the minute, clamored to hear his music and to purchase any product that carried his name or likeness. Sales of every record in Williams's catalog soared to the point that, as *Billboard* magazine reported on January 17, MGM Records' pressing plant was "having difficulty keeping up with the demand." In the three weeks following Williams's death, his music publisher, Acuff-Rose, reported that it had sold a combined ten thousand copies of his two song folios, which each typically sold seven hundred copies per month, and besieged radio disc jockeys struggled to satisfy listeners' countless requests for Williams's records by either "block-programming" them in two-hour segments or playing one record every fifteen minutes. Marveling at the surge in consumer demand engendered by his death, his musical collaborator and publisher Fred Rose, along with MGM Records president and general manager Frank Walker, spearheaded the marketing of the late singer's music, promising fans that there would be a continuing stream of new Williams releases drawn from recordings in the MGM vaults.

Yet another indication of Williams's extraordinary posthumous appeal was the proliferation of commercially recorded tribute songs honoring his life and mourning his death. The first and most popular such disc was Jack Cardwell's "The Death of Hank Williams," released in mid-January 1953. By the end of that year, no fewer than nineteen others had joined it on the market, including Ernest Tubb's "Hank, It Will Never Be the Same without You," which provides the title for this section. Such recordings initiated a trend that continues to this day in the form of songs that are either about or include references to Williams.

In addition to purchasing records, song folios, and other products related to their late singing idol, many grieving fans felt compelled to commit their thoughts to paper. Some fifteen thousand sent sympathy cards and messages to Williams's mother and family, and the scores of letters received by Montgomery and Nashville newspapers reveal the deeply personal ways in which individuals of every age, from across the United States and beyond its borders, responded to Williams's death. For many fans, Williams seemed to have been more like a friend or a family member than a distant and inaccessible radio performer and recording artist. These frequently poignant testaments lent credence to the emerging characterization of Williams as a poet of the common people.

The mass outpouring of public grief, the spike in posthumous record sales, the rash of tribute songs, and the flood of heartfelt editorials and letters were striking, but the fate of the recently deceased star's legacy nevertheless remained uncertain in 1953. Despite predictions in the immediate wake of his death that he would never be forgotten and that his songs would live forever, the notion that the late Hank Williams was destined for musical immortality was far from a foregone conclusion.

| 12 |

Mystery Shrouds Death of Singer Hank Williams

After sixty years, the final hours of Hank Williams's life remain a mystery. According to his death certificate, he passed away at seven o'clock on the morning of January 1, 1953, in Oak Hill, West Virginia. But both the date and the site are in question, as he may actually have died in the late hours of December 31, 1952, and at any spot along the snowy stretch of highway between Knoxville, Tennessee, where he and his driver had checked into a hotel for a few hours, and Oak Hill, where he was pronounced dead at the local hospital. The following front-page article, excerpted from the *Knoxville Journal*, is the first of dozens of such pieces to address the intriguing questions about the exact timing of Williams's death. It raises the possibility, based on Tennessee Highway Patrolman Swan H. Kitts's eyewitness account, that the singer may have expired several hours before being officially pronounced dead in Oak Hill.[*] Another revelation reported here is that, during the brief layover in Knoxville, a local doctor had given Williams two injections of what, although not disclosed in this article, turned out to be vitamin B-12 laced with a small amount of morphine.

Hank Williams, the hillbilly singer who made Nashville his headquarters, was found dead in the back seat of his chauffeur-driven automobile in West Virginia yesterday, but officers are investigating the possibility that he was dead six hours earlier when his speeding car was stopped by a highway patrolman at Blaine, [Tennessee], near Rutledge.

SOURCE   "Mystery Shrouds Death of Singer Hank Williams," *Knoxville Journal*, January 2, 1953.
[*] A few days after Williams's death, Kitts conducted a full investigation of the incident he describes below, but his official report was subsequently misplaced and did not come to the attention of Williams's biographers until it was first published in Doug Morris's article, "Hank Williams' Death Still Issue," in the December 15, 1982, issue of the *Knoxville Journal*.

54

Highway Patrol Cpl. Swann [Swan] Kitts said he saw Williams lying in the back seat when the patrolman stopped the car hours before Williams' death was reported.

"I told the driver, Charles Harold Carr of Montgomery, Ala., that Williams looked dead, but I did not press the point when Carr explained that Williams had been given two sedatives by a Knoxville physician."

The death of the 37-year-old [sic] ballad singer whose income is said to exceed $100,000 a year at first was attributed to a heart attack, but West Virginia authorities said an autopsy would be performed to determine the exact cause.

It was the chauffeur who reported Williams' death. He told officers that while going through West Virginia to a Canton, Ohio, New Year's [Day] theater engagement, he stopped the car and found that the "sleeping" singer was cold. He raced six miles to Oak Hill Hospital, Carr said, but Williams was pronounced dead upon arrival at the hospital shortly before 7 a.m.

Patrolman Kitts said last night that Williams did not awaken during the discussion in which he took the chauffeur to task for speeding. Carr paid a $25 fine and [court] costs at Rutledge on a charge of speeding. The car was stopped at Blaine after it almost collided with a highway patrol car, Kitts said.

Williams, singer and composer often called "King of the Hillbillies" by his followers, had been scheduled to make a personal appearance in Charleston, W. Va., but the plane on which he was traveling was grounded in Knoxville because bad weather prevented a landing at the West Virginia city.

Williams and Carr then set out for another engagement in Canton, O., by automobile after Williams consulted a physician here and was given two injections to enable him to sleep, according to Carr.

Carr, 18, said the 29-year-old singer had been in ill health for some time. He said a relief driver, Donald Surface, was picked up in Bluefield, W. Va., at 5:30 a.m. When Carr, following a nap, attempted to awaken Williams between Beckley and Oak Hill he could not do so.

| 13 |

H. B. Teeter: Hank Williams Had Premonition of Death

A standard element of Hank Williams lore holds that he foresaw his impending death. Some have offered as evidence the fact that at the time he died his single "I'll Never Get Out of This World Alive" was scaling the Top Ten record charts, while others have pointed to the disturbing dream he reportedly had, on the eve of his final road trip, in which he claimed to have seen "God comin' down the road after me." *Nashville Tennessean* feature writer H. B. Teeter's front-page article, published one day after Williams's death, appears to be the first printed account to make this otherworldly claim on behalf of the singer. Teeter (dates unknown) ranges well beyond the supernatural, however, providing several quotations and anecdotes that not only offered insights into Williams's life and personality, but also were subsequently used in the construction of his legend, a process that, as this article reveals, was already well underway.

Hank Williams—the lonesome Alabama country boy who rose to fame and riches with an $8 guitar and a melancholy voice—had a premonition of his own death several months ago.

He told me: "I will never live long enough for you to write a story about me."

This statement came out in a series of interviews I had with the country song writer and singer whose records sold in the millions.

CAREER WAS FABULOUS

Yesterday, while he was en route to Canton, Ohio, for a personal appearance, death came to the singer-writer whose career was one of the shortest—and most fabulous—in American music.

Charles Carr, chauffeur for the radio and recording star, said the 29-year-old Williams became unconscious in his automobile near Oak Hill, W. Va.

"I thought he was asleep," Carr said. "I reached over and touched him. He was cold."

SOURCE   H. B. Teeter, "Hank Williams Had Premonition of Death," *Nashville Tennessean*, January 2, 1953. © 1953, *The Tennessean*. Reprinted with permission.

WAS DEAD ON ARRIVAL

Williams—in semi-retirement since a serious illness and back operation—was pronounced dead on arrival at an Oak Hill hospital. The body is to be returned to Montgomery, Ala., where funeral services are incomplete.

An inquest into his death will be held today.

In the music world, Williams' death brought memorial programs throughout the nation.

The lank, lean and lonesome singer was credited last night with "breaking the barrier between the country and popular music fields."

Murray Nash, associated with Acuff-Rose, publishers of music, said:

"With Hank Williams' passing the American music field has lost one of its greatest writers and artists."

"Seldom is anyone considered as being the top in both classifications. But for the past few years, Hank Williams has held this distinction."

SOLD PEANUTS, SHINED SHOES

Williams, who was recently separated from WSM "for failure to make appearances," was a resident of Montgomery, Ala. As a youth he sold peanuts and shined shoes, meanwhile strumming on a guitar under the guidance of an aged Negro resident of his home town.

At 14, Williams organized his own country band. He played on radio stations in Alabama and Louisiana.

"I guess I kinda resisted formal education," Williams once said. "I picked and sang at night and I reckon I must have slept through my classes."

Williams liked to indicate his lack of formal education. In his songs, window is "winder," help is "hep," invitation is "invertation," picture is "pitcher."

SONGS SOLD FAST

But the songs he wrote in the few years of his career sold an estimated 10,000,000 records.

Jack Norman of Nashville, his attorney, financial advisor, and friend, said last night:

"This nation has lost a great poet and composer. His was the genius that proved there is no line of demarcation between the popular music field and the country field."

A psychiatrist once described Williams "as the most lonesome, the saddest, most tortured and frustrated of individuals."

"I'M SO LONESOME..."

It was because of this trait, many believed, that Williams wrote and made such songs as "Long Gone Lonesome Blues," "I'm So Lonesome I Could Cry," "Jambalaya," "Cold, Cold Heart," and "I Dreamed of Mama Last Night." One of his latest was "I'll Never Get Out of This World Alive."

Almost 100 of his songs came into national prominence.

But misfortune dogged him throughout his life, friends said last night, even with success beyond an entertainer's fondest dream.

As a youth, Williams said, he stood outside a small town motion picture theater and couldn't find the dime to enter.

"I think that's where he got his cowboy complex," a fellow entertainer said yesterday. "He never sang western songs, but he called his outfit the 'Drifting Cowboys.' He started a store which features western costumes and his own western clothing wardrobe was elaborate."

Williams came to Nashville about five years ago, riding from Shreveport, La., by bus. He walked into the office of Fred Rose, Nashville composer, and sang a few of his songs.

DIDN'T BELIEVE HIM

Rose said that, frankly, he didn't believe the lean, drawling country boy had written the songs.

"Let me give you an imaginary situation and see what kind of a song you write," Rose said. "Come back with the song as soon as you can."

The situation Rose outlined had to do with an impoverished youth who had lost his sweetheart. Williams came back with "Mansion on the Hill," which proved to be one of his most popular songs.

Although he was branded "temperamental" by close friends, Williams never forgot his fans. Although he did not appear to be sturdy, he once stood knee deep in snow for two hours signing autographs with Ernest Tubb in Amarillo, Texas, where the two country stars appeared before 18,000 persons.

TOLD OFF BERLE

The Williams philosophy was unique. Once he told Milton Berle, the comedian who likes to get into everybody's act: "Mr. Berle, if you come on this stage with me, I'll wrap this guitar around your head."

Berle didn't come on the stage with Williams that night.

This incident was told [to] me by Williams one night at his former home on Franklin Road, the home he said "music built for me." At that time, Williams was in blue jeans, bending over a small record player. Beside him was a stack of recordings of his own songs, recorded by Jo Stafford, Frankie Lane [Laine], Guy Mitchell and others.

WAS OFTEN BROKE

Although Williams made approximately $1,000,000 in his brief career,* it was not unusual for him to "be flat broke."

As a composer, Williams was so prolific that he invented an alter-ego, "Luke the Drifter," who narrated some of the songs closest to the composer's heart.

"These are for the take-home trade," Williams said. "I don't like for these songs to make the juke boxes. They are mostly sad songs about mother, funerals, death and men with broken hearts."

His philosophy was that men in taverns, hearing his recitations, would either break down and cry or start a free-for-all fight.

Bill Matthews, organizer of the Jordanaires,† believes Williams was one of the greatest hymn writers of modern times. The country singer had a deep religious strain which came to the surface in such hymns as "I Saw the Light."

PUT IT ON TAPE

Nash said last night Williams never actually "wrote" a song. He did not try to compose. He spent many hours before a tape recorder, never putting the song down in words until it was well in his mind. He once recorded 15 [radio] transcriptions without [a] script, without a stutter, ad-libbing all the while.

Although he was six feet tall, Williams weighed hardly more than 140 pounds. Rose, who worked closely with Williams, recognized him as "a natural poet whose songs just came out of him." Williams credited the Nashvillian song writer with giving him the "breaks" that brought him fame in the world of American music. [...]

WAS DIVORCED

Williams was employed by KWKH in Shreveport, La., after his separation from the "Grand Ole Opry." Before leaving here he was divorced by Mrs. Audra [Audrey] Mae Williams, who had sometimes been his stage partner. On Oct. 19, on the stage of the municipal auditorium in New Orleans, he was married to the former Miss Billie Jones of Bossier City, La.

---

* Williams's income appears to have been considerably less, perhaps only half of this amount.
† A white southern gospel quartet, formed in 1948, best known as the background vocal group for Elvis Presley as well as for numerous Nashville country stars.

He explained: "All the folks want to see me [get] married, and all of them can't get in the auditorium at once."

Jimmie Davis, the ex-governor of Louisiana, is fond of telling how he brought one of his songs—not too successful—to Hank Williams. Williams put "Lonesome Whistle" into the top brackets by re-writing the words and singing it in his melancholy style.

"If anything is typical of Hank Williams, it is the sadness of a lonesome soul, singing his heart out," one entertainer said yesterday.

~~~~~~

| 14 |

Joe Azbell: Hank's Funeral Is Far Largest in All Montgomery's History

Any doubts about the size and devotion of Hank Williams's audience were dramatically dispelled by the massive public response to his death. Held on the chilly Sunday afternoon of January 4, 1953, the singer's funeral was attended by some three thousand mourners who packed the Montgomery City Auditorium, while a crowd estimated at between 15,000 and 20,000 gathered outside and thousands of others waited at Oakwood Cemetery Annex to pay their last respects. It was the largest funeral in Montgomery's history and remains one of the largest in the history of the American South.

In the account excerpted below, *Montgomery Advertiser* city editor Joe Azbell (1927–1995) notes not only the size of the crowd but also its diversity, including the presence of some two hundred African American mourners in the auditorium's segregated balcony seating. In the eulogy, which was broadcast along with the rest of the funeral service on two local radio stations, Dr. Henry L. Lyon, Jr. (1907–1985), the conservative pastor of Montgomery's Highland Avenue Baptist Church, advanced an anticommunist Cold War variation of the "Populist Poet" theme, emphasizing that, above all, Williams offered "a human, heart-felt message" and embodied Americans' God-given "freedom to succeed."

"When he played on his guitar, he played on the heart-strings of millions of Americans." Dr. Henry L. Lyons [Lyon], pastor of the Highland Avenue Baptist Church, spoke this line as he officiated at the last and greatest packed house for

---

SOURCE   Joe Azbell, "Hank's Funeral Is Far Largest in All Montgomery's History," *Montgomery Advertiser*, January 5, 1953. Reprinted courtesy of the *Montgomery Advertiser*.

Hank Williams here yesterday when silent thousands filed past his open casket and top folk artists twanged out his requiem in hill-billy hymns.

It was a strong statement and true. It bore some reason why 15,000 to 20,000 people, shoving, pushing, waiting, jammed Perry Street, the city auditorium, and the entire City Hall block to look upon the body of this famed singer and composer as he lay in a spotless white suit in a gray casket near the flower-curtained stage where once he had appeared as a singer.

Even in death, Hank Williams set records. Never before in the history of his hometown of Montgomery had so many turned out for a funeral service. They came from everywhere, dressed in their Sunday best, babies in their arms, hobbling on crutches and canes, Negroes, Jews, Catholics, Protestants, small children, and wrinkled faced old men and women. Some brought their lunch, arrived at 9 a.m., seated themselves in the auditorium, and refused to move until the services ended at 3:30 p.m.

They sat solemnly, only the squawls [*sic*] of babies, the rasping of coughs, and [the] soft shuffle of feet breaking the silence, many weeping. Others holding their heads low. All of them ready to spend this Sunday to say, "We'll miss you, Hank."

FILED PAST CASKET

Thousands, handkerchiefs to their faces, hats in hands, slowly passed the casket, beset on one side by two large floral wreaths in guitar shapes, one with silver strings, two purple-toned lamps in the back, and a white Bible-shaped floral design to the side, a tiny white Bible in his hand, a small silk pillow near.

As the people marched down one aisle, past the casket, and out a side door, scores more pushed their way forward to glance at the body. One woman knelt on her knees, cried, stepped away from the casket, and fell to the floor in a faint. She was carried to an automobile at the rear of the auditorium by firemen and revived. "He's gone...gone," she repeated again and again. Three other women fainted during the services, but were revived.

A crowd of several thousands were left standing in the snapping cold as the services began at 2:30 p.m. Ernest Tubb, a friend of Williams, began the ceremony with the soft tones of "Beyond the Sunset" and as he reached the words of the "autumn leaves turning brown" there was complete silence. The Southwind Singers, a Negro quartet, sang a spiritual. In the balcony section where about 200 Negroes sat, eyes became watery and many knelt before their seats.

Dr. Lyons began his message, reading the 23rd Psalm, I Corinthians 15:50–58, and John 14:1–7, verses, and the audience lifted their heads. It seemed as if the lights in the auditorium were dimmed lightly. Many broke through the doorway, stood against the walls. The sobbing of the audience could be heard as the minister finished the last words of the Biblical verses.

Roy Acuff, dressed in his western-type attire, came on the stage, moved to the microphone, attempted to introduce the other 12 singers and musicians, [and] finally gave up, saying: "I am so moved I can't remember their names...they've been with me for years."

Then the slow, flowing melody of "I Saw The Light" echoed across the auditorium and into the mob-packed streets. Acuff tried to express his feelings for Hank Williams: "All I can say is he was one of the finest young men that we ever knew."

MUSICIANS CRY

The "Peace In The Valley" of which Dr. Lyon said "all men search" was told in a song sung by Red Foley. Backstage, Jimmy Dickins [Dickens] broke into tears and the other musicians and singers sobbed audibly but none spoke.

Outside the crowds showed restlessness. They packed closer to the door, many pressed their faces to the glass, begging for a look inside, others lifting children to their shoulders. Others left to go to automobiles to turn on radios to hear the service.

An old friend of Williams, the Rev. Talmadge Smith, pastor of the Ramer Baptist Church, in a prayer asked that the "Lord look down on and bless his mother in her grief and give her the strength to go and find in Christ the spiritual comfort that can come only from Him."

Dr. Lyons, dressed in a blue suit, moved to the microphone, and speaking in a soft voice, began his message:

"Hank Williams, the singing idol of millions of American, has just answered the call of the 'last round-up.' Even so, if this world should last a thousand years, Hank shall remain dear to millions of hearts. I cannot preach the funeral of Hank Williams. It has already been preached in music and song on the radio—listened to by millions of admiring Americans since the sad message of his death was announced Thursday. The preacher of the message—Hank Williams, the congregation—the American people. His life is a real personification of what can happen in this country to one little, insignificant speck of humanity. [...] We thank God for our great American country which gives us the privilege to sing like we want to sing and the privilege to listen to our own special kind of music—enjoying it with the entirety of our beings."

"Millions and millions will never tire of the genuine heart appeal of his songs. As long as we have America with its freedom to succeed, we will have our Hank Williams to inspire us in the midst of life's hardships."

"A GREAT AMERICAN"

"Hank Williams was a great American. What was the secret of his greatness? Listen, I'll tell you what it was—he had a message. It was swelling in him like a great body of water behind a massive dam. It was a message of the heart—Hank Williams's heart. Deep down in the citadel of his inner-being, there was desire, burden, fear, ambition, reverse after reverse, bitter disappointment, joy, success, sympathy, love for people. It was all there in Hank's heart. The break had to come, it did come. It came with Hank Williams playing on his guitar, singing only as a freeborn American can sing. When Hank played on his guitar, he played on the heart-strings of millions of Americans. They listened to Hank over the radio in their homes, in the bus station, in the car driving along the highway, in prison, in the office. They listened everywhere—white and colored, rich and poor, the illiterate and the educated, the young and the old. Yes, we all listened and we'll still listen. Why? Hank had a message. This message was written in the language of all the people. It was a message of the things that everyone feels—life itself. Years ago, one of America's greatest doctors said, 'If you have something which represents a genuine need of humanity, though you live in a cottage deep in the forest, mankind will beat a trail to your door.'[†] Hank Williams did have something humanity universally needs—a song with a human, heart-felt message."

Just before the benediction, the Statesmen Quartet sang "Precious Memories" and the services ended as the crowd waited quietly as the family moved out behind the casket. Outside, thousands formed a line of march that stretched for two-and-one-half city blocks through which the procession moved on its way to Oakwood Cemetery Annex. Many raced for their automobiles to go to the cemetery before the others arrived.

In the rush out of the auditorium, a woman fainted. In the streets, many got on top of automobiles and others moved to second floor viewing points to see the procession.

MAJORITY WERE FANS

Many were curiosity seekers at the funeral but by far, the majority were Hank Williams fans. They stood in line for hours. They waited in the crowds. Some went without lunch. Many came from Atlanta, Birmingham, Mobile, Nashville, Luverne, Georgiana, and whistle stops.

Three floral company trucks were required to move the scores of wreaths to the cemetery. Fire Chief R. L. Lampley and Assistant Police Chief Marvin Stanley, who directed the 100 firemen and policemen who kept order in the auditorium and streets, estimated the crowd at 15,000 to 20,000 at the time of the funeral but "other thousands came and left."

[†] A misquotation of a famous statement attributed to Ralph Waldo Emerson (1803–1882), the celebrated American essayist and poet.

The service was broadcast over Montgomery stations, dozens of tape recordings were made and photographers and newsmen were present from several Southern newspapers, wire services, and magazines. Flash bulbs popped everywhere but photographers said they were uncertain to photograph the huge mob.

Big-time folk music people filed past the casket for a last look of the country boy who had been great among them.

Ray Price, WSM Grand Ole Opera singer; Webb Pierce, another great in the folk music world; Carl Smith, who now holds the spot formerly occupied by Williams at WSM; June Carter of the famous Carter Sisters team; Bill Monroe, veteran performer in radio; Johnnie and Jack, a famous pair of singers; and "Little Jimmie [Jimmy] Dickens," one of Hank's best friends in Nashville, who cried almost constantly. [...]

As Acuff stopped at the casket he bent close to the body and whispered, "Good bye, Hank."

Hank's original Drifting Cowboys furnished the background music for singers. [...]

His wife, Mrs. Billie Jones Williams of Ocean [Bossier] City, La., was in the front row along with his ex-wife, Mrs. Audrey Williams of Nashville.

MARRIED IN NEW ORLEANS

It was less [than] three months ago, Oct. 19, that Williams married again in the City Auditorium at New Orleans. Many of the musicians at his funeral played the wedding music then. He married Billie twice on the stage that day—once for the benefit of the throng who couldn't see the first ceremony.

In filing for divorce early last year in Nashville, Mrs. Audrey Williams estimated her husband's 1951 income at more than $90,000.

Williams combined a nasal, undulating voice that could wring extra syllables from words with an amazing capacity for just sitting down and composing a new song. [...]

For the fans who thought his death brought an end to his songs and singing, his publishers had good news.

"Hank wrote, recorded and sang a lot of songs we haven't released yet," said [Fred] Rose at the funeral today.

"I can't say how many. It's a trade secret, but you'll be hearing Hank right along for some time."

| 15 |

Selected Newspaper Editorials

Editorials reacting to Hank Williams's death appeared in several southern newspapers, particularly in Montgomery and Nashville. Because the editorial writers were upper-middle-class individuals discussing a largely working-class phenomenon, they approached the late singer-songwriter and his music from a cultural distance. But, for the most part, they viewed him with sympathy, recognizing that millions of fans drew inspiration from his songs and deeply grieved his passing. The *Alabama Journal* editorialist offers a lone dissenting voice among the five southern editorials reprinted below, expressing a disdainful attitude toward "hillbilly" music that was shared by many Americans, even southerners, at the time.

In contrast, few newspapers outside of Williams's native South published editorials immediately following his death. It was instead the newswire service reports of his funeral that sparked commentary from non-southern newspapers. The final three editorials appeared in response to the memorial service and the spectacular crowd it drew, a phenomenon that surprised and puzzled observers unfamiliar with the radio and recording star and his songs. Like their southern counterparts, however, these writers attempt to explain Hank Williams's remarkable popularity and to assess the cultural significance of country music.

"MONTGOMERY'S FAMOUS FOLK SINGER"

ALABAMA JOURNAL (MONTGOMERY), JANUARY 2, 1953[*]

The passing of the hill-billy folk singer, Hank Williams, takes away a nationally famous Montgomery son.

While there have been many native sons who have figured more prominently in political and business circles, the young man who, only a few years ago was singing over a local radio station, achieved international fame in four short years.

His rise to fame was sensational. His voice was no greater than many other Montgomerians who are amateur vocalists. It was what he did with that voice that made him famous in his field of music. As a composer of folk music, the kind which some might call corny, he was among the country's best. There is not a juke box or a dance band in the nation which hasn't played and replayed a Hank Williams tune.

---

[*] Reprinted courtesy of the *Montgomery Advertiser.*

Today on every radio station and from every bandstand in the country, the current Williams hit "Jambalaya" plays forth.

His name is a by-word among that large segment of America which takes delight in the kind of music he wrote and sang.

Hank Williams' only claim to fame was a tricky voice and the ability to put on paper the lyrics and music of something which publishing and recording companies were eager to buy. This was enough to make his death a news story of national consequence.

"HANK WILLIAMS"

NASHVILLE BANNER, JANUARY 2, 1953

Hank Williams touched with song a multitude of hearts, and there is sadness at his passing…a star that burned brightly in the music firmament, only to fall at the peak of its brilliance.

His was the unusual gift of seeing, and feeling, life's repertoire of deepest sentiment—of translating it into language and melody, and with it tugging at a million heartstrings. A natural musician, he wove a fabric of songs as colorful—in pathos, in humor, in romantic vein, in hymn-type exhortation—as was his own personality.

His life was tragic in some particulars, but not, certainly, in lack of friends. Nor in default on gratitude to those countless thousands drawn to him as admirers and fans.

The news of his death occasions wide regret. Nashville and Middle Tennessee, where his star shined in its ascendency, feel it as a deep, personal loss.

"MR. HANK WILLIAMS"

NASHVILLE TENNESSEAN, JANUARY 3, 1953

It is a tragic fact that Mr. Hank Williams was never able to bring to his own life the satisfaction that he gave to so many others with his contributions to the fields of folk and popular music.

The professional career he carved out in his brief life was nothing short of fabulous. Once an unknown and impoverished farm boy, he parlayed an $8 guitar, a melancholy voice and a feeling talent for composition into national fame and a handsome income. Not only admired for his personal performances, he was credited by many with "breaking the barrier between the country and popular music fields."

For all this, however, he was never at peace with himself. Once described by a psychiatrist "as the most lonesome, the saddest, most tortured and frustrated of individuals," he was called "temperamental" by his close friends.

But it is said that, whatever his other shortcomings and troubles, he never forgot his fans, who can be numbered in the thousands. Among these admirers—many of whom are found here in Middle Tennessee where Mr. Williams gained his first prominence—his death is counted a distinct loss.

"HANK WILLIAMS"

MONTGOMERY ADVERTISER, JANUARY 3, 1953[†]

In appraising the life of Hank Williams, it is unimportant whether you liked his songs, whether in your opinion he created ugliness or beauty. The important thing is that he made millions of people happy, and no amount of quibbling over the artistic merit of his life's worth can erase that.

That Hank had a certain order of poetic genius is attested by the legions of those to whom his songs contained truths about life. For those people the words and music of Hank Williams were eternal verities such as the words of Keats are to others.

He was racked by physical and emotional afflictions, and these, coupled with his gift of song, made him kin to millions. He brought them relief and gayety, and that is a blessed work in a somber world.

"AT THE CEMETERY"

MONTGOMERY ADVERTISER, JANUARY 6, 1953

Never in the long history of this town have so many thronged the funeral of a citizen as they did in the case of Hank Williams. Bankers, jurists, physicians, writers, governors and philanthropists have been returned unto dust in Montgomery, but the coffin of none was followed as was that of the dead singer.

It is an example of the extent to which people take into their hearts their entertainers and how personal the relationship can become. The death of actress Jean Harlow put a load so heavy on the telephone wires as to blow the fuses—more calls than were occasioned by Pearl Harbor.

Again, it was the death on August 23, 1926 of Rudolf Valentino, the screen lover. It is recorded in Stanley Walker's *Mrs. Astor's Horse*[‡] that Valentino's death occasioned a high mass at a Rio de Janeiro cathedral. [...]

And there, of course, is a difference between Valentino's grip on his public and Hank's appeal. The star of *The Sheik* was hot love galloping across the Arabian sands on a stallion, a captive beauty lashed to his saddle. He was "love itself" and his appeal was almost entirely to women.

[†] This and the following editorial reprinted courtesy of the *Montgomery Advertiser*.

[‡] A 1935 collection of sensationalist profiles of the rich and famous.

But Hank's appeal was to men and women, young and old. Yesterday hundreds remained about his plot in the cemetery. Reporters asked them about their attachment to him and their answer was that he could express the things they felt.

"ART AND HILLBILLY MUSIC"
KANSAS CITY (MO.) TIMES, JANUARY 6, 1953

There are many answers to questions about what constitutes music, poetry and art in general and some of the views are in disagreement. Yet the sort of thing that drew a throng of 20,000 to the funeral of Hank Williams, hillbilly composer, in Alabama, is not easily subject to challenge.

That Williams touched a popular chord can hardly be denied. Here in America we have a lusty and variegated audience, and there is plenty of room for tolerance by both the people who run from a guitar and those who are drawn to it as if by a musical magnet.

We can't write off all of our ballads and folk music as tawdry or unworthy. Even some of the rhymes mothers sing to their babies, simple jingles centuries old, are strangely moving or soothing. Any tune that touches the heart has something good in it. And there is sound authority for calling it art.

"A GREAT SINGER PASSES"
SPOKANE (WASH.) DAILY CHRONICLE, JANUARY 8, 1953

Hank Williams was not a great musician by the yardstick of symphony and opera, but he won the hearts of a multitude as Stephen Foster did.

The young hillbilly composer wrote and sang his way to fame in six short years. His compositions were tuneful and colorful.

Why did his body lie in the large Montgomery, Ala., municipal auditorium? Why did 20,000 fellow Americans come to pay him a last tribute? Why did weeping break out audibly during the service? Why did tears stream down the faces of musicians who played the funeral music on fiddles and guitars?

Because Hank Williams' tunes went straight to the hearts of his hearers, and if the paraphrase is acceptable let it be said that he who writes the songs of a people is greater than he who taketh a city.[5]

"A NEW CATEGORY OF NATIONAL HERO"
HARTFORD (CONN.) COURANT, JANUARY 12, 1953

Students of hillbilly music were grief stricken the other day when one of the more accomplished composers of this type of music died suddenly. But before

---

[5] A reference to Proverbs 16:32.

you say sardonically that it should happen to more of them, let us point out that this particular young man was still in his twenties and already had several resounding hits to his credit. He was the creator of *Jambalaya* which, if you have ears, you have doubtless heard not once but dozens of times. You know. Big doings down on the bayou.

In addition to *Jambalaya* young Hank Williams also wrote *Cold, Cold Heart* and *Hey, Good Looking*, all of which were distinctive enough, and so superior to the average run of hillbilly lamentations, that they became popular hits.

Although hillbilly music has a certain vogue here, it is nothing compared with its popularity in other sections, particularly the South and southeastern parts of the country. The singer of hillbilly ballads in these areas becomes something like the movie stars of old. For example, it became the privilege of a famous hillbilly star like Roy Acuff to sing the final hymn at the bier of Hank Williams.

There is probably a link between most hillbilly music and early American folk songs. The greater part produced today is almost similar in its simplicity. It would be fine if American tastes became more widely cultivated to something better. But the opposite seems to be true. Slowly but surely the cult of the hillbilly spreads over the land. Not even a great general or statesman now gets the monetary rewards of a hillbilly singer in life, nor earns half the grief he gets in death. In some sections at least, the hillbilly singer is a new category of national hero.

~~~~~~

| 16 |

Allen Rankin: So Long, Hank. Hear You Later

The shift to a grimmer tone in the posthumous writings about Hank Williams is illustrated in this heartfelt tribute, published on the day of his funeral, by longtime *Montgomery Advertiser* columnist Allen Rankin. Rankin (1917–1991), who had previously touted Williams in the local press by emphasizing the singer's professional success (no. 3), here recalls the late hillbilly singer as a physically and emotionally tormented musical genius who wrote songs primarily as a means of personal catharsis. Sharply critical of those who would demean or dismiss country music, Rankin boldly compares him to Oscar Hammerstein II, the masterful lyricist of the Broadway musical. While Rankin overlooks Williams's troubles with alcohol and drugs and understates his commercial motives, the

SOURCE Allen Rankin, "Rankin File: So Long, Hank. Hear You Later," *Montgomery Advertiser-Alabama Journal*, January 4, 1953. Reprinted courtesy of the *Montgomery Advertiser*.

columnist clearly recognizes the inner turmoil that inspired much of the star's greatest work and that would become an essential ingredient of his growing legend.

So long, Hank.

It is significant that we can say just "Hank" and practically everyone in the South will know we mean Hank Williams, the "old master" of the "country-type" song, Hank the Hillbilly Hammerstein.

What other Hank is there—or was there? It will be hard to get used to speaking of you in the past. Your fatal heart attack this week was more shocking to us because you had just told us how you were going to "sit [sic] the woods on fire" in 1953. You'd have done it too, Hank. You've been doing it every year since 1947, when you wrote a song requesting a hound dog to "Move It On Over" for you in the doghouse.

We don't know whether the hound moved it on over or not, but the big-time did.

How lucky that you could spring from anonymity to fame at 23. That in the six brief years since—before death cut you down at 29—you could become an international sensation.

Lucky for you, Hank, for how you loved it, fame! The fat rolls of bills, the 10-gallon hats and Texas boots, the bespangled shirts, and the five Cadillacs—a different-colored Cadillac to match as many moods!

Lucky for the world, too, Hank, because you had what it takes. And what it takes is what people want. They didn't put up with your temperament, your eccentricities and, occasionally, your brooding ways, for nothing, Hank. Nuh-uhh. You gave them something in return, namely a phenomenal 125 Williams songs in six years! For two solid years your songs were never out of the top 10 on Hillbilly's Weekly Hit Parade. Perhaps you gave too much. For it is what you used to call "the busting out" inside of you, the obsession to catch down on paper and wax all the thousands of lyrics and melodies that reeled through your brain, that helped kill you young. It is often so with turbulent souls.

TRUE BARD, '47 TO '53

In your field you were a genius, Hank. Lesser writers squeeze their hearts all their lives to try to eke out one or two meager songs. Songs by the thousands boiled up in you. You would have "busted" if you couldn't have let them out. In the end you did "bust" with the birthpangs of them.

We wonder if enough people know what you were really like or [what] you really felt. There are still a few superior people, ignorant enough to smile down their noses at hillbilly music. They haven't realized that "country" and "western" music is perhaps America's most original and typical contribution to the arts; that hillbilly writers are our most honest, sincere and accurate recorders of American ways and feelings.

You were the best and most remarkable of them all, Hank. We know of no one who can touch you. You were the reverse of a hack. I have never known you to write a song just to please a publisher or to make money. You wrote only what you felt boil up inside you. You wrote only about what happened to you and the people around you.

So you were not just a hillbilly (you hated the name) or even a "country singer" (which you liked to be called). For the six years that you sang best, you were an honest-to-God troubadour, a bard of the type that once chronicled heart-feelings and events of the Middle Ages.

STREET VENDOR WITH DREAMS

You had a fine genius for getting down to the basic feelings of people and setting them to music, and you personally had a lot to set down:

The days when you were a peanut vendor here, a kid following around an old Negro guitarist named "Teetot." His twanging and wailings of "The Lovesick Blues" were magic to you. You had to learn how to howl like that yourself. You had to sing about how you grew up on a Georgiana farm, on "land so poor and yeller, you had to sit on a sack of fertilizer to raise an umbrella."

You had to record the day you rode in your grandmother's funeral and it was "Six More Miles" to the graveyard.

But you did not become the Hillbilly Hammerstein by being all melancholy. People weren't all that way and so you weren't. When you had troubles you grinned at them in your songs.

As a kid, you paid 50 cents a week till you finally got a $9 guitar, and the night you got it paid for, you had to "ruin it over a fella's head" to save your life in a honkytonk brawl. Fortunately, you soon managed [to acquire] another guitar, Hank. And no one, who (as you said of yourself) "couldn't read a note except in my heart," ever got further with one.

SLEPT THROUGH SCHOOL

Ironically, the things that made you a great troubadour wore you out too fast. You were not, for instance, an exemplary schoolboy at Lanier.* You couldn't

---

* Montgomery's Sidney Lanier High School, which Williams briefly attended as a sixteen-year-old sophomore, before dropping out, in October 1939, to pursue a musical career.

have been. You got through playing the all-night honkytonk circuits just in time to make it to class by 8:30. Naturally, you had to sleep sometime, and so you slept through school hours. Luckily your sleep was sound in English class. A bit of language polish might have ruined the wonderful, natural speech of your singing.

It is not odd, either, that you did not grow up to be a conservative, civic-minded luncheon club member. Few troubadours ever do. However, I know of several occasions when you turned over a check for $500 or $1,000—what difference did it make to you?—to hospitals or other charities.

You had a remarkable, Hammersteinian ear, for what was clean or clever in our rural language. Flowery, stilted phrases offended you. The worst thing you could think to say about a fancy lyricist was, "He's no good atall [sic]. He writes just like Shakespeare."

On the other hand, the highest compliment you could pay a song, yours or anyone else's, was: "Say, that's really great! It's really maudlin!"

You had a theory that if a singer "suffered" on the stage—howled, shed real tears and at times quivered all over—his audience would "suffer better" with him.

"Suffering" was no problem to you, Hank. Many a night you were hurting so much with neuritis or your last spinal operation that your voice and knees would have shaken anyway, without acting effort.

WARM, WARM HEARTS

Hank, your "Cold, Cold Heart" was a good song, a fine song. I remember when you wrote it. You were "all messed up inside," you said, as you so often were. "Cold, Cold Heart" wasn't a catch phrase that came to you for the money it would bring. You meant every word of it, from the bottom of your soul. You meant all your songs, and the ones you meant most were the great ones. That they happened to be hits was incidental to you.

"Jumbalaya" [sic] was like that. If I don't miss my guess, you were blue at the time it came to you. You needed something gay to cheer you up. So did a few million other people. And so "Jumbalaya" became a 15-record song-smash.

Fifty-three was going to be a great year for you, Hank. You had a new, beautiful wife. You were more settled, happier. Except for that pain that had paralyzed you the week before, you were feeling fine. You were going to "sit [sic] the woods on fire."

Well, you are going to do that anyway, for a long time to come. You won't be making any more personal appearances before mobs of 19,000 fans. You won't be causing any more lady fans to swoon. But right now your '53 hits are beginning to rollick from the juke boxes. They mock the fact that a boy named Hank Williams is dead at 29.

The prettiest thing about it is that they always will. Where people are young or old, happy or sad, in love or out, your better songs will go on playing.

We still sing songs that were written by real troubadours 1,500 years ago. And you were, and are, a real troubadour, Hank.

~~~~~~

| 17 |

Selected Letters to the Editor

In the wake of Hank Williams's sudden death, the *Montgomery Advertiser* and its afternoon affiliate, the *Alabama Journal*, were inundated by mail from fans across the nation who wrote to request photographs of the late country star and souvenir copies of newspaper editions containing articles about him. On January 7, in a front-page notice titled "Did You Know Hank Williams?" the *Advertiser* urged readers who "saw, spoke to, or knew anything about Hank Williams in any way to send in their reminiscences of the singer." The paper also announced that the fifty people submitting the best accounts would receive the sheet music of an unidentified forthcoming Williams song, courtesy of his music publisher, Acuff-Rose. Eventually, the *Advertiser* published some three dozen such letters from his fans and acquaintances, while collectively the *Alabama Journal* and the *Nashville Tennessean*—which also received many letters from grieving readers— printed a half-dozen or so more. The following sampling appeared in the eight weeks following Williams's death. Like the editorials that ran in these same newspapers (no. 15), many of these letters cast the late radio and recording star as a "Populist Poet," endowed with the ability to express the emotions and long- ings of ordinary people. Consistently, they reveal how deeply Hank Williams and his songs touched his fans' lives.

"SONGS FROM THE HEART"
ALABAMA JOURNAL (MONTGOMERY), JANUARY 6, 1953*
Editor, Alabama Journal,

"Our Hank" was the confidant of human nature. The South's guitar-playing troubadour wrote and sang songs that came from the heart. To him the gods of joy and sadness opened their infinite book of heartfelt lyrics.

Hank had an instinctive feeling for the type of expression that appears in actual folk music. His songs have the necessary appeal to make them survive

---

* Reprinted courtesy of the *Montgomery Advertiser*.

beyond their present popularity. To the rest of the nation, Hank Williams ranks with the South's best loved musicians and composers of "hill-billy" hit tunes.

As Americans, far and near, grow to know him better, the quality in Hank that most impresses all of us is his kindness—being helpful to others. His kindness extended to all humanity. And people who love folk music will sing "Our Hank's" songs, as long as human life knows joy and sadness, as long as human hearts are touched by tears and laughter, and human souls cherish all that is lovely and of good report.

J. Mitchell Pilcher
Montgomery

"WE LOVED YOU, HANK"

NASHVILLE TENNESSEAN, JANUARY 7, 1953

To the Editor:

Jan. 2, 1953. A thick fog of rain settled around our house in the early morning hours. No one expected to hear that Hank Williams, the beloved country song-writer and singer, had suddenly passed away on New Year's Day.

We listened to the sad news and prayed that it was all a mistake, Hank. But there comes a time when reality tells us that our fears are real and that's when we face the truth. There was no mistake; our beloved Hank was dead.

There were tears in our eyes as we got ready for school, Hank. We didn't want to talk about it, but occasionally one of us would look at the other and say, "I wish it wasn't true."

At school, we went to our classes as usual and recited our lessons, but when we looked across the aisle at a schoolmate, there was a sad expression on his face and we knew he was mourning for you, Hank.

Yes, Hank, America is mourning for you. We loved you and your ever popular songs.

We looked at the papers, when they arrived at school, Hank, and there was the sad story of your death. We cut out the story and carefully placed it in our book, so when we went home we could paste it in our scrapbook to keep forever.

In assembly, we bowed our heads and prayed silently: "Dear God, please bless Hank Williams, as he lies a corpse. Please take him to Heaven with you, O, Lord, where he will be happy in his mansion of gold. We have lost one of the best singers and song-writers in the world, but we'll meet him in Heaven someday. Amen."

As we worked in the school cafeteria, we sang, "I've got a mansion just over the hilltop," as a memorial to you, Hank. We know that you've got a mansion in Heaven and that you've gone from us to live in that mansion. And we pray that you will be very happy in your new home.

We read in the paper that you were the most lonesome, the saddest, most tortured and frustrated person that ever lived. Oh, Hank, why were you so lonesome and lost?

As this dark, dreary day comes to a close, we shall also close our message to you. Even though we never saw you in person, we loved you, Hank.

Retha Mae Brewer, 19
Nettie Jean Brewer, 14
Hohenwald, Tenn.

"LOST A FRIEND"

NASHVILLE TENNESSEAN, JANUARY 7, 1953

To the Editor:

Many have lost a means of entertainment.

Hank Williams traveled with me on many a pleasant mile and sang for me many pleasant hours.

During his short life his greatest accomplishment was bringing pleasure to his fellow man.

May he find the peace and happiness he seemed to seek. May the world appreciate this man who did so much when he was so pained and sick.

I feel I have actually lost a friend.

Alex E. Jones
Clarksville, Tenn.

"HE WAS NOT PREJUDICED"

MONTGOMERY ADVERTISER-ALABAMA JOURNAL, JANUARY 11, 1953[*]

The few little things I know about Hank add up to a lot, because he thought as much of a poor man as he did a rich man, and he (would) just as soon speak to a colored man, woman or child as he would a white man.

One thing I remember about him is the way he carried his shoulders with each quick stride. If it was the first time he had ever seen you, he would talk to you just as well as he would someone he had known all of his life, and (he) would tell you where he was going or supposed to be (going) just like it was as much your business as it was his.

Like one day he said to me: "I'm supposed to be at the courthouse but it looks like I'm late, and I don't know what the judge is going to do to me."

Everywhere you would see him, someone would hallow [sic]...and say, "Hi Hank," or "How are you doing, Hank?"

---

[*] This and the following two letters reprinted courtesy of the *Montgomery Advertiser*.

I'll always remember him as the man…who didn't let popularity put his head above any other man's head.

Jackson J. Boddle
Prattville, Ala.

"CAPABLE ARTIST"

MONTGOMERY ADVERTISER-ALABAMA JOURNAL, JANUARY 11, 1953

To the average modern musician, frequently called "jazz men," and also to the serious musician, often called "Squares or Longhairs," folk music or "hillbilly" music is not to their taste. When Hank Williams played and sang to us (Local 479 AMF‡) at the Musicians' Party, Sunday, Dec. 28, [1952] all of us, including the above two groups, were there. We listened attentively as if attending a concert by Benny Goodman or hearing the cultivated voice of some operatic star. We forgot our talent, technical skill and musical training; we truly enjoyed every note of song done by this capable artist.

This last appearance here in his home town was not public and I only met him once, and had a few pleasant words with him. However, his magnetic personality—plain and honest as it was—will be a lasting memory to all who were present. His was a God-given talent projecting through him into his music and lyrics. They will last forever and be a glowing part of our American heritage.

Tom Hewlett
President of Local 479 AFM
Montgomery, Ala.

"HANK WILLIAMS IN THE LAND OF WAGNER"

MONTGOMERY ADVERTISER, FEBRUARY 24, 1953

Editor, The Advertiser:

As we have received so many clippings of Hank Williams' death from the States, I thought it might be of interest to you about how we people over here felt about Hank.

There are three reasons my husband and I are interested in hearing all we can about Hank. One is that my husband was also born close to Georgiana, Ala. Another is that I have personally known Hank since about 1938. The most important reason is that we both love hillbilly music, and [are] not ashamed of it, and Hank was our favorite singer.

---

‡ The American Federation of Musicians, an international union of professional musicians in the United States and Canada founded in 1896.

I asked at the PX[s] for records by Hank Williams and the German Fraulein said in broken English, "Hank, he dead, we heard on radio." I stood there for a moment and then I began to feel weak, a sick feeling in the pit of my stomach. The only thing I can compare it to is the day I was listening to the radio and heard about FDR. And I don't think it's wrong to compare the two, as they both were well known and loved by the public. Hank was [the] No. 2 boy on hillbilly records on AFN[¶] in 1952 and he was No. 1 in '51. He was well liked by all the GIs, and Germans also. We all felt the loss very much.

Mrs. Edgar B. Hanks
Wiesbaden, Germany

| 18 |

Frank Walker: Letter to Hank Williams

Prominent among those who publicly mourned Hank Williams's unexpected passing were music industry insiders, particularly Frank B. Walker (1889–1963), president and general manager of MGM Records, who had signed him to a recording contract in 1947. Walker claimed that he had reworked his customary New Year's Day letter to Williams to create this tribute, addressed to the late recording star in care of "Song Writers' Paradise." Walker's sentimental dispatch was widely published in country music fan magazines and music industry publications, and *Billboard* went so far as to pronounce it "one of the finest eulogies ever written." It also graced the back cover of MGM's *Hank Williams Memorial Album*, which appeared in March 1953. At the personal request of Williams's mother, Lillie Stone, MGM also released an abridged recorded version, titled "The Last Letter," by Jimmy Swan, a Hattiesburg, Mississippi, disc jockey and aspiring country singer who had known Williams personally. Despite a glowing review from *Billboard*, Swan's recitation failed to make much of an impression in a country music record market then saturated with Hank Williams tribute songs.

January 1, 1953
(New Year's Day)
Mr. Hank Williams
c/o Song Writers' Paradise

SOURCE "Frank Walker's Letter to Hank Williams," *Cash Box*, January 17, 1953, p. 25.
[s] Post Exchange, general-goods retail stores located on U.S. army bases.
[¶] American Forces Network, an information and entertainment radio network whose broadcasts served U.S. servicemen and their families stationed at bases overseas.

Dear Hank:

You see it was my intention to write you today as has been my custom for many years past. We've been great friends, you and I, and I've always enjoyed writing you on New Year's Day, referring to the year just past, but particularly looking forward to things as I might see them in the New Year.

Only yesterday I was thinking of some of the little things I would mention in my letter, but somehow I think I'll have to change the letter a bit for an hour or so ago I received a phone call from Nashville. It was rather a sad call too, Hank, for it told me that you had died early this morning. I don't know much about the circumstances and it really doesn't matter, does it? What does matter, though, is that the World is ever so much better for the fact that you have lived with us, even for such a short time.

Please forgive me, Hank, for including in this note one or two of the little things I was going to mention in my regular letter. I wanted to tell you that undoubtedly the year 1952 was your greatest year—I would have reminded you of those great songs "Cold, Cold Heart," "Half As Much," "Settin' The Woods On Fire," "You Win Again," "Jambalaya," and lots of others. I wanted to say that I agree with you that the two songs to be released late in January of the New Year are definitely the greatest you have ever written. You know, the novelty one and that tremendous ballad.* I would have told you, and I believe it, that 1953 would prove, what I've known for so long, that you are one of the world's greatest writers of songs—powerful songs, songs of the heart, songs with a message, songs of the Hills and Plains. And I wouldn't have forgotten to mention too the plans we had in mind—that you would write a series of those wonderful religious songs, the kind you started some years back and which you so loved to do. I would have reminded you too of that day in Baltimore several years ago when you said "You know, Mr. Walker, you and I both came from the country, our names, Hank and Frank, rhyme pretty good too, we ain't gonna have any trouble—ever," and we didn't, Hank, did we?

Yes, Hank, I had so many, many things I wanted to write you about today but somehow it's just a little bit harder saying them than I thought it would be. I know I was going to tell you that I was putting out country songs before you were born, and how happy I am to have been allowed to stay around to hear the wonderful ones that you wrote and sung. I'm sure I would have told you that I so wanted to be around for quite a while yet to hear some more of them.

Remember the time the newspaper man asked you how you wrote a song? I'll never forget your answer—"I just sit down for a few minutes, do a little

---

* A reference, respectively, to "Kaw-Liga" and "Your Cheatin' Heart," both of which became posthumous No. 1 hits for Williams.

thinking about things, and God writes them for me." You were so right, Hank, and do you know I think HE wanted to have you just a bit closer to him, Nashville's pretty far away, so HE just sent word this morning, Hank, that HE wanted you with him. You're going to be kept busy too, there's lots of work to be done way up there for we aren't improving too much here on earth. You'll be writing for the greatest singers too, the Angels, they're so wonderful—I know they'll want you to join them.

I'm sure that I was going to say I think you are a fabulous fellow, a wonderful writer, a sensational singer, a great genius, but I've said all of that in previous letters. Of course, I'll miss you, Hank, that's natural for we've been pretty close to each other down thru the years, but honestly I'm not too unhappy for I must rejoice with you at the tremendous opportunity you will have to do good for others. Don't forget your millions of friends; we'll be thinking a lot about you, so please remember us too.

I guess that's about all I have to write about on this New Year's Day, Hank. Thanks so much for being with us, and until I see you again,

HAPPY NEW YEAR, HANK.

Your Pal,
Frank Walker

Cover of *Hank Williams Memorial Souvenir Program*, 1954. Courtesy of the Alabama Department of Archives and History, Montgomery, Alabama.

Part III

~~~~~~

"Hank Williams Won't Die"
The Legend Emerges (1953–1964)

After the media attention surrounding Hank Williams's death and funeral subsided and his posthumous hit records dropped from the charts, there would have been every reason to expect that interest in him would diminish and that his memory and music would gradually be relegated to a largely forgotten past. "A couple of years after Hank died, we thought the 'legend,' too, was pretty much dead," recalled Jerry Rivers, who played fiddle in Williams's Drifting Cowboys Band. Yet not only did the late hillbilly star continue to command the attention of journalists and record buyers, but by the mid-1960s, the Nashville music establishment and even the Hollywood film industry had confirmed his status as a monumental figure who embodied and indeed transcended the genre of country music. As the title of a 1959 article in *Climax*, a men's adventure magazine, proclaimed, "Hank Williams Won't Die."

One catalyst behind Williams's ascension to legendary status was the sustained sales of his recordings, which MGM had repackaged with great success in more than thirty long-playing albums by 1965. But the ongoing fascination reflected more than merely record buyers' continued interest in his music. Writers and journalists from a variety of backgrounds were drawn to his story, each seeking the elusive answer to one essential question: Just who was Hank Williams? Was he a tragic musical genius worthy of reverence? Or, as more sordid details about his private life came to light, was he an irresponsible hedonist deserving only of pity or scorn? Did the truth lie somewhere between these extremes, or was it located somewhere else altogether?

Not surprisingly, Williams's immediate family members, who maintained not only a personal but also a financial interest in protecting his legacy, endeavored to promote a highly positive, wholesome posthumous image. Their writings introduced two new literary interpretations, that of the "Model Family Man"—which depicted Williams as a loving and dutiful son, a loyal brother, and a faithful husband and father—and, relatedly, that of the "Lay Preacher"—which presented him as a devout Christian who evangelized through his music. In an example of the first representation, his ex-wife Audrey Williams rhapsodized in newspaper articles about the undying love she and Williams shared, conveniently omitting any mention of their two divorces or his second marriage. But this interpretation found its fullest expression in his mother Lillie Stone's 1953 booklet *Our Hank Williams, "The Drifting Cowboy," as Told by His Mother to Allen Rankin*, an idealized, factually dubious account that, until more authoritative biographies appeared two decades later, served as the chief source of information about the singer's early life. For her part, his sister Irene Williams Smith assisted in the family's campaign of projecting a sentimentalized image of Williams through a regular column she wrote in the 1950s for the fan magazine *Country Song Roundup*.

While family members were publicly defining Williams as a devoted Christian and a caring and sensitive human being, an entirely different breed of writers advanced a third and equally durable interpretation, that of the "Tabloid Celebrity," which held Williams to be an unsympathetic, even depraved figure. Elements of this theme had first emerged only days after his funeral, in newspaper reports covering the bitter legal feud that erupted between Williams's mother and his widow over his estate, and then resurfaced in March, in the more sensational accounts of the Oklahoma state legislature's investigation into the criminal activities of Horace "Toby" Marshall, the quack doctor who supplied Williams with the prescription drugs that, in all likelihood, contributed to his death. But the fullest and most shocking presentations of the "Tabloid Celebrity" theme appeared in the profiles produced for celebrity scandal sheets and men's adventure magazines, the most lurid of which, Sanford Mabrie's 1955 *Behind the Scene* exposé, "The Strange Life and Death of Hank Williams," is reprinted below in its entirety. While it is tempting to dismiss these tabloid and pulp magazine articles for their sensationalism and sometimes outlandish claims, they nevertheless represented an important addition to the expanding body of Hank Williams literature. Not only did their appearance indicate broad popular interest in the most intimate details of Williams's life, but for a time, these articles constituted the only writings about him based on any significant amount of primary research. Moreover, several of Williams's later biographers accepted and presented as fact some of the more salacious, unsubstantiated revelations and anecdotes found in these accounts.

Meanwhile, in yet another, parallel development, Williams increasingly came to be recognized as a towering artist whose life and work embodied the essence of the nation's musical tradition, an interpretation that we term the "American Icon." The initial steps in this transformation occurred at the grassroots level with commemorative events such as Montgomery's short-lived "Hank Williams Memorial Day" celebrations, which began in 1954. By the end of the decade, however, as local interest in such events waned, the task of memorializing Williams shifted to Nashville, where, in 1958, representatives from the industry's various sectors had formed the Country Music Association (CMA) as a means of aggressively marketing the music nationwide. Consequently, Nashville industry insiders began touting country music as a genuine American folk art that crossed boundaries of genre, region, and class. Hank Williams proved an ideal symbol for this promotional campaign, which the Nashville music establishment itself officially acknowledged with his 1961 induction into the CMA's new Country Music Hall of Fame (now the Country Music Hall of Fame and Museum). Williams's rising stature was perhaps best expressed by veteran music journalist and CMA charter member, Charlie Lamb, who, in the liner notes to MGM Records' 1961 album, *Hank Williams' Greatest Hits*, not only proclaimed him to be the very "image of country music," but further asserted that his songs had become "a part of our American heritage."

This phase of the Hank Williams literature culminated with MGM Studio's 1964 biopic, *Your Cheatin' Heart*. Its screenplay, a scene of which is transcribed below, uneasily combined all the existing literary interpretations into a single package, but in the end emphasized the "Model Family Man" interpretation by revising and sanitizing Williams's final months. A milestone in the development of Williams's image, the movie's release might also have marked the end of any serious interest in the late star. Dead for more than a decade, safely ensconced in the Country Music Hall of Fame, his life story touchingly encapsulated in a Hollywood feature film, Hank Williams could reasonably have been regarded as a country music legend who, despite the CMA's best marketing efforts, had little continuing relevance to an American culture and music scene that were changing with disorienting speed.

| 19 |

Audrey Williams (as told to the *Montgomery Advertiser*): Hank's First Wife Tells Up and Downs of Marriage

Five days after Hank Williams's funeral, his ex-wife Audrey (1923–1975) made a bombshell announcement. Before his death, she told reporters, Hank had secretly planned to divorce his then-wife Billie Jean and to remarry Audrey sometime in early 1953, a claim that Billie Jean predictably dismissed as "preposterous." Thus began Audrey's public crusade to establish herself as Hank Williams's legitimate widow, a role she would expertly play—and from which she would handsomely profit—for the remainder of her life. Within five months of her former husband's death, she launched a tour of the eastern United States with an all-female hillbilly band, the Drifting Cowgirls, billing herself as "Mrs. Hank Williams"—"The Girl for whom the Late, Great Hank Williams Wrote His Famous Songs!" Meanwhile, Billie Jean embarked on a whirlwind musical tour of her own, also billing herself as "Mrs. Hank Williams." But in August 1953, as part of a $30,000 settlement she accepted from Williams's estate, she agreed to yield that coveted title exclusively to Audrey.

Only days after she revealed her ex-husband's supposed plans to remarry her, Audrey published this "as-told-to" article in the *Montgomery Advertiser*. In what was clearly another effort to place herself at the center of her ex-husband's biography, she describes her relationship with him as a one-of-a-kind love affair in which she served as his musical partner and songwriting muse. Although the byline identifies her as the "First Wife of Hank Williams," nowhere in the article

SOURCE   Audrey Williams (as told to *The Advertiser*), "Hank's First Wife Tells Up and Downs of Marriage," *Montgomery Advertiser*, January 13, 1953. Reprinted courtesy of the *Montgomery Advertiser*.

does Audrey mention that she and Williams were divorced at the time of his death, an omission that, when considered alongside the accusations she leveled in her 1952 divorce complaint (no. 9), indicates her determination to revise her relationship with Hank Williams in order to stake her claim to his legacy and to advance her own career.

There could never be another love like that of Hank Williams and myself.

I felt like that the day I married him in 1943 [*sic*], and I still feel the same way.

I met Hank one night in 1942* when he played for a medicine show in my home town, Banks, Ala.

Someone introduced us after the show and I knew immediately that here was the one person in the world who could make my dreams come true.

Prior to meeting Hank, nothing very exciting had ever happened to me.

I was born in the little community of Banks, just below Brundidge, and had attended Pike County schools most of my life.

Playing basketball on the Brundidge High School team covers just about the highest spot in my career until that time.

My father's family are all musicians—six boys and one girl.

When I was ten years old, my father bought me a guitar, but until I met Hank, the instrument meant little to me.

Soon afterwards, though, music became one of my greatest interests.

"HAD A DATE"

Hank and I had a date the night after I met him, and the second night he proposed.

I didn't believe he was serious, of course, but I was attracted enough to join his band a few weeks later as a singer.

Pretty soon, he said "I love you" so often that I got to believing it. I had wanted to believe it [for] a long time.

We were married about a year after our first meeting.

After our marriage, I kept singing with the band, and filling in when one of the musicians would be absent.

I also booked shows for the band, took up tickets and did any odd job that came to hand.

Hank and I didn't have much in those days. I washed his clothes—and later when we could afford it—I designed his stage clothes.

---

* Biographer Colin Escott dates the couple's first meeting to "the late summer of 1943."

When Hank hit the big-time just after the war, we moved to Nashville, and I signed contracts with the same people as Hank. I signed with him on MGM Records, with Acuff-Rose Publishing Co., and with the radio stations.

Hank and I had the good and bad—both financially and in love.

We were separated several times in the early years of our marriage. Show life is hard when one is trying to get a start. Nights without sleep, days of drudgery, and short tempers don't promote better marriage relationships.

Hank always used to say he wrote his songs for me.

"You are my inspiration," he said.

I do know that some of his best "suffering" songs were written during the times we were separated.

"Cold, Cold Heart" was one of them.

And I always went back.

I went back because I knew that the heart of Hank Williams was great. He was [a] genius if there ever was [a] genius.

I knew he would never hurt me or anyone else knowingly.

He was often misunderstood because his emotions and his thinking and his feelings were so much deeper than the average person.

But his love was even deeper. It can never be written on paper. Words won't express him or his life.

Somehow, even in the beginning, I knew that Hank Williams would be on top of [his field].[†] [All my childhood dreams] had been built, as most girls' dreams are, around being a star myself, and of marrying a star of the stage.

FORETOLD HIS FAME

The night I first met him, I could visualize him as the top star of the Grand Ole Opry. He looked as if he belonged there.

I also knew that I would eventually marry him.

[I felt the night I met Hank] that all my dreams had come true, and I realized it more and more as our courtship continued.

Even after marriage, and through difficult times, it kept pulling me back to him when other senses told me to stay away.

The dream was good—it was true.

Everything I ever wanted or could desire, I found in Hank Williams.

[†] Parts of this and the next sentence, as well as one in a following paragraph, are out of sequence in the original article due to typographical error. The words in brackets indicate where, we, the editors, have rearranged these parts according to what we believe was the author's intent.

The heights of joy could not be told, or even imagined, of the happiness I have known as his wife.

Nothing can ever take that away from me.

Since he is gone, his memory is still like the beautiful dream he made come true for me.

I will try to carry on where he left off.

The world of music was his—I am making it mine.

My band will be the Drifting Cowgirls in memory of his Drifting Cowboys.

And I will try to find happiness in the world in which he found it and gave it to me.

| 20 |

Mrs. W. W. Stone (with Allen Rankin): Excerpt from *Our Hank Williams, "The Drifting Cowboy,"* as Told by His Mother to Allen Rankin

Hank Williams's biographers have had few good things to say about his mother, Lillie Stone (1898–1955), but all agree that she was a formidable woman. Born Jessie Lillie Belle Skipper in Butler County, Alabama, she married Elonzo Huble "Lon" Williams, a native of nearby Lowndes County, in 1916, when she was eighteen years old and he was nearly twenty-five. Because of the nature of Lon's work as a log train engineer, the Williams family moved frequently among the lumber-mill towns and logging camps in south-central Alabama. In 1930, Lon, a World War I veteran, entered the Veterans Administration Hospital in Pensacola, Florida, to begin more than nine years of treatment for what Lillie later claimed was "shell shock," but which was actually a brain aneurism that paralyzed his face and slurred his speech. The following year, Lillie and her two children, Irene and Hiram, or "Hank," moved to Georgiana, where she supported the family through a variety of occupations and odd jobs such as sewing and canning. Four years later, Lillie moved the family to Greenville, the Butler County seat, and then, in 1937, to Montgomery, where she operated a series of boardinghouses.

Although most accounts concede that Lillie was hardworking and ambitious, and a relatively stabilizing force within her household, she has also been

SOURCE   Mrs. W. W. Stone, with Allen Rankin, *Our Hank Williams, "The Drifting Cowboy," as Told by His Mother to Allen Rankin* (Montgomery, Ala.: Philbert Publications, 1953), unpaginated.

described as domineering and grasping. According to former neighbors and her son's ex–band members, she physically abused her husbands (she apparently married and divorced at least three times), sometimes stole money from Hank when he was passed-out drunk, and occasionally even got into fistfights with him. Whether motivated by greed, as many believed, or by love, as her daughter Irene insisted, Lillie assumed the roles of business manager and booking agent for her son and his band, serving in that capacity between about 1939 and 1942, when Hank left home for wartime work in the Mobile, Alabama, shipyards.

After her son's death, Lillie maneuvered herself into being named administrator of his estate, and, under the terms of an October 1952 agreement, gained custody of his illegitimate daughter, Antha Belle Jett (now known as Jett Williams), who was born two days after his funeral. In 1954, Lillie legally adopted the infant and rechristened her Cathy Yvone Stone. That same year, in an effort to keep her late son's memory alive, she converted his old bedroom in her Montgomery boardinghouse into a public shrine. Lillie died of an apparent heart attack on February 26, 1955, and was buried beside her son in Montgomery's Oakwood Cemetery Annex.

In March 1953, just three months after her son's death, Lillie published *Our Hank Williams, "The Drifting Cowboy," as Told by His Mother to Allen Rankin*. The sixteen-page booklet, which sold for one dollar chiefly by mail order, grew out of her 1,600-*word Montgomery Advertiser* article, "I Remember Hank as a Little Boy," published on January 11, 1953, and probably ghostwritten by Rankin (1917–1991), a columnist for the newspaper. A romanticized and self-aggrandizing but nonetheless influential depiction of her son's life, *Our Hank Williams* represents not only the first biography of Hank Williams, but also one of his family's earliest published attempts to mold his posthumous reputation.

I hope you will like this little memento of Hank Williams, "The Drifting Cowboy"—

Hank, they tell me, was one of the most successful and popular Hillbilly singers and songwriters who ever lived.

It warms my heart to know you are Hank's friend and fan because I am the best friend and fan Hank ever had. I am his mother—and he was my only son.[*]
It was a great loss to the world when Hank died suddenly last New Year's Day. It was a greater loss to me.

---

[*] Researchers Steve A. Maze and Brian Turpen have both independently confirmed that Lon and Lillie Williams had another son, Earnest Huble Williams, who was born prematurely on July 5, 1921, and died two days later.

But Hank isn't really dead. He put his whole heart into his songs and I feel that his songs will go on longer than you and I. They will be sung as long as people live, fall in love, feel joy and sorrow and music.

Probably you know what makes Hank's songs great. He never wrote a song except from the depths of his heart. Maybe you didn't know that Hank wrote about 125 song hits in the past five years and didn't know a note of music. He used to say, "I never wrote a note except in my heart."

And that was true. In all his life I never knew my son, Hank, to just sit down and write a song. He wrote them, he said, "because they just come bustin' out." If people liked his songs, he was glad—but he would have written and sung them anyway because he felt them so much he just had to sing them. He would "bust" he said, if he didn't. [...]

All his life his words poured out like people, not books, spoke them.

Hank was seventeen when one day he came home looking sheepish. "You know what makes songs, Mama?" he asked.

"No," I said. "What?"

"Love," he said. "It's love that makes the best songs."

Hank's love-at-first-sight was Audrey Shepherd [Sheppard], a tall, pretty blonde girl he had met while playing a medicine show at Banks, Alabama. His statement was more correct than he knew.

Never in the history of "country music" were so many songs to pour out of the love of one boy for one girl as in the case of Hank and Audrey.

Audrey soon became Mrs. Williams. They loved each other like lovers in old ballads love and out of their joys, troubles, spats and trials came dozens and scores of love ballads of the Twentieth Century—Hank's best love songs. "They'll Never Take Her Love From Me,"[†] "Why Don't You Love Me? (Like You Used To Do)" and dozens more. Then finally the beautiful "Cold, Cold Heart" and "You Win Again."

They say the course of true love never runs smoothly. Certainly it didn't in this case.

One day they'd leave each other—"forever"—and the next day they'd be back in each other's arms, having a big cry—both of them—and collaborating on the latest sad song Hank had written about their "parting."

You could know just how Hank and Audrey were getting along at all times by listening to his latest hits on records and radio. If the songs were sad he and Audrey were at "outs"; if they were gay they were "at ins."

[†] Williams did not write this song, as the authors seem to suggest; it was written by Leon Payne (1917–1969), a fellow country singer and songwriter perhaps most famous for penning the song "Lost Highway," which Williams also recorded.

I must admit I was a little jealous at times. Not really. I'm joking. Hank's Mother was always his first girl, and he never forgot it. He was always as sweet and kind to me as anybody could be. He wrote many "mother songs" to me. One was "Last Night I Heard You Crying In Your Sleep."

I don't know whether you know how religious my son was. His most serious songs were his hymns and he meant them so much he would often shed tears while composing and recording them. Some of my favorites from his beautiful hymns are "I Saw The Light"—(it's the one they sang at his funeral)—"Wealth Won't Save Your Soul," "A House of Gold," and "When God Comes and Gathers His Jewels."

I suppose Hank was a sort of preacher at heart. Maybe all real artists who try to portray beauty and truth are. Anyway, he was never happier or more himself than when he was talking to music like he did on his "Luke the Drifter"‡ records.

How grave and sad his voice could be as he spoke some solemn truth to music and made his serious recordings in the middle of the night. The talking record he liked best, I think, was his "Men With Broken Hearts."

"Look," he'd say about somebody who was broke or down-and-out or being called a criminal in the newspapers, "that man's the same man today as he was when he was in the chips, in the good graces of people, ain't he? Why do they think he's so different now? He's got the same heart now as always."

That's the way Hank was. He loved everybody and fought for the underdog. [...]

His songs [...] brought him access to many of the better things in life, but most of all, I think he loved his children—Audrey's daughter, Lycretia [Lycrecia], age eleven, and their little four-year-old son, Randall, whom he called "Bocephus."

Hank used to like to sign off his radio shows by saying, "Beings the Good Lord's willing and the creeks don't rise, I'll be with you in a minute, Bocephus." And he usually was.

But Hank was wearing himself out by working too hard, hours too long, and the obsession to capture for himself and the world all the thousands of words and melodies that flew through his mind.

With all of his traveling he had developed a spinal injury. He had to have an operation. Some people thought that the way Hank trembled and "suffered"

---

‡ The pseudonym Williams used on fourteen recordings consisting chiefly of moralizing recitations and talking blues, including "The Funeral," "Pictures from Life's Other Side," and "Ramblin' Man."

over a song was part of his act but his friends knew that the "act" was real. He was suffering continuously.

His health broke under the strain as did his marriage. Right here "Cold, Cold Heart" was a smash hit, but there was heartbreak behind it. Hank and Audrey were getting a divorce. Then "Jambalaya," that gay song of life on the Louisiana Bayou, came out. But Hank was far from gay. His body was sick but his only thought was to provide enjoyment for his fans.

Hank visited me several times in those last days. How proud he was that no matter where he went or what he did, he had Mama and home to come back to.

He acted gay, kept putting up a bold front to the last, but he was nearly at the end of the line and looking back, somehow he must have realized it.

Death struck suddenly and dramatically as 1952 was passing and the New Year coming in. While other people were hailing in the New Year—many of them with Hank's songs—he died in his sleep as he was being driven through West Virginia on the way to an Ohio appearance.

They say you never appreciate your friends until a time like this. Hank's and my friends have been my greatest consolation. Twenty thousand of them, most of them weeping, tried to press into the Montgomery City Hall [*sic*] for his funeral. At our home in Montgomery, I have received many thousands of letters of sympathy from all states and nearly every foreign country.

Hank had, and has, friends, all right—a world full of them.

I feel, too, that Hank isn't really dead—not as long as he has friends like you who will remember and sing his songs. I believe Hank will live as long as people sing of their joys and sorrows. Hank's songs were his real heart which poured over and became music—music that will go on echoing in the great lasting heart of humanity.

And that is good. For them to live on is what Hank wanted more than anything.

~~~~~~

| 21 |

Was Singer a Suicide?

Because Hank Williams's death occurred unexpectedly and under mysterious circumstances, it has inspired all manner of theories, rumors, and

---

SOURCE "Was Singer a Suicide?" *Oklahoma City Times*, March 18, 1953.

speculation.* In March 1953, Horace R. "Toby" Marshall (1910–1972), a self-described "alcoholic-narcotic therapist" who treated Williams in the final weeks of his life, gained extensive media attention by claiming that his former patient had become so despondent that he might have actually committed suicide. The two had first met in Oklahoma City, apparently in mid-October 1952, when a local promoter summoned Marshall to help Williams "sober up" for a concert. Impressed with his services, Williams hired him as his personal physician, unaware that the so-called doctor had purchased his bogus medical diploma through the mail. In reality, as biographer Bill Koon writes, the charlatan Marshall served as "little more than a drug contact" who "kept Hank in amphetamines, Seconal, chloral hydrate, and morphine." Shortly after the singer's death, Marshall brazenly submitted a $736.39 bill for his services to Williams's family.

Out on parole on a forgery conviction, Marshall came under the suspicion of Oklahoma authorities when his estranged wife died in March 1953 after taking drugs he had prescribed. He was arrested and then called to testify before a special Oklahoma legislative committee charged with investigating the state's illegal narcotics traffic. The probe into Marshall's medical practices—as well as the press coverage of the investigative hearings—expanded after he submitted a list of patients that included Williams's name. Under the committee's questioning, Marshall admitted to prescribing chloral hydrate, a powerful, often addictive sedative, for Williams on December 22, 1953, and confirmed that the singer had filled and then refilled the prescription at a Montgomery, Alabama, pharmacy. Far from accepting any responsibility for the singer's death, however, Marshall maintained that he had endeavored conscientiously to save the suicidal Williams's life. In contrast, Williams's widow, Billie Jean, who had interrupted a nationwide singing tour to appear before the committee, testified that she believed that the drugs Marshall had illegally prescribed contributed to her husband's death.

The front-page article reprinted below is only one of numerous newspaper and wire service reports covering these legislative hearings. Often bearing sensational headlines such as "Singer Given Leopard Drug," "Song Writer's Widow Called in Dope Probe," and "Pretty Witness Tells Hillbilly's Bizarre Story," these articles offered some of the earliest public revelations of Williams's drug abuse and raised further questions about the official cause of his death. Moreover, during the next few years, these accounts would serve as grist for the nation's tabloid magazines and give a veneer of legitimacy to their tawdry allegations about Williams.

---

* On January 6, 1953, in perhaps the most bizarre example, the *Montgomery Advertiser* reported that a rumor then circulating in the city claimed that the recently deceased singer had been "suffering from a rare disease which was turning his body to stone."

A confidential letter, in which mystery man Horace R. "Toby" Marshall claims Hank Williams may have committed suicide to escape "parasites" and "fair weather friends," was revealed Wednesday.

Marshall, who reads the Bible, spouts medical terms, talks like a doctor, but admits he never went beyond high school, said Williams told him he intended "to destroy the Hank Williams that was making the money they (fair weather friends and relatives) were getting."

Williams, 29-year-old "Sinatra" of the hillbilly set, was treated extensively for alcoholism by Marshall for almost three months before his death January 1.

PAROLE OFFICE RELEASES IT

[...] Marshall's letter, written to Campbell LeFlore, pardon and parole officer, January 7, was disclosed by LeFlore Wednesday following testimony by Williams' widow before a legislative narcotics investigating committee Tuesday night.

Nineteen-year-old[†] Billie Jean Williams, a shapely brunette with a southern drawl, who has traded on her husband's name in nightclub singing engagements since he died, said she suspected Marshall of contributing to his death.

HEADED FOR SKIDROW

But Marshall, whose parole on a forgery count was revoked last week, set forth a different version in his letter of explanation to LeFlore.

Sprinkling his narrative with medical terms, the 43-year-old Marshall[‡] told a story of long vigils over Williams during drunken periods and a sustained effort to prevent him from sinking to performances "for nickels and dimes on skidrow."

He said he first met Williams in early October [1952] when he was called in to sober up the recording star during an Oklahoma City performance.

AGENT'S LETTER QUOTED

Marshall, a former drunkard, who set himself up as a "noted alcohol therapist," said the October meeting was the beginning of a relationship which grew closer up to Williams' death.

---

† She was actually twenty years old.
‡ Marshall, whose Social Security registration indicates he was born on March 20, 1910, was two days shy of his forty-third birthday when this article was published.

(He presented to LeFlore a letter from Mrs. Delbert F. Cravens, a local booking agent, in which she praised Marshall for telling Williams of the "laws of principle, ethics, and the moral law of rightness in living.")

Marshall's letter reads, "Although he (Williams) had a multiplicity of emotional problems, basically he was a very lonely person, and couldn't stand being alone."

FAIR WEATHER FRIENDS?

"This was expressed in his music. This, in spite of the fact he had a host of fair weather friends, most of whom were parasites who fawned on him, played up to him, kept him supplied with liquor and women, and usually wound up by getting to him for a chunk of money."

"He informed me that his second wife (Billie Jean) was really taking him to the cleaners..."

Marshall added, "Now it occurs to me that perhaps Hank got to mulling things over in his mind and, having a very persuasive personality, he might just have talked the doctor in Knoxville out of enough stuff (barbiturates) to kick himself off."

GRADUAL DECAY NOTED

The letter was filled with information which the committee, headed by Rep. Robert O. Cunningham, has struggled to extract from Marshall in a number of hearings. He will be held in Oklahoma County jail until the committee is through with him, then be remanded to the state penitentiary to serve out his two-year forgery term.

He told a story of gradual decay on the part of his patient, Williams, whom he accompanied on several personal appearance tours.

"I can't overlook the fact that...he had been on a rapid decline. Most of his bookings were of the honky-tonk beer joint variety that he simply hated."

WIFE ALSO DEAD

"If he came to this conclusion (suicide)...he still had enough prestige left as a star to make a first-class production out of it...whereas, six months from now, unless he pulled himself back up into some high-class bookings, he might have been playing for nickels and dimes on skidrow."

Marshall has been an object of double interest to the committee. His 48-year-old wife, Fay, died March 3 at Albuquerque, N.M., after he had "prescribed" a headache medicine for her. Her death was diagnosed as a cerebral hemorrhage.

$35 FOR A DIPLOMA

Marshall professed heartbreak from her death, which he said he did not know about until more than a week later.

He said he learned a new philosophy of life in San Quentin prison, where he served for armed robbery "and the Scriptures took on new meaning."

He later paid $35 for a fake diploma bearing his name from the "Chicago School of Applied Science."

PRISON REPORT EYED

After hearing the nightclub singer tell about her husband's death Tuesday night, the house narcotics investigating committee prepared to look at reports that dope is getting inside the state prison at McAlester. [...]

Tuesday night's hearing drew the biggest crowd of any thus far. Spectators filled the capitol hearing room and stood on tables in the hall.

The session broke up at 2:10 a.m. and there were still 70 or 80 spectators, "a good comfortable crowd," Cunningham said.

| 22 |

Eli Waldron: The Death of Hank Williams

This article, excerpted from the first of a two-part series on country music published in the *Reporter*, ranks as a milestone in the literature on Hank Williams. Although Williams had been interviewed previously for articles about country music in *Pathfinder* and *Nation's Business*, this piece marks the first time a journalist from a prominent national magazine dedicated to political and cultural commentary considered him worthy of a full-fledged profile. But rather than touting the singer's posthumous commercial appeal, as was the trend in contemporaneous newspapers and entertainment industry trade journals, author Eli Waldron (1916–1980) sketches a decidedly unflattering portrait of Williams that anticipates the even more sordid articles soon to appear in scandal sheets and pulp magazines.*

SOURCE   Eli Waldron, "Country Music I.: The Death of Hank Williams," *Reporter*, May 19, 1955, pp. 35–37.
* Waldron himself recycled much of this article to create a more sensationalistic profile of Williams for a pulp magazine: "The Life and Death of a Country Singer," *Coronet*, February 1956, pp. 40–44.

To his credit, Waldron includes information that had been previously omitted from Williams's story, including Fred Rose's significant role in his songwriting success, his second marriage to Billie Jean (Jones) Eshliman, and details about the drugs that he used on the night he died. On the other hand, Waldron repeats several chronological errors and dubious claims found in Lillie Stone's 1953 booklet, *Our Hank Williams*, from which he culled much of his biographical material. Even more striking is his tone of smug detachment, which reflects the American literati's dismissive attitude during the 1950s toward Hank Williams and the entire Nashville country music industry.

Hank Williams, the country singer, drew his last breath at about three in the morning of January 1, 1953, leaving behind him fifteen million mourning fans of hillbilly music, a considerable fortune, a wife, an ex-wife, two children, and a devoted mother.

At the time of his unexpected demise, Williams, who for four years on radio and juke box had rivaled even the great Roy Acuff in the extent and depth of his popularity, was reclining in the back seat of an automobile on his way to a New Year's Day engagement at Canton, Ohio. The previous evening Williams's plane had been forced down at Knoxville by bad weather,[†] and he had checked into a hotel there to get some rest. Since sleep had been denied him for several years, he at once called a physician, who at once gave him a small, easeful squirt of morphine. With the narcotic floating around inside him, smoky and cool, he managed to lie still for a few hours. Then the thin, spectral figure, six feet tall, half bald at twenty-nine, hollow-eyed and pale, staggered up out of bed and got into the hired car that was waiting for him. For exactly a year now, he had been altogether crazed by drink, narcotics, and the torture of sleeplessness.

The end of all this lay up the road just a few hours away. Two hundred miles out of Knoxville, at Oak Hill, Virginia [*sic*], the chauffeur stopped the car, tried to awaken Williams, and noticed that he "felt cold." He *was* cold. He was dead.

The autopsy revealed traces of alcohol in Williams's veins but no sign of the sedation administered by the Knoxville physician. Nor did it reveal, as many thought it might, any residuum of the chloral hydrate the singer had been regularly consuming. After an inquest, the death of Hank Williams was put down to a heart attack.

[‡] Prior to the Canton engagement, Williams was booked to appear at two New Year's Eve shows in Charleston, West Virginia, which Waldron fails to mention. He also incorrectly states the details of Williams's aborted flight, which actually originated in Knoxville but was forced to return because of inclement weather at the Charleston airport.

Williams returned to his home town of Montgomery, Alabama, feet first, there to participate, in a subdued and most un-Williams-like way, in the greatest emotional orgy in the city's history since the inauguration of Jefferson Davis. Three thousand people stampeded the Municipal Auditorium to view the body and join in the keening and the wild singing, and thousands more milled around outside. Roy Acuff and his Smoky Mountain Boys were there and Ernest Tubb and Carl Smith and two or three hundred other more or less famous pickers and singers. Hank Williams's first wife, his second wife, his mother, his cousins, his son Bocephus,‡ and his stepdaughter Lycretia [Lycrecia] occupied the mourners' bench. The stage was banked with floral offerings in the shapes of guitars, wreaths, and memory pillows. The whole scene was illumined by the balefully silent explosions of flash bulbs. The photographers covered the whole thing from beginning to end, scuttling about below the stage and around the bier and the floral offerings, getting shots of the relatives in various grief-stricken poses, shots of the corpse, and shots of the preacher as he delivered the broadcast sermon. Some of these photographs were later offered for sale but were sternly suppressed by Williams's agents.

"I SAW THE LIGHT"

The competition to capitalize on the death of Hank Williams continued on through the exequies§ and long after he had been laid away for keeps. Williams had written a great number of songs—"Cold Cold Heart," "Jambalaya," "Your Cheatin' Heart," and "Kawliga" are a few of the titles—and most of them were hits. His gross income in 1951 was around $175,000 and in 1952 around $200,000. According to experts in the field of hillbilly music, he would have earned half a million dollars in 1953—that is, if he had been around to cash in on the publicity attending his death. Simply alive, he might have earned half that.

In any event the royalties-to-be from unpublished songs and unreleased records represented an unknown but undeniably vast and mouth-watering sum of money. As an acquaintance of Williams's put it recently, "It was like a five-million-dollar horse suddenly being turned loose. That horse has been rampaging up and down the country ever since, from Shreveport to Montgomery to Nashville, tearing up the earth and raring and screaming. And everybody trying to lay hands on it at once, clawing at each other and kicking and swearing. I tell you it's so disgusting I don't even want to talk about it, don't want to

---

‡ A reference to Randall Hank Williams (b. 1949), better known as Hank Williams, Jr.
§ Funeral ceremonies.

think about it." He, too, was a country singer and he spoke with deep feeling. Most of the other country singers—or hillbilly singers, to use the less elegant term—felt the same way.

These "disgusting" activities had begun immediately. In Canton, for example, where he had been scheduled to appear on the afternoon of the day that turned out to be the day of his death, William's manager,[*] a small, dark, adaptable man, leaped nimbly and expertly into the breach, ordered a spotlight thrown on the empty stage, and called for a record of "I Saw the Light," one of Williams's best-loved religious songs. The audience rose to its feet, weeping copiously, and joined in.

The move was hailed as "excellent showmanship" by the inner circle of hillbilly managers and agents who make their home in Nashville.

To the delight of a number of other interested parties, it was evident that Williams dead might be a much more valuable property than Williams alive. At any rate, more manageable. Alive he had been an irresponsible drunk, an incorrigible egomaniac, a man who could never be relied upon to keep his engagements and who, when he kept them, would more than likely have to be propped up in the wings until it was time for him to wobble out to the microphone, and who then, to the further agony and embarrassment of bookers, managers, and houseowners, might survey his audience contemptuously and tell them to go to hell, to go get their money back because he wasn't going to sing.

But now he was dead and safe, and the haymaking had begun. From Canton the spotlight quickly shifted to Montgomery, where after the funeral there was a free-for-all fight for Williams's briefcase, which contained one of two things—either two or three million dollars' worth of unpublished songs or his dirty laundry. It didn't really matter which. The possession of the briefcase was of extreme importance for its strategic and symbolic value, and whoever seized it and held it—either Williams's first wife or his second wife or his mother or his publisher, Acuff-Rose of Nashville—would stand in a strong position in the litigious huggermugger that was already beginning to shape up. Acuff-Rose came up with the briefcase and after a quick peek announced that Hank Williams had left a hundred songs to posterity. This was a surprising statement, since Williams could neither read nor write music; could, in fact, scarcely manage his own name, and was not in the habit of getting this far ahead of the game anyway. But it didn't matter—nothing mattered at this point. 1953 was destined anyway to be a great Williams year on the juke boxes. And even today, if Acuff-Rose of Nashville and M-G-M Records of New

---

[*] A reference to noted promoter and manager A. V. "Bam" Bamford (1909–2003).

York could somehow contrive to get Williams's dirty laundry to spin at 45 RPM, they'd make a fortune on that too. Williams had ten million fans in this country and another five million abroad. They literally, quite literally, worshiped him.

HANK'S BEST GIRL

His mother, Mrs. W. W. Stone, worshiped him no less. Having interred her son, she promptly sat down with a Montgomery newspaper columnist and dashed off a two-thousand word pamphlet with pictures, "Our Hank Williams." The foreword gives the flavor of the thing: "Our Hank Williams is an account of the Drifting Cowboy's Life, as told by his mother, Mrs. W. W. Stone, to Allen Rankin. One dollar is the price placed on this booklet and it must not sell for more. Violations will be prosecuted. For [a] copy of this booklet mail $1 to Our Hank Williams, Montgomery, Alabama."

The story, as told to Mr. Rankin, revealed that Hank was born in 1923 in Mount Olive, Alabama, that at the age of five the family moved to Georgiana, nine miles away, where Hank sold peanuts, shined shoes, and learned to play the guitar from a Negro street singer named Teetot. At twelve, now living in Montgomery, he won an amateur-night prize at the Empire Theater with "The WPA Blues" and began playing the honkytonks. At thirteen he had his own string band, "The Drifting Cowboys," and a year later was playing over Montgomery's Station WSFA. At seventeen he married Audrey Shepherd [Sheppard], a cool-eyed blond whom he had met while playing a medicine show at Banks, Alabama.[||]

"I must admit I was a little jealous at times," Mrs. Stone told Mr. Rankin. "Not really. I'm joking. Hank's Mother was always his first girl, and he never forgot it. He was always as sweet and kind to me as anybody could be. He wrote many 'mother songs' to me—'Last Night I Heard You Crying In Your Sleep,' 'I've Just Told Mama Goodbye,' and many others..."

Hank and Audrey set up house keeping with Mrs. Stone (then Mrs. Williams) and the going was rough. At nineteen, in despair, he gave up playing altogether and took a job in a Mobile shipyard. That was 1942. But his mother had faith in him. She rented a car and went to every schoolhouse and nightclub in the Montgomery area. She booked Hank solid for sixty days. Three weeks after her son's departure for Mobile, she appeared in the shipyard with the datebook in her hand. "When Hank saw the datebook for those shows he gave me the sweetest smile I've ever seen and said, 'Thank God, Mother. You have

---

[||] Williams was actually twenty-one-years old when he married Audrey in December 1944.

made me the happiest boy in the world.'" And he threw away his riveting gun for good and picked up his guitar once more.**

Three years later, in 1946, he had made a few recordings for an obscure company called Sterling Records, and about this time he got the break he had been waiting for. According to the Stone-Rankin pamphlet, he was joking with his wife Audrey one day and she asked him what he'd do if he came home too late and she locked him out. He thought about this for a moment and said, "I'd go out and tell that little dog to move it on over in the doghouse." And then he thought about *this* for a moment and sat down and picked out a "rollicking" song called "Move It On Over."

He sent "Move It On Over" to Acuff-Rose, and the Rose half of the firm liked it and summoned the composer to Nashville. Fred Rose, an old-timer in show business and nobody's fool, said to Williams, "It's good but how do I know you wrote it? Here, I'll give you a test. Take this situation: There's a girl who marries a rich boy instead of the poor boy who lives in a cabin. Go in the room there and see if you can make a song out of that." Hank went into the room, thought about this situation for a while, and emerged thirty minutes later, singing "A Mansion on the Hill."†† This made two hits on his first day with the firm.

As Williams's publisher and the partner in one of the country's most prosperous music-publishing companies, Rose figures prominently in the Williams legend. His was the patient, unpublicized work of shaping the singer's lyrics, sharpening them, and giving them the particular timely point and barb they needed to get into the public mind and stay fastened there. Not a few people regard this as a work of genius in itself. "Kawliga," for example, a tremendous hit in 1952 [*sic*], began with Williams as the usual dull and customary recital of unrequited love—this time among the Cherokees in Alabama—and ended with Rose as a lively little ditty about unrequited love between a pair of wooden Indians.

The rest, so to speak, is history. Williams was a great success on the "Louisiana Hayride" program over Shreveport's Station KWKH. From there he moved into Nashville on WSM's "Grand Ole Opry," which, in the country-music field, is about as big as the big time gets. He had ten million listeners to sing to every Saturday night, and during the past four years of his life there was hardly a week when he didn't have a song among the top ten in the nation.

But success destroyed him. On January 1, 1952, exactly a year before he died, he left his wife, his Cadillacs, and his fancy new Nashville home. In September

---

** Williams worked off and on at the Alabama Dry Dock and Shipbuilding Company in Mobile between late 1942 and mid-1944, according to most biographers.
†† This story, long since debunked as fiction, appears in Stone's *Our Hank Williams*, as do several of the other questionable anecdotes that Waldron relates here.

he was booted out of the Grand Ole Opry[‡‡] and sent into that limbo from which, they say, country singers never return. Four months later he was dead.

ONE WIDOW TOO MANY

There was a great deal, of course, that Mrs. Stone did *not* tell Mr. Rankin— Hank's habit of packing a pistol in the back of his belt, for instance, and shooting up hotel rooms. Hank, drunk and screaming, throwing wads of money on the floor and stamping on it in a rage. And then she ignored Hank's second wife completely in her little biography. Shortly after leaving Nashville, Hank divorced Audrey[§§] and married a Miss Billie Jones of Houston, or perhaps Dallas, a cute little thing with two blue eyes, at least one of which was out for the future. Hank's mother did not like the second Mrs. Hank Williams, who did not care very much, in turn, for the first Mrs. Hank Williams, who did, however, in her turn harbor an affection for her former mother-in-law. The two young ladies hit the trail at about the same time after the funeral, each "singing the songs of the deceased" for all she was worth. Dressed in cowgirl outfits, each billed herself as Mrs. Hank Williams and sang two or three painfully memorized songs in Hank's old sobbing manner to Hank's old lachrymose fans. But this was one Mrs. Hank Williams too many, even for the notoriously insatiable hillbilly circuit. Miss Billie Jones of Houston, or perhaps Dallas, fired an injunction at the first Mrs. Hank Williams, who was forced to resume her tour as Mrs. Audrey Williams. She, however, placed a sizable ad in *Billboard*, the amusement magazine, explaining that Audrey Williams was the one, the only, the original, the bona fide Mrs. Hank Williams.

~~~~~~

| 23 |

Sanford Mabrie: The Strange Life and Death of Hank Williams

Country music stars rarely attracted the notice of 1950s scandal magazines, such as *Confidential*, *Behind the Scene*, *Naked Truth*, *Private Affairs*, and *Uncensored*. Huge newsstand sellers during their mid-1950s heyday, these inexpensive,

---

SOURCE Sanford Mabrie, "The Strange Life and Death of Hank Williams," *Behind the Scene*, September 1955, pp. 28–29, 47–48.

‡‡ Williams was fired from the *Opry* in August 1952.

§§ Williams was still residing in Nashville and performing on the *Opry* when his and Audrey's divorce was finalized in late May 1952.

lowbrow publications typically featured titillating gossip about the sex lives of Hollywood stars, exposés of professional sports "rackets," and disclosures of political scandals. This lurid profile of Hank Williams, written by Sanford Mabrie (almost certainly a pseudonym), exceeds any previous—or, for that matter, almost all later—published descriptions of the late country music star's alleged transgressions. Mabrie's salacious tone, shocking charges, and lack of verifiable sources understandably outraged Williams's friends and family members, who immediately leaped to his defense. Despite their best efforts to discredit the piece, however, Mabrie's article became the prototype for the tabloid version of Williams's life, an interpretation that would appear in several other pulp magazine articles in the mid- to late 1950s and then, in the 1970s and 1980s, would resurface under a more respectable guise in major biographies and articles.

It was about 12:30 A.M. on the morning of January 1, 1953, when Hank Williams, the nation's favorite country singer, climbed into the back seat of a chauffeur-driven hired limousine.

He was still feeling good from the effects of the shot of morphine a local doctor had given him when bad weather forced his plane down at Knoxville.

As the tall, skinny 29-year-old hillbilly stretched his long legs in the back of the car trying to relax, he thought he was on his way to keep a New Year's Day singing date at Canton, Ohio. Actually he was speeding to keep an appointment with destiny.

The chauffeur, who had been warned to expect anything with Williams in the car, was a little disappointed. Nary a peep came from his famous passenger.

They had been rolling along for some time now—it was 3 A.M. and they were going through Oak Hill, Virginia [sic]—when the driver decided to break the monotony of the trip by starting his own conversation.* Williams didn't respond.

The chauffeur knew the singer wasn't sleeping, as he could see through the rear view mirror that Williams' eyes were open. So he tried again, this time talking much louder. He could have used a fog horn for all the good it would have done him.

A LIFE OF CONTRADICTIONS

Hank Williams, the singing idol of millions, the writer of such big hits as *Cheatin' Heart, Cold, Cold, Heart, Jumbalaya* [sic], *Last Night I Heard You Crying*, to mention just a few of the hundreds he composed, was dead!

It's only fitting that Williams' death should have been as sudden, spectacular and controversial as his life. The autopsy showed no trace of the shot of

---

* Actually, the time of this incident would have been shortly before 7:00 a.m.

morphine and very little evidence of the quarts of whiskey he had consumed shortly before his trip to the promised land.

Although it still brings nothing but raised eyebrows in the trade, the official records say that he suffered a fatal heart attack.

Hank Williams had lived a life of contradiction. The countless millions of fans who knew him only from his records pictured him as the wholesome country boy who wouldn't recognize a bad thought or deed if one came up and hit him square in the face.

Those who saw him perform in person thought he was an eccentric, excusing his outbursts of temper, which often included cursing out the audience and walking off the stage in the middle of a tune, as big city showmanship.

But those who worked with him and knew him intimately considered him nothing but a perpetual pain.

That is, except for his mother, Mrs. W. W. Stone, who, till this day,[†] swears that Hank had been the epitome of godliness, graciousness, kindness, and unselfishness. And of course that's exactly what he might have been to her—or at least, should have been.

No other person was as responsible for this illiterate, ex-shoeshine boy's success than his mother. Although he had been performing professionally since he was 13, until he finally clicked 9 years later in 1946, the going was always tough.

He would have quit many times if it hadn't been for her. And it was more than just encouragement she gave him. She actually went out and found singing engagements for him.

AN ILL-TEMPERED EGOMANIAC

But to less biased bystanders, such as his first and second wives, Audrey Shepard [Sheppard] Williams and Billie Jones Williams, Hank was an ill-tempered, surly, illogical egomaniac who was interested only in morphine, heroin, whiskey, and himself—in the order named.

It's their version of the country singer that's backed up by most of the late hillbilly's associates.

Oddly enough, Hank Williams' records and songs have become even more popular than ever since his death and because of this his publishers, Acuff-Rose, and his recording studio, M-G-M Records, have been doing everything possible to squelch any BEHIND THE SCENE stories on the singer.

A close acquaintance (Hank had no real friends), another country singer who strangely enough bears a striking resemblance to Williams, even to the

---

[†] Williams's mother had been dead some six months at the time Mabrie's exposé appeared.

balding dome, suggests that incurable insomnia might have been the cause of all his trouble.

"Hank went for as long as 70 to 75 hours at a stretch without any sleep," he told us. "I'm not saying this is what turned him to whiskey and dope but his sleepless condition, aggravated by long bouts with John Barleycorn and the needle, made him capable of terrifying acts that either made no sense or were in bad taste."

At a rehearsal for a theater date in Nashville, Tenn., the bandleader merely suggested to Hank, who was drunk as usual, that he sing a little softer and save his voice for the performance. This so incensed Williams that he picked up his trusty guitar and splintered it over the maestro's cranium.

The maestro, a 6-foot ex-football player, didn't dig this kind of treatment even from a headliner and with a left hook flattened our "hero."

You might have thought that this would have made Hank more respectful of bandleaders, or at least the big ones, but during an actual performance in Montgomery, Ala., he stopped in the middle of a song and for no apparent reason spat right into the eye of the orchestra leader.

NO WELCOME MAT

Williams became such a problem to work with during personal appearances, especially in the year before his death, that he was finding fewer and fewer bookings. Shortly before his death, despite all his song hits, he was given the bum's rush from the radio program, *Grand Ole Opry*, the high spot in the country music field, broadcast over Nashville's WSM.

Getting the "bum's rush" was nothing new for Hank. Hotels had been giving it to him for years, and for a real weird reason. Unhappy Hank, the paragon of the plains, always toted several six-shooters, and when he was in his cups, got his kicks shooting up hotel rooms.

Many was the night that Hank's associates leaped underneath tables and dove underneath the beds, trying to escape hot lead. Hank was a pitiful sight, glassy-eyed, full of dope, with trembling hands, firing bullet after bullet in every direction.

One particular cold November afternoon in 1951, in a swanky Chattanooga hotel, the late troubadour went a little too far and almost paid for it with his life.

A pretty chambermaid, Sally Fields, was ordered by the management to clean Hank's room. She had heard about his reputation and was frightened at the prospects of the encounter. But they promised her a big tip and she finally agreed.

When she reached his room, she cautiously knocked. There was no answer. Happy in the thought that he was out, she opened the door with her pass-key. But he was anything but out. There he was, sitting in an armchair, giving himself a shot of morphine.

When Williams saw her he went berserk. Yanking a gun off the table, he aimed it directly at her head. The trigger clicked on an empty cylinder. He squeezed it again, and once more, nothing happened.

VICTIM STRIKES BACK

By this time the panic-stricken maid managed to get her hands on a heavy floor lamp which she smashed over his head. Hank dropped like a stunned cow. Blood was streaming down the side of his face.

The girl was certain that she had killed him. Frightened, she raced out of the room, out of the hotel and never stopped running until she reached the depot and boarded the first train out of town.

Hank remained unconscious and undiscovered for several hours. He might have stayed there forever had it not been for the manager of the hall where he was scheduled to sing that night. He stopped by to make sure that Williams was still sober enough to go through with the engagement.

He found Hank more dead than alive and rushed him to a hospital, where they managed to revive and patch him up in time for the performance. The manager—who had no love for Williams—refused to say what he would have done if he had found Williams in the same condition and the singer had not been under contract to him.

After this incident, Hank swore off using the six-shooter. But the very next week, he was up to his old tricks in a hotel room in Birmingham, Ala.

The hotel had a collection of beautifully framed portraits hanging in its hallways. The doped-up Williams lifted as many as he could carry and lined them up at one end of his room as in a shooting gallery.

Then he tried to put a bullet through the eyes of each one of them. In his shaky condition, the pictures were the only things in the room he *didn't* hit.

There were no dull days with Hank. His activities in hotel rooms weren't confined to the firing of firearms. He also liked to stage private concerts there for girls, especially the really young ones.

Hank went in for the 14- and 15-year-olds who would follow him up to his hotel room after a public appearance, naively believing all they were going to get was his autograph.

In one town, a peeping tom, who had a high-powered pair of binoculars trained on her idol's room, was so shocked at what she saw, that she called the police. When they broke into Williams' locked room, they found him playing a guitar accompaniment for a 15-year-old's strip tease. The girl had nothing left to take off but her skin.

A SUCCESSION OF PAY-OFFS

The police had him dead to rights this time, but one thing saved the country boy's hide. The girl turned out to be the Mayor's daughter and with elections coming up, he couldn't afford a scandal, either.

Other times Williams wasn't quite so lucky. His habit of mauling minors kept everyone financially involved with him in a state of consternation.

Much of Hank's earnings went down the drain paying off somebody's family to make sure the case stayed out of court and out of the papers.

Among his more normal eccentricities was his love for fast and flashy automobiles. That is, if you call normal having, as it's been said, a different colored car for every day in the week and several two-tone jobs for Sundays.

But Hank Williams had his good moments, too. He never forgot his desperately poor boyhood. Born in Mt. Olive, Ala., his family kept moving about searching for a better life.

But all the homes young Hank knew were the same—wretched and ugly and filled with the horror of emptiness and poverty. It was necessity that forced him to try to capitalize on his natural singing talent at such an early age.

And it's very possible that the miserable side-street saloon, where he picked up nickels and dimes entertaining drunkards, pimps, whores and degenerates of every description, thwarted his perspective of life.

But because he never forgot what it meant to be hungry, he never shunned a worthwhile benefit and sometimes appeared at as many as four charity affairs in one week at the cost of cancelling lucrative engagements that stood in the way.

ALWAYS GOOD FOR A TOUCH

At one time a fellow performer in the art of frantic-antics had a streak of hard luck. His wife and 2 children were ill and required expert and expensive medical aid. He was about to lose his home and car to the creditors and there was no immediate work or money in sight.

Williams heard of this and called him long distance to ask him how much was needed. The down-and-out singer, trying not to sound desperate, jokingly replied he needed about $5,000. In the next mail he received a check for the same amount.

Another time Williams heard about a church in Tennessee that was badly in need of repairs. A messenger flew to the little town the same day and delivered

$1,000 to the minister. There was one stipulation attached to the donation. Hank insisted upon anonymity.

There's also the story of the little Negro shoe shine boy in Alabama who badly needed an operation. Williams remembered another little Negro shoe shine boy who had taught him many songs,‡ and in his memory, sent the cripple's family $1,500.

No matter in what condition he was, Hank was the softest touch in the world. Anybody who possessed a good spiel or had any kind of hard-luck story could beat him out of a couple of hundred dollars.

Williams was even kinder to those who were making a fortune off him through publishing his music and making his records. For them, he couldn't have picked a better moment to die.

There's no question, at the rate he was going, that it was only a matter of time before the whole world found out about his uncontrollable love affairs with morphine and booze. This would have ended his popularity and a very profitable part of their business.

Instead when he died, there were millions and millions of Hank Williams fans who wept and mourned.

And when his body was taken to Municipal Stadium [sic] in Montgomery, Ala., thousands upon thousands of his followers and admirers came to pay their last respects.

Today, almost 3 years later, with the truth about Williams still so well guarded, the late country singer and his works are more popular than ever. At the expense of his ruined body, twisted mind, and two wives, he became a great star and national institution.

Don't think too harshly of him. The person he hurt most of all was himself!

| 24 |

Ed Linn: The Short Life of Hank Williams

Saga was one of several men's adventure magazines, along with *True*, *Argosy*, and *Stag*, that flourished in the 1950s and 1960s. Known in the publishing trade as "armpit slicks" and "sweats," these pulp magazines featured colorful covers and, inside, purportedly true stories of war, adventure, and intrigue, all designed

SOURCE   Ed Linn, "The Short Life of Hank Williams," *Saga*, January 1957, pp. 8, 10–11, 87–88.
‡ Apparently a reference to Rufus "Tee-Tot" Payne.

to cater to what was an almost exclusively blue-collar male readership. In this rather unlikely print venue, free-lance journalist Ed Linn (1922–2000)—best known as the co-author of such professional baseball memoirs as Bill Veeck's *VEECK—As in Wreck* (1962) and Leo Durocher's *Nice Guys Finish Last* (1975)— made an early and significant contribution to the Hank Williams literature. A boon for future biographers despite its occasional factual and chronological errors, Linn's lengthy profile contains revealing recollections gathered from Williams's fellow performers and industry associates while their memories of him were still relatively fresh. The article also includes a wealth of previously unpublished anecdotes that have since become essential elements of Williams's life story. Unlike previous authors, who often wrote dismissively about the late singer and country music for news magazines or tabloids, Linn exhibits a healthy respect for both his subject and the music, as the excerpt below reveals. While acknowledging Williams's failings, Linn refuses to dwell on only the squalid aspects of the singer's life and instead emphasizes some of Williams's values that the magazine's working-class male readers may have shared, particularly his disdain for authority, tendency toward fatalism, and generosity toward others.

"I'm nothing but a drunkard," Hank Williams once cried out to an old, respected friend. "Why do people expect me to be anything else?" And then he laughed his dry, bitter laugh and said: "You think I'm a drunkard? Hell, you should of seen my old man!"

Hank Williams was always quick to blame his troubles, particularly his deep-bred, gnawing bitterness, upon an unhappy childhood. His most vivid memory seemed to be of standing in front of a movie house in Montgomery, Alabama, a scrawny little boy with a shoeshine box thrown over one shoulder and not so much as a dime in his pocket to get him into the show.

In later years, when he had become the overpowering figure in the world of country music and was making close to a quarter of a million dollars a year, he would never return to Montgomery without bringing along two Cadillacs. Not one Cadillac; two Cadillacs. Hank was showing them.

Once, while he was sharing a Montgomery hotel room with Ernie [Ernest] Tubb, another hillbilly singer, he received a phone call from a local banker. Tubb, hearing Hank's voice go cold before he hung up, asked him what was wrong.

"He invited me up to his house for dinner," Hank said grimly.

"Well, what's the matter with that?"

"Look," Hank said, "I've known that guy all my life. When I was starving in this town, the sonofabitch wouldn't buy me a hamburger. Now there's nothing too good for me. What's the matter, ain't I the same guy?"

Tubb ("I'm Walking the Floor Over You") tried to tell him that in this imperfect world recognition had to be earned. "You've got to take people the way they are," Tubb said. "Not the way you'd like them to be. You've achieved something. Why don't you enjoy the way you're treated now, instead of brooding about the way it used to be?"

But Hank could never forget the way it used to be. When most of us return to the home of our childhood, we are astonished to see how it has shrunk. Hank's childhood home seemed to grow larger through the years.

After he had become a leading recording "artist" with MGM Records, Hank was signed to a contract with MGM Pictures without even being put to the inconvenience of a screen test. When he was brought to Hollywood to discuss his first picture with Dore Schary, he was understandably excited. Now, Schary, as production head of MGM, is possessed of powers that should rightly belong only to God. Men with that kind of power become accustomed to being treated—to put it as mildly as possible—with civility.

As Hank walked into the lush executive offices, he was hoping to make a good impression. But immediately that strong desire set up an even stronger reaction. Hank was damned if he was going to suck up to anybody, just because it was someone who could help him—*especially* because it was someone who could help him.

Disdaining the ordinary courtesy of removing his white ten-gallon hat, Hank slouched down into his chair, stretched out his feet and glared at Schary. All questions were answered with grunts or sneers.

The interview over, Hank walked out into the sunny Culver City lot. At the gate stood a shoeshine boy. Hank stopped suddenly, reached into his pocket and handed the startled boy a five-dollar bill. Then he went out and got drunk. When MGM tried to get in touch with him again, he was spectacularly indisposed. Thus began and ended the movie career of Hank Williams.

The other great influence in Hank's personal life was, of course, his wife Audrey, to whom most of his songs—in the purest Hollywood tradition—were directed. To those who were aware of the nature of the stormy seven-year marriage—the arguments and the amnesties, the recriminations and the reconciliations—their day-by-day relationship could be charted in Hank's songs: "I Can't Get You Off My Mind"; "I'm a Long Gone Daddy"; "Please Don't Let Me Love You"; "They'll Never Take Her Love From Me"; "I'm So Lonesome I Could Cry"; "There'll Be No Teardrops Tonight"; "Weary Blues From Waitin'"; "Someday You'll Call My Name (and I won't answer)" [sic]; "I Won't Be Home No More"; "I Can't Escape From You."

From "Baby, We're Really in Love" to "Alone and Forsaken."

Once, when Audrey was in the hospital after a break with Hank, he went to visit her along with her daughter from a previous marriage, Lycretia [Lycrecia], and the girl's governess. Audrey turned her face to the wall, and Hank told the governess: "She's got the coldest heart I've ever seen." The result, of course, was "Cold, Cold Heart."

Audrey finally left him after he burst into the house, following a New Year's Eve party, and shot at her four times.* Hank lived exactly one year after that; a year almost to the second. It was a tortured journey Hank took that year, for he was dying, bit by bit, every step of the way.

Hank Williams was born in an old log cabin back in the scrub country, nine miles from Georgiana, Alabama. [...] For his seventh or eighth birthday, Hank's mother bought him a $3.50 guitar. And Hank's future was staked out. He began to tag after an old Negro streetsinger, called "Tee-tot," aping his chords and his music. This has led to the theory that there was much of the Negro lamentation mixed into Hank's undeniably sad and bitter music. But as a friend of Hank's—a professional man outside the music world—says: "That kind of theory can be pressed too far. The Negro lamentation was based on economic and racial persecution. It was *Old Man River just keeps rolling along* and *Thirty days in jail and my face turned to the wall*. There was nothing the Negro could do, the songs said, but endure. The back-country whites feel defeated but they also feel there is something they should be able to do about it. Their defeat is a personal defeat. Hank Williams, with that hard core of bitterness, communicated that personal defeat. He was an alcoholic and he had no more morals than an alley cat; he knew it and it tore him apart. He was totally uneducated—almost illiterate—and he felt those limitations keenly. He shouldn't have, of course. He was a pure poet; education would have probably ruined him. He put down his own feelings, simply and movingly."

The essential tragedy of Hank Williams was that the same poetic feeling that produced his songs and lifted him to success also tortured him and led him, inevitably and inexorably, to disaster. An unfeeling man would have drank and caroused and savored the memory. Hank cursed himself. He had much to curse himself about. When sober, he was a modest, considerate companion. Drunk, he was a mean, moody, raving egomaniac.

While appearing in a Las Vegas cabaret, Hank ran across a juke box which did not feature any of his songs or records. He took a cab to a juke-box distributing house, bought the best machine they handled, stocked it entirely with his own numbers, and had them deliver it—and himself—to the cabaret.

---

* Audrey Williams, in her unpublished memoir, dates this incident to December 30, 1951.

"Throw that other one out," he told the owner. "This one's got records worth playing." [...]

He was known, too—when he had nibbled on the grape when the sun was upon it[†]—to walk off a stage after telling the audience that they were unworthy to be honored by the presence of such as he. He had, of course, a far more interesting way of phrasing it.

It is worth pointing out, before we go any further, that for every time Hank went on a stage while he was drunk, he went on a stage sober a hundred times. His audiences loved him; so much so that in a *Down Beat* poll conducted a year after his death, he was voted the most popular country and western performer of all time. They were with Hank from the moment he stepped onstage until the moment he left them with a promise to see them again: "If the Good Lord's willin' and the creek don't rise," or with his word for the day: "Don't worry about anythin', because it ain't gonna be all right no how."

Don Helms ("Little Miss Blue Eyes"), an electric [steel] guitarist who started out with Hank back in the early years of the Drifting Cowboys, says: "There's been a lot of rotten stuff written about Hank since he died. Some of it's true, a lot of it isn't. But even a true story can be told two ways. One is the way we tell them when we get together and start talking about Hank. With affection. You can put the same stories down in black and white and make him look, to people who didn't know him, like a degraded sot. He wasn't. He was kind and generous to a lot of people who didn't deserve it."

The proof seems to be that he was almost universally liked. Ernie Tubb says: "Emphasize one thing. Hank had an unusual consideration for his fellow man. He had great feeling for unfortunates, and he was moved deeply by anybody else's misfortune."

Hank Williams, in fact, seemed to be drawn to sorrow. [...] It almost seemed at times as if he felt more comfortable with sadness than with joy.

| 25 |

Irene Williams Smith: Three "Hank's Corner" Columns from *Country Song Roundup*

Within days of Hank Williams's death, his sister Irene Williams Smith (1922–1995) began what would become her lifelong campaign to protect and preserve his

---

SOURCE   Irene Williams Smith, "Hank's Corner," *Country Song Roundup*, March 1955–June 1957.
[†] That is, when Williams had been drinking or was drunk.

memory. Thirteen months older than Hank, Irene developed a close bond with her brother during their childhood, and, beginning around 1938, she served as the first booking agent, manager, and female singer for his original Drifting Cowboys band. During the 1940s, by her own account, she and Hank grew apart as each of them started families of their own and moved away from Montgomery, Alabama. Later, however, her status as the late star's sister created an opportunity for her to write a semi-regular column titled "Hank's Corner" for the fan magazine *Country Song Roundup*. Over the course of eighteen columns published between 1955 and 1959, some of them written in the form of letters to her departed brother, Smith presented to readers the Hank Williams she remembered—or at least the one she wanted the public to remember. She sought to convey those qualities that, in her view, had defined him—his deep compassion, his godliness, his ability to touch people through song, and his essential loneliness. Smith worked equally hard to shield her brother's memory from his detractors, particularly those who published scurrilous articles in the tabloid magazines of the day. She especially resented slighting references to his childhood poverty and went out of her way to credit their mother Lillie with having instilled in Hank the values that made him the remarkable artist he became. Throughout the remainder of her life, Smith expanded upon these themes in her writings, one of which is reprinted elsewhere in this reader (no. 33). As her brother's chief commemorator and staunchest defender, she played a pivotal role in the shaping of his legacy.

MARCH 1955 (P. 24)
(This is the first in a series of articles to be written especially for COUNTRY SONG ROUNDUP by Mrs. J. T. Smith, of Portsmouth, Va., sister of the late and great Hank Williams.)

Whenever I meet someone for the first time, there is always one question that they never fail to ask me: "Which of Hank's songs do you like best?" Of course I like all of them but, like everyone, I do have a favorite, "Men Of Broken Hearts." Perhaps you will think it strange that of all his happy songs I should pick for my favorite one of the saddest of all. Why? Well, to me, "Men Of Broken Hearts" is Hank.

To me this song contains Hank's philosophy of life. If you stop and think about it, we really don't have the right to criticize and condemn our fellow man (how much happier each of us would be if we remembered that!). Just think how wonderful it would be if we stopped every time we saw some poor lost soul walking or staggering blindly down the way of life and said to ourselves, "But for the Grace of God it could be us instead of him."

I have heard the expression "No Account Bum" so many times, but how many times have I stopped and talked to that person only to find that here in this pitiful shell dwelled a man that was or had been at one time far from a "bum." Like Hank said, "Some were paupers, some were kings and some were masters of the arts."

Do you know that I can never remember hearing my brother say an unkind thing about another person? No, he was not perfect, but he just didn't believe in kicking a man when he was already down, and he didn't believe in saying something about a fellow to get him down or make him drop his head in shame.

He was much closer to God than any of us realized. It has been said that Hank had a Message, and I think that there is a Message in a number of his songs. But in "Men Of Broken Hearts," he had a Message as old as time: "Love thy fellow man—and no matter what he does, try to understand."

FEBRUARY 1957 (P. 8)
Hi! A lot has happened since I last wrote this column. I went to Montgomery, Alabama, on September 17th, and we did have a small graveside service in memory of Hank. I believe that it was one of the most beautiful and most impressive services I have ever attended. Thank you [to those] who came so far to be with us.

There is one question that I have been asked so often that I feel I owe it to you all to answer it. "Are all the things that are being written about Hank true?"

No, they could not possibly be. To have done all the things that he has been accused of doing, Hank would had to have lived a hundred years, and I doubt that even then he would have been able to do it all. Let's face it; for a long time Hank's name has been news. Anything that has had his name on it has interested you readers, and you have bought the magazines bearing stories about him. Many of these writers have written about Hank without having ever tried to find out the truth about him or his life. They have taken one incident that they have heard about and have blown it up as though this was his whole life. Yes, Hank drank, but he did not spend his whole life drunk. He was in terrible pain the last two years of his life and was given sedatives by the doctors for this pain. But Hank was not a dope addict, and as far as I know he never pitched a wild dope party in his life.

Basically, Hank was a clean, honest man. He tried to do unto others the way he would have had them do unto him more than any person I have ever met. I only wish that there were more Hank Williamses in this world—frankly I think that it would be just a little bit better place in which to live. Perhaps you will say—and naturally so—that, after all, I am his sister, but if you will listen to his music you will get to know the real Hank Williams, and you won't find him to be the kind of person these people are writing about.

Another question that so many of you have asked—and perhaps I have done wrong not to answer—is, "Were Hank and Audrey divorced?"

Yes, they were, and had Hank lived there is little doubt in my mind that they would have stayed divorced. [...]

May God bless each of you. Please keep writing, as I enjoy every one of your letters even though I never have been able to answer every one of them. We are moving, so please note our new address, 920 Avon Street, Dallas, Texas.

Love,
Irene Williams Smith

JUNE 1957 (P. 28)

Dear Hank,

It has been four years now since you left us for a better home. Every day you seem to be with us more and more. Your records continue to sell and be played and loved by so many here in our country as well as foreign countries. So many men in the service have carried your records overseas with them that you have become popular not only here but in most of the world. Honey, it is amazing to me the influence you continue to have on the lives of so many young people— and, honey, it is a good influence because they want to write and sing songs the way you did. I get so many letters from youngsters that want to leave the world just a little better place to live just like you did. Honey, an uncle of ours told you once that God meant for you to be a preacher. I feel like you did just as much good as you would have done if you had been one.

Hank, today someone asked me if it makes me sad to hear your records. No, I just always listen and feel real proud that I had the privilege of being your sister and of knowing and loving you. I read an article recently that said we came from poor, ignorant white trash. Yep! We were poor—financially, that is—but not ignorant and not trash. Now, Hank, what do you think that person would call trash? Be kinda interesting to know, wouldn't it?

Lots have happened since God called you to be with Him. Your son is growing into a handsome fine young man. Some of your friends have left us to be with you and Fred [Rose] and Mama. Of those still around several are getting more popular all the time, especially Ray Price,[*] but you always knew that he would make it. As for me and my family, we are fine. John[†] gets taller, looks and acts more like you every day.

---

[*] Country singer (b. 1926), who was a protégé and onetime housemate of Williams.
[†] Irene's son, John Tillman Smith, Jr. (b. 1943).

Hank, lots of folks didn't really get to know and understand you when you were with us, but [those] that did shall continue to profit from having known and understood you. We are so thankful that there are still so many of your songs to be released, and are also so very grateful for those that have already been released. Hank, I didn't believe that you ever knew just how much people loved you. I hope that you know now, and somehow I feel that you do.

"So long, Hank; you and Mama make a place for me." "We three," it always was and always will be.

God bless each of you.
Irene Williams Smith
920 North Avon
Dallas, Texas

~~~~~~

| 26 |

Charlie Lamb: Liner Notes to *Hank Williams' Greatest Hits*

A legendary Nashville editor, publisher, music journalist, promoter, and general jack-of-all-trades, Charlie Lamb (1921–2012) played an essential role in marketing country music to mainstream America during his fifty-plus-year career. Hank Williams was an important component in this promotional campaign, as Lamb reveals in the album liner notes below. Gone, in Lamb's carefully crafted portrayal, is the business-savvy and upwardly mobile "Organization Man" celebrated in the newspaper and trade press accounts published during Williams's lifetime. Also banished is the hedonistic, self-destructive "Tabloid Celebrity" featured in the scandal and pulp magazine stories of the mid- to late 1950s. In their place stands another Hank Williams, the humble country boy whose universal, marrow-of-life music knows no boundaries of time, place, or genre.

If Madison Avenue admen set out to create an "image" for country music, they would never top Hank Williams.

Hank Williams *is* the image of country music.

However, it doesn't end there. The words and music that poured out of this star-crossed troubadour dot the musical landscape of that unique bordertown of musicdom which is both pop and country.

SOURCE   Charlie Lamb, liner notes to *Hank Williams' Greatest Hits* (MGM Records E3918, 1961).

Almost a decade ago Hank Williams died...but that is not a completely true statement. Hank left so much behind him, it is difficult to say that he really died on that New Year's Day in 1953.

The spirit of this wandering minstrel walks the hallowed boards of the Grand Ole Opry every Saturday night as *his* songs are sung and played. And too, the record industry blooms with the evergreens which sprung effervescently from the soul of the sad-faced cowboy.

The love, happiness, misery and lonesomeness Hank wrote and sang about will disappear before the baleful balladeer from Montgomery will be forgotten.

Whether he was spotlighted in his tight-cut show outfit at the Ryman Auditorium* in Nashville...or whether he was strumming and crooning over the turbulent backdrop of a boisterous café...or whether he was sitting in the back seat of an automobile scribbling a fresh inspiration on the back of an envelope...or whether he was lounging on the banks of a placid Bayou deep in Louisiana Cajun country with a hound dog for a companion...no matter where he was and no matter whom he was with, he was always the same compassionate symbol of humility.

This is Hank Williams the man—the image of country music. In the early 30's he ran barefooted across the Alabama lowlands with nothing but ragged blue jeans and a heavy tan to keep him warm. He was an eight year old plunking a cheap guitar, unaware that he was the heir-apparent to the folk-music throne.

But even as the King of Country Music, Hank retained the childhood simplicity and humility of his farm boy days.

Analyzing and explaining the success of his songs is another matter. Some say that when Hank Williams died, the Legend was born and his songs became great.

Some say Hank just had a way of saying what other men could only think deep in their hearts. This is true, but it's not the whole story.

To explain the secret of the Alabama Troubadour's triumph, perhaps we should slip back through time and recapture a moment of his life.

Standing before a radio microphone in the WSM studios, Hank was asked which of his songs was his favorite. With his guitar slung to one side, his white Stetson in hand, he hunched forward and in his quiet drawl said, "I don't have any favorite. I reckon a man feels something special for EVERY song he writes."

That's the key—Hank felt something "special" for every song he wrote.

---

* Home to the *Grand Ole Opry* radio broadcasts between 1943 and 1974.

And what songs!! America has sung them in the corn fields of Iowa; in the factories of Michigan; in the smog of Los Angeles and they still ring from juke boxes and radios everywhere. Country artists will go on recording Hank's material…and so will the big pop artists. And so the Legend grows. Hank's heirs will make more money than he ever did in his lifetime.

However, making money was the least of Hank's worries. Lyrics, not loot, were his life. Music, not money. And the music he made has become a part of our American heritage.

The kind of wealth that mattered to that easy-going, country-bred poet is stamped in vinylite on the two sides of this album, "Hank Williams' Greatest Hits."

Inside this cover is a wealth of musical Americana that no record library should be without. The immortal Hank Williams singing about his mythical Kaw-liga…the teardrops, cold hearts, lonesome days and honky tonkin' nights of broken love that Hank seemed to have such a deep feeling and understanding for. In this album are what MGM Records considers the 14 greatest songs ever turned out by the greatest of them all—Hank Williams.

As you listen, you may hear the phantom voice of Hank himself saying, "Thank you kindly for listenin', neighbor."

| 27 |

Stanford Whitmore: Excerpt from the Screenplay for *Your Cheatin' Heart*

Plans for a cinematic version of Hank Williams's life story emerged only weeks after his death, when his ex-wife Audrey sought to sell the movie rights to a Hollywood studio. MGM Studios, the logical choice, optioned the film, but complications with the script and casting delayed production until 1963, when B-movie producer Sam Katzman—who was known around Hollywood as the "King of Schlock"—took over the project. In short order, Katzman commissioned a script from veteran television screenwriter Stanford Whitmore (b. 1925) and selected George Hamilton to play Hank Williams (after Elvis Presley had rejected the role). The songs on the biopic's soundtrack, which consisted of "Nashville Sound" versions of Williams's hits, were sung by his fifteen-year-old son, Hank Williams, Jr., reportedly at Audrey's insistence.

SOURCE Stanford Whitmore, screenplay for *Your Cheatin' Heart* (MGM Studios, 1964), in the Margaret Herrick Library, the Academy of Motion Pictures Arts and Sciences, Beverly Hills, California. Used by permission of Warner Bros. Entertainment Inc.

Whitmore's script for *Your Cheatin' Heart* follows the general contours of Williams's biography but severely distorts the trajectory of his musical career and contains many glaring errors and omissions. In the film, for example, Williams never sings his breakthrough hit, "Lovesick Blues," presumably because Acuff-Rose, which licensed all the songs for the movie, did not own the copyright. Nor does the film mention his divorce from Audrey and his second marriage to Billie Jean Eshliman, who unsuccessfully sued its producers for defamation. As an interpretation of the hillbilly star's life, however, *Your Cheatin' Heart* offers a fable about the perils of success, a lesson relevant at the time to both the Nashville country music industry, then seeking to balance a reverence for its rustic roots with its status as a modern and lucrative commercial enterprise, and Williams's fans, many of whom had grown up poor in the rural South and were coming to grips with their own upward mobility amid the nation's postwar prosperity. Thus, in the following emblematic scene, a drunken Williams—who is hobbling with the aid of a cane due to a painful back injury—expresses his fears that if he accepts his newfound affluence, he might lose his authentic self, "a poor boy from the country" whom his adoring fans pay to see and hear.

NASHVILLE MANSION SCENE, CA. EARLY 1952

Int[erior] Bedroom—Audrey paces as Hank is seated on couch at right—CAMERA TRUCKS in as Audrey moves to b.g. [background]—she stands, hand on hip, as Hank [. . .] turns, looks back toward her—she turns facing him as he rises and moves toward her—follows her as she paces toward f.g. [foreground]—CAMERA TRUCKS in again as he gestures to her—moves around her as she turns from him—CAMERA PANS right, then PANS left as she keeps turning from him—he pulls her around to him [. . .]—CAMERA TRUCKS back as she moves forward and PANS right as she crosses—leans over near fireplace [. . .]—

Audrey: Everything I've done—I am only doing it to better ourselves.
Hank: That's exactly what's wrong, Miss Biggity of Nineteen Fifty-two! Time and place—when and where and who—you are! I know exactly what's goin' on in that mind of yours. *[mimicking Audrey]* "Hank, I know we started out as just a couple of poor kids from Alabama, but people change." Well, they don't! Are you so dumb you can't understand that? Who do you think the people come to hear—some slick-haired, fancy Dan, from New York City? They come to hear one of their own—a poor boy from the country.

Audrey: Is that why your records are selling so well in Detroit, in Chicago, Los Angeles—?

Hank: Well, that don't make no difference. The point is what I was... *(shakes his head)* I am, and I always will be!

Audrey: *(shakes her head also)* You know, that's one tune of yours that I am *sick to death* of hearin'. Just a poor country boy—draggin' your heels all the way, and when you get to the top, you act like you sneaked in the back door, and somebody's goin' to throw you out any minute! Maybe you like feelin' that way! *(continuing with her outburst)* Maybe you like earnin' money, so you can throw it all away, like it was blood money!

Hank: All your talkin'—'n' you don't understand nothin'.

Audrey: *(grows emotional and shakes her head)* Hank, I understand this—I can't go on livin' like this.

Hank: *(leans forward, grinning a bit, after looking [at the lavishly furnished bedroom])* Meanin' what?

Audrey: Meanin' I have tried—and I will continue to try—to be a good wife and a mother... but I am not going to be a *nurse!*

Hank: Well, you treat me like I got a disease!

Audrey: *(turns to mirror behind fireplace, facing b.g. in exasperation)* Oh!

Audrey faces mirror over fireplace at right as CAMERA TRUCKS in and around to left as Hank crosses and opens door of closet—points to his suits hanging up—Audrey puts hand on hip and turns to f.g.—gestures—Hank moves into closet and tosses out his suits—

Hank: Who messed up my things?

Audrey: I—uh—messed up your things!

Hank: A man works his head off and a woman comes along and jes' takes over his property!

Int. Closet—Hank lifts up his cane and knocks down clothes from neatly arranged rack—tosses apparel about—leans over and picks up fallen cane and moves toward door—pulls out another suit and moves toward adjoining room with it—

Hank: Now! Now, maybe I can find things the way I want them!

Int. Bedroom—Hank comes forward from closet, carrying suit—CAMERA TRUCKS back ahead of him as he strides forward—tosses suit down at left—

Hank: Now, that ought to make a great suit for Jefferson [their butler], huh?

CAMERA TRUCKS back to right as he moves to another closet at right, while Audrey is seen seated at dressing table at right—he turns to her as he is about to enter her closet—

Audrey: You'd better stay out of there.

Hank: *(leans over her, gesturing)* Do you know somethin', Queenie? The only thing missin' here is a crown. Perfume—you got enough... *(takes his hand and knocks all the bottles from dressing table)* to float a battleship! *(Audrey reacts, rising—she reaches after him as he digs into her jewel box and tries to restrain him)* And them jewels—!

CAMERA PANS left as he flings her across room, and she lands on couch—PANS down to left—

Audrey: Oh!

CS [Center Stage]—Hank looks down—CAMERA TRUCKS back to left as he crosses to Audrey who remains on couch—CAMERA PANS down as he stretches out his hand—she adjusts pillow and gestures—he gestures also, as she shakes her head—

Hank: After another successful year, like this, and I'm goin' to end up in the poor house!

Audrey: I should be wearin' flour sacks and no shoes.

Hank: Well, that's not a bad idea.

Audrey: You'd like your wife to look like that?

Hank: Well, I'd recognize her then! Ohhh.

CAMERA PANS up as Hank straightens—then as he moves o.s. [off-screen] in left fg., CAMERA TRUCKS in and PANS down to Audrey who sits up and reacts as she looks o.s. in left fg.—

Audrey: Who ever put it in your mind that it's a sin to be rich and famous?

Hank: I don't reckon it's a sin, but why me? Women shovin' babies at me to touch...crippled people—what do they think I am—a walking shrine? I got a hard enough time tryin' to save myself.

CS—Audrey looks up from couch, then she rises—CAMERA PANS up to right—
PANS her left as she crosses to door, trying to prevent Hank from leaving—she puts
her hand to his face, trying to soothe him—tugs on his jacket—

Audrey: Honey—nothin's wrong with us that a long vacation wouldn't cure.
Just—just the two of us! Like it used to be! No more records and no more
personal appearances—.

Hank: *(edges his way to the door and [leaves] as she watches)* Don't wait up for
me. 'Cause you're goin' to get awful old and ugly.

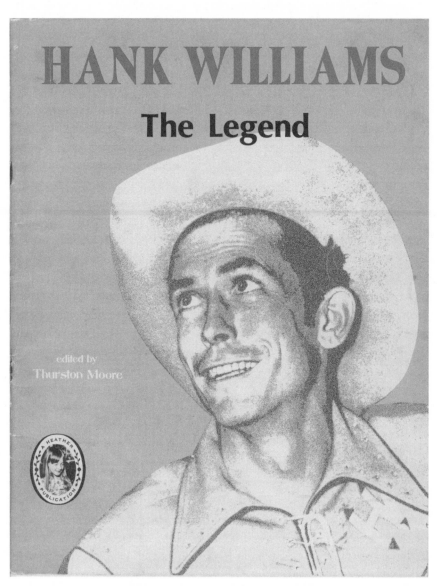

Cover of Thurston Moore's edited collection, *Hank Williams, The Legend*, 1972. Courtesy of Heather Enterprises, Inc. and Thurston Moore.

Part IV

~~~~~~

Bringing the Legend to Life
The Search for the "Real" Hank Williams (1965–1974)

Beginning in the late 1960s, a renewed interest in Hank Williams fueled a torrent of writing, a development that paralleled the dramatic upswing in country music's popularity. According to *Look* magazine's 1971 special country music issue, titled "Hillbilly No More: Country Music Sweeps the U.S.A.," the genre's fans now ranged from "truck drivers...and housewives to White House staffers and college kids." Encompassing everything from the contemporary "Countrypolitan" of singers such as Lynn Anderson and Charlie Rich to the sensitive, poetic stylings of singer-songwriters like Kris Kristofferson and Tom T. Hall to the harder-edged Bakersfield sound of Buck Owens and Merle Haggard, country music had burst out of its traditional domains—the rural South and "hillbilly" enclaves in industrial cities—to claim millions of fans across the nation. By the late 1960s, one of every five radio stations in the United States programmed country music exclusively, and the syndicated television variety show *Hee Haw*, which premiered on CBS in 1969, posted respectable ratings in New York, Chicago, and Los Angeles. Amid the political and social upheaval of the civil rights movement, women's liberation, Vietnam War protests, and the sixties counterculture, country music, rightly or wrongly, came to be identified with the conservative "silent majority," what *Look* called "middle-Americans...the ones the Republic can depend upon to pay their taxes, to send their sons faithfully to war," whom "country music assures...that they still matter." Country music's soaring popularity represented the culmination of the Nashville industry's efforts to garner national respect for its product, a point on which *Look* agreed. "The Nashville Sound is a misnomer," the magazine explained. "Country music is really the American Sound." Coinciding with the national media's discovery of country music's newfound success, writers from a variety of backgrounds rediscovered Hank Williams and firmly established him as the music's most studied, revered, and important historical figure.

Between 1965 and 1974, this revival of interest in the late country star either introduced or advanced three additional interpretations in the literature. The first of these, the "Ordinary Guy," appeared in a series of writings that chipped away, often unintentionally, at the legendary elements of Williams's story in order to present his more commonplace, human qualities. Not surprisingly, this theme figured particularly prominently in published memoirs by his family members and bandmates, beginning with ex-Drifting Cowboys fiddler Jerry Rivers's *Hank Williams: From Life to Legend* (1967) (an excerpt from which is not included below due to copyright restrictions). Rivers's recollections, along with subsequent efforts by Don Helms, Joe Pennington, and other onetime Drifting Cowboys, rendered Williams a more accessible figure by presenting him as a typical, self-taught southern musician who happened to achieve enormous commercial success thanks to years of hard work, endless touring, and dedication to the craft of songwriting. These writings also provided indispensable source material for later scholarly and journalistic accounts of Williams's life. Rivers's book, for example, contained not only his reminiscences of working alongside the country star between 1949 and 1952, but also the first comprehensive discography and bibliography devoted to him, plus a series of previously unpublished photographs.

Easily the most popular and influential account of Williams published during this period, however, was Roger M. Williams's *Sing a Sad Song: The Life of Hank Williams* (1970), the first full-length interpretative biography of the star. Roger Williams (no relation), a journalist by training, assembled the book from long-ignored primary sources and his own interviews with the singer's family members, friends, and music industry associates. Most important, his biography extended the "American Icon" theme, first introduced by the Nashville music establishment in the early 1960s. In what has become the most durable and widely embraced interpretation of Hank Williams, the "American Icon" recognized the hillbilly star as a musical giant whose talents, fame, and significance placed him in an elite cultural category reserved for only a select group of nationally renowned artists. The broad but still developing contours of yet another significant interpretation were outlined in Ralph J. Gleason's 1969 *Rolling Stone* article "Hank Williams, Roy Acuff, and Then God!!," which, with its references to Williams's drinking and drug abuse, validated the country star's bohemian credentials for the magazine's counterculture readers and anticipated the new rock criticism. As a fully developed concept since the 1970s, this "Rock 'n' Roll Pioneer" theme celebrated Williams's role as a godfather of rock music, noting with approval his unruly behavior and his uncompromisingly innovative musical style.

Another landmark contribution to the literature published during this period was *High Lonesome World: The Death and Life of a Country Music Singer* (1969), by award-winning Alabama novelist and short-story writer Babs H. Deal. (No excerpt could be included in this reader due to copyright restrictions.) The first novel based on Hank Williams's biography, *High Lonesome World* chronicled the misspent life of an Alabama country-and-western star named Wade Coley, a stereotypically temperamental, tortured artist who destroys himself with alcohol and drugs and, in his descent, disrupts the lives of those around him. Before the novel even begins, Coley has died at the age of thirty, in the backseat of a chauffeured Cadillac, in a mid-January snowstorm on his way to a show in Memphis, Tennessee. The story of his meteoric rise to stardom and his equally rapid decline is recounted, using a *Citizen Kane*-like technique, in a series of reminiscences by twelve characters, each of whom offers distinctive insights into the enigmatic Coley. Employing barely fictionalized details from the Hank Williams saga, *High Lonesome World* prefigured the many novels, short stories, and plays depicting the late country star, in some form or fashion, that would follow.

The late 1960s and early 1970s clearly represented a turning point in the development of Hank Williams's posthumous literary reputation. While some writers produced the first serious biographies of the country star or sought to strip away the legendary elements that had accumulated about him, others began to approach him from entirely new perspectives, arguing—explicitly or implicitly—for his historical and cultural significance beyond the restrictive bounds of region or musical genre. By the end of this period, the onetime "King of the Hillbillies" was well en route to becoming a revered American institution.

| 28 |

Bill C. Malone: Excerpt from *Country Music, U.S.A.: A Fifty-Year History*

This selection originally appeared in Bill C. Malone's landmark 1968 book, *Country Music, U.S.A.: A Fifty-Year History*, the first comprehensive study of country music by an academic historian. A revision of Malone's doctoral dissertation at the University of Texas at Austin, *Country Music, U.S.A.* ranks as one of the most critically and commercially successful books ever written about any genre of American popular music, and, now in its third revised edition, it remains what one critic has hailed as "the original, territory-defining bible of country music history." In the book's section on Hank Williams, a scholarly update of the "Organization Man" interpretation, Malone maps out what would thereafter be accepted as the major milestones of Williams's life story, from his impoverished Alabama childhood, through his rise to Nashville stardom, to his death en route to Canton, Ohio. More important, Malone parallels the trajectory of Williams's career with the rising fortunes of the postwar Nashville country music industry.

In many ways, Malone's accounts of country music and of Hank Williams in particular reflect his own life story. Malone (b. 1934) grew up a self-described "tenant farmer's son" who spent his early childhood on an East Texas cotton farm, where his musical family introduced him to old-time country music and folk songs. From Malone's perspective, the music he heard and sang as a child represented a cherished cultural inheritance and the genuine folk music of his people, the southern white working class. During World War II, Malone's family moved to the prosperous oil town of Tyler, Texas, where he saw Williams perform in 1949 when the *Louisiana Hayride* broadcast a show from the local high school auditorium. Over the ensuing years, Malone went on to become a noted historian, a university

SOURCE Bill C. Malone, *Country Music, U.S.A.: A Fifty-Year History* (Austin: University of Texas Press, 1968), 232–233, 239, 240–241. © 1968 by Bill C. Malone. Used by permission of the author and the University of Texas Press.

professor, and the nation's foremost authority on country music. In the excerpt below, Malone credits Williams with inspiring other honky-tonk singers and furthering country music's popularity, but, in the end, he views Williams with some ambivalence, even melancholy, for his role in "diluting its rural purity" and, in doing so, hastening the end of its "Golden Age."

The individual who most successfully spanned the gulf between country and popular music was King Hiram "Hank" Williams,* who along with Jimmie Rodgers and Fred Rose constituted the triumvirate first elected to country music's Hall of Fame.[1] Williams was the symbol of country music's postwar upsurge, and his sudden death in 1953 signified the ending of the boom period. His early death solidified the legend that had already begun during his lifetime.

It is paradoxical that Hank Williams, whose compositions were more readily accepted by popular-music practitioners than any other country writer's, was more firmly grounded in the rural tradition than most other hillbilly performers. In the influences that worked upon him, in his early upbringing, and in his mode of musical expression, Williams reflected the inherited traditions of the rural South and the forces that have strived to urbanize it. He is, therefore, an interesting fusion of the old with the new; he was a rural singer who had the talent (or knack) to create compositions acceptable to people outside the rural tradition. But, at the same time, his career came at a fortuitous moment when country music was gaining wider public acceptance and when the commercial entertainment world was devoting greater attention to country songs. Despite his talents, Williams would not have gained fame as a popular songwriter had he lived during an earlier period. The preceding decades had not been propitious for such a development. As it was, Williams rode to prosperity and fame on the crest of the postwar wave that spread country music throughout the nation, and, as much as any one man, he inaugurated the movement that, despite his own immersion in the rural tradition, served to becloud country music's unique identity. [...]

Country music would probably have followed the course that it did even had Williams lived, but, coming as it did at the beginning of a new era, his death symbolized the closing of country music's "high" period. It is ironic that Williams, whose style was so firmly grounded in rural tradition, did more than any other individual to modify the traditional music forms and broaden the music's

---

* According to Lon Williams, his son was christened King Hiram, after the Phoenician king of Tyre mentioned in the Bible in 2 Samuel and 1 Kings, although Hank's birth certificate, which Lillie belatedly registered with the state of Alabama in 1934, lists his name as only Hiram, which was misspelled "Hiriam."

base of acceptance, thereby diluting its rural purity. Williams' success at song composition gained a wider acceptance for country music and, furthering the advances made by "The Tennessee Waltz,"[†] served to batter down the tenuous walls between popular and country music. [...]

For approximately one year after Williams' death, country styles did not change materially. The songs played on radios and juke boxes still were characterized by the honky-tonk beat and the sounds of the fiddle and steel guitar. New singers continued to appear, to earn hefty incomes, and to gain glittering success. Some of them, like Ray Price and George Jones (both from Texas), received their inspiration from Hank Williams.[2] A few, like Marty Robbins of Arizona and Jim Reeves from Texas, used a soft, semi-crooning style somewhat suggestive of Eddy Arnold. The most successful country performer in the year immediately following Williams' death was a wailing honky-tonk singer from Monroe, Louisiana, Webb Pierce. Recording for Decca, Pierce produced twenty-one consecutive "hits," or songs that sold over 100,000 [copies]. [...] Using standard honky-tonk instrumentation featured by a "crying" steel guitar, Pierce occupied the position vacated by Williams and catapulted himself first to the Louisiana Hayride and later to the Grand Ole Opry.[3] In short, Pierce was only one of several country entertainers who continued to produced hit records and attract large followings. But no one could capture the public imagination as Williams had.

NOTES

1 The "official" Hall of Fame created by the Country Music Association [...] .

2 Both singers have acknowledged their debts to Williams (interview with Ray Price, Austin, Texas, March 2, 1962; interview with George Jones, Austin, Texas, August 16, 1962).

3 Information on Pierce was obtained from Linnell Gentry, *A History and Encyclopedia of Country, Western, and Gospel Music* (Nashville: McQuiddy Press, 1961), 288; *Billboard, The World of Country Music* (New York, 1963), 192–199; interview with James Denny (of Cedarwood Publishing Company), Nashville, Tennessee, August 25, 1961; and a letter to the author from Bob Pinson, Santa Clara, California, September 4, 1966.

[†] Written by country-and-western bandleader Pee Wee King (born Julius Frank Anthony Kuczynski) (1914–2000) and Henry Ellis "Redd" Stewart (1923–2003), the vocalist in King's band, "Tennessee Waltz" ranks as country music's best-selling crossover hit, most notably in singer Patti Page's lush cover version, which topped the pop music charts for nine weeks in late 1950 and early 1951.

| 29 |

Joe Azbell: No Direction Signs Exist

While Hank Williams's stature among scholars and journalists continued to grow, and his fan base expanded across the globe, in many ways he remained a prophet without honor in his hometown of Montgomery, Alabama. In the years just after his death, the city hosted the occasional commemorative celebration, including Hank Williams Memorial Day, an extravagant two-day affair in September 1954, with a massive parade that attracted more than 60,000 spectators. By the late 1960s, however, civic leaders showed little interest in the late hillbilly star. In this 1968 article, veteran local newspaperman Joe Azbell (1927-1995) expresses his long-held conviction that a memorial center dedicated to the singer would draw thousands of tourists to Montgomery. But despite Azbell's efforts, more than two decades would pass before a statue of Williams was unveiled in Montgomery (1991) and even longer before a museum devoted to him opened downtown (1999). Meanwhile, Hank Williams's hilltop grave became an increasingly popular shrine for country music fans, attracting, according to a 2006 newspaper report, an estimated 100,000 visitors a year. Memorial ceremonies commemorating the late country star are still held there twice a year, on January 1, the anniversary of his death, and September 17, his birthday.

Montgomery has a tourist attraction that puts Six Flags over Georgia, the Battleship Alabama and Rock City* in the cool, cool shade. It goes untouched, ignored, unscratched, unpublicized. It is a crying shame.

What is this attraction? The grave of Hank Williams. The grave of the guitar-strumming man, the legend, the hometown boy whose music speaks in plain words the sorrows, the loves, the tribulations, the deeply-felt emotions of sharecroppers, village storekeepers, truck drivers, truck stop waitresses, millionaires, teachers, doctors, professors, politicians—rednecks in Hickey Freeman† suits and washpot-faded overalls—for there is a little redneck in all of us.

Hank is buried here. His body lies in a grave on the windy hillside of Oakwood [Cemetery] Annex. A monument, black lettered in stone, sits

---

SOURCE   Joe Azbell, "No Direction Signs Exist," *Montgomery Independent*, September 12, 1968. Reprinted by permission of the *Montgomery Independent*.
* A famous roadside attraction atop Lookout Mountain in Georgia, best known for its ubiquitous "See Rock City" advertisements painted on the roofs of barns in the South and Midwest.
† A nationally known brand of traditional-style men's suits.

atop the grave. It was designed by Willie Gayle when he was associated with L. C. Henley[‡] and before he became the national managing director of the Dale Carnegie Organization.[§] Gayle did a superb job with the monument. Gayle designed it and Henley built it to tell a stone story of Hank. There are music sheet covers of Hank's songs carved into the stone and two big musical notes. There is a metallic picture of Hank with his guitar on his knee and the words, "Praise the Lord, I saw the light" from one of his songs. There are the stone boots and the cowboy Stetson [hat] branded with HW, his initials. Hank would have liked the stone. Willie Gayle designed it as Hank would have wanted it to look. Emotional in its simplicity—like his songs.

To reach the grave, you drive up a dirt road, gravel spitting under the tires, past neat rows of graves of British cadets.[¶] You must park in the road. Off to the north are Newtown slums, factories, City Maintenance Shops and the Old City Jail that Negroes call the "Big Rock." Tourists have to hunt for the grave but they find it. Thousands of them each year.

They come and stand there quietly. Some cry. But mostly they stand and look down at the chained-in grave. It is as if they are hearing the words of Hank's music come up from a departed soul—"Cold, Cold Heart," "Kawliga," "Your Cheating Heart," and the hymn, "I Saw the Light." They stand there and hum these songs as if they are touching the spirit of a man who suffered their sufferings, who knew the loneliness of their loneliness, who hitchhiked the long, lonely roads of life, lost, forlorn, troubled.

They want something from Hank to take back home. A chunk of dirt. A piece of stone. Sometimes a rock. And there are those who steal part of the monument. "We spend hundreds of dollars every year to replace things and maintain the grave site," lamented Robert Stewart, Montgomery attorney for the Hank Williams Estate. "It is a problem. People love his memory."

There is no direction sign on the highways that Hank is buried here. None at the cemetery. There is nothing in the tourist advertisements. They ask the

---

[‡] Owner of Henley's Memorial Company, a Montgomery, Alabama, monuments firm.

[§] International business organization offering training in self-improvement, salesmanship, and public speaking founded in 1912 by its namesake, Dale Carnegie (1888–1955), author of the best-selling self-help book, *How to Win Friends and Influence People* (1936).

[¶] A reference to the nearly eighty Royal Air Force cadets buried in the cemetery who died during pilot training at nearby Maxwell Field or at other Southeast Air Corps Training Center sites during World War II.

service station man, the waitress, the dime store clerk. They bring flowers, potted plants. They take rolls of snapshots.

For years I have been convinced hundreds of thousands of people would visit a memorial center for Hank Williams. When I have mentioned a memorial center to friends they have smiled. They know I, too, love his music because I knew him as a person or maybe it's the redneck in me.

Music publisher Fred Rose once told me that my articles in the Montgomery Advertiser did as much to keep Hank's memory alive as anything else. Rose was wrong. Hank's music kept his memory alive. My articles simply sold newspapers.

It is true that Hank's funeral almost cost me my job as a newspaperman [at the Advertiser]. Photographer Albert Kraus [...] went with me to Hank's funeral.

There were 25,000 people packed around the City Auditorium. They came to mourn the death of an old friend, dead at 29 [....] [Inside, mourners] filed by the casket. They touched his suit. They took flowers from the casket. Some put little bouquets of flowers there. Old women and old men in their Sunday best, young boys and girls, reverent and quiet, the beautiful and the ugly, the great blistered. They cried without shame. They felt a part of their own emotions were lying in the flower-decked coffin because Hank's music spoke what was in their hearts.

When I went back to the newspaper that afternoon, the makeup editor asked me: "How much space do you want on page one for the funeral?" I looked over at him. "All of it!" I said. He flinched. "All of it?" I nodded.‖ He rubbed a hand across his mouth. "I guess you know what you're doing?" Kraus brought the pictures. I wrote the story.

The next morning publisher R. F. Hudson, Sr., one of the greatest men I have ever known, called me at home. He was fuming.

"Did you put all of that stuff on the front page—the whole front page?" I said I did. "When you come down, see me in my office!"

A few minutes later, R. F. Hudson, Jr., called me. "What in the world possessed you?" he said. All I could think to say was "Hank deserved it." Hudson Jr. understood newspapering. "I'll try to smooth it over with Dad. He thinks you have ruined the newspaper."

‖ Contrary to Azbell's claim, only about one-third of the front page of the *Montgomery Avertiser*'s January 5, 1953, edition was devoted to Williams's funeral, and most of the coverage consisted of the photographs Kraus had taken at the services.

Later when I reached the newspaper I had decided to try Nashville for my next newspaper job. I walked into the office of R. F. Hudson, Jr. He looked up, then ordered me to sit down.

Shaking his head he finally said: "You may be saved yet." He dialed for A. D. Potter, circulation manager, to come to his office and left me sitting there without a word. When Potter arrived, Hudson asked him: "Are we still getting the calls?"

"I never saw anything like it," Potter said. "We've sold out of papers. It's amazing!"

"I'll take responsibility. Go to work and get all you can on Williams," Hudson said.

As it turned out, more copies of the Montgomery Advertiser were sold of that issue than any edition in the newspaper's history. The issue was reprinted. Orders came in from throughout the world. For six weeks we collected and published material on Hank's life. Now [almost] sixteen years later with [the] release of the movie, "Your Cheating Heart" starring George Hamilton with songs by Hank Jr., and the continuing popularity of his music, Hank goes on living in the hearts of millions. That issue is a collector's item but no copies are available.

Few recognized the immense popularity of Hank's music in those days in 1951 [*sic*]. It was difficult for him to get a personal appearance engagement. People in Montgomery even yet cannot recognize what a Hank Williams memorial would mean to our city.

I asked attorney Stewart if it would be possible for the bodies of Hank, his mother, Mrs. Lillian Stone,** and his niece to be moved to a center if it were built. "I cannot presume to speak for the family," he said, "but I believe they would be interested if a suitable center and museum to honor his memory were constructed."

The July issue of Harper's Magazine carried a graphic article on "The Grand Old Opry" by Larry L. King. Discussing a tour of Nashville, King wrote: "Our longest pause was at the home of Audrey Williams, widow of the legendary Hank. 'That 1952 Cadillac in the driveway is the one Hank Williams died in…' our guide said prompting the greatest camera action since Iwo Jima…"††

** Although it was not her birth name, Williams's mother went by "Lillian" later in life, and, in fact, her gravestone, which is located next to her son's in Montgomery's Oakwood Cemetery Annex, reads "Lillian Skipper Williams."

†† A reference to the iconic World War II photograph taken on February 23, 1945, depicting five U.S. Marines, along with one Navy corpsman, raising the United States flag atop Mount Suribachi during the Battle of Iwo Jima.

If they pause the longest in Nashville to see the automobile in which Hank died, it makes sense they would visit Montgomery to see a Hank Williams Museum and Memorial Center where he is buried.

Montgomery would benefit. Most important it would pay honor to a man and his music who spoke to [the] hearts of millions.

~~~~~~

| 30 |

Ralph J. Gleason: Perspectives: Hank Williams, Roy Acuff and Then God!!

An unexpected development in the growth of Hank Williams's posthumous popularity occurred during the late 1960s and early 1970s, when his aging audience was augmented by a new generation of fans, particularly high school and college students drawn to the sixties counterculture. Their parents may have enjoyed the singer's records, or, more likely, "crossover" pop versions of his songs, but for many young people he became a symbol of rebellion against the "Establishment" and the embodiment of bohemian artistry achieved through intense suffering and the consciousness-altering use of drugs and alcohol.

Magazine profiles of Williams, especially those appearing in alternative and rock music publications, played a key role in cultivating new audiences for his music and in advancing the "Rock 'n' Roll Pioneer" interpretation. One such pivotal article, which provides an early, inchoate version of this theme, was penned by Ralph J. Gleason (1917–1975), a longtime San Francisco newspaper columnist, music critic, author, and co-founder, in 1967, of *Rolling Stone* magazine. Although he principally covered jazz and pop music at the time, Gleason interviewed Williams in Oakland, California, in mid-April 1952, and published the results in his weekly *San Francisco Chronicle* newspaper column seven weeks later.* That piece was a standard "Organization Man" profile typical of the articles published about the country star during his lifetime.

Seventeen years later, Gleason drew upon his recollections of that interview, along with those of a Williams concert he had attended at a nearby San Pablo

---

SOURCE   Ralph J. Gleason, "Perspectives: Hank Williams, Roy Acuff and Then God!!" *Rolling Stone*, June 28, 1969, p. 32. © Rolling Stone LLC 1969. All Rights Reserved. Reprinted by permission.

* Ralph J. Gleason, "The Rhythm Section: 'A Song Ain't Nothin' But a Story Just Wrote with Music to It,'" *San Francisco Chronicle*, June 1, 1952.

dance hall, to produce the famous 1969 *Rolling Stone* article featured below. Like the earlier column, Gleason's article contains several illuminating quotations from Williams. The original piece, however, did not include the review of Williams's show found here. Nor, significantly, did it mention his frail, pallid appearance or his pill popping and whiskey drinking. In a seismic shift within the Hank Williams literature, what in the 1950s had been deemed scandalous behavior suitable for discussion only in tabloids and pulp magazines was now routinely accepted, even celebrated, by the alternative and rock music press of the 1960s.

Hank Williams came out of the bathroom carrying a glass of water. He was lean, slightly stooped over and long-jawed. He shook hands quickly, then went over to the top of the bureau, swept off a handful of pills and deftly dropped them, one at a time, with short, expert slugs from the glass.

I didn't really know doodley-britt about country-western music except that I dug Ernest Tubbs [Tubb] and T. Texas Tyler and thought that "You Two Timed Me One Time Too Often" was a great song. But I was writing about popular music for the San Francisco Chronicle and Hank Williams was by God popular and a fat-ish man with big glasses named Wally Elliott, who doubled as a C&W[†] disc jockey under the *nomme du disque*[‡] of Longhorn Joe, was presenting Williams in several one nighters. So I went to talk to him.

The bathroom was in the Leamington Hotel which is the biggest hotel in Oakland and could have been any one of the standard Muhlebach or old Statler hotels anywhere in the U.S., the salesman's shelter. All I knew about Hank Williams was that he made records as Luke the Drifter[§] and under his own name and had sold millions and he sure wrote good songs. I was a little surprised by the pills, but then he looked pale and thin and had deep-set eyes and might have been hung over for all I knew. It was June, 1952,[¶] six months before he died in that car's back seat on New Year's Day, with everybody denying the first report that it was from an overdose.

So he threw the pill boxes in his suitcase, and we went down to the coffee shop. Hank Williams talked and ate breakfast and I wrote it down.

[†] An abbreviation for "country and western."

[‡] A French phrase, usually spelled *nom de disque*, literally meaning "disc name"; it typically refers to a recording artist's pseudonym.

[§] The pseudonym under which Williams's MGM recordings of sermonizing recitations and talking blues were released.

[¶] Based upon Williams's touring schedule, Gleason's interview with the singer occurred in mid-April, rather than in June, 1952, making it some eight-and-a-half months before Williams's death.

"I've been singing ever since I can remember," he said. He was 29 then,[||] doing 200 one-nighters a year and grossing over $400,000, he said. "My mother was an organist at Mt. Olive, Alabama, and my earliest memory is sittin' on that organ stool by her and hollerin'. I must have been five, six years old and louder than anybody else."

"I learned to play the git-tar from an old colored man in the streets of Montgomery.[**] He was named Tetot and he played in a colored street band. They had a washtub bass. You ever seen one of them? Well, it had a hole in the middle with a broom handle stuck in it and a rope for the strings."

"I was shinin' shoes and sellin' newspapers and followin' this ole Nigrah around to get him to teach me to play the git-tar. I'd give him 15¢ or whatever I could get a hold of for a lesson. When I was about eight years old, I got my first git-tar. A second hand $3.50 git-tar my mother bought me. Then I got a jazz horn[††] and played both of them at dances and had a band when I was 14 or 15."

Hank went on the air on WSFA in Montgomery when he was still in school and, after he met Fred Rose, he cut his first records for Sterling. "One session, $90 for four sides including 'Never Again Will I Knock On Your Door.'"

That started it all. MGM signed him. He starred with the C&W radio programs for years and had an incredible string of hit records in the days of the 78 rpm disc and his songs were recorded by many other performers, too.

"A good song is a good song," Hank said as he ate. "And if I'm lucky enough to write it, well ... ! I get more kick out of writing than I do singing. I reckon I've written a thousand songs and had over 300 published."[‡‡]

Hank surprised me by referring to his music as "folk music." "Folk music is sincere. There ain't nuthin' phony about it. When a folk singer sings a sad song, he's sad. He means it. The tunes are simple and easy to remember and the singers, they're sincere about them."

"I don't say I ever write for popularity. I check a song by its lyrics. A song ain't nuthin' in the world but a story just wrote with music to it. I can't sing 'Rag

---

[||] Williams was twenty-eight years old at the time of this interview, not twenty-nine, as Gleason notes.

[**] Most biographers believe that Williams's boyhood musical association with Rufus "Tee-Tot" Payne took place in Georgiana or, more likely, Greenville, prior to the Williams family's move to Montgomery in 1937.

[††] Biographer Roger M. Williams speculates that this was probably "a kazoo sort of thing you could play a tune on simply [by] humming into it."

[‡‡] Williams's claim of having more than 300 published songs to his credit is an exaggeration, and his assertion of having written one thousand songs in total appears to be even more wildly overblown.

Mop' or 'Mairzy Doats.'⁵⁵ But the best way for me to get a hit is to do something I don't like. I've been offered some of the biggest songs to sing and turned them down. There ain't *nobody* can pick songs. Because I say it's good, don't mean it'll sell."

"I like Johnny [Johnnie] Ray.¶¶ He's sincere and shows he's sincere. That's the reason he's popular. He sounds to me like he means it. What I mean by sincerity, Roy Acuff is the best example. He's the biggest singer the music ever knew. You booked him and you didn't worry about crowds. For drawing power in the South, it was Roy Acuff and then God!! He done it with 'Wabash Cannonball' and with 'Great Speckled Bird.' He'd stand up there singing, tears running down his cheeks."

Acuff was his idol and Fred Rose his inspiration. "Fred Rose, it was my good fortune to be associated with him. He came to Nashville to laugh and he heard Acuff and said, 'By God, he means it!'"

Sipping coffee and talking, Hank went on about now forgotten singers like Bill Darnell, about Roy Acuff and Fred Rose and Ernest Tubbs and Bing Crosby, about "Wheel of Fortune" and "I Love You So Much It Hurts Me."

Pretty soon Wally Elliott looked at his watch and said he had to take Hank off somewhere to plug that night's show: Hank was looking a little better now, the paleness under the close shaven jaws had been replaced with some color and wasn't quite so peaked.

So they split and I split and later that night I drove out to San Pablo Hall which is 'way out past El Cerrito and Richmond and almost to Vallejo. San Pablo Avenue, possibly the longest main street in the world, runs for almost 20 miles from downtown Oakland on out there and in 1952 there were no freeways. When you got to San Pablo, it looked like every place else only a little raunchier, and San Pablo Hall was a one story white building on a lot a block off the Avenue. You parked in the mud and walked past a tree up to the door and inside there was a long room with a bandstand at one end and a bar in an annex at one side.

Wally Elliott, who had been wearing a business suit in the afternoon and looked like one of Ralph Williams'|||| Ford salesmen, was a Western dude now,

---

⁵⁵ Two best-selling pop novelty songs: the Ames Brothers scored a *Billboard* No. 1 hit in 1950 with their version of "Rag Mop," while the Merry Macs topped the charts six years earlier with their recording of the nonsensical "Mairzy Doats."

¶¶ An American popular singer, songwriter, and pianist (1927–1990), best known for his signature song, "Cry," which was a No. 1 hit for eleven weeks on *Billboard*'s charts in 1952.

|||| Owner of Ralph Williams Ford, a large Encino, California, automobile dealership; his television commercials, for which he served as the on-screen pitchman, were prominent on Los Angeles stations throughout much of the 1960s.

with full Grand Ole Opry regalia, Stetson hat, hand made boots. The whole bit. The band was terrible. I only remember that about them and shortly after I got there Hank Williams went on. He looked just like he looked at the hotel except that now he had a Western hat and a guitar. When he sang, he looked like he squeezed himself to get the notes out sometimes and he seemed shorter somehow than when we were talking in the coffee shop.

He did them all, all his hits, "Jambalaya,"*** "Lovesick Blues," "Move It On Over." I don't remember him singing any of the Luke the Drifter religious songs. Not even "I Saw the Light." But he did the barrelhouse blues and the bar room ballads, "Cold, Cold Heart" and "Hey, Good Lookin'" and "Your Cheatin' Heart."†††

And he had that *thing*. He made them scream when he sang and that audience was shipped right up from Enid or Wichita Falls intact (like Elia Kazan shipped the bit players for *Baby Doll* up from the Deep South to Long Island for a scene). There were lots of those blondes you see at C&W affairs, the kind of hair that mother never had and nature never grew and the tight skirts that won't quit and the guys looking barbershop neat but still with a touch of dust on them. "Shit-kicker dances" the outside world called them then but some great people came through to play for them and this time it was Hank Williams and the Driftin' Cowboys it said, but I believe now (as I suspected then) that the only Driftin' Cowboy was Hank.

At the intermission, it was impossible to talk to him. He was a little stoned and didn't seem to remember our conversation earlier in the day and the party was beginning to get a little rough. They were whiskey drinkers and so I gave them room, looked around a while and then went on back out.

Six months [*sic*] later when I read he had died I remembered him saying in that Oakland hotel coffee shop, how much he loved his Tennessee ranch but how little time he got to spend there because he was on the road so much. "Last time I was there it rained," he said sourly. And then he added that he was stocking the ranch with cattle and his ambition someday was to retire there and watch "them cattle work while I write songs an' fish."

He never did, of course. I had no idea how tortured a man he was when I saw him. It came through more in his performance. He didn't cry but he could make *you* cry, and when he sang "Lovesick Blues" you knew he meant it.

*** Williams did not record "Jambalaya (On the Bayou)" until June 13, 1952, almost two months after the show Gleason attended. It is possible, although unlikely, that the singer performed the song that night at part of his set.

††† Gleason also appears to be mistaken here about "Your Cheatin' Heart." Williams almost certainly did not perform the song at this show since, according to biographer Colin Escott, he did not finish writing it until mid-August 1952, more than four months later.

So he died in the back seat of a car en route from one gig to another, from one ratty dance hall to another ratty dance hall, while the world gradually came to sing his songs and his Hollywood-ized life was shown and reshown on late night TV and the court fight for his estate went on for years. Still goes on, I think, that legal fight, like some ghost walking the pine hills for eternity.

~~~~~~

| 31 |

Roger M. Williams: Excerpt from *Sing a Sad Song: The Life of Hank Williams*

Until Roger M. Williams published his critically acclaimed *Sing a Sad Song: The Life of Hank Williams* in 1970, neither Hank Williams nor, for that matter, any country star had ever been the subject of a serious full-length biography. Born in New York City and educated at Amherst College, Williams (b. 1934) (no relation), like many of the journalists who wrote about Hank Williams in the 1960s and 1970s, was not a native southerner. While serving in *Time* magazine's Atlanta bureau, he decided to write a biography after hearing "larger-than-life" stories about the late country star from a fellow reporter who once covered the Nashville music beat. For more than two decades, the resulting book, *Sing a Sad Song*, would remain the most authoritative account of Hank Williams's life.

In its early chapters, Roger Williams fills in much of what was previously unknown about Hank Williams's early life, including details about his parents' background and marriage, his childhood in south-central Alabama, and his relationship with his musical mentor, Rufus "Tee-Tot" Payne. Throughout the book, the author seeks to account for the roots of his subject's unique appeal as a performer and songwriter, and to uncover the reasons for his self-destructive behavior, especially his alcoholism. In the conclusion, excerpted below, he identifies several of the essential elements that contributed to Hank Williams's continuing popularity in the decades after his death, particularly the undying devotion of his fans worldwide. Besides showing the ways that Montgomery and Nashville, for better or worse, attempted to preserve his memory, Roger Williams also addresses the controversy over MGM Records' audio enhancement of the singer's original recordings, which many fans view as sacrilege, but which nevertheless

SOURCE   Roger M. Williams, *Sing a Sad Song: The Life of Hank Williams* (New York: Doubleday, 1970), 265–268, 271–273, 274–275. © 1970, 1973, 1981 by Roger M. Williams. Used with permission of the University of Illinois Press.

"helps keep the legend alive." So enduring is Hank Williams's appeal, Roger Williams proclaims, "it will last as long as country music itself."

Estimates of fifteen million Hank Williams fans are by no means inflated. A few other country music artists—Jimmie Rodgers, Roy Acuff—have had as many. The remarkable thing about Hank's fans is their unending devotion to the man and his music and their efforts in keeping the legend alive. Their ranks have been swelled by millions of other people too young to recall Hank's life and times but captivated by his music nonetheless.

Who are the fans? People from every section of the country—indeed, of the world—from every walk of life, of every musical taste. Because Hank's songs spanned the country and pop fields, his enthusiasts span them too. He is even considered, along with a select few other country artists, acceptable to most folk music fans. When guitar pickers gather, one will inevitably say, "Let's do this old Hank Williams song...." (The song will not be a commercial hit like "Your Cheatin' Heart" but a hymn or one of the less-celebrated ballads of unrequited love.)

The whole process, legend and money-making and durability of music, has been greatly aided by what Roy Acuff calls Hank's "very timely death." Like James Dean, Hank died at a most propitious time: in Hank's case, after he had rocketed to the top of his field, then fallen and was striving to regain the heights again. It is no surprise that this story, involved as it was with love and alcohol and loneliness, has touched the hearts of millions. Coupled with the man's songs, it will last as long as country music itself.

The efforts, both commercial and non-commercial, to perpetuate Hank have been so successful that large numbers of people think he is still alive. The Grand Ole Opry, [former Drifting Cowboys fiddler] Jerry Rivers notes, still gets requests from Japan (where Hank has always been popular) to "Send Mr. Hank Williams to sing for us."

One of the reasons for this apparently endless appeal is the ever-widening circle of artists who record Hank's songs. They range from country to pop to folk to soul and even jazz, and they include various sub-species within those categories. "Your Cheatin' Heart," for example, has been recorded by such diverse types as Ray Anthony, Ramsey Lewis, Frankie Avalon, Roberta Sherwood, Fats Domino, Ray Charles, Les Paul and Mary Ford, and the Pete King Chorale, not to mention a dozen or two country artists—some seventy-five artists in all. A song getting this kind of recording action finds its way onto a lot of turntables that would not touch a pure country number.

M-G-M itself has catered to this broad market. Its catalogue includes a version of Hank Williams' songs for just about everybody. For the real devotee, there is album after album of Hank and the Drifting Cowboys—the genuine, original stuff; for followers of Hank and Audrey and all that, an album called "Mr. and Mrs. Hank Williams," featuring their duets; for those partial to a smoother sound, a couple of albums offering the songs done sweetly with strings; for fans of Hank, Jr., albums with his voice superimposed on that of his father, in one of those "recording miracles" we are blessed with these days; and for everybody, the usual run of "Unforgettable" and "Immortal" albums, plus one that capitalizes on what M-G-M seems to regard as Hank's third Coming— "The Legend Lives Anew." If the company had the Beatles or the Boston Pops under contract, there would surely be Williams albums by them too.

The slicked-up, fully orchestrated reissues of Hank's music have not found universal approval. Using strings, horns, and vocal groups as back-ing for country singers is a matter of controversy within the trade these days. "We can only have praise for the few remaining A&R men who have resisted the modem approach and continue to record their artists with simple backing," wrote Everett Corbin, editor of Nashville's *Music City News*, in the fall of 1967. Corbin lamented that country music will continue to be modernized "unless there are enough country music fans left to rally to its cause."

The modernized treatment of Hank Williams is largely the work of Jim Vi-enneau, an M-G-M Records executive who is also the nephew of the late Frank Walker.[*] Vienneau, according to some observers, has "revitalized" Williams' music. According to others, he has defiled it. "Perhaps the worst thing ever to happen to country music is the recording of the late Hank Williams with strings," wrote an English enthusiast, John Atkins, in a letter to *Music City News*. "Hank was one of the most gifted and talented men ever to grace this earth.... His music will live on forever in its ORIGINAL FORM, and anything short of this can only serve to tarnish his memory."

Adding strings to Hank's singing, said Atkins indignantly, "is about as rea-sonable as someone painting a mustache on the *Mona Lisa* to bring it up to date. Hank Williams' recordings, too, are a work of art, and they need no alter-ation or addition. Never again will there be a singer and composer as great as Hank Williams, and he will live on forever as the greatest country singer of all time, and not as someone who merely fronted an orchestra as M-G-M would have some people believe."

---

[*] Founding president and general manager of MGM Records (1889–1963), who, in 1947, signed Williams to a recording contract and subsequently served as one of his mentors. See no. 18.

M-G-M, Acuff-Rose, and others with a commercial interest in the Hank Williams legend do not fret over such criticism. It helps keep the legend alive. It also proves what they have long believed: that the markets for Hank's music are many and varied. One man's "mustache on the *Mona Lisa*" is another man's favorite album. You take your choice, and you pay your money.

Successful as the efforts at "revitalizing" the music have been, the simple versions of Hank's songs remain the most popular. At times the popularity has been awesome. In the late 1950s, in many areas, Hank's records were outselling those of the phenomenon of the day, Elvis Presley. Radio stations from Georgia to Texas were reporting Hank still leading the pack in requests from listeners. [...]

For a while in Montgomery, civic boosters—and real fans too—worked hard to keep the legend alive. In September of 1954, to honor Hank's birthday, the Alcazar Temple of the Shrine sponsored a two-day memorial celebration. Sixty thousand people packed the sidewalks to watch the opening parade, which included among the marchers three governors, Alabama governor-elect Jim Folsom, Alabama senator Lister Hill, and more than fifty country artists. Ten thousand people came to the first show, at which everyone paid to get in and no one was paid to perform. The money, of course, went to Shrine charities, but the local businessmen got in their plugs too. "You are invited to read your souvenir program carefully," read the program forward, "so you may know the business firms of Montgomery who have made this book possible." Willie Gayle's marble monument was dramatically unveiled to the singing of "I Saw the Light," then placed at the graveside in a solemn ceremony. Another memorial celebration, on a slightly smaller scale, was held three years later.

Nowadays Montgomery residents usually take visitors to see two historic sites: the spot at the top of the capitol steps where Jefferson Davis took the oath as president of the Confederacy; and Hank Williams' grave in Oakwood Cemetery Annex. The grave is about the only memorial to Hank remaining. Lilly's old boardinghouses have given way to new buildings. The Empire Theater, where Hank sang his "WPA Blues," is still operating, but it takes no special cognizance of that occasion. The civic boosters now let Hank's anniversaries go by without fanfare, perhaps because business is good anyway; they have not even put up markers directing people to Oakwood Cemetery Annex.

Yet the people come, many thousands of them every year. They ask directions at gas stations and cafés, and they drive slowly up the red dirt road leading into the cemetery. Often they have to hunt up the cemetery caretaker, a Negro named Willie Embry, to locate the grave site, because again there are no signs and because the grave, monument and all, is almost indistinguishable from its neighbors until one is standing in front of it.

The grave has been the target of various forms of vandalism over the years, with people stealing the small urns or digging up plants or chipping souvenir pieces from the monument as if it were Plymouth Rock. In December of 1969, after a long spell without incident, the urns and the marble cowboy hat were stolen. They were recovered, undamaged, the following day.

Nonetheless, Hank's grave remains the best-kept in the annex. The Montgomery attorney who represents his estate replaces the stolen material and tips caretaker Embry to make sure the plot is always neat. Audrey regularly sends fresh flowers, which are placed in a yellow pot with a card reading, "From Audrey and the children." On warm weekends, the dirt road often is lined with cars, the grave surrounded by visitors. "There's been some drop off," says Willie Embry with a chuckle. "You can nearly count the cars that come now."

Not long ago, a young gravedigger stopped his work nearby to point out for a visitor some of the details of Hank's grave. "I know a lot of boys around here who carried him home when he was drunk," he said. Then he shook his head and added, "Hank Williams ain't never gonna die in Montgomery."

Nor in Nashville. [...] The czars of Nashville's music industry have not seen fit to make shrines out of the hotels Hank got drunk in and the sanitariums he dried out in, but that would hardly be in keeping with the image the industry tries to project. They have chosen instead to memorialize him through the Country Music Hall of Fame and Museum, an historical-promotional enterprise housed in a tastefully modernistic structure on Record Row. The Hall of Fame, which features color pictures and recordings and artifacts of some sixty artists, has attracted almost one million paying visitors, plus innumerable nonpaying school children, since it opened in April, 1967. The visitors are almost reverent as they make their way through the treasures. Souvenir snitching is unheard of, as Dorothy Gable, the attendant, explains:

"When we put Gentleman Jim Reeves' clothes on a manikin and placed it right in the open, we were told, 'People will cut the fringe off his jacket, you watch.' Well, it hasn't happened. If this were a rhythm and blues or rock and roll place, maybe it would. But the people who came in here are devoted to these artists. Why I believe if our visitors saw somebody taking something, they'd knock him down."

Only a few of Hank's possessions are in the museum; the rest, visitors are told, are "tied up in litigation." There is a guitar to be inspected plus a handful of pictures and a book of his songs with Japanese lyrics. Most visitors, however, prefer to stand silently in front of his plaque or his picture in the "Artists' Gallery." "The first remark you usually hear is, 'Isn't it a shame he died so young?'" says Dorothy Gable. "Once in a while you hear, 'Isn't it a shame the way he died?' but then the same person adds, 'But he must have had a reason.'" [...]

So the legend lives—in records and royalties, in simple, stirring memorials as well as in hokey, tasteless ones. It shows no sign of dying; sustained by commercial interests and by a legion of fans, old and new, it may live forever. Yet the life remains more intriguing than the legend, as any great life must. To the average fan, it is a dimly perceived blend of color and chaos, joy and anguish, with an awesome, mysterious end. The fan doesn't know why Hank burned himself out at twenty-nine, but he knows it was a terrible waste. And he knows, as the people who visit the Hall of Fame know, that Hank "must have had a reason."

~~~~~~

| 32 |

David Halberstam: Hank Williams Remembered

For more than four decades, David Halberstam (1934–2007) was one of America's leading journalists and authors. Halberstam first rose to national prominence in 1964 when his critical reporting on U.S. military efforts in South Vietnam for the *New York Times* earned him a Pulitzer Prize. He followed with a trio of books about the Vietnam War, including his breakthrough best-seller, *The Best and the Brightest* (1972). A prolific writer, he published dozens of magazine articles and more than twenty books covering a wide range of contemporary and historical topics, including the Korean War, the civil rights movement, and professional sports. At first glance, Halberstam, the Bronx-born, Harvard-educated grandson of Eastern European Jewish immigrants, may seem an unlikely candidate to write about Hank Williams, but he was, in fact, no stranger to country music. In one of his first newspaper jobs in the late 1950s, Halberstam had covered the music beat for the *Nashville Tennessean*.

An important milestone in the Hank Williams's literature, Halberstam's essay below originally appeared in *Look* magazine's July 13, 1971, special issue on country music. In it, he compares the late country star to other doomed celebrities, such as Marilyn Monroe and James Dean, whose short, troubled lives embody what the author paradoxically terms the "American cult of the failure of success."[*] By placing Williams on a par with these pop icons, Halberstam

---

SOURCE   David Halberstam, "Hank Williams Remembered," *Look*, July 13, 1971, p. 42. Used by permission of Jean Halberstam.
[*] In a 1962 essay in *Down Beat* magazine titled "Billie Holiday: The Voice of Jazz," noted jazz critic Leonard Feather had similarly speculated that Holiday's posthumous popularity might "reflect the peculiarly American death cult that has earned for James Dean, Charlie Parker, Lester Young, and Hank Williams more publicity posthumously than they earned alive."

anticipates by several years a new wave of journalists, music critics, and scholars who would similarly elevate the hillbilly singer to America's cultural pantheon.

The air-conditioned tourist bus pulls up in front of the house on Franklin Road in Nashville. The guide, practiced, friendly, begins his pitch: "Folks, this here is the Hank Williams house." They pay little attention, they know the history better than he. It is part of their lore. They are already busy loading cameras. "Folks, notice the fence. Those notes on that fence are the very notes from *Lovesick Blues*, Hank's first big hit." On he talks, the cameras clicking away. "Hank died," the guide continues, "at the age of 29, on New Year's Day in 1953."

New Year's Day, 1953? Can it be that long ago? Can it be that he would be 47 this year?[†] And what would he be like now—bald, pudgy in the middle, his sharp, reedy voice gone mellow, his songs backed by violins, pianos and worse? On the late-night talk shows beamed from New York, and dressed in Continental-cut suits? No, it is inconceivable; certainly the faithful, drawn to this particular pilgrimage, would not have him that way. No, he belongs to them now, a legend, better than a tarnished middle-aged reality. He is special, one of those searing American talents who burn themselves out, like comets, so fast; the talent and the unhappiness mixed together, propelling them forward, but talents and problems so great they could never be controlled. Bix Beiderbecke, James Dean, Charley [Charlie] Parker, Marilyn Monroe, Janis Joplin. And Hank Williams. Personal lives fatefully and fatally interwoven with professional lives; the anguish just as real offstage as on. Quick success and quick destruction. The American cult of the failure of success.

Hiram Hank Williams. He was the very embodiment of this particular soil and culture. Son of a railroad man in a small Alabama town, his early years marked by depression, poverty and a broken home; a country boy in love with nothing but his guitar, scrounging lessons from anyone who would teach him. He learned to play and sing the blues from Rufus Payne, a poor Negro street singer nicknamed Teetot. The payment was about 30 cents a lesson and sometimes less. At 13, he formed his own band, at 14, he was singing on a Montgomery, Ala., radio station, already traveling the Alabama backcountry singing with his band, making sure that the boys carried blackjacks because Saturday night could be rough, too many good old boys drinking too much good old whiskey and Coke.

---

† Had he lived, Williams would have turned forty-eight-years old on September 17, 1971.

He wrote his own songs, clear and simple ones, marked by an almost elegant purity of language. By the time he was 23, in 1947, he was writing songs for a Nashville company. That was halfway to the big dream of every country boy, to get in the pickup truck, drive to Nashville, talk his way past the Grand Ole Opry receptionist, pluck a few notes, and sign a contract.

They were a little slow to sign him on at the Opry because they heard there was a drinking problem there. Finally, in 1949, they let him sing. He was 26,[‡] awkward and gangling, looking like a good meal and a little love would do him. That night he sang *Lovesick Blues*, and they tore the Opry apart; he sang and sang, they forced six encores from him, and there might have been more but other people had to sing, too, and finally Red Foley, the master of ceremonies, put a stop to it, made a little speech promising this boy would be back. It was a special kind of dream come true, as much for the audience as for him. If it was possible for him, then perhaps one day it was possible for them too.

He was not handsome and he was certainly not even a country-style crooner; indeed it could even be argued that he did not have a particularly good voice. But he was of these people, he reflected them and their hardships. Hillbilly music, at its best, is the simple music of proud, poor people scratching hard to make a living off a difficult soil. Their struggles are not against affluence but against their poverty and the problems caused by poverty, their women problems and their whiskey problems. The songs are not the softer, tranquilizing June-moon rhymes of the North. They are, rather, a more visceral, plaintive call. Hank Williams was their genius. His own life had been harsh, and his style reflected it. His voice was not easy, he retained an edge of pain in it; if anything, he exploited that sense of hurt. It was the music of white hill-country culture, with a tone of Negro blues thrown in. White soul music.

His songs poured out one after another. *Cold, Cold Heart, Your Cheatin' Heart, I'm So Lonesome I Could Cry, Hey, Good Lookin', Jambalaya, You Win Again, I Can't Help It (If I'm Still in Love with You), Why Don't You Love Me, Lonesome Whistle.* His success was immediate, and it was a special kind of success, for in addition to holding the deep affection of the regular Opry fans, he was also something rare, the hillbilly singer with a genuine following among a surprising number of intellectuals. There were jobs everywhere. Traveling with his band in a Cadillac through the night, he had no time to stop and sleep at a motel, writing his songs in the back seat of the car.

---

‡ Williams was a little more than three months shy of his twenty-sixth birthday when he made his debut on the *Grand Ole Opry* in June 1949.

As his success mounted, so did his torment. He began to drink heavily, and an always shaky marriage began to fall apart. He showed up at concerts half drunk, sometimes completely drunk, sometimes he didn't show at all. The instinct for self-destruction seemed only to feed his popularity; it was more proof than ever that he was one of them, that his pain was real. It showed that he did not just sing of pain and then retire at night to an easy life in the big city surrounded by fancy people doing fancy things. The failure of his marriage provided some of his best songs ("The news is out all over town / That you've been seen a-runnin' 'round / I know that I should leave, but then / I just can't go, you win again / This heart of mine could never see / What ev'ybody knew but me / Just trusting you was my great sin / What can I do, you win again.").

There were more concerts and more drinks. An old back injury was aggravated, and he began to take drugs, pop pills. His thin frame, 6'2"[s] and 140 pounds in the best of times, seemed more gaunt than ever; his face, more haunted. By late 1951, just two years after he had exploded on the country-music scene, he was coming apart. He was missing too many concerts and bodyguards were assigned, unsuccessfully, to keep him off whiskey. His marriage died early in 1952, and later that year he was fired from the Opry.

The decline was almost as fast as the ascension had been. He went to Shreveport, a notch below the Opry in the country-music world, to see if he could make it back. He found a new wife, this one 19 years old,[¶] and since they were a little down on their luck, their marriage became a public ceremony, with Hank and his bride getting gifts and presents in return for the public performance—two shows, an afternoon rehearsal, an evening marriage. He started to come back, his young wife fighting to stop his drinking. His health seemed to be slipping away. So, classically, in the country style, he did not go to a real doctor, but to a convicted forger with a faked medical certificate. The quack reassured him and, more important, helped make whiskey and drugs available.

In late December of 1952, he finally got a major booking for New Year's Day in Canton, Ohio. A chance to start anew. It was bad weather, and a young friend was hired to drive the Cadillac from Montgomery to Canton. Hank was in back, mixing whiskey with chloral hydrate. They found him that way, dead at the age of 29, on New Year's Day, the life gone, the legend born, the legend of the comet lasting longer in our folk history than if somehow they had managed to discipline that raw talent, temper his passions, assuage his fears, and turn him into just another middle-aged singer.

―――

[s] In a 1952 *Country Song Roundup* interview, Williams claimed to be six feet tall.
[¶] Born on June 6, 1932, Billie Jean (Jones) Eshliman was actually twenty years old at the time of her marriage to Williams.

| 33 |

Irene Williams Smith: My Treasured Life with a Beloved Brother (1972)

References to the supernatural occur frequently in the Hank Williams literature, ranging from stories about his alleged premonition of his own death to accounts of sightings of his ghost. In this selection, Irene Williams Smith recalls her own eerie omen of her brother's passing. Smith wrote this piece for *Hank Williams, The Legend* (1972), a pioneering anthology edited by Thurston Moore that features a curious mixture of fan magazine pieces, newspaper clippings, family and friends' recollections, album liner notes, poems, an occasional scholarly article and tabloid exposé, a bibliography and discography, and even recipes for jambalaya and crawfish pie. But, by far, the most fascinating selection in the volume is Smith's revealing essay.

Smith (1922–1995), a longtime Dallas, Texas, real estate agent and civic leader, led a troubled life that, in some respects, paralleled that of her famous brother. At the time she wrote this piece, she was serving an eight-year sentence in a federal prison. In October 1969, Smith was convicted of attempting to smuggle drugs into the United States from Mexico. She protested her innocence, claiming that she knew nothing about the seven million dollars' worth of cocaine concealed in the automobile she had been driving for a friend. This "friend" turned out to be Edgar Babe, the alias of Jorge Juan Lemos Garcia, who was also charged in the case and with whom, her attorney stated, Smith was "madly in love." Smith's poignant explanation for her plight harkened back to a major theme of her brother's songs. "I know it's difficult to believe," she told reporters, "but you just have to be a 47-year-old woman so lonely you just don't know what to do." Even from her prison cell, however, Smith tenaciously guarded her brother's memory. In "My Treasured Life with a Beloved Brother," she offers a spirited defense of both her mother and her famous sibling similar to those she had made in her 1950s "Hank's Corner" columns for *Country Song Roundup* (no. 25), but this time with an added twist of the occult.

During my brother Hank's lifetime, he and I were bound by very strong extrasensory perception ties. No matter how many miles separated us, we were

SOURCE   Irene Williams Smith, "My Treasured Life with a Beloved Brother," in *Hank Williams, The Legend*, ed. Thurston Moore (Denver, Colo.: Heather Enterprises, 1972), 5–6, 7. © 1972 Heather Enterprises, Inc. Reprinted by permission of Thurston Moore.

often aware of one another's thoughts. I would like to share with you a little of our life together as children and some of the experiences I have had since his death.

On December 31, 1952, I was living with my husband and children in the Naval Housing Project in Portsmouth, Virginia. All during the day, I had a strange feeling of doom.

The last time I had seen Hank was just a couple of months before when he had played a show in Jacksonville, Florida, and had visited with us in our home at Jacksonville Beach.

Throughout the month of December, I had wondered about Hank and had wanted so much to see and talk with him because the last time I had seen him was after the last show in Jacksonville when we had gone to dinner with his manager.

At dinner, Hank said he was tired and was going to his hotel instead of back to the Beach with us. We said goodbye. As he walked away, down the street, I called to him, ran to where he was, hugged him and said, "Goodbye. I love you very much." Then I walked back to where my husband and children and Hank's manager were standing. I said to them, "I will never see him alive again. He is dying and he knows it."

The night of the 31st, my family and I were invited to spend the evening with another Navy couple and their two children. We four adults were laughing and talking. The children had long ago gotten sleepy and been put to bed. Just as the television announcer said, "Happy New Year," I turned to my husband and began to sob. "Please take me home. Hank is dead. I must get packed and ready to leave for Alabama." Of course, everyone was shocked, feeling, I am sure, that I had lost my mind.

Finally, at two o'clock, I was able to convince my husband that it was time to awaken the children and leave. Earlier during the evening, my daughter had spilled hot chocolate on the clothes she would need to travel in. I washed these before going to bed. I retired fully aware that morning would bring news of Hank's death.

At 8:30 the following morning, we were awakened by a Virginia highway patrolman with a message for me to go to the nearest telephone and call my mother-in-law. When I got her on the phone, I said, "Mama Smith, what time did Hank die and where is my mother?" She said, "Honey, how did you know? The news has not been released yet. Your mother is on her way to Oak Hill, West Virginia, to claim Hank's body. We don't know what happened yet."

I hung up the telephone in a daze. The highway patrolman took me back to the Housing Project. I went first to our friend's home to ask if she would take the children and I to Norfolk to catch a train for Montgomery. When she opened the door, I said, "Mary!" but that was as far as I got, because I lost my voice. When I could finally speak, I explained that what I had said the night before was true and that I needed her help.

The children and I left a few hours later by train to say goodbye for the last time to one of the few people who has ever really understood me.

In 1954, we were transferred to Dallas, Texas, where I decided to become a businesswoman. I went into the real estate business, and became so engrossed that it became the most important thing in my life.

In 1961, my husband and I were divorced. After our divorce, I became more and more interested in psychic phenomena. I joined a group that met weekly to discuss the different psychic sciences.

In the spring of 1969, a couple of friends dropped by one evening to discuss psychic phenomena. During the course of the evening, my friends decided to set up the Ouija Board they had brought with them. They began to get messages almost immediately. One of the Spirits contacted told them that Hank was there and wanted to talk with me.

For the next forty-five minutes, I asked questions and wrote them down along with the answers. We discussed a man with whom I was deeply in love. Hank told me that he was not good for me, and that to continue our relationship could only end in disaster for me.

Two months later, I attended two séances where once again Hank spoke with me through the Medium conducting the séance. Both times he begged me to forget the man I loved. He went on to tell me that even though I had neither seen nor heard from him [the man] in several months that I would hear from him soon and that he would invite me to join him in Mexico. Hank warned me not to go to Mexico, whatever I did. Both séances were recorded by friends in Dallas.

I was deeply in love, when the call came less than two months later. I left immediately to join the man I loved in Mexico. Most of you know the rest of the story. All I can say is that no one would have understood better than Hank. Despite his warning, love is eternal, and if you truly love, you go when called.

Less than a week after I left for Mexico, I was arrested in Laredo, Texas. For the past two years, I have been an inmate in the Federal Reformatory for Women in Alderson, West Virginia, just a few miles* from where Hank was found dead in the back seat of his car in the early hours of January 1, 1953.

---

* Alderson is some seventy miles from Oak Hill, West Virginia, where her brother had been pronounced dead.

Many times during the past twenty-seven months, I have thanked God for the things taught us by our mother when we were growing up. Our mother loved us dearly. There were times when we were cold, hungry and without proper clothes. Yet, there was never a time when we were without love.

Hank and I learned early that we had to help make a living. Our dad entered a Veterans' Hospital when Hank was five and I was six.[†] We picked cotton and strawberries, and sold peanuts on the street. Hank shined shoes, while I sold Christmas cards and cosmetics house-to-house.

When Hank was seven or eight years old, we lived in Georgiana, Alabama. There was an elderly black man, Tee Tot, that had a street band. They made their living playing up and down the street, passing the hat for collection.

Hank began to follow them everywhere they went, begging Tee Tot to teach him just one more chord. After more than forty years, I can still hear Tee Tot say, "Please, Little White Boss, run away! 'Dis ole man is tired. Can't teach you today." But Hank was persistent, and it was this wonderful old man that did teach him to play.

To provide for us, Mother worked very hard as a practical nurse, canning plant supervisor, and doing sewing for others. When Hank was twelve, we moved to Montgomery, Alabama, where there were more opportunities for Mother to earn a living. She began to run a boarding house. Our mother was one of the most dynamic women I have ever known; her word was her bond. If you made her angry, you had a wildcat on your hands, yet she could be as gentle as a lamb. For one of her children or for a friend, she would turn the world up-side-down. She worked hard all of her life, very seldom thinking of herself, always thinking of others.

After Hank got together his first band at the age of thirteen, Mother was always there to lend a helping hand, buy instruments, provide transportation, furnish a place for the boys to live, and to provide food.

When I was fourteen and fifteen, I booked shows, sang with the band, sold tickets, and traveled with them. Hank and I had a favorite number that we always did, "A Paper of Pine."[‡] As booking agent and performer, I always made more money than Hank. You can imagine some of the discussions this brought about. [...]

[†] According to the generally accepted chronology of Hank Williams's life, Smith appears to be in error here, as well as at several other points in this essay, regarding the years of certain events and her and her brother's ages at the time of those events.

[‡] Apparently, a typographical error in reference to "A Paper of Pins," a widely known American folk song.

In 1942, I started working at the Aviation Cadet Detachment, Gunter Field, Montgomery, Alabama. Because I worked five days a week, I stopped going with Hank to shows. By this time, he had met and fallen in love with Audrey. She and Mother booked shows. Audrey began to sing with the band and Mother sold tickets.

Our paths began to part. I got married, had a son and a daughter; Hank and Audrey got married and had a son. I left Montgomery to join my husband in Seattle, Washington, and Hank and Audrey moved to Shreveport, Louisiana, where he and his Drifting Cowboys became hits on the Louisiana Hayride. [...]

There have been many things written about Hank these past twenty years—both good and bad. To me, he was a great person. He loved people; he understood and truly cared for his fellow travelers. He wrote and sang from his soul. He knew what it was to have loved and lost; to have suffered the pain of the death of a loved one; to have watched as the heart within a loved one died. He knew what it was to feel the ice of a cold, cold heart.

You see, Hank and I were not protected from life as children. There is no protection or blinders when you work with and live with all types of people. We lived life realistically, yet we were taught, by example, to find something good in every person and every situation. We learned that nothing is ever so bad that it couldn't be worse. We were taught to make life's real hard knocks into stepping stones, not stumbling blocks. [...]

For several years, I wrote a column for Country Song Roundup entitled "Hi, Hank" [sic]. May I end this visit with you by writing once again a few words to Hank?

Hi, Hank,

Forty-eight years ago, you joined my life. Only twenty-nine of those years were you here in life, yet in death, you have never left my side. You are always near to lend a helping hand, to guide and protect. No, I don't always listen. I wouldn't be here [in prison] if I did. Yet, even here, you are ever on hand.

How many times can I hear little bits of wisdom, as though you have spoken: "Don't be so hasty in your decisions"; "Remain calm"; "Don't lose your temper"; "Be understanding"; "Love"; "Understand." Conscience? Perhaps! Yet, they are the things you would say.

Thank God for you and our mother. When I came to prison only a few miles from where you died, I was so ashamed of the shame I felt I had brought to your name that I could hardly hold my head up. I cried all the time. I cried a river of tears.

Then one day, it was as though I could hear you say, "Smile! I understand. You are where and as God would have you be. There is much to be done here that only you can see. There are tears to be dried, and hearts to be made lighter. There needs to be someone to care, as only you care."

I don't cry so much anymore. I am proud to be your sister, and to have shared a part of your life.

Hank, continue to walk slowly down that long, long road. Someday, I will follow you, but not until I have done that for which I came, just as you finished that for which you were sent. What a great reunion that will be!

How wonderful to have learned at our mother's knee to love and care about others, to see and to listen. Sure, it is painful, but he who feels no pain neither feels joy, because he has become the walking dead.

So long, Hank! I know you understand my not listening to your warnings. Thank you for caring enough to try.

"Have I Told You Lately That I Love You?"[§] I do.

Irene

~~~~~~

| 34 |

Harry E. Rockwell: Excerpt from *Beneath the Applause (A Story about Country & Western Music and Its Stars—Written by a Fan)*

Originally a fan of the pop singers and swing bands of the 1940s, small-town Pennsylvania printer and composer Harry E. Rockwell (1921–1986) developed a passion for country music around 1952, after purchasing a pair of Hank Williams's MGM records. As his interest deepened, Rockwell began research aimed, as he put it, at learning "everything I could about the stars and their music and songs." The result was *Beneath the Applause (A Story about Country & Western Music and Its Stars—Written by a Fan)*, a rare, privately published booklet that described his pilgrimages to the *Grand Ole Opry* and to several other historic country music-related sites.

SOURCE   Harry E. Rockwell, *Beneath the Applause (A Story about Country & Western Music and Its Stars—Written by a Fan)* (Chambersburg, Pa.: privately published, 1973), 13–15, 16–17. © 1973 Harry E. Rockwell. Used by permission of Gregory E. Rockwell.
§ A reference to a classic 1945 country song written by Scotty Wiseman (1909–1981), one half of the popular *National Barn Dance* husband-and-wife duo, Lulu Belle and Scotty.

Hank Williams was one of the author's favorite singers, and in *Beneath the Applause*, Rockwell chronicles the visits he and his young son made to places associated with the legendary star, including Georgiana and Greenville, Alabama, and Oak Hill, West Virginia. Along the way, he recounts his conversations with an assortment of local residents who either knew or had some connection to Williams. Of particular interest is the following excerpt in which Rockwell describes an extended August 1969 interview he conducted with the star's elderly father, Elonzo Huble "Lon" Williams, in McWilliams, Alabama, a little more than a year before Lon's death.

An insubstantial, shadowy figure in Hank Williams biographies, the elder Williams (1891–1970) has generally been depicted as an impoverished sharecropper, henpecked husband, and unambitious drunk who, debilitated by a mysterious wartime injury, eagerly abandoned his family for the peace and quiet of a veterans' hospital when Hank was just six years old. Many biographers have insinuated that Lon Williams was personally responsible for his son's later self-destructive behavior, because his nearly decade-long hospitalization left the boy adrift and without the guidance of a proper male role model. In this considerate, heartfelt portrait, however, Rockwell reveals a far more sympathetic Lon Williams, portraying him as a proud and dignified individual who, despite his ex-wife Lillie's machinations, had attempted to maintain a close relationship with his famous son and who, as a result, was able to offer revealing insights about him.

After driving approximately 20 miles, we came to the small tranquil village [of McWilliams] which is situated in the wooded section of Alabama where lumbering is the main industry. [. . .]

As we drove into the driveway of the pale gray shingled, modest looking home, which fit the description given to us, I noticed an elderly, gray haired man, wearing a western type hat sitting in a rocker on the front porch.

After we were properly parked, I asked if he was Hank Williams' father and he immediately answered that he was and asked us to come in and sit down, which we quickly and excitedly did. [. . .]

I was still beaming with excitement when our conversation began with the elderly gentleman informing me that his name was Elonzo H. Williams and [that he] was usually called "Lonnie," a nickname, by his friends and associates.

He informed me that he has been married twice. Besides his present wife, he was first married to Lillian Skip [Skipper] Williams, who was Hank's mother, and that they had a daughter, Irene, who was born about fifteen months before her brother. [. . .] The proud father stated that his famous son's name was Hiram Williams and besides the nickname "Hank," he was called "Skeets" when he was very small and later "Herky."

Mr. Williams stated that he and Lillian Williams were divorced when Hiram was 18 years old and Irene was 19. After the divorce, his former wife married three more times and was divorced as often. For many years she preferred to be called Mrs. Stone which was one of her latter husbands' name. [...]

I asked Mr. Williams a question that had been puzzling me since finding out that he was still living, and that was, why he was not mentioned in many of the stories published about his son and why he had been reported as being dead long before Hank's career had become such a great success?

He replied, "I don't know for sure. The boy's mother, Lillian, and I didn't get along too well." The elder Mr. Williams continued by telling me that he had served with the U.S. Army during World War I and was sent to France. While there he got in a fight with another G.I. over a French girl. After a short argument, the other soldier struck him across the side of his face with a wine bottle, knocking him to the floor. Then his opponent kicked him in the jaw before he could get to his feet.

"Lonnie" Williams said he was unconscious for a short time and was taken to a base hospital where he spent about a week, then returned to duty with seemingly no ill effects.

Back home, many years later, his face and jaw became very painful and eventually paralyzed. As soon as possible, he went to The Louisiana Veterans Hospital at Alexandria, Louisiana,* because he was unable to talk, and this condition continued for seven long years, which he was compelled to spend in the medical institution.

Mr. Williams told me that he was awarded a pension by the government for his disability which he used for the support of his two children and Mrs. Williams. Because of a continued poor relationship between him and his wife, Elonzo Williams said that shortly after he was hospitalized, Lillian took the children along with the household belongings and moved to Georgiana, where she worked as a practical nurse and took in roomers. [...]

About a year or more later, Mrs. Lillian Williams and the children moved to Greenville where she, again, opened a rooming and boarding house. Several years later, they departed from the Greenville County Seat City for Montgomery, the state capital, occupied again with a rooming and boarding business. [...]

Mr. Williams further stated that after the nerves of his face were repaired and he could speak again, he later returned to the hospital in Louisiana and

---

* According to Colin Escott, Lon Williams first entered a veterans' hospital in Pensacola, Florida, in 1930, but at some later, undetermined point was transferred to one in Alexandria, Louisiana.

spent some time in the Mississippi Veteran's [*sic*] Hospital in Gulfport, Mississippi, as he had a gallbladder operation and later surgery for a prostrate condition.

During his confinement in Louisiana, Hiram was permitted by his mother to visit him on one occasion and when the boy was fourteen he went to see his father in the Gulfport hospital.

Elonzo Williams explained that because of the boy's mother transferring from town to town, and her different marriages, it became difficult to keep in touch with him. The boy wasn't disciplined too much and his father admitted that he had heard reports about him being introduced to the bottle at an early age.

Mr. Williams further stated that he couldn't explain why his name was constantly withheld from the public after Hank had become famous. He, also, couldn't explain why, when he was connected with his son, he was referred to as being dead. He did say that the boy's mother was probably responsible for most of it because of her unkind attitude towards him [Lon]. He said that he felt this feeling was also installed [*sic*] in "Miss Audrey" by the mother. (This is the name Mr. Williams used constantly when he referred to Audrey Williams who was Hank's former wife.)

I remember during my conversation with Mr. Williams, when I had expressed my admiration for the verse that Audrey had written which, in turn, was carved on the back of the beautiful gravestone at the top of her former husband's gravesite, Lonnie Williams said, "Yes, it's a pity 'Miss Audrey' couldn't have given him some of those flowers while he could of smelled them."

He had told me earlier that his son and Audrey didn't always get along too well. He said that Hank had always recognized him as his father, during his younger life and after he became famous. He said he felt that his son was under pressure from his mother to stay away from him when he was in his teens and later after his marriage, but he always managed to keep in touch. [...]

My visit continued, as he showed me pictures and newspaper clippings of his son that I had never seen before.

I asked him if he knew what made his son such a good writer of so many wonderful songs and if he or the boy's mother ever played musical instruments or whether they had ever had any natural endowments for music? He answered by telling me that Lillian Williams liked to play the old "peddle" or "pump-type" organ and that Hank would sit nearby and listen to her playing and singing when he was a small lad.

Elonzo Williams continued his answer, as he told me that he had played a jew's harp when Hank and Irene were very young. He said, "I can remember those kids begging and pestering me to play that old thing every evening as soon as I would get home from work. Sometimes it would be hard to find time to eat and get some of my work done around the house, but they would enjoy singing and dancing as I played what they thought was music in them days." He ended this part of our conversation, as he referred to his son's music and writing skill, by saying, "I guess he just had the talent and ability for it." [...]

He said that Hank, his band, "The Drifting Cowboys," and "Miss Audrey" occasionally spent the night at his home when they were in the vicinity. "I spent one weekend at Hiram's home near Nashville and on Saturday I was invited to The Grand Ole Opry and that is the only time I have ever seen it," Mr. Williams said. "The following day we went to Kentucky Lake and done some fishing," he continued. [...]

A very emphatic and important question concerning Hank Williams' life had been resting in the back of my mind for many years and I thought this was an opportune time and place to have it answered.

I knew Hank's father would be an ideal person to ask and receive a satisfactory answer, but was still a little hesitant, as I asked him what he knew about his son's association with drink and narcotics. I wanted to know if some of the tales I had heard were false rumors or the truth.

The man answered me by saying, "I know there has been stories about Hiram drinking during his teens, but as I have told you before, because of his mother marrying several times after our divorce and her moving from place to place, I was unable to keep in touch with him on a regular basis. I will truthfully say that I had never seen him drinking then, but I saw him doing it when he was in his twenties, but never getting drunk from it."

The entertainer's father continued, "I've heard that the boy drank a lot during the last couple years of his life and this was during the period when he was really going somewhere and he must of used 'dope' because this is the word that a doctor used at the St. Jude Hospital in Montgomery."

Mr. Williams explained that this doctor had phoned him several times asking for permission to bring Hank to his home for a rest, but Mrs. Stone, the boy's mother, had always intervened and wouldn't allow it.

Elonzo Williams said, "Then, one day during the spring of 1952, Hiram called me and asked me to come to his mother's house in Montgomery and bring him back to my home here in McWilliams. This was after 'Miss Audrey' and him had separated as the boy was in a poor mental condition and I knew this, from the way he talked on the phone, so I got ready as soon as possible, and drove to Montgomery."

"Lonnie" Williams then stated that something must have happened at Mrs. Stone's home between the time his son had called him and when he arrived at the house in Montgomery, because he said to me, "I was surprised when

I parked near the house because they were carrying Hiram on a stretcher and putting him in the ambulance from St. Jude Hospital."

He continued, "I followed them to the hospital and to Hiram's room, but wasn't able to talk to him because he was unconscious, but the doctor who had called me several times came over to me as Mrs. Stone was standing nearby listening." Mr. Williams continued, "I told the doctor that the boy had called me earlier that day and asked me to come and get him, and was shocked when the doctor told me to leave Hiram at the hospital until he could get the 'dope' out of him. The doctor said the boy had enough 'dope' in him to kill a mule, then the boy's mother said that he had only two beers and two aspirins all day. The doctor asked her if she was sure that it was aspirin that she had given Hiram."

After listening to these unknown facts concerning Hank's life, I asked his father for his opinions as to why his son had these frequent bouts with liquor and dope and if he thought they were chiefly due to the pain and misery of his bad back?

He answered by stating that his son had a bad back for a long time—not from the time that a horse was supposed to have thrown him. But, he said that Hiram had a swollen spot on his back since he was a small boy, and later in his life, surgery was performed near the spine, but this left the back in a worse condition with more pain than before.

Hank Williams' father explained that his opinion as to the cause of his son's drinking and narcotic escapades were not due to the back condition as much as the laborious routine he was being urged into and utterly pushed to produce more songs, plus his increased public appearance schedule. [...]

It had been a very enjoyable and rewarding day. Twilight was approaching, and I knew it was time to end this very interesting meeting with Hank Williams' father, but there was one more thing that he wanted me to see as we were preparing to depart.

He seemed very proud, as he handed me a letter he had received recently from the governor of Alabama. This message stated that the state of Alabama was planning to build a shrine in honor of his son, who is still recognized by that state as its most distinguished descendant. It hasn't been decided where this memorial will be erected, but it is planned to remove Hank's remains from The Oak Ridge [sic] Cemetery in Montgomery and transfer them to the site of the shrine. Since the writing of this story this might already have been done.[†]

Elonzo Williams was highly pleased to receive the governor's letter and happy that someone has finally consulted him for information about his son. He is also very gratified that he is finally being recognized as the male parent of the great troubadour, Hiram "Hank" Williams.

[†] This memorial, which was to be built in the shape of a sixty-foot-tall cowboy boot, never received funding from the Alabama state legislature.

After putting a few words of "Lonnie's" voice on tape, we reluctantly said "goodbye" to one of the nicest and most respectable persons I have ever had the pleasure of meeting.

~~~~~~

| 35 |

Henry Pleasants: Excerpt from *The Great American Popular Singers*

One of the first classical music scholars to take Hank Williams seriously was Henry Pleasants (1910–2000), an internationally renowned musicologist and author of twelve books who, while working as a *New York Times* music correspondent, also served as an American spy in Cold War Europe during the 1950s and early 1960s. Unusual among classical music critics of his generation, Pleasants harbored a deep appreciation for popular music and particularly for jazz, which he championed in his controversial book *The Agony of Modern Music* (1955) and elsewhere as the "true" art music of the twentieth century. In *The Great American Popular Singers* he profiles twenty-two diverse performers whom he believed were "the most accomplished, the most innovative and the most influential" of the twentieth century, a roster that ranged from Al Jolson and Bing Crosby to Ray Charles and Elvis Presley. Pleasants also devotes a chapter to Hank Williams, one of only three country music artists he profiles (the others are Jimmie Rodgers and Johnny Cash). Largely free of musical jargon and written in a clear and accessible style, Pleasant's essay on Williams ranks as the first and still one of the best technical evaluations of the hillbilly star's artistry as an unlettered yet innovative and versatile singer and songwriter.

Measured against any conventional criteria either of songwriting or of singing, Hank's appeal makes no sense. Take the voice itself, for example. Words have failed just about everyone who has tried to describe it. The most successful effort I have seen came from a writer in the *Alabama Journal* who suggested, when a $1,000 music scholarship was established in Hank's memory at the University of Alabama, that among the qualifications of a recipient should be a voice "like the whine of an electric saw going through pine timber."

The writer may have been referring to sounds Hank's voice makes on certain closed vowels as they occur in such words as *could, would, look, love, me* and *see.*

SOURCE   Henry Pleasants, *The Great American Popular Singers* (New York: Simon and Schuster, 1974), 229–230, 232–233, 235–236. © 1974 Henry Pleasants. Reprinted with the permission of Simon and Schuster, Inc.

Those vowels emerge as though they had become lodged between the vocal cords en route from lungs to throat. Or one thinks of a man trying to sing with a fishbone stuck somewhere between pharynx and larynx. Then there is the nasality in such words as *clown, town, around, want, die, cry, when, then, heart, part, shame, name,* etcetera, not to mention a curious and characteristic quaver, not quite vibrato and not quite tremolo, suggesting a kind of feedback from overloaded muscles in the throat, which is probably what it was. Play any Hank Williams record to [an] opera buff, or even a Frank Sinatra fan, and you will clear the room.

Hank was musically illiterate and no more than barely literate when it came to reading and writing. The only musical schooling he ever had was from a black street singer, Rufe Payne, nicknamed Tee-tot, in Greenville, Alabama. That schooling did not include notation. "I have never read a note or written one," Hank told *Montgomery Advertiser* columnist Allen Rankin in 1951. "I can't. I don't know one note from another." His literary reading was confined to comics, which he called "goof books." His vocabulary was small. He knew nothing of grammar. His spelling was atrocious. He dropped out of high school in his sophomore year—when he was nineteen!*

It was similar with Hank Williams as a poet. He has been called a hillbilly Shakespeare. He was a hillbilly, all right, in the generic country-music sense of the term. His language, not to speak of his versification, was anything but Shakespearean. Those simple, homespun ditties about cheating hearts, cold hearts, honky-tonks, doghouses and hobos, with their dubious rhymes and faulty, faltering meter—is one to take this as poetry, as Shakespearean?

It is tempting to suggest that it was precisely these deficiencies that accounted for his greatness. But they have been shared by millions of young men, including country singers and songwriters. One might, however, put it the other way around and suggest that he would never have achieved greatness without the deficiencies. Lack of schooling did not inhibit his poetic imagination. It simply kept him down to earth, where his listeners lived. Hank knew it. "You write just like Shakespeare," he once told an aspiring lyricist, "and if you don't watch out you'll be buried in the same grave with him." [...]

What distinguished Williams' verses and singing was the lack of pretension and an extraordinary perception of event and feeling, articulated in a vernacular as picturesque as it was ordinary and simple. "If you're gonna sing a song," he used to say, "sing 'em somethin' they can understand."

---

* According to biographer Colin Escott, Williams dropped out of high school in October 1939, the month after he turned sixteen.

Within the limits of a rudimentary vocabulary he was linguistically both inventive and resourceful. A delightful example is "Move It On Over," a song about a man who comes home late, finds that he has been locked out (his wife has even changed the lock), and crawls into the doghouse, telling the occupant to "move it on over." Hank uses twelve synonyms for *move*, two to a verse: *get, scoot, ease, drag, pack, tote, scratch, shake, slide, sneak, shove* and *sweep*. One should say, perhaps, that he uses twelve words as synonyms. The distinction between a synonym and a word simply pressed into service as a synonym is not one that would have troubled him.

As a songwriter he was always more concerned with words than with melody. If he got the words he wanted, the melody seemed to take care of itself. He was not a distinguished or even a particularly inventive melodist. The tunes are as simple, even primitive, as the conventional tonic-subdominant-dominant chords that support them. One remembers them only in association with the words—and with the way he sang the words. That is what is remarkable about them. Hank's melodies were the music of language. His singing issued from the same linguistic source.

Formal vocal cultivation would have been as disastrous to his singing as formal literary schooling would have been to his writing. Having none, and having no vocal pretensions or vanity, he was free to match voice to song without worrying about conventionally accepted criteria of what constitutes an admissible vocal sound. That his voice was capable of adaptation to a remarkable variety of songs and subjects makes it difficult to describe, simply as a voice. One feels that he had a different voice for each song, or as if versification and vocalization sprang from the same lyrical impulse, as they almost certainly did.

On a song like "Ramblin' Man," for example, with its long, mournful, upward glides, he stays in the lower register and sounds almost like a basso—and quite a lot like a distant train whistle. On bright up-tempo numbers such as "Hey, Good Lookin'" and "Settin' the Woods on Fire," he elects a higher area of his range and sounds like a tenor. Actually, the voice was a light baritone, with an unexceptional range of about an octave and a sixth, from an A below to an F above.

Within that range he could achieve an extraordinary variety of character and color. Some of this variety is illusory, deriving from imaginative and resourceful ornamentation rather than from alteration of timbre. In his use of ornamentation, and in the kinds of ornament he used, he was unique among country singers. It is of no little significance that in nothing I have ever read about him is there any mention of ornamentation at all. His ornaments grew so naturally, apparently so inevitably, out of word, context and phrase that they do not emerge conspicuously as ornaments. They are not, strictly speaking, ornamental. They are organic.

This is almost true even of so prominent a device as falsetto. Hank Williams could, and sometimes did, introduce yodeling breaks in the manner of Jimmie Rodgers, and as carried on after Rodgers' death by Ernest Tubb. His "Long Gone Lonesome Blues," for example, comes close to being a prototypical twelve-bar blue yodel in the Rodgers style. But more characteristic of Williams is the rapid yodeling alternation of falsetto and normal voice within the phrase, or even within the time span of a single note, the effect being that of a birdlike warble, its function at once ornamental and expressive. A spectacular example is his recording of "Lovesick Blues."

Possibly because this song was not his own, but an old vaudeville number from the 1920s, he indulged in something closer to sheer vocal virtuosity than was his wont in music of his own inspiration. He simply drenched it with falsetto cascades, leaping back and forth easily and accurately over a wide variety of intervals. It is a rollicking display of vocal agility, unprecedented, in my experience, in the work of any other singer, but reproduced nowadays with astonishing fidelity by that admirable black country singer Charley Pride.

An important difference between falsetto as used by Jimmie Rodgers on the one hand and by Hank Williams on the other is the area of the vocal range in which it is employed. With Rodgers it was almost always an upward extension of his natural range, taking him up to the D flat above high C. With Williams it was produced within the natural range, which probably accounts for the ease with which he shifted back and forth between falsetto and normal voice, achieving an effect rather like a weathercock[†] in a whirlwind.

He turned this facility into an important and distinctive device. That crack, or catch, which gave a mournful, soulful, sometimes lugubrious inflection to so much of his articulation and phrasing—a kind of tearjerk, as it were—was accomplished by attacking a note in falsetto, then switching instantly to normal voice. Most singers of any category would find this difficult, if not impossible. To Hank Williams it seems to have come naturally. Probably because it came naturally, he never abused it.

[†] A weathervane, particularly one shaped like a rooster.

But it was not alone his gifts and accomplishments as vocalist, lyricist and public performer that gave to his art those special qualities which have kept his memory and his music alive over a score of years spanning the most explosive era of stylistic evolution—and revolution—in the brief history of Afro-American music. With him more than with most singers, even the finest, the music was the man. That is probably why, as he matured, he ever more rarely sang anyone else's songs.

Music, it would seem, was not so much an extension of his personality as a personal fulfillment, inevitably transitory. Except in the creative act of fashioning the song and performing it, and in the flush of an audience's— or record producer's—response, it was also unsatisfactory. The adjective most commonly employed by those who knew him is "lonely." Another, significantly, is "bitter."

It may well have been just this element of bitterness that excluded, in his songs, the sentimentality characteristic of much country music. Certainly it distinguished his special vein of lyricism from that of Jimmie Rodgers, whose voice and songs, on records and radio, were Hank's earliest musical inspiration. There was nothing of the "dear old South," or "dear old pal of mine," or "dear Mother of mine" in Hank Williams' repertoire, and probably nothing of it in his nature, either. Jimmie Rodgers was an amiable fellow. Hank Williams wasn't—except on stage.

No one seems ever really to have known him, least of all, probably, Hank Williams himself. Jim Denny, until his death in 1963 the general manager of [the] *Grand Ole Opry*, and head of its Artists' Service,‡ who experienced much of the best and the worst of Hank, once said of him, "I never knew anybody I liked better than Hank, but I don't think I ever really got close to him. I don't know if anyone really could."

His audiences, maybe. Only to them could he, or would he, reveal himself. Says Allen Rankin:

> He didn't have much personality except when he was singing. That's when his real personality came out. He'd come slopping and slouching out on stage, limp as a dishrag. But when he picked up the guitar and started to sing, it was like a charge of electricity had gone through him. He became three feet taller.

---

‡ WSM's booking department, sometimes referred to as the Artists Service Bureau, organized in 1934.

As with [Al] Jolson and Frank Sinatra, so with Hank Williams, too, the life of a public performer was the only one he knew or ever wanted to know. He worked for a year and a half (in 1942–44) for the Alabama Drydock and Shipbuilding Company in Mobile as a welder. Even then, at nineteen, he already had six years of public performance behind him, and while working at the shipyard he moonlighted as a musician in the Mobile area. After that, he never earned another nickel or dime that he didn't sing for, play for or write for.

Cover of Al Bock's *I Saw the Light: The Gospel Life of Hank Williams*, 1977. Courtesy of Stephen Bock.

Part V

~~~~~~

Scenes from the Lost Highway
Shedding Light on the Dark Side (1975–1984)

The years 1975 to 1984 marked a decade of remarkable vitality in the writing about Hank Williams, spearheaded by the emergence of popular music criticism as a viable literary endeavor. Beginning in the mid-1960s, a new generation of music critics came of age, many of whom, steeped in the sixties counterculture, were influenced by the frenetic and personal literary styles of Beat writers, New Journalism practitioners, and smart, hip film critics. Inspired by the literary freedom accorded them by alternative publications, these critics were, above all, determined to write seriously about rock music, and they found outlets for their often edgy, inventive writing in several new magazines, beginning with *Crawdaddy!* (founded in 1966), but most importantly in *Rolling Stone* (1967) and *Creem* (1969). Here, the "new rock critics" discovered a readership of literate fans who likewise considered rock 'n' roll an art form worthy of passionate intellectual engagement and debate.

A key mission of the new rock critics was to establish the music's historical lineage, a task that involved determining which musicians of the "pre-rock" era either contributed to the development of rock 'n' roll or embodied its ideal. Several of the new critics speculated on country music's place in rock history and, in particular, sought to pinpoint where Hank Williams fit into that tradition. To some he was the culmination of an older, more circumscribed musical era, while to others he was a trailblazing pioneer of rock 'n' roll. At the same time, rock and country-rock musicians of the 1970s—John Fogerty, Linda Ronstadt, Dave Edmonds, and George Thorogood, among them—were recording commercially and artistically successful covers of Williams's songs. Thus, however uncertain critics might have been regarding Williams's precise place in rock music's genealogy, its artists and their fans seemed eager to accept his prominent standing within that tradition.

Meanwhile, mainstream country music writing received an infusion of this rock criticism when several of the new critics began contributing to *Country Music* (founded in 1972), a glossy, handsomely designed, New York–based monthly magazine that stood at the cutting edge of country music journalism. Several smaller-circulation regional periodicals also covered the contemporary country scene, including *Country Rambler* (1976), based in Niles, Illinois, and *Texas Music* (also 1976), published in Dallas, Texas. In such magazines, the new critics stressed the close kinship between Hank Williams and country music's emerging "Outlaw" movement. By the mid-1970s, a cohort of dissident artists led by Texas singer-songwriters Waylon Jennings and Willie Nelson were in rebellion against Nashville and its producer-dominated "Countrypolitan" sound. Among other things, these performers demanded the same artistic independence (selecting their own material and recording studios, for example) enjoyed by the era's leading rock stars. Simultaneously, they sought to forge a new cultural identity for country music that combined a reverence for tradition and cowboy imagery with the "redneck chic" of southern rock and the drug-fueled decadence of the sixties counterculture. For these artists and the music critics who championed them, Hank Williams came to reign as the "Original Outlaw," an uncompromising artist and unapologetic user of drugs and alcohol who openly scorned the Nashville establishment. In their admiring eyes, as Michael Bane noted in *The Outlaws: Revolution in Country Music* (1978), even Williams's death ranked as something of an existential victory over the bland forces of conformity, consumerism, and mediocrity.

As popular and influential as it might have been during its heyday, the "Original Outlaw" interpretation was far from unopposed. The Hank Williams lionized by the Outlaws proudly and willfully defied social conventions, regardless of the consequences. But this is not the Hank Williams recalled by those who knew him personally, as the writing reprinted or excerpted below by his family members and friends clearly showed. In her account, his widow Billie Jean Horton intimated that the overbearing, grasping personalities of Williams's mother and his first wife Audrey were likely responsible for hastening his demise. Hank Williams, Jr., too young at the time of Hank Sr.'s death to have many firsthand memories of him, speculated that his father was a "haunted" man destroyed by his own "demons," while friends, family, and associates "stood by, unwilling or unable to help." And Minnie Pearl, perhaps the nearest thing to a close friend that the deeply reserved and suspicious Williams possessed, likened him during the final year of his life to a man ravaged by a terminal disease, dragged toward destruction by unknowable forces "deep in his psyche." The Hank Williams we see in these accounts is not an "Outlaw," cavalierly flouting the demands and expectations of others while casually tossing his life away.

He is much more the "Tragic Hero," a musical genius brought to ruin by inner and outer forces beyond his ability to comprehend or control.

Still other writers acknowledged Williams's many personal failings while implicitly or explicitly rejecting the "Original Outlaw" explanation of his life and behavior. Completely at odds with contemporary celebrations of hedonism and excess, Al Bock argued that Williams and his music were best understood within an evangelical Christian framework. His biography, *I Saw the Light: The Gospel Life of Hank Williams* (1977), offered the fullest articulation of the "Lay Preacher" theme that originated in the early 1950s. In Bock's view, Williams's drug and alcohol abuse were not examples of rebellion but symptoms of the weakness that kept him from completely embracing his religious faith. Two years later, Jay Caress followed with *Hank Williams: Country Music's Tragic King* (1979), a biography that, as its title suggests, encapsulated another long-standing interpretation of the country star, that of the "Tragic Hero."

Meanwhile, academics became increasingly fascinated with Williams, and this period witnessed both the first scholarly article and the first scholarly biography devoted to him: Larry Powell's "Hank Williams: Loneliness and Psychological Alienation," which appeared in the Fall 1975 issue of the *Journal of Country Music* (founded in 1971); and George William Koon's *Hank Williams: A Bio-Bibliography* (1983), respectively. And in 1978, Robert K. Krishef provided a telling indication of the broadening interest in the Alabama singer-songwriter when he published the first and, to date, only book-length biography of Williams for young readers. Although none of these works advanced an "Original Outlaw" explanation of Williams per se, neither did they shy away from considering the sordid aspects of his private life.

If there has been a "bombshell" in the Hank Williams literature, surely it was Chet Flippo's book, *Your Cheatin Heart: A Biography of Hank Williams* (1981), which, at first glance, seemed to represent the culmination of the "Original Outlaw" interpretation of the star. Flippo's Williams is an angry, embittered man, filled with self-loathing and contempt for the world, who goes about the business of destroying himself with chilling abandon. But in this nihilistic incarnation—lost, amoral, agonizing, and hopeless—Williams is more a prisoner of his own poisoned motivations and resentments than a conscious rebel. And so in the end this controversial characterization hewed more closely to the "Tabloid Celebrity" of the 1950s than to the "Original Outlaw" interpretation in vogue when Flippo wrote his biography. Yet for all that, Flippo managed to create a far more sympathetic Hank Williams than ever appeared in the pages of the scandal sheets and pulp magazines.

By the middle of the 1980s, then, Hank Williams was generating interest among an increasingly diverse group of writers engaged in an effort to determine his significance, to assess his influence, to locate his place within American culture, or simply just to understand him as a human being. Disagreements flourished, as existing interpretations were revised and expanded and new paradigms were developed, but all writers agreed that he was important, however that importance was defined. More than thirty years after his death, Hank Williams was steadily moving into the mainstream of American cultural consciousness.

| 36 |

Greil Marcus: Excerpt from *Mystery Train: Images of America in Rock 'n' Roll Music*

One of the most prominent "new rock critics" is Greil Marcus, author of the influential 1975 book *Mystery Train: Images of America in Rock 'n' Roll*. As much as any single writer of the 1970s, Marcus (b. 1945) elevated rock criticism from the level of pop journalism to that of a respectable literary pursuit. Born in San Francisco, he graduated from the University of California, Berkeley; worked as a music columnist at the *San Francisco Express-Times*, a pioneering alternative weekly; served as *Rolling Stone* magazine's first record review editor; then became an editor at *Creem* magazine in 1970.

As Marcus explains in the book's introduction, *Mystery Train* constitutes his "attempt to broaden the context in which the music is heard; to deal with rock 'n' roll not as youth culture, or counter culture, but simply as American culture." In its expression of contradictory longings for both independence and community, Marcus argues that rock 'n' roll echoes these two classic themes found in the most enduring American literature, from Alexis de Tocqueville through Herman Melville and Walt Whitman to Mark Twain. The most remarkable chapter of *Mystery Train* is its lengthy concluding essay, "Elvis: Presliad," in which the author addresses the essential cultural differences between Hank Williams and Elvis Presley. In drawing a sharp distinction between Williams and the conservative limits of country music, on one side, and Presley and the adventurous spirit of rock 'n' roll, on the other, Marcus established the parameters of the debate about Hank Williams's musical legacy for many of the critics who followed see, for example, nos. 43 and 55.

SOURCE Greil Marcus, *Mystery Train: Images of America in Rock 'n' Roll Music* (New York: E. P. Dutton, 1975), 148, 149–53. © 1975, 1982, 1990, 1997, 2008 by Greil Marcus. Used by permission of Greil Marcus.

They called Elvis the Hillbilly Cat in the beginning; he came out of a stepchild culture (in the South, white trash; to the rest of America, a caricature of Bilbo* and moonshine) that for all it shared with the rest of America had its own shape and integrity. As a poor white Southern boy, Elvis created a personal culture out of the hillbilly world that was his as a given. Ultimately, he made that personal culture public in such an explosive way that he transformed not only his own culture, but America's. I want to look at that hillbilly landscape for a bit—to get a sense of how Elvis drew on his context.

It was, as Southern chambers of commerce have never tired of saying, A Land of Contrasts. The fundamental contrast, of course, could not have been more obvious: black and white. Always at the root of Southern fantasy, Southern music, and Southern politics, the black man was poised in the early fifties for an overdue invasion of American life, in fantasy, music, and politics. As the North scurried to deal with him, the South would be pushed farther and farther into the weirdness and madness its best artists had been trying to exorcise from the time of [Edgar Allan] Poe on down. Its politics would dissolve into night-riding and hysteria; its fantasies would be dull for all their gaudy paranoia. Only the music got away clean.

The North, powered by the Protestant ethic, had set men free by making them strangers; the poor man's South that Elvis knew took strength from community.

The community was based on a marginal economy that demanded cooperation, loyalty, and obedience for the achievement of anything resembling a good life; it was organized by religion, morals, and music. Music helped hold the community together, and carried the traditions and shared values that dramatized a sense of place. Music gave pleasure, wisdom, and shelter. [...]

Music was also an escape from the community, and music revealed its underside. There were always people who could not join, no matter how they might want to: tramps, whores, rounders, idiots, criminals. The most vital were singers: not the neighbors who brought out their fiddles and guitars for country picnics, as Elvis used to do, or those who sang in church, as he did also, but the professionals. They were men who bridged the gap between the community's sentimentalized idea of itself, and the outside world and the forbidden; artists who could take the community beyond itself because they had the talent and the nerve to transcend it. Often doomed, traveling throughout the South enjoying sins and freedoms the community had surrendered out of necessity or never known at all, they were too ambitious, ornery, or simply different to fit in.

---

* Theodore G. Bilbo (1877–1947), a notoriously racist Mississippi politician, whose name has become synonymous with white supremacy.

The Carter Family, in the twenties, were the first to record the old songs eve-ryone knew, to make the shared musical culture concrete, and their music drew a circle around the community. They celebrated the landscape (especially the Clinch Mountains that ringed their home), found strength in a feel for death because it was the only certainty, laughed a bit, and promised to leave the hillbilly home they helped build only on a gospel ship. Jimmie Rodgers, their contemporary, simply hopped a train. He was every boy who ever ran away from home, hanging out in the railroad yards, bumming around with black minstrels, pushing out the limits of his life. *He* celebrated long tall mamas that rubbed his back and licked his neck just to cure the cough that killed him;[†] he bragged about gunplay on Beale Street; he sang real blues, played jazz with Louis Armstrong, and though there was melancholy in his soul, his smile was a good one. He sounded like a man who could make a home for himself any-where. There's so much *room* in this country, he seemed to be saying, so many things to do—how could an honest man be satisfied to live within the frontiers he was born to?

Outside of the community because of the way they lived, the singers were tied to it as symbols of its secret hopes, of its fantasies of escape and union with the black man, of its fears of transgressing the moral and social limits that promised peace of mind. Singers could present the extremes of emotion, risk, pleasure, sex, and violence that the community was meant to control; they were often alcoholic or worse, lacking a real family, drifters in a world where roots were life. Sometimes the singer tantalized the community with his outlaw lib-erty; dying young, he finally justified the community by his inability to survive outside of it. More often than not, the singer's resistance dissolved into senti-ment. Reconversion is the central country music comeback strategy, and many have returned to the fold after a brief fling with the devil, singing songs of virtue, fidelity, and God, as if to prove that sin only hid a deeper piety—or that there was no way out.

By the late forties and early fifties, Hank Williams had inherited Jimmie Rodgers' role as the central figure in the music, but he added an enormous reservation: that margin of loneliness in Rodgers' America had grown into a world of utter tragedy. Williams sang for a community to which he could not belong; he sang to a God in whom he could not quite believe; even his many songs of good times and good lovin' seemed to lose their reality. There were plenty of jokes in his repertoire, novelties like "Kaw-Liga" (the tale of unre-quited love between two cigar store Indians); he traveled Rodgers' road, but for Williams, that road was a lost highway. Beneath the surface of his forced smiles

---

[†] A reference to Rodgers's tuberculosis.

and his light, easy sound, Hank Williams was kin to Robert Johnson in a way that the new black singers of his day were not. Their music, coming out of New Orleans, out of Sam Phillips' Memphis studio and washing down from Chicago, was loud, fiercely electric, raucous, bleeding with lust and menace and loss. The rhythmic force that was the practical legacy of Robert Johnson had evolved into a music that overwhelmed *his* reservations; the rough spirit of the new blues, city R&B, rolled right over his nihilism. Its message was clear: What life doesn't give me, I'll take.

Hank Williams was a poet of limits, fear, and failure; he went as deeply into one dimension of the country world as anyone could, gave it beauty, gave it dignity. What was missing was that part of the hillbilly soul Rodgers had celebrated, something Williams' music obscured, but which his realism could not express and the community's moralism could not contain: excitement, rage, fantasy, delight—the feeling, summed up in a sentence by W. J. Cash‡ from *The Mind of the South*, that "even the Southern physical world was a kind of cosmic conspiracy against reality in favor of romance"; that even if Elvis's South was filled with Puritans, it was also filled with natural-born hedonists, and the same people were both.

> To lie on his back for days and weeks [Cash writes of the hillbilly], storing power as the air he breathed stores power under the hot sun of August, and then to explode, as that air explodes in a thunderstorm, in a violent outburst of emotion—in such a fashion would he make life not only tolerable, but infinitely sweet.

In the fifties we can hardly find that moment in white music, before Elvis. Hank Williams was not all there was to fifties country, but his style was so pervasive, so effective, carrying so much weight, that it closed off the possibilities of breaking loose just as the new black music helped open them up. Not his gayest tunes, not "Move It on Over," "Honky Tonkin'," or "Hey Good Lookin'," can match this blazing passage from Cash, even if those songs share its subject:

> To go into town on Saturday afternoon and night, to stroll with the throng, to gape at the well-dressed and the big automobiles, to bathe in the holiday cacophony...maybe to have a drink, maybe to get drunk, to laugh with the passing girls, to pick them up if you had a car, or to go swaggering or

---

‡ Wilbur Joseph "W. J." Cash (1900–1941), a noted South Carolina–born journalist and author of *The Mind of the South* (1941), which was hailed by contemporary critics, especially liberals, as a landmark study of southern culture.

hesitating into the hotels with the corridors saturated with the smell of bichloride of mercury, or the secret, steamy bawdy houses; maybe to have a fight, maybe against the cops, maybe to end, whooping and god-damning, in the jailhouse . . . .

The momentum is missing; that will to throw yourself all the way after something better with no real worry about how you are going to make it home. And it was this spirit, full-blown and bragging, that was to find its voice in Elvis's new blues and the rockabilly fever he kicked off all over the young white South. Once Elvis broke down the door, dozens more would be fighting their way through. Out of nowhere there would be Carl Perkins, looking modest enough and sounding for all the world as if he was having fun for the first time in his life, chopping his guitar with a new kind of urgency and yelling: "Now Dan got happy and he started ravin'—He jerked out his razor but he wasn't shavin'"—

He hollered R-R-RAVE ON chillen, I'm with ya!
RAVE ON CATS he cried
It's almost dawn and the cops're gone
Let's <u>allllllll</u> get dixie fried!

Country music (like the blues, which was more damned and more honestly hedonistic than country had ever been) was music for a whole community, cutting across lines of age, if not class. This could have meant an openly expressed sense of diversity for each child, man, and woman, as it did with the blues. But country spoke to a community fearful of anything of the sort, withdrawing into itself, using music as a bond that linked all together for better or for worse, with a sense that what was shared was less important than the crucial fact of sharing. How could parents hope to keep their children if their kids' whole sense of what it meant to live—which is what we get from music when we are closest to it—held promises the parents could never keep?

The songs of country music, and most deeply, its even, narrow sound, had to subject the children to the heartbreak of their parents: the father who couldn't feed his family, the wife who lost her husband to a honky-tonk angel or a bottle, the family that lost everything to a suicide or a farm spinning off into one more bad year, the horror of loneliness in a world that was meant to banish that if nothing else. Behind that uneasy grin, this is Hank Williams' America; the romance is only a night call.

Such a musical community is beautiful, but it is not hard to see how it could be intolerable. All that hedonism was dragged down in country music; a deep sense of fear and resignation confined it, as perhaps it almost had to, in a land overshadowed by fundamentalist religion, where original sin was just another name for the facts of life.

~~~~~~

| 37 |

Billie Jean Horton: Fear and Loathing at Hank's Funeral

Hank Williams earned nearly $70,000 in record sales and songwriting royalties in 1952 alone, yet surprisingly, when he died in 1953, his estate was valued at only $13,329.* But he also left behind at least ninety unpublished songs, whose eventual income from recording and publishing royalties, one newspaper reported, "could run into hundreds of thousands of dollars." Because Williams left no will, a family feud quickly erupted over the settlement of his estate. His funeral created a highly combustible situation by bringing together four combative individuals, each angling for advantage. In short order, though, his ex-wife Audrey Williams, his sister Irene Williams Smith, and his mother Lillie Stone closed ranks against a relative newcomer to the saga—his twenty-year-old widow, Billie Jean (Jones) Williams (b. 1932). In June 1952, the stunning redhead first captured the singer's attention backstage at the *Grand Ole Opry*, where she had arrived from Bossier City, Louisiana, as the girlfriend of up-and-coming country star Faron Young. Williams "appropriated" Billie Jean from Young—reportedly at gunpoint—and, after a whirlwind four-month courtship, they were married in a small private ceremony in Minden, Louisiana, on October 18, 1952, and then twice again the following day on the stage of the New Orleans Municipal Auditorium, before a combined paying audience of some 14,000 spectators.

In the intrafamily battle that raged in the immediate aftermath of Williams's death, his mother Lillie questioned whether Billie Jean's divorce from her first husband had been final at the time she married Williams, while Billie Jean clashed with Audrey over which woman should be legitimately crowned "Mrs. Hank Williams." Eventually, in August 1953, Billie Jean relinquished all rights to the estate in exchange for a $30,000 settlement. The following month, she married rising country singer Johnny Horton, then a regular on

---

SOURCE   Billie Jean Horton, "Fear and Loathing at Hank's Funeral," *Texas Music*, June 1976, pp. 45–46. Used by permission.
* Considering his six-figure earnings over the previous few years, this figure is a paltry amount, but it is worth noting that it represents a relatively substantial sum: approximately $107,000, in inflation-adjusted 2010 dollars.

the *Louisiana Hayride*, who, like Hank Williams, was destined to die young after achieving stardom.

Twenty-three years later, Billie Jean recounted the tensions that crackled within her former mother-in-law's Montgomery boardinghouse as the respective members of the Williams family gathered for the singer's funeral. Billie Jean's brassy personality is much in evidence in this June 1976 cover story for the short-lived alternative magazine *Texas Music*, as she describes the behind-the-scenes jockeying for position—occasionally escalating into physical violence—that took place among the four determined women.

I'll never forget the funeral—Hank's.

It reminded me of the rebirth of the Hadacol Show.† Everybody wanted to "sang." And did. For us who was hurtin', it just left us lingering on for hours, having to sit silently looking at Hank. Cold. Still. Dreading the inevitable—puttin' him in the ground, throwing dirt on him. Dreadin' the coffin lid to shut because you knew you'd never see his face again.

Hank was afraid of the dark and graves. He wouldn't have wanted to be in that cold, dark ground.

If I hadn't been broke, country, a child and ignorant, I would've brought him home to the bayou in Louisiana. Being broke was my biggest handicap. I figure if I'd had money I would have had a lot of knowledgeable doers—arm breakers, mind benders, and so on. But as it was, my daddy took me back home from Alabama on the Greyhound bus. It was proper though, since I went to Nashville on a Greyhound when I met Hank. Pride never enters the mind of a broken heart. Hank was gone—the buzzards had started to pick at his leavin's. All I really wanted was some of his personal belongings, and the weddin' ring I gave him. I never got them—possession is nine-tenths of the law, and just about everything we owned was in his mother's house, since that's where we were staying when he died. A lot of things nobody wants is still in storage in Alabama—I may go acallin' one day—for my wedding ring. And, if I don't get it, well, I might go acallin' again. For his body. I gave up his fortunes when he

---

† A reference to the Hadacol Caravan, a spectacular, big-budget medicine show that, in 1950 and again in 1951, traversed the South and lower Midwest by rail promoting a quack "vitamin supplement" called Hadacol invented and marketed by Louisiana state senator Dudley J. LeBlanc (1894–1971). Hank Williams performed with the 1951 Hadacol show, as did Milton Berle, Bob Hope, Jimmy Durante, Carmen Miranda, Minnie Pearl, and other nationally known stars.

died. But I don't believe that contract said a thing about his body! Well, that could lead to another story…back to this one…

By "buzzards" I mean Mrs. Stone, his mother; Irene Smith, Hank's sister; and Audrey, his ex-wife.

Hank's mother—of whose love we didn't share for each other naturally— died in a year,‡ so she didn't reap the wealth she took. Irene, Hank's sister, harvested a better crop as administrator of the Alabama estate and went into the real estate business in Dallas—that is, until peddling cocaine got to paying better. Right after that girl was voted Woman of the Year,§ she got herself caught carrying a few million dollars worth of goodies over the border at Laredo. The feds frowned on that. She got eight years. She's out now—just recently.¶

Mr. Williams, Hank's dad, just stayed in the background. Nobody seemed to care about him, not even the press. But that's understandable since he'd spent 10 years of his life in a VA hospital after being gassed fighting for his country in World War One. Mrs. Stone divorced him and kept on marrying. I cared about him, Hank's daddy, in my heart, but since I didn't know him well—just met him at the funeral, and he was a quiet man—I didn't know how he felt toward me. Hank and I had gone to see him and his wife and daughter Christmas day [1952] and they weren't home. Four years ago I finally made my mind up to see him. I called the Skippers, Hank's cousins, to pick me up and take me to see him. I wanted to know Hank's father. He died the day before I got there.‖ His wife told me at the funeral that he spoke of me often. Hank has a stepsister, Leila, that is a carbon copy of Hank.

Now that Audrey is dead (of natural causes) only time will tell which turn Randall Jr.'s** (Hank Jr.) mind will take. Junior had all the strikes against him, being raised by a domineering mother like Audrey, who wanted fame for Junior too—with the fortune that goes with it. But she ended up losing both. She died—in hock to the IRS and deserted by Junior, who had gone through two wives himself. In self defense, Junior has moved to Alabama. Surely, by now he must know why Hank Sr. was running—you can never keep up with what you're supposed to be. Audrey is better off—she couldn't have faced old age and time takes its toll with all of us. I can't complain. I've just kept on hookin'

‡ Lillie Stone died on February 26, 1955, a little more than two years after her son.
§ Probably a reference to a Dallas neighborhood award Smith received in May 1967, when she was named "Oak Cliff Woman of the Month" in recognition of her "wide-range of civic and business interests…and for her dedication to the preservation of her brother's music."
¶ For more information on Smith's arrest and conviction, see no. 33.
‖ Lon Williams died in McWillliams, Alabama, on October 22, 1970.
** Although he performs under the stage name Hank Williams, Jr., Randall Hank Williams is not technically a "junior."

it. When my time's up, I hope I'm backstage somewhere listening to Willie Nelson singing "Amazing Grace."

While Hank's body lay in state for all cameras to view in his mother's living room, she and I were fightin' (fists) in the bathroom and elsewhere. She was so big—[a] good six-foot and no less than 250 pounds—I had to get up on the commode to slap her. But my daddy had taught me in the South that they was never too big. I guess I believed him, since I haven't changed yet.

All the fighting was taking place because during mine and Hank's marriage she hassled him for money and, hell, she had more than he did because Audrey got it all when they divorced. I put my foot down: no more money—immediately I made a friend. We were staying with her during Christmas until December 30th [1952]. Hank left to do two personals. I flew home to Louisiana to visit my parents. He died the next night. The chauffeur called me at my dad's house. I called her—Hank's mother—she had some plane-chartering money. I didn't. She beat me to his body and took all his personal effects, including my wedding ring off his finger. She had hidden his car. With money, God knows, you can do anything. (God ain't alone; I came to know it too.)

I never saw Hank's car again. My brother and an ambulance took his body back to Alabama. Meantime, my dad said I would need a lawyer. He was with me in Oak Hill, West Virginia, where I went to get Hank. I didn't know any lawyers, except the dude who got my divorce from my first husband. But, 'though I didn't know much about lawyers, I knew he wasn't much brighter than me, and that was bad. So, from Oak Hill I called a firm Hank had retained in Shreveport. I gave them a few details by phone as to the happenings thus far and, like any good firm, they sent a young lawyer to Montgomery, Alabama, and he was there when I got there. Naturally they thought I was a fat cat, or soon would be; so, we divided up the house: The old lady, Audrey, back in the picture again (all money should stick together—in this case they deserved each other), Irene, and other grievers with high-priced attorneys, was on one side of the house—a hall in between—and me and my family and one lawyer (brand new at lawyering) was on the other side.

Someone decided we should be notified when the other party was viewing Hank's body. But somehow the old lady and I met up first in the restroom. On with the hair-pulling!

My dad had enough money for one hotel room. My entire family stayed in there. I didn't know any better, so the day they finally decided to bury Hank, my family and I went to the auditorium and finally got a seat in the middle. Then someone told the head honcho of the funeral who I was and he moved me up to the front row. I couldn't figure out why I deserved such a good seat when those people couldn't even get in the door! But when I saw Audrey sittin' on the front row—other side—I figured there was something to it.

I didn't send any flowers 'cause I didn't have the money. And I didn't print no sign on no touchstone at the grave either. All I wanted to do was get the hell out of there. We did—back to my dad's shotgun house in Louisiana, where I'd come from....

Sure was dull without Hank buggin' mamma to cook him some biscuits and sorghum syrup.

| 38 |

Michael Bane: Excerpt from *The Outlaws: Revolution in Country Music*

Members of the 1970s Outlaw movement saw themselves as the natural heirs to Hank Williams's legacy. Given his legendary stature as a singer, songwriter, and performer who had supposedly demonstrated his integrity by refusing to kowtow to the Nashville establishment, they embraced him as a powerful symbol in their own struggles for artistic freedom. Consequently, not only did they write and record songs about him, but they eagerly sought to live out the Williams myth of the rebellious, hard-living hillbilly singer. In his genre-defining 1978 book, *The Outlaws: Revolution in Country Music*, journalist Michael Bane (b. 1950) chronicles the rise of this musical movement and profiles several of its leading figures. In the excerpt below, he notes the "two-edged" nature of Williams's influence, lamenting that so many self-defined Outlaws saw it as almost an artistic duty to pursue stardom along the self-destructive path trod by their doomed idol.

Nashville had its first run-in with rampant Outlaw-ism almost thirty years ago, when a skinny scarecrow of a kid from Alabama changed country music from a quaint Appalachian pastime into a national craze, in the process changing what country music was and what it could ever hope to be. For the performers who followed him, Hank Williams' ghost laid with almost tangible feeling over their careers. Hank Williams' music set the tone for country music for decades; his widespread acceptance among non-country fans and his national

---

SOURCE Michael Bane, *The Outlaws: Revolution in Country Music* (New York: Country Music Magazine Press, 1978), 14, 16–17, 19. Used by permission of Michael Bane.

prominence set the standards for future country stars; he pioneered the singer-songwriter concept, which had such a profound effect on country music that Nashville is still trembling; in short, in his less than five years [*sic*] on the music scene, Hank Williams became *the* role model, past and present, for a country singer.

Ole Hank has become so much a part of the Nashville cultural unconscious and the country music landscape that his myth is recycled constantly, at a seemingly ever-increasing rate. In any given year, the following echoes of Ole Hank are more than likely to occur: At least one Hank Williams song goes to the top of the charts; at least one Hank Williams "tribute" album is released by a major country star; at least one song about Ole Hank is recorded. In 1976, for example, Moe Bandy recorded "I'm Sorry For You, My Friend" (Hank Williams song), John Denver and Michael Murphey recorded "Mansion On The Hill" (another Hank Williams song), Ray Price also recorded "Mansion On The Hill" (just one song on his *Me 'N' Hank* album), Waylon Jennings recorded "Are You Sure Hank Done It This Way?" Moe Bandy recorded "Hank Williams You Wrote My Life," and Hank Williams, Jr. recorded "Living Proof" and "Daddy," both songs about his daddy and the trials and tribulations of being his daddy's son.

Hank's impact on Nashville (and particularly on the people who came to be called "Outlaws") runs deeper than the evergreen nature of his music. In "Hank Williams You Wrote My Life," Moe Bandy summed it up as well as it's ever been done:

We've never met, I know, and yet
I know you well my friend
And if ever I get to heaven on high
I hope you'll shake my hand

You wrote "Your Cheatin' Heart" about
A gal like my first ex-wife
You moaned the blues for me and for you
Hank Williams, you wrote my life

Bandy's lines speak of a very personal heritage from Ole Hank, and that's the point: Hank's most profound impact was not found among the countless imitators who dominated country music for years after his death, but among the young pickers who saw genius go down in flames while his friends and admirers stood on the sidelines, studiously ignoring the smoke (one long-time Nashville observer who knew Hank commented, "He had no friends until he died. Those people on the Opry didn't give a shit"). The example Hank left those young pickers was, for the first time in country music, a page from the Bible according to Hollywood: Live fast, die young, and leave a beautiful corpse.

The saddest thing, perhaps, was that for Hank there really didn't seem to be any other ending. When he arrived in Nashville in 1946 (just seven years before his death), he had been roaring since he was twelve years old, when he had entered his first talent contest back home in Montgomery, Alabama, singing his own "The W.P.A. Blues." By the time he was fifteen, he was hitting the brutal north Alabama honky tonk circuit with a band he called the Drifting Cowboys. Driven by a bitter childhood—he had been raised by his mother after his father left for a veteran's [sic] hospital—he was, according to his biographer, Roger M. Williams, a virtual alcoholic before his twentieth birthday. Then there were the pills, begun to ease a chronically bad back and soon seen as an end in themselves. When he came to Nashville in 1946 to audition for Fred Rose of the powerful Acuff-Rose song publishing company, he brought with him the natural, stunning ability to drive a simple song straight into the gut, to bypass the head and score an immediate, direct hit on the emotions. He was best, perhaps, at evoking despair—no country songwriter before or since has been able to express such pain with such eloquence. [...]

But the legacy of Ole Hank remains a two-edged sword. For all the good that he and his music did, he did give country music a *tragic* figure to revere and follow. He provided a prototype for the hard-living, hard-drinking, got-no-future-but-I'm-sure-as-hell-on-my-way hillbilly singer, and that prototype launched a thousand singers who wanted to do it "just like Ole Hank done it." He launched the era of the miserable hillbilly, the *artiste* who must suffer first, then create. There's this nagging feeling in Nashville, even today, that, well, so what if he *died* doing it, Hank's route is still the only way to go. If you want to write about life, you understand, you've got to get down and *roar*; you've got to *live* until you either just plumb pass out or leave a real nice corpse and a whole bunch of pretty country songs.

There's a lot of that feeling in the new Nashville music, the music of the people called Outlaws. Waylon [Jennings] and Willie [Nelson] and Tompall [Glaser] and the others, you can be sure, have heard that midnight train whining low, and if Hank Williams wrote anybody's life, it's theirs. They are faithful to Ole Hank's spirit and style—the only difference is that, so far, they have all managed to survive.

| 39 |

Al Bock: Excerpt from *I Saw the Light: The Gospel Life of Hank Williams*

Although the depiction of Hank Williams as the founding father of country music's Outlaw movement dominated much of the writing about him during the mid- to late 1970s, a rival and dramatically different interpretation cast him as a devout evangelical Christian. Perhaps no piece of writing better expressed this view than *I Saw the Light: The Gospel Life of Hank Williams* (1977), by Alan W. Bock (1943–2011), a longtime libertarian newspaper columnist, magazine writer, syndicated radio talk-show host, and author. Filled with scriptural passages and based upon what Bock calls "prayerful study" of his subject, *I Saw the Light* examines Williams's religious beliefs and their influence on his life and music. Despite the singer's indifference to organized religion and his history of substance abuse, Bock presents him as having had a "deep personal commitment to Christianity," and contends that "all of Hank Williams' gospel songs were consistent with the fundamental Christian faith which was at the root of his life." In making such claims, Bock echoes Lillie Stone's and Irene Williams Smith's earlier portraits of Williams as, at heart, a folk preacher and evangelist. But in the following excerpt Bock also speculates that ultimately the singer's faith might not have been strong enough to enable him to overcome the daunting challenges he faced or to achieve true happiness.

There can be little doubt that Hank Williams is one of the towering figures of American music, an artist whose music and legend continue to grow in popularity and influence more than twenty years after his tragic death in 1953 at the age of 29. [...] Yet in all the Hank Williams lore, one element seems to be missing or underplayed, and that is the subject of this book. We have had tales of drinking and tragedy, of pills and emotional immaturity. But what are we told of Hank Williams' religious life, of his personal beliefs about God and Jesus Christ? What role did his religion play in his life? Just what were his religious convictions and how did they influence his life and his music?

SOURCE   Al Bock, *I Saw the Light: The Gospel Life of Hank Williams* (Nashville, Tenn.: Green Valley Record Store, 1977), 1, 2–3, 4, 5, 6–7, 147, 148, 152–53. Used by permission of Stephen Bock.

It is easy to understand the reluctance of people on both sides to deal with Hank Williams' religion. On the one hand, those attracted by the myth of the brilliant songwriter who lived a hedonistic life of wine, women and song, don't want to deal with the fact that, whatever his personal shortcomings or actions, Hank had a deep personal commitment to Christianity. It seems out of character, especially for those who see Christianity as a stern, forbidding and joyless religion. Those who have the false view that God's function is to look down, see who is having fun and try to stop it are not eager to take note of the role of Christianity in such a freewheeling life as Hank Williams'.

On the other hand, many Christians are a little reluctant to embrace a man like Hank Williams as one of their own. Whether your particular brand of Christianity involves teetotaling or temperance, no Christian doctrine endorses the kind of unrestrained drinking which characterized an alcoholic like Hank Williams. Many people still do not understand that alcoholism is a physical disease rather than a moral weakness. Even if we understand that, do we want to associate Christianity with a man who got involved in so many well-publicized excesses? [...]

One can understand a certain reluctance to deal with Hank Williams' Christian faith in very much depth. But if we are to consider Hank as a whole man, we cannot ignore it. Like the Lord's Prayer's statement about forgiveness, it is to be found right there in the middle of the thing. Hank Williams wrote about 125 songs, more than two dozen were hymns and sacred songs. Among them is the classic "I Saw the Light," which is one of the greatest gospel songs of all time, beloved by every gospel singer for its expression of the exuberance and joy which is to be found in the fellowship of Jesus. [...]

Hank Williams not only believed in the Christian faith, he had a well-informed knowledge of what that faith was, and of what Jesus promises to those who will follow Him. If he wrote the songs strictly for their commercial appeal, or because he sometimes had some vaguely mystical or religious feelings, there would almost certainly be parts of the gospel songs which would be out of line with fundamental Christian belief. There is plenty of songwriting and literature which has a humanitarian or even religious overtone to it which is not in line with Christian doctrine. One thinks of many of today's modern "gurus," whose work is humanitarian in character and religious in some senses, but not Christian. Hank Williams' religious songs were smack in the mainstream of Christian teaching and belief. [...]

What this knowledge about Hank Williams gives us is a new perspective from which to consider his life and his artistic output. [...] Many artists can be appreciated without considering their religion, but in almost every case knowledge of their religious beliefs lends an important dimension to our understanding of them. [...] Any country music fan loves Hank Williams' singing and appreciates his songs. But when we understand the depth and sincerity of his Christian faith we can look at his songs in new ways, and get new meanings from them. I am not saying that Christianity was the central fact of Hank Williams' life. Which of us is able to judge the inner workings of another man's soul? But I do believe that Christianity was an important part of his life, and that if we don't understand that fact, we get a distorted picture of the man rather than a rounded picture of the whole man. [...]

Just what plan and purpose God had for Hank Williams only God knows for sure. But through his gift and his career Hank Williams was in some measure an evangelist, a witness to the faith, a teacher and preacher. [...] There's no evidence that he seriously doubted the basic Christian beliefs. But he didn't take everything that Christianity offers. I don't believe that he made a full life-commitment to Jesus, that he ever turned his entire life over to the Lord's will. [...]

It may well be that Hank Williams was simply not aware of the deeper levels of faith which are possible to a Christian. There are plenty of churches which will let Christians be comfortable with regular attendance and regular donations. Many Christians are never challenged to deepen their personal commitment and reliance on Jesus. It is quite likely that Hank never fully understood what kind of reliance on God is required to break the vicious cycle of alcoholism. He was a hardworking, busy man, and demands on his time were even greater after he achieved great success in music. It may be that in his short life he simply did not find or make the time to seek out the ways by which Jesus could come into his life more fully. [...]

Hank Williams believed. Yet he still had problems with his marriage, troubles with his career, and a deep, gnawing loneliness at the core of his being. He found that financial and professional success didn't take away that bitter loneliness. Money didn't bring him happiness.

He must have had some sense that the answer to his loneliness and fears and troubles lay in a full commitment to Jesus Christ. He had to have some knowledge of that to write and perform the gospel songs as he did. Yet, apparently, he did not reach out and take the full measure of spiritual strength and personal fulfillment which Christ has to offer. This is the real tragedy of Hank Williams' life—that he had some knowledge of our Lord, but didn't have the full knowledge which could have filled his life with fulfillment and joy. He had fulfillment and happiness some of the time. By the standards of the world he had all he could have wanted.

Yet, it seems, he didn't reach out and take everything which Jesus Christ had to give. He took part of it. He had a great gift, and he used that gift (or perhaps the Lord used it) to help spread the word about the salvation which

Jesus has in store for others. Yet he didn't take all of it for himself. He had it within his grasp, but there was more available for the asking. Perhaps it would have meant a happier life for this gifted, talented, delightful yet troubled genius, Hank Williams.

~~~~~~

| 40 |

Hank Williams, Jr. (with Michael Bane): Excerpt from *Living Proof: An Autobiography*

Born Randall Hank Williams in Shreveport, Louisiana, Hank "Bocephus" Williams, Jr. (b. 1949) was only three-and-a-half-years old when his father died and so has few memories of him. A stage performer from the age of eight, Hank Jr. began his now-fifty-plus years in the music business as a gifted impersonator, singing his late father's classic songs and mimicking his voice and mannerisms. His career, Colin Escott notes, was "orchestrated by his mother, Audrey, who saw in Hank Jr. an opportunity to sustain the legend [of Hank Sr.] in which she had such a huge financial and personal stake." Hank Jr. debuted on the *Grand Ole Opry* at the age of eleven, signed a $100,000-a-year contract with MGM Records (Hank Sr.'s label) three years later, and scored a No. 5 hit in 1964 with his debut recording, a cover of his father's song, "Long Gone Lonesome Blues." He went on to record a million-selling soundtrack album for the biopic of his father's life, *Your Cheatin' Heart* (1964), and a series of other successful MGM albums featuring the elder Williams's material. He even cut two albums as Luke the Drifter, Jr., a reincarnation of his father's musical alter ego. But Hank Jr. eventually grew disillusioned with his role as a tribute act and, like his father before him, fell into heavy drug and alcohol abuse. By the time he was in his early twenties, he wondered if he too would die young.

With the release of his watershed album *Hank Williams, Jr. & Friends* (1975), the younger Williams began to chart his own course as a country-rock singer, songwriter, and musician. A near-fatal mountain climbing accident in Montana in 1975 temporarily derailed his career, but he managed to return to the stage only nine months later. From that point on, Hank Jr. primarily played his own music, although his ambivalent relationship with his father's legacy remained a frequent theme of his songs. By the late 1970s, he had emerged as one of the leading voices of the Outlaws. Hank Jr. went on to enjoy tremendous success in

SOURCE   Hank Williams, Jr., with Michael Bane, *Living Proof: An Autobiography* (New York: G. P. Putnam's Sons, 1979), 61–64. © 1979 by Hank Williams, Jr., with Michael Bane. Permission granted by Lowenstein Associates, Inc.

the 1980s, releasing eleven studio albums and three volumes of greatest hits, and winning a combined five Entertainer of the Year Awards from the Academy of Country Music and the Country Music Association.

His memoir, *Living Proof: An Autobiography*, co-written with Michael Bane, appeared in 1979 and inspired a 1983 made-for-television movie (with former *Waltons* star Richard Thomas in the lead role). Much of the book recounts Hank Jr.'s struggles to emerge from his father's long shadow and to establish his own identity as a performer.* In the excerpt below, from the chapter titled "Daddy," he provides a refreshingly candid, clear-eyed assessment of both his father and mother, while also offering some thoughtful commentary about what he calls "the Cult of Hank Williams."

Daddy was haunted by his genius, and when the blues came around at midnight he had no place to turn, no one to grab ahold [*sic*] of. His life was marked by strong women, first Lilly, his mother, then Audrey, his wife, and I'd be lying if I didn't admit that they pushed. Lord, how they pushed!

Maybe he needed the pushing. There are questions I'd like to have discussed with him, answers I wished I knew. His relationship with my mother was stormy. She hated his drinking and belittled the fact that he could never be the person she thought he should be. They fought, bitterly and sometimes in public, but there was always a reconciliation at the end. That is, right up until the very end.

The problem was (I think) that despite the hangers-on, well-wishers, managers, wife, and what have you, nobody ever gave the slightest thought to helping Daddy cope with his success. He was successful beyond his wildest imagination, and that was the problem. Literally, beyond his wildest imagination, and he couldn't imagine what to do next.

On the balance, though, times were more private then than they are now, and Daddy guarded his privacy fanatically. No one would even *think* about telling him that he drank too much or he was ruining his career and his life. Maybe it's still the same way now—who counseled Elvis in his final days?

I was born May 26, 1949, in Shreveport, and the next month Daddy got his long awaited shot at the Grand Ole Opry. The Opry had been very leery of allowing him to perform, because they'd heard all the stories of his wild and wooly ways, but he had too many hit records to ignore.

---

* For a detailed discussion of this phase of Hank Jr.'s career, see no. 51.

The performance went down as one of the great moments in country music history, and he walked off the stage as the biggest star country music had ever known.

Three years later he was dead.

What happened was those demons caught up with him, hounded him and finally ran him into the ground. He became a parody of himself, and his fans began coming to his concerts, perversely to see if he could really stand on stage through the whole thing without falling off. Yet he did go on—the promoters *made* him go on. Whether the people were paying to see Hank Williams sing or to see him die a little bit on stage didn't make a damn bit of difference, as long as the people were paying.

In 1951 Daddy's "Cold, Cold Heart" became a million-selling pop hit for Tony Bennett.

The next year, Daddy was fired from the Grand Ole Opry and sent back in shame to the Louisiana Hayride in Shreveport.

The very promoters who'd forced him on stage refused to book him any longer, because he was a "drunk."

The top record of 1952 was Daddy's "Jambalaya."[†]

Finally, even Mother had had enough, and she filed for divorce. Ever the businesswoman, she demanded—and got—fifty percent of the future royalties to his songs. Hank moved out of the house on Franklin Road and into an apartment with another aspiring singer named Ray Price. The divorce was final in May 1952, and even then he never stopped begging her to take him back.

Not even after he decided to get married again. He'd met Billie Jean Jones Eshlimar [Eshliman] backstage while he was still at the Opry, and Billie Jean was seeing Faron Young. Daddy proposed in the autumn, and he and Billie Jean were married not once, but *three* times: once by a justice of the peace in New Orleans [*sic*], then twice on stage in Shreveport [*sic*] before the paying customers. Twice, because the first performance was sold out.

It was pathetic.

Daddy had gotten a good booking for New Year's Day in Canton, Ohio, and he left early to drive through a blinding snowstorm that had blanketed Tennessee that weekend.[‡] Daddy had hired a driver named Charles Carr to drive him to Canton and had talked him into stopping along the way for Daddy

---

[†] According to *Billboard*, the top country-and-western record of 1952 was Hank Thompson's "Wild Side of Life," in both retail sales and jukebox play. Williams's "Jambalaya (On the Bayou)" ranked third and eighth, respectively, on those charts.

[‡] Several of these details of Hank Williams's last trip conflict with those presented in his major biographies.

to get a shot of painkiller for his back. Carr began to worry that Hank was lying so quietly, and in Oak Hill, West Virginia, he stopped to check.

Daddy was dead.

The autopsy said heart failure linked to excessive drinking, and so it was.

His biggest song of 1953 was "I'll Never Get Out of This World Alive."[§]

Mother claimed until the day she died that she and Hank had decided to get back together, just as soon as he got back from Ohio, and I'll always believe that.

Nashville was left in the lurch—what to do now that the legend was dead?

That question happened to coincide with the same question asked by my mother, and the answers came out the same. Nashville wholeheartedly adopted the Cult of Hank Williams, and the way Hank done it became, quite honestly, the only way to go.

To hear the tributes, one would think that the entire city took turns kissing Daddy while he was still alive. Everybody loved Hank. Everybody worried over his, ahem, "excesses." Everybody tried to help him.

While he was alive, he was despised and envied; after he died, he was some kind of saint. And that's exactly how Nashville decided to treat Daddy—country music's first authentic saint.

I was the chosen son.

But, underneath all the squeaky clean tributes and the "Hank Williams, bless his name" from the stage of the Grand Ole Opry, there was a whole other Hank Williams myth being born. It's a myth that I ran right smack into, and it changed my life.

Simply this: A lot of people were not nearly as blind as the powers-that-be in Nashville thought they were, and what they saw wasn't the same as what they heard described from the stage of the Grand Ole Opry. What they saw was a great man slipping into a maelstrom of drugs and liquor while his "friends" stood by, unwilling or unable to help. A whole new generation of singers and songwriters, inspired by the Hank Williams story, were trapped along the sidelines while every cliché in the book came true. Money couldn't buy happiness. Suffering led to flights of genius. Business success led to personal failure. He lived fast, died young, and left a beautiful corpse.

While the city boys mourned the passing of James Dean, the rebel without a cause, the country boys were mourning the death of their own rebel and wondering about his causes. It was a time, in the early 1950s, of martyrs.

[§] Although Williams's recording of this song was a posthumous No. 1 hit for one week in late January 1953, three of his other hits enjoyed better chart success, including "Kaw-Liga," which occupied the top spot for thirteen weeks, earning it the honor of being named *Billboard*'s Top Country and Western Record of 1953.

While the Opry was piously evoking Hank the Saint, Hank the Hellraiser was capturing the soul of country music. It's still that way today.

Gotta go down in flames? Gotta die young? Gotta drink till you can't stand on stage anymore? I've heard it all my life, folks, and I'm not buying any more.

~~~~~~

| 41 |

Minnie Pearl (with Joan Dew): Excerpt from *Minnie Pearl: An Autobiography*

Of all Hank Williams's fellow *Grand Ole Opry* cast members, Minnie Pearl perhaps knew him best. Certainly, none of them has reminisced about him more eloquently or insightfully. Minnie Pearl was the stage name and alter ego of Sarah Ophelia (Colley) Cannon (1912–1996), a classically trained actress and drama coach originally from Centerville, Tennessee, who won international acclaim as a country comedian on the *Grand Ole Opry* between 1940 and 1991, and later, between 1969 and 1991, on television's *Hee Haw*. She spent her entire professional career playing a naive, gangly, man-hungry country spinster best known for her trademark top-of-the-lungs greeting of "How-dee! I'm just so proud to be here!" and the price tag dangling from her straw hat. Pearl was inducted into the Country Music Hall of Fame in 1975 as, in the words of the bronze plaque honoring her, "the first country music humorist to be known and loved worldwide."

In her 1980 memoir, *Minnie Pearl: An Autobiography*, written with Joan Dew, Pearl devotes a chapter to Hank Williams, and her thoughtful and by then well-rehearsed anecdotes are often extensively quoted in other authors' writings about him. Pearl paints a darker and more disturbing portrait of the singer in her memoir than she did in a 1954 *Montgomery Advertiser* interview she gave on the occasion of the first Hank Williams Memorial Day.[*] In the earlier piece, she had praised the universal appeal of his music and his captivating power as a stage performer while recalling little-known aspects of his personality. Shifting historical perspectives and a more tolerant cultural climate no doubt allowed her to be more candid in 1980 than she had been a quarter century earlier.

SOURCE Minnie Pearl, with Joan Dew, *Minnie Pearl: An Autobiography* (New York: Simon and Schuster, 1980), 210–16. Used by permission.
[*] James K. Hutsell, "Minnie Pearl Describes Hank Williams as She Knew Him in Opry," *Montgomery Advertiser*, September 5, 1954.

I had first met Hank Williams during World War II. It wasn't long after the Camel Caravan,[†] when I was still with Pee Wee King. We were playing Dothan, Alabama, and Pee Wee had asked us to go down to the local radio station that afternoon to do a promotion spot. I had a severe sore throat. I was hoarse and had no business being there, but we never thought of not working because we were sick. [. . .]

When we walked into the lobby of the radio station, which was upstairs in an old building, I noticed a couple sitting there. The man looked like he was down on his luck. He was wearing a tan suit, boots and a cowboy hat that was slightly soiled. He was tall, thin—terribly thin—and hollow-eyed. He appeared to be in his early twenties. The woman was a very attractive blonde with beautiful skin and a good figure. Pee Wee introduced them as Hank and Audrey Williams. I had never heard of Hank Williams, but Pee Wee had. He had negotiated with him to buy a song for Becky Barfield called "I Am Praying for the Day That Peace Will Come." Pee Wee gave him $20 for the song.

Many people have asked me if I experienced a prescience of his greatness when I met Hank. I didn't feel anything. When I met Brenda Lee I felt it. I knew instantly that that child had something very special. But I haven't felt it often, and I didn't feel it with Hank. Of course, I hadn't seen him perform. He was living in Montgomery then, working clubs locally, and he had come to Dothan just to see Pee Wee and sell his song. I do remember being touched by the sight of him because he was so pitifully thin.

I mentioned to Audrey that I was sick, and she offered to take me to a doctor, saying she knew one in Dothan. She was very kind. She and I went alone, leaving the others at the radio station. When we went out to get into their car, I noticed the fender was smashed. She said, "We had an accident recently, and we've been so busy we just haven't had time to put the car in the shop and get it fixed."

It didn't appear to be a recent dent, and I surmised they simply didn't have the money to fix the fender. But she was too proud to say so. Audrey was a very proud woman, and I think this time she was showing wifely pride to cover for Hank. I believe she was terribly in love with him then, although people said later that she wasn't. Thinking back on the looks she gave him and the manner

---

[†] A traveling revue, sponsored by the R. J. Reynolds Tobacco Company (the manufacturer of Camel cigarettes) and comprised of some two dozen *Grand Ole Opry* stars, that was organized to provide entertainment for U.S. military personnel during the early years of World War II. The Camel Caravan on which both Pearl and King performed ended in December 1942, and biographer Colin Escott has suggested that this first meeting between Pearl and Williams occurred sometime in the late summer or early fall of 1943.

in which she tried to protect him, I think she loved him deeply, and there was no doubt about his love for her.

It was one of the tragedies of our business that Audrey and Hank had such a star-crossed romance. Their marriage ended bitterly in a divorce about a year before he died, and a number of people in country music were critical of her. They thought she aggravated Hank's alcohol problem. But I think his sickness went way back to childhood, long before Audrey came into his life. I always liked her, and I mourned her death, just as I mourned his.

It wasn't long before we were all hearing a great deal about Hank Williams. When he hit, he exploded. He was the biggest thing country music had ever seen, and the fans absolutely adored him. His charisma on stage was unsurpassed. Elvis later had that effect on an audience, but in the beginning most of his fans were teenage girls who responded to his gyrations as much as to his music. Hank appealed to all ages, and both sexes, and he didn't have to move a finger.

The first time I actually saw him work was on a tour in 1948[‡] when [my husband] Henry [Cannon][§] and one of his pilots flew us out West in a DC-3. Hank had not joined the Opry then, but was working on [the] Louisiana Hayride, a popular country show from Shreveport. I recognized him as being the man I'd met in Dothan, but he was a different person. He was alert and bright-eyed, with a fine wardrobe and a clean white hat. He was on his way.

Oscar Davis, the promoter of the tour, had set Hank to go on just before I did. As I said, I'd never seen him perform, although I had heard him sing on the radio. His song "Lovesick Blues" was already on the charts.

When the time came for him to work, I went to the wings to watch him. He ambled out on stage with his guitar and started singing. An excitement seemed to spread through the crowd, continuing to grow as he sang several songs. By the time he got to his last number the excitement had grown to a fever pitch. The crowd would not let him leave the stage. The rest of us on the show might as well have stayed at the airport—especially me, who had to follow him.

After umpteen encores they finally got Hank off and me on. It was not one of my better shows. They still wanted more of Hank! And I didn't blame them. The man had something indefinable, something that made an audience crave more.

[‡] If Pearl's following recollection of Williams's "Lovesick Blues" being on the record charts at the time of this western tour is correct, then the year was 1949, since his recording of this song was not released until February of that year and did not chart until early the following month. Colin Escott dates the tour that Pearl describes to mid- to late April 1949.

[§] Henry R. Cannon (1917–1997), Pearl's husband and business manager, was a pilot who operated a Nashville-based chartered flight service that often flew Opry stars to show dates.

I told Oscar after the show—and every other promoter after that—"*Never* put me on after Hank Williams!" And I never followed him again.

Bob Hope had a similar experience with Hank when we were in Louisville working the Hadacol Tour.¶ Bob had been brought in especially for that show. As a superstar of radio and movies, they naturally set him to close [the show]. Everyone was amazed (everyone except us hillbillies) when Hope had to wait, and wait, and wait, and wait, while Hank took encore after encore. Hank finally walked out on stage without his guitar and said very simply, "Folks, I thank you a lot, but we've got a mighty big act waitin' to come on, so I'd better leave."

After Hank joined the Opry in 1949, he and I worked together frequently and we became close friends. I adored him. Then Henry began flying him and they became very close. I think he considered Henry one of the few people he could trust implicitly. They had some great times together, and they also had some serious moments when Hank would open up and be uncharacteristically revealing about himself. He wrote "Jambalaya" on one of his flights with Henry.

Hank once made the most incredible remark I ever heard anyone make about their mother. He told us he used to get into a lot of honky-tonk brawls when he was still a kid living at home. One night a guy beat him up so badly he was left for dead in a roadhouse parking lot. A cab driver had been called by someone else, and when he pulled in to pick up his fare the headlights hit Hank, lying there unconscious in a pool of blood. The cabbie recognized him and took him home to his mother. She looked at his wounds, then said, "First we get you sewed up; then we go get him." Hank said, "Minnie, there ain't nobody in the world I'd rather have alongside me in a fight than my mama with a broken beer bottle in her hand." He said it as though it was nothing out of the ordinary at all.

Through his songs of heartbreak and loneliness, and his tragic personal life, Hank's image became one of a sad, hopeless man. But he was actually one of the funniest men I ever knew. He had a wry sense of humor, much like Henry's (which might be one of the reasons they took to one another so readily), and he loved to tell stories on people. He never played the star. He was always close to his band members, and they were very fond of him.

I like to remember Hank as he was at his peak—with a twinkle in his eyes, his wardrobe immaculate, and *killing* them with his show and his unforgettable songs. But something he said to me the last time we were alone will always stick in my mind. It was a horrible day.

¶ See footnote in no. 37.

Hank, Ernest Tubb and I were booked to play San Diego.‖ I had flown out alone after the Opry Saturday night because Henry had a charter flight. I went over to the auditorium about 2:30, and the people were already coming in for the three o'clock matinee. Ernest and Hank were arriving from Bakersfield, where they had played the night before. I was surprised they weren't in yet, because their musicians had to set up. [...] The promoter was already walking the floor. Then word came that Tubb had had car trouble and that Hank was in really bad shape physically. But they were on their way. The promoter waited as long as he could—the crowd was growing more restless by the minute—then asked me if I'd go on and open. I had never opened a show, but I felt sorry for the man so I agreed. I told the audience that car trouble had delayed the others, then I started telling gags with one ear tuned to backstage so I could hear them come in. Finally, after about 15 minutes, I heard the musicians arrive, so I told the crowd I'd let Ernest Tubb reopen the show and I'd be back later.

I got off just in time to see this pathetic, emaciated, haunted-looking, tragic figure of a man being assisted through the stage door—not too gently—by a male nurse. The male nurse had undoubtedly had enough problems with Hank to warrant being impatient with him, but it upset me to see my friend handled that way. When you love a child you don't want the child to be treated roughly, even if he's being a brat, and that's the way I felt about Hank. He was like a pitiful lost child to me, and I had never seen him in as bad shape as he was that day. I ran to him and hugged him. He threw his arms around me and clung to me, crying. I tried to comfort him, to tell him that everything was going to be all right, just as you would try to comfort a child crying in the dark. No one will ever know what tortured dreams he had. Perhaps all of life was a bad dream to Hank. By this time he was killing himself with drugs and alcohol, and his mind had undoubtedly been severely affected.

It broke my heart to see this incredibly talented, sweet man in the depths of despair and pain, and I begged the promoter not to put him on. It was so *cruel*. They wouldn't have put a man dying of cancer out there on stage for people to gawk at. Nowadays a star of that caliber would have a manager, or someone in authority, who wouldn't allow him to be seen in that condition. But in those days management and career guidance as it is known in Hollywood hadn't reached country music, and the hillbillies were on their own.

The promoter was determined Hank Williams was going to perform that day if he had to carry him out there on a stretcher. They started pouring coffee

---

‖ In at least one earlier tape-recorded interview, Pearl places the famous incident she relates here in El Paso, Texas, while some researchers claim this episode actually occurred in Sacramento, California.

down him. They walked him back and forth. They dunked his face in cold water. Finally they somehow got him into his wardrobe and steered him toward the stage. It was pathetic. It tore me apart to see him out there trying to sing, his voice cracking, hanging on to the microphone for dear life, a sickening caricature of the superb, magnetic performer he had been at the height of his career.

The audience was not kind. I could understand their disappointment and sympathize with them. They had paid to see *Hank Williams*, not this sad, sick man who belonged in a hospital. But I was angry with them, too. I wanted them to show more empathy for him in his condition, even if the illness was self-inflicted.

After the show the promoter told me he wanted me and his wife to drive Hank around town until the next performance at 8 p.m. to keep an eye on him. Hopefully, he would sober up in that time. "He'll do what you tell him to do," the man said. He obviously hadn't had much experience with anyone strung out on pills and whiskey. In the state Hank was in, he wouldn't have listened to his own mother. But I went along because I didn't want him left alone with these people who didn't love him, who saw him as a piece of merchandise they'd bought for the day.

That was the longest automobile ride I've ever had in my life. We actually drove around for only a couple of hours, but it seemed like an eternity. Hank was *really* hurting by then. They had already kept him off the stuff for four or five hours and his body was craving help. He kept asking us to stop the car, trying to come up with every excuse he could think of to get us to pull over. He was all bent over in the front seat, his hair in disarray, hunched forward with his thin arms crossed tightly over his abdomen.

I was trying to think of *anything* that would take his mind off whiskey, so I said, "Come on, Hank. Let's sing." I started singing "I Saw the Light," a gospel song he had written several years earlier. He joined in, his voice cracking and off-key, then suddenly he stopped and looked at me. He put his hand on mine and said, *"That's just it, Minnie. There ain't no light. It's all dark."*

It was the pitiful cry of a man alone at his road's end. He lived about six months after that, and no one knows how much more suffering and hell he went through before he died on New Year's Eve [*sic*], 1953. The autopsy said he died of an overdose of pills and alcohol,** but I think those were the instruments of his death, not the cause. The cause lay somewhere deep in his psyche, and only God knows what went on there.

** This statement is at odds with Williams's official cause of death, as reported on his death certificate.

It's difficult to realize he was only 29 years old when he died, because his body was so worn from all the abuse he'd given it. There's no telling what heights he could have reached had he been able to straighten himself out and enjoy a normal lifespan. He was one of the most prolific songwriters ever born, and there is little doubt that he had many, many more hit songs left in his mind and heart when he died.

Henry and I feel privileged that we were around him during his happy times and saw more of that side than we did the other. It's odd, but neither of us ever saw Hank take a drink. Nor did we ever see him use drugs of any kind. We were around him many times when we knew he was under the influence of something, but we never knew what. Over the years he has been immortalized and is now considered a legend in our business. He would have found that amusing. He was just a regular funny ole boy raised in Alabama, as down to earth as dirt. But he had that awesome talent. We've never seen another like him in country music, and I doubt we ever will.

~~~~~~

| 42 |

Chet Flippo: Excerpt from *Your Cheatin' Heart: A Biography of Hank Williams*

Of all the major biographies of the famous singer, Chet Flippo's *Your Cheatin' Heart: A Biography of Hank Williams* (1981) remains the most shocking, riveting, and controversial. Flippo not only portrays Williams as a reckless and irresponsible alcoholic, drug addict, and womanizer, but also describes him secretly purchasing songs from other songwriters, exhibiting open contempt for his audience, and relentlessly abusing his family, friends, and band members. Sullen, profane, and cynical, Flippo's Hank Williams carries deep psychological scars from his impoverished childhood and broken home, and bitterly resents his mother Lillie and his wife Audrey. Oddly, Flippo still manages to elicit readers' sympathy for his subject, who comes across as a damaged individual trapped by forces beyond his control or comprehension, and incapable of finding solace or joy.

A native of Fort Worth, Texas, Flippo (1943–2013) recalled first hearing Williams on the radio during the summer of 1951. Some twenty-five years later, while working as an editor at *Rolling Stone* magazine, he decided to write a

SOURCE   Chet Flippo, *Your Cheatin' Heart: A Biography of Hank Williams* (New York: Simon and Schuster, 1981), 165–69. © 1981 Chet Flippo. Used by permission.

biography of the country music star at the suggestion of a book editor, and then spent three years researching the project. In the process, Flippo uncovered a wealth of previously unused sources, some of which contained startling information: medical reports that identified Williams's painful congenital spinal condition; accounts that suggested Paul Gilley, a Kentucky college basketball player, had written early versions of several of Williams's best-loved songs; Oklahoma state legislature files that detailed the criminal activities of Toby Marshall, the quack doctor who supplied Williams with the lethal drug chloral hydrate; and even the last scribbled lyrics that Williams ever wrote, which were found on the floorboard of the car in which he died. These discoveries notwithstanding, Flippo believed that his book would have constituted "just another fan story" had he not also acquired access to Audrey Williams's unpublished memoir and private papers, which detail her tempestuous relationship with her husband.

Flippo employs a narrative technique that he calls "extrapolation," in which he recreates Williams's thoughts and reconstructs entire conversations. The result is a book that crackles, as Flippo put it, with the "immediacy and fire" that he believed the legendary singer's life deserved. It also generated considerable controversy. No less a figure than Johnny Cash, for example, took to the pages of *Country Music* magazine to criticize what he called a "cheap shot" of a biography and its grossly distorted, one-sided portrayal of Williams. Yet Flippo staunchly defended his work, insisting in one interview, "There is no incident in this book that didn't happen."

Published at a time when scandalous celebrity exposés were becoming increasingly common, *Your Cheatin' Heart* exerted little observable effect on Williams's posthumous popularity and, if anything, enhanced his stature among many of his fans, who somehow identified with the doomed star that Flippo managed to bring to life. As shown in this excerpt depicting his subject on tour in mid- to late 1951, Flippo grippingly recreates Hank Williams's sad, sordid, and inexorable decline.

Hank was back out on the road in a fury: if nothing else, he still had his audience. He was performing with an intensity that the [Drifting] Cowboys hadn't known was there, a reservoir of energy above his usual effort. Offstage, he spoke little. He was moody, his band decided.

He was also having to pay off a few people to hush certain things up in the area of offstage behavior. In Chattanooga, a hotel maid went into his room to clean and found him putting a needle into his arm. When he saw her, he reached for a pistol, aimed at her and pulled the trigger. The gun misfired, and she knocked him out with a lamp over the head. In Birmingham, he gathered framed portraits from the hotel's hallway, lined them up, and used them for target practice. Police caught him in his hotel room with a fifteen-year-old girl, who was stripping for him while he played guitar. The police everywhere were usually pretty tolerant of him, but his cases of entertaining minor girls cost him a little bit.* He started telling police he was actually Herman P. Willis,† which didn't always work, or that he was George Morgan,‡ which did work several times. He would sing Morgan's hit "Candy Kisses" to prove that was who he was. Morgan was furious when he found out that he was acquiring a police record, but he was afraid of Hank.

Hank's board of directors—WSM, Acuff-Rose, the Opry, Audrey, and Lilly— saw that Hank was meeting his touring obligations and that looked fine to them. He didn't seem to be writing songs and was not recording at all. He and Pappy [Fred Rose] didn't talk often. Sometimes when they did, the talk was distant and abrupt, like the time Hank threatened to leave both M-G-M and Acuff-Rose.

"Go ahead, Hank, if you're so goddamn independent," Pappy snapped.

"Now, Pappy, I was just kiddin'."

"Well, I *wasn't.*"

That had scared Hank a little. He used to stand up to Pappy. When he first brought his Drifting Cowboys in to recording sessions with him instead of using studio musicians the way they had done before, Pappy objected. Hank had stood up for his Cowboys.

"Pappy, if these boys are good enough to play on stage with me, they're good enough to be on record with me. Besides, I got to sleep with these boys on the road."

He had won that argument, just like he had won some earlier ones about song selection and even about very minor things. Hank pronounced the word "picture" as "pitcher" and couldn't change that and insisted on recording it that way, over Pappy's objections.

But now Pappy sounded... *indifferent.* Was it just Hank's imagination, or were things kind of conspiring against him? Bad luck seemed to be always a step ahead of him. It had scared him in New York when he'd finally sobered up and heard what he'd done. He and Don Helms§ had flown up to do "Hey, Good Lookin'" on The Kate Smith Show. At first they wouldn't let him bring any of his musicians up but he had told them he had to have Shag and his steel guitar

---

* These anecdotes originally appeared in Sanford Mabrie's 1955 *Behind the Scene* exposé, "The Strange Life and Death of Hank Williams" (no. 23).

† A pseudonym Williams often used to register in hotels in order to maintain his privacy.

‡ A fellow *Grand Ole Opry* star (1924–1975), whom, according to several accounts, Williams despised.

§ The Drifting Cowboys' steel guitarist (1927–2008), whom Williams called "Shag," in reference to Helms's longer-than-fashionable wavy hair.

or it wouldn't sound like Hank Williams. Hank didn't like New York City a damn bit, to start with. He had almost gotten into fights with a couple of waiters in restaurants who tried to make him take off his hat. Then he'd gotten drunk. M-G-M's [president and general manager] Frank Walker came over to Hank's suite at the Savoy Hotel, and Hank got to fooling around and shoved Walker, who fell against the radiator and hit his head and knocked himself out. Hank was too drunk to notice. The hotel maid came in to turn down the bed and found two figures laid out on the floor—one with a bloodied head—and called for help. Hank was bitterly ashamed when he came around and learned what had happened. He had let himself down, had let his weaknesses betray him. He quit drinking for a while. But now and again he had to have the drugs, when his back was aching so and he would call home five times a day and Audrey was never there. Morphine could dull the ache pretty quickly.

Hank snored on. The woman got out of the bed and threw up in the direction of the wastebasket, thin ropy strings of whiskey and brown foam streaking the rug. When the convulsions from her dry heaves finally stopped, she rolled over in a ball and cursed Hank Williams. Some fuckin' king of country music...can't even get it up...fuckin' drunk...just wants a blowjob...fucker will by Gawd pay for this. She knee-crawled into the bathroom and threw up a cupful of foam, hauled herself to her knees by the sink and threw cold water over her face. When she could walk, she located her step-ins and dress. On her way out of the room, she rifled Hank's pockets and came up with $437. Shoulda been more. Cocksucker.

If he moved, the pain moved and got worse. So he tried to will his aching body to lie still. Mercifully, the light was off and the curtain was drawn over the window. Still, what little light there was hurt his eyes when he opened them. He had no idea where he was, not even what city he was in, or what time it was or even what day. The last thing he remembered was staggering onstage in Oklahoma City. Or was it San Antonio? All the goddamn cities looked the same to him these days. He barely remembered that the doctor had given him a shot of something in his left arm, and he could still feel a slight sting there where he had had to dig around with the syringe before finding a vein that would accept the needle. He remembered holding onto the microphone stand to keep from falling off the stage and looking down off the low wooden stage into the first few rows of people and seeing the mockery and derision in some of those eyes. He remembered singing "Jambalaya."¶ Or was it "Lovesick [Blues]"? And

---

¶ While in this excerpt Flippo appears to be discussing the year 1951, his reference to "Jambalaya (On the Bayou)" appears confused, since Williams did not record the song until June 1952.

forgetting the words; the goddamn words were there in his mind but they slid around somehow and just wouldn't make it down to his voice, goddamn it. He had tried to explain to the people how he felt. But they could never know.

He squeezed his eyes tight, so tight that he saw stars flashing under his swollen eyelids and tried to forget that. He tried to pretend that he was invisible, like he would sometimes do at parties, when he would hide under a coffee table or squeeze into a corner and then no one could see him and if someone did talk to him he would just say, "This ain't' ole Hank. Ole Hank done left. I'm George Morgan." Or sometimes he would be Herman P. Willis, which was his favorite. The other person would be named Herman, too. That way, they could never get to him.

He thought maybe if he became invisible, the pain would have no body to inhabit and would go away. He gripped the chenille bedspread and willed himself invisible. It wasn't working. The pain spread and seemed like a white ball of heat broiling throughout his right side. It was swollen and throbbing. His lower back was a huge needle of pain. He could feel his swollen liver pressing against his ribs. He felt around on the floor with his right hand. Thank God. There was some beer left that was still fairly cold. He sat up long enough— goddamn, the pain!—to find the church key and popped a bottle of Jax and drank half in one long swallow and praised God that it stayed down. He grabbed another bottle and lay back and pressed the cold bottle against his aching liver. That helped some. Oh God. What now? He couldn't take a deep breath without it hurting, he couldn't goddamn move. He prayed to sweet Jesus that he didn't have to play a show somewhere that night; it would kill him, he knew it would, if he had to do that. Please God, let me rest, he prayed. Involuntarily he began weeping, silently, the tears coursing down his gaunt, unshaven cheeks. Dear God, sweet Jesus, just let me *live*, let me live to see my sweet baby boy, my little Bocephus.‖ God, I'll do anything for you, I'll quit drinking, I'll go to church but please dear God drive out this pain and let me *live*.

Where did things go wrong? He and Audrey had been happy once, they were a real family, and he had his horses and dogs and could go fishing. And the crowds loved him, goddammit! They loved ole Hank. Nobody but nobody could follow him on stage, not even that goddamn Bob Hope on the Hadacol Caravan.** Nobody could close a show like ole Hank.

It was just that constant pain in his back, that fucking stabbing pain that would sometimes drive him to his knees with tears of pain. It wouldn't leave him alone. And Audrey—that motherfucking whore of a bitch Audrey who

---

‖ Williams's nickname for his infant son, Randall (Hank Williams, Jr.) (b. 1949).

** See footnote in no. 37.

wouldn't leave him alone and spent twice what he made and was running around with everything in pants in Nashville, he was sure of that. He ought to kill her and just be done with it. The worst mistake he ever made—no, the second worst, the fucking worst one was marrying the bitch—was letting her get up on stage and sing with him. The cunt couldn't carry a tune in a wheelbarrow, but she thought she was singing like a goddamn bird. A fucking buzzard. Yeah, like a fucking ugly turkey buzzard. Jesus. If he killed Audrey, Lilly would come after him with the wrath of God and he was more scared of Lilly than of Audrey. You can't kill your mother. You could get away with killing your wife—people would understand that—but not your sweet old mother. If only he could disappear, just become invisible like The Shadow,‡‡ it would all be so easy. Maybe just vanish into the bayous down in south Louisiana with the Cajuns. Now *there* were some goddamn people who appreciated ole Hank. Gumbo and beer on Saturday night. Maybe they would hide ole Hank while he just kinda rested up and got his strength back. But then he wouldn't be able to see little Bocephus. What the fuck was he gonna do?

He heard the door open and could hear a soft footfall on the wooden floor. He opened one eye and flinched and cursed. Goddamn. All he could see swimming into his blurred field of vision was the doctor. And he was opening his goddamn black bag and taking out a needle.

"Hank. How ya feel, son? You gotta be onstage in an hour."

Hank wept.

~~~~~~

| 43 |

John Morthland: Excerpt from *The Best of Country Music*

While Greil Marcus contended that Hank Williams represented an older, conservative southern musical tradition distinct from rock 'n' roll (no. 36), other critics, such as *Rolling Stone's* record editor Dave Marsh, considered the singer one of rock music's earliest pioneers and most influential artists. For John Morthland, though, Williams's most important quality was the degree to

---

SOURCE John Morthland, *The Best of Country Music* (Garden City, N.Y.: Doubleday, 1984), 203–5. Reprinted with the permission of John Morthland.

‡‡ A mysterious crime-fighting hero who appeared in a popular radio program between 1930 and 1954, as well as in a series of contemporaneous pulp novels, detective magazines, comic books, low-budget films, and movie serials.

which he ultimately transcended music altogether, and served as a transitional figure who hastened the South's integration into the American mainstream.

Morthland (b. 1947) grew up in San Bernardino, California, and, while still in high school, made a name for himself by becoming the first American reporter to interview the Rolling Stones during the band's initial U.S. tour. He went on to attend the University of California, Berkeley, where Greil Marcus, then an editor at *Rolling Stone*, befriended him and, in 1969, hired him as a record reviewer. After Morthland moved to *Creem* magazine in 1974, his interest turned increasingly to introducing country music, and especially Hank Williams, to the literate rock fans who made up the bulk of the magazine's readership. As part of this mission, he published *The Best of Country Music* (1984), "a critical history" of the genre in the form of a consumer guide to its essential albums. In this excerpt, a review of Time-Life's three-LP boxed set, *Hank Williams: Country & Western Classics* (1981), Morthland generally concurs with Marcus's interpretation of Williams as an artist who failed to overcome the cultural limitations of his class and region. Rather than depicting him as a tragic figure, though, Morthland, instead elevates him to heroic status. Hank Williams may never have achieved crossover stardom, but by the time he died, Morthland asserts, "for better or worse, he had brought the modern world into country music, and then he had brought country music into the modern world."

In listening to this [boxed set], I'm struck mainly by how inadequate criticism is in pinning down Hank's music and his power. Instead, I keep thinking of the way his songs were used in the movie *The Last Picture Show** both to orchestrate the isolation of those small-town characters and to reinforce the fact that even in what appear to be dead-end situations, lives and dreams go on, with people doing the best they can whether they understand or not what's happening to them.

Hank's music is mainly about limits, and you can take that several ways. Most obviously, "Honkin Tonkin'," "Hey, Good Lookin'," "Honky Tonk Blues," "Settin' the Woods on Fire" and others all aim for a good time on Saturday night, but it's nothing symbolic or metaphorical, and really not even anything special. That's all they *dare* aim for, because in the grinding, numbing poverty of the rural South that produced Hank Williams, release or escape could never be more than temporary.

---

* A 1971 Academy Award–winning film, directed by Peter Bogdanovich and based on Larry Mc-Murtry's semi-autobiographical 1966 novel of that same title. The movie's soundtrack employed nine Hank Williams recordings (as well as Tony Bennett's cover version of Williams's "Cold, Cold Heart") in order to evoke its setting of a small, desolate north Texas town during 1951–1952.

Then there were the limits set up by the feudalistic system that was the Grand Ole Opry, which was the only show in town. The Opry resisted hiring Hank Williams at first because of his drinking, and then hired him only when he'd become so popular there was no choice. Still, the powers behind the Opry seemed to keep their fingers crossed that he'd fail, and they moved swiftly to fire him when he did. Once he was safely dead, the same people lionized him because now he was no threat. (He was elected to the [Country Music] Hall of Fame in 1961.) The fans represented still more limits. He had started out just like them, white working folks scraping to get by, and though they didn't begrudge him his success—they welcomed it, for it held out hope to them, too—they did not want him to ever rise above them, though he could hardly help it under the circumstances. It was a double bind, but one he could appreciate, for he knew all about double binds; his marriage, the bad back that hampered him all his life and probably caused some of his erratic behavior, the dependencies on drugs and liquor, all gave him plenty of experience in that department.

Hank was a child of the transitional South. You could hear it in his music, which echoed everything from traditional Appalachian string-band music to the most modern pop-oriented performers. You could hear it in his lyrics, which utilized both archaic language obsolete since he was a child and the latest slang. But most of all, you could hear it in the stories he told. Here was the postwar American South, hurtling from a rural to an urban culture, from agrarian to industrial, from underdeveloped to technological, from oral traditions to mass media. It was unsettling, disorienting. And here was a man who didn't speak to those issues directly, but spoke in terms of the turmoil in his personal life, and did so in a style that made it appear he was talking to each person in his audience on an individual basis. Of course these people would understand that one-to-one approach best, because that was the way their culture had always communicated best. And what this man was saying was that his life was a shambles, he had no control over anything, everything was going too fast, he was torn up from his roots and on a treadmill he couldn't escape.

Williams gave shape, gave a certain kind of proud and defiant dignity, to those fears. But he was frail, both physically and emotionally, and he had little education or training in dealing with the larger world around him. He could never really overcome those fears and obstacles, wasn't really equipped to even give it a very good try (and might not have bothered had he been able to). In articulating them so well, though, he took country music, as people then knew it, as far as it could go—and then those limits rose up again. His songs were being covered regularly by pop artists, which Hank loved because he craved both the money and the respectability such cover versions brought him. But he

202 | SCENES FROM THE LOST HIGHWAY

was never able to even consider going pop himself—he was too hillbilly. In a working-class South that had, since Reconstruction, gotten used to abuse and exploitation from the North, that was as big a victory as Hank Williams could win at the time, but it was a significant start; for better or for worse, he had brought the modern world into country music, and then he had brought country music into the modern world. That, as much as any other reason, is why 25,000 people came to his funeral in Montgomery, Alabama, after he died in the back seat of his car on his way to a January 1, 1953, gig in Canton, Ohio.

When Jimmy Carter was elected President in 1976, I remember the commentary, nearly all of it pure drivel, about how this meant the South was finally being integrated into the rest of the country. But Carter, though he did have traditional southern traits, was also a nuclear engineer, a bureaucrat, and a technocrat who in most respects had been integrated into the American mainstream long ago, I thought. His ascendance wasn't the beginning of something new so much as it was the culmination, or confirmation, of a process that had begun three decades earlier with Hank Williams as much as anyone else.

HANK WILLIAMS

THE COMPLETE LYRICS

Including the LOST LYRICS to COUNTRY CLASSICS, and
the FIRST PUBLICATION of the LOST SONGS
by the KING of COUNTRY MUSIC

DON CUSIC | EDITOR

Cover of Don Cusic's book, *Hank Williams: The Complete Lyrics*, 1993. Courtesy of Don Cusic.

Part VI

~~~~~~

"Gone But Not Forgotten Blues"
Entering the American Mainstream (1985–1994)

Between 1985 and 1994, interest in Hank Williams escalated on a variety of fronts. For years MGM record executives had sought to "update" the late country star's recordings by adding artificial stereo sound and overdubbed instrumentation in the form of string sections and choruses (see no. 31 for Roger Williams's discussion of this process). But in 1972, Williams's recordings were acquired—some might say rescued—by the newly formed Dutch-German conglomerate PolyGram. Six years later, its subsidiary, Polydor Records, began to restore his musical legacy by returning his unmodified recordings to the market. Between 1985 and 1989, in the most exhaustive compilation to that point, the label released an ambitious series of eight double-LP sets that presented, in chronological order, all of Williams's then-known studio recordings and many of his nonsession recordings, remastered and in their original, undubbed form. Polydor followed up in 1990 with *Hank Williams: The Original Singles Collection...Plus*, a three-CD, eighty-four-track boxed set. In addition, the Country Music Foundation issued an album of his "demos" in 1985 and another of his earliest recordings the following year, while in 1993 Mercury Records released a two-CD set of Williams's "Health and Happiness Show" radio transcriptions. In 1989, the Country Music Foundation also co-produced a sixty-minute television tribute that originally aired on PBS, titled *In the Hank Williams Tradition*, which included commentary and performances by a roster of past and present country music luminaries. Meanwhile, Williams made headlines with his 1987 induction into the Rock and Roll Hall of Fame, and earned the top spot in *Life* magazine's special 1994 issue, the "100 Most Important People in the History of Country." But his rising stature was evident even beyond the music world. In an example of widespread approbation that few would have imagined possible only twenty years earlier, the U.S. Postal Service honored Williams with a 1993 commemorative postage stamp.

Clearly, mainstream assessments of once-derided "hillbilly" music in general and of Hank Williams in particular were changing dramatically. This was especially evident in the academic world, where the now-legendary country star became, for the first time ever, the subject of sustained scholarly attention. The 1980s and 1990s witnessed a new wave of humanities scholarship that bridged traditional disciplinary boundaries while employing a variety of theoretical approaches and methodologies. Scholars in American Studies, as well as those in cultural studies and the "new" social history, frequently analyzed marginalized groups and popular culture in order to challenge traditional, top-down historical narratives that focused on political and military leaders, and stressed social and cultural consensus. For some of these interdisciplinary scholars, Hank Williams and his songs illustrated significant yet overlooked themes in post–World War II American history. While approaching him with varied political agendas and from different scholarly perspectives, academic writers tended to expand on the "Populist Poet" theme, viewing Williams's life and songs as representative, in many respects, of the experiences of ordinary white working people in the twentieth-century American South.

Meanwhile, the struggle continued among nonacademics to define Williams as a human being and an artist. Was he a modified version of the "Model Family Man," as his stepdaughter Lycrecia Williams and long-lost daughter Jett Williams both suggested in their respective memoirs, *Still in Love with You: The Story of Hank and Audrey Williams* (1989) and *Ain't Nothing as Sweet as My Baby: The Story of Hank Williams' Lost Daughter* (1990)? Or was he, as others would have him, an early, trendsetting model of a debauched rock 'n' roller? While his immense talents as a songwriter were unquestioned, could Williams be better conceived of as a poet rather than as simply a lyricist? Such questions continued to elude definitive answers.

These were, however, just the sort of answers that Colin Escott promised to provide in his critically acclaimed *Hank Williams: The Biography* (1994), written with the assistance of George Merritt and William MacEwen. Escott's thorough research and his dogged determination to hew closely to the facts, he claimed, allowed him to debunk myths and "reclaim the real Hank Williams." While he did not ignore the scandalous details of the star's personal life, such matters were of secondary concern to Escott. By subordinating Williams's personal troubles to his professional achievements, Escott ended up offering a variation of the "Organization Man" interpretation. Generally downplaying the notion of Williams as an artist of unique creativity, Escott instead grounded the singer's story in the specific conditions of the mid-twentieth-century country music business. Thus, in producing what he hoped would be the final word on his subject, Escott harkened back, ironically, to the very theme that had dominated the press coverage during Hank Williams's lifetime: his central role as a representative of the early postwar Nashville music industry.

| 44 |

Kent Blaser: "Pictures from Life's Other Side": Hank Williams, Country Music, and Popular Culture in America

Since at least the time of the American Revolution, one of this nation's cherished patriotic creeds has been the belief in a distinctive "American character," a key feature of which is a strong sense of optimism. The decade of the 1950s, in particular, appears to epitomize this principle and was long conceived, both in scholarly studies and the public imagination, as an era of ideological consensus and upbeat self-confidence, with an attendant saccharine popular culture reflecting the country's mood. In his 1985 article excerpted below, however, Kent Blaser (1949–2010), then a history professor at Wayne State University, challenges such *Happy Days* interpretations of 1950s America through a close analysis of Hank Williams's life, career, and, above all, his songs. As Blaser points out, Williams's national popularity at mid-century reveals the existence of another America, an America drawn to the themes of sadness, loneliness, and fatalism that coursed through his musical catalog. A watershed in the Hank Williams literature, Blaser's article ranks among the first scholarly studies to analyze the country singer-songwriter as representing broad themes that characterized postwar American social and cultural history. In the ensuing decades, a lengthening parade of scholars, including Bill Koon, Curtis W. Ellison, Cecelia Tichi, and Barbara Ching, to name only a handful, would also find Williams's life and music fruitful subjects of academic study.

SOURCE   Kent Blaser, "'Pictures from Life's Other Side': Hank Williams, Country Music, and Popular Culture in America," *South Atlantic Quarterly* 84 (Winter 1985): 12, 16, 23–25, 26. Copyright 1985, Duke University Press. All rights reserved. Used by permission of the publisher.

"Pictures from Life's Other Side" is one of Williams's songs. A sentimental, mawkish "talkie"* about people defeated by life and "gone bad," it is not one of his better or more memorable efforts. In fact, the song was released under an alias, Luke the Drifter, a ploy Williams sometimes used for material that seemed in some way out of character or below his usual standards. But the importance of this particular title will become obvious as this story unfolds. [...] This essay proposes an alternative look at American society in the 1950s, using the career and popularity of Hank Williams as a vantage point from which to view the scene, and suggests that the postwar years are an apt focal point for reexamining the larger issue of American popular culture generally. [...]

The first impressions one is likely to receive from most of his music are sadness, lonesomeness, unhappiness, and a strong sense of fatalism. To make a difficult attempt at categorizing and quantifying intractable material, of fifty of Williams's most important songs, all but five deal with relationships between the sexes.[1] Of these forty-five, almost one-third involve the protagonist being left by the woman with whom he is in love. Other major themes include marriages or relationships in which both members' love has grown cold (11 percent); failure to find love, or unrequited love (14 percent); and "evil woman" songs describing a kind of love-hate relationship with a woman who treats the singer badly (16 percent). There are a scattering of rambling or hobo songs, drinking songs, a prison song, hymns, and seven novelty or miscellaneous songs, of which four describe general marital or personal problems, like the broken romance between the two wooden Indians in "Kaw-Liga." Of the fifty total, eight are moderately cheerful, upbeat songs, but five of these are in the honky-tonk, let's-have-a-party-and-get-drunk genre. All in all, there are *three* songs that deal in a reasonably positive way with love and the prospects for future happiness.[2]

Williams's music, then, was hardly a paean to American optimism, innocence, and the good life. A pet phrase, which he used as a signature to close many of his concerts, was "don't worry about nothin', 'cause it ain't gonna be all right no how." Even his titles reveal deep roots in the blues, the southern black music that contradicts in almost every way the typical popular-culture image of the 1950s. His songs include "Cold, Cold Heart," "The Blues Come Around," "Weary Blues From Waitin'," "Lovesick Blues," "Never Been So Lonesome," "Moanin' the Blues," "Long Gone Lonesome Blues," "I Don't Care If Tomorrow Never Comes," and "I'll Never Get Out of This World Alive." The first known song he wrote was titled "WPA Blues."

---

* A recitation, or spoken-word recording.

Williams is especially associated with a kind of music called "honky-tonk," a blend of country and blues that emerged from the rural South in the 1920s and 1930s. The "honky-tonk hero" (to use a phrase from a recent hit) is one of the major figures in Williams's songs. And the values portrayed often suggest the kind of rebellion against bourgeois morality that supposedly became a part of popular music only with the emergence of folk music and the birth of rock and roll later in the 1950s and 1960s.[3] Casual romance, living from day to day, a rejection of traditional morality are all parts of the honky-tonk life.

Indeed, in a variety of ways, Williams went out of his way to flaunt traditional ideas of "proper" behavior, marital bliss, and middle-class values generally. "Mind Your Own Business" relates the stormy relationship Williams had with his first wife and not too subtly chastises people who pry into his private life. From the beginning authorities at the [Grand Ole] Opry worried that Williams's reputation would damage their clean-cut family image. Williams and the Opry maintained, at best, an uneasy relationship until he was finally fired for drunkenness and missed engagements.

Williams did, of course, partake of some of the traditional popular culture of the 1950s. He styled himself after that quintessential American symbol of individualism, innocence, and optimism—the cowboy. He wore ostentatiously western clothes and called his band the Drifting Cowboys; he even ran away to join a rodeo as a teenager. All of this was perhaps sincere enough, but it was also almost entirely superficial. Williams sang almost no true western songs. Both his career and his music were a direct contradiction to the squeaky-clean cowboy image cultivated by the famous singing cowboys and western movie stars of the period—Roy Rogers, Gene Autry, or William Boyd (Hopalong Cassidy). As mentioned earlier, Williams wrote religious music, but surprisingly for an era and audience usually viewed as extremely religious, Williams's sacred songs were not among his top sellers, even though some of them have later come to be recognized as classics of the genre. Most of Williams's listeners apparently preferred honky-tonking, drinking, and frustrated love as themes.

Of course, "somebody-done-somebody-wrong" songs and "look-how-rotten-things-are-let's-get-drunk" songs are standards of country music generally.[4] Williams was unique only in the intensity and talent with which he pursued the theme, and in his wide popularity. It hardly appears coincidental that blues, country music, and Hank Williams all originated in the rural South. This may support C. Vann Woodward's contention that the South was long atypical in having a sense of defeat, pessimism, and irony not present in most of American culture.[5] But the fact that Williams brought country blues to a receptive, national audience in the 1950s, an audience that cut through the sectional limitations of earlier traditional country music, suggests that more of the nation was ready to tune in to such emotions and ideas than has usually been recognized. If Williams had fifteen million devoted fans, it was because his music told them something many of them knew was true—that life was not all easy and all right. Heartbreak and lonesomeness were part of it too, and people liked Williams for singing about it, and for living it.

So, where does all of this leave us in terms of popular culture in the 1950s? I certainly do not want to imply that previous perspectives on popular culture in the 1950s are wrong—only that there are some important alternatives. [...] Hank Williams's music gives us some "pictures from life's other side." His popularity suggests that sympathy with this "underground" aspect of popular culture was still significant in the 1950s, and more pervasive than is often realized. He had a wide appeal, and it was an appeal that penetrated to the supposed core of American culture—small town, rural, middle class America. At the very least this should make us wary of stereotyping too glibly *the* popular mind or culture of American society. Some Americans in the 1950s may indeed have been listening to Lawrence Welk, Billy Graham, Norman Vincent Peale, or Walt Disney, and singing along to popular songs that urged them to "accentuate the positive."[†] But many were also fans of Hank Williams—getting drunk, grinding his hips and swooning on stage, exuding what one critic called "raw sexual primitivism,"[6] and singing songs like "Mansion on the Hill" and "Wealth Won't Save Your Soul" that had transparent class and social implications. Williams represents tensions, traditions, and currents of the 1950s that have been too much ignored. His songs at least remind us that there was indeed an "other side" to American society. The 1950s weren't "Happy Days"[‡] for everyone.

NOTES

1 The sources for the following are Melvin Shatack [Shestack], ed., *The Songs of Hank Williams* (Nashville, n.d.); Joel Whilburn [Whitburn], *Top Country and Western Records, 1949–71* (Menomonee Falls, Wis., 1972); and the discography in Roger M. Williams's *Sing a Sad Song: The Life of Hank Williams* (New York, 1970).

[†] A reference to the upbeat 1944 pop song "Ac-Cent-Tchu-Ate the Positive," written by lyricist Johnny Mercer (1909–1976) and composer Harold Arlen (1905–1986).
[‡] A popular television sitcom, which aired on ABC between 1974 and 1984, that presented an idealized version of 1950s America.

2 This is almost identical to the findings of another study of the content of country songs generally. Dorothy A. Hortsman [Horstman], *Sing Your Heart Out, Country Boy* (New York, 1975).

3 See Herbert Goldberg, "Contemporary Popular Music," *Journal of Popular Culture* (Winter 1971 [1970]): 579–89, and [Douglas T.] Miller and [Marion] Novak [Nowak], *The Fifties[: The Way We Really Were]* [(Garden City, N.Y., 1977)], pp. 291–314.

4 See Hortsman, *Sing Your Heart Out [sic]*; Dean [Tudor] and Nancy Tudor, *Grass Roots Music* (Littleton, Colo., 1979); Ann Nietzke, "Doin' Somebody Wrong," *Human Behavior* (November 1975): 64–69; Eli Waldron, "Country Music I: The Death of Hank Williams," *Reporter*, 19 May 1955, 35–37; and [Nelson King] "Hillbilly Music Leaves the Hills," *Good Housekeeping*, June 1954, [18], for an interview with D. J. Nelson King.

5 C. Vann Woodward, *The Burden of Southern History* (Baton Rouge, 1970), pp. 213–33.

6 Tudor and Tudor, *Grass Roots Music*, p. 215.

| 45 |

Richard Leppert and George Lipsitz: "Everybody's Lonesome for Somebody": Age, the Body and Experience in the Music of Hank Williams

Anyone who saw Hank Williams in the last two years of his life was immediately struck by his haggard physical appearance. Although he was only in his late twenties, his emaciated and stooped frame, sunken cheeks, and thinning hair made him look old beyond his years. In the selection below, excerpted from an article originally published in the British academic journal *Popular Music*, musicologist Richard Leppert (b. 1943) and historian George Lipsitz (b. 1947), then colleagues at the University of Minnesota, describe how Williams's damaged body not only exemplified the maladies routinely suffered by poor, rural southerners, but also represented a rebuke to the nation's sturdy masculine ideal. As this excerpt demonstrates, the scholarly study of Hank Williams benefited from the disciplinary interplay that produced the field of cultural studies, and Leppert

---

SOURCE Richard Leppert and George Lipsitz, "'Everybody's Lonesome for Somebody': Age, the Body and Experience in the Music of Hank Williams," *Popular Music* 9 (October 1990): 260–61, 263, 266. Copyright © Cambridge University Press 1990. Reprinted with the permission of Cambridge University Press.

and Lipsitz's analysis marks an ambitious and imaginative addition to the academic literature on the country star that flourished in the 1980s and 1990s.

AGE AND HISTORICISATION OF THE BODY

Hank Williams began his career as a child prodigy and ended it as a still young man who appeared years older than his age. [...] Despite Williams's short life and the relative brevity of his career, among the more striking aspects of his work as a lyricist, composer and performer were the multiple and complex encodings of both age and experience as played out on the ground of the individual human body, both physically and psychically. Significantly, he located his work within a context that invariably posited that body not in the transcendence of timeless/universal humanism, but in the history of rural southern poor and working class America in the mid-twentieth century.

The concept of youth is largely taken as a "natural"—and not constructed—category in American middle-class culture today. But in the early post-war years (especially among the rural poor) the concept had little bearing on life as it was lived, as Williams's own typical experience as a child labourer illustrates. To be young was essentially to be an even less reliable wage slave than one's parents, in a setting when obtaining work at all ages was a necessity for survival. Hank Williams lived out his short life within this larger reality; he lived out his decade as an "official" of-age adult under still more complex circumstances, during a decade of traumatic post-war change in America in general, and in the rural South in particular. In this respect, his experience paralleled that of a generation of young men—and women—who came of age during [World War II] (where, in the field, a twenty-six-year-old might commonly be referred to as the Old Man) and who confronted the jolting realities of an atomic peace immediately re-defined in terms of Cold War and economic upheaval, massive migrations from the land to the emerging suburbs, and changing prescriptions for family life and for relations among races, classes and genders. [...]

At twenty-three, as at twenty-nine, Williams was a chronologically young man long past youth—indeed, a man who seemingly never experienced youth, as was borne out by his physical appearance. At six feet in height he was not especially tall, but his thin body (140 lbs.), and the hats he perpetually wore (to cover his thinning hair about which he was sensitive [Williams 1981, p. 144]), made him look taller: he stood out. Toward the end of his life he was haggard, gaunt, physically wrecked. He began drinking by the time he was eleven (ibid., p. 15), a habit he continued with few interruptions for the rest of his life, compounded by drug use in his later years (amphetamines and Seconal, the sedative chloral hydrate, and morphine). He had a form of spina bifida which exacerbated his chronic back pain and, near the end, hepatitis and a heart condition; and he suffered from malnutrition—when drinking heavily he did not eat, sometimes for days on end (ibid., pp. 175, 205, 207; Koon 1983, p. 50). His body could never properly fill out his expensive tailor-made suits (evident even in the posed publicity shots).

The appearance of Williams's body marked the urgency of age as a central category in his work, especially in a culture where increasingly prescriptive post-war expectations of bodily and behavioural propriety were being forged. It was well known that Hank Williams lived his life on the edge. His music masked none of it. His songs about failed love followed closely the dismal history of his marriages—and his innumerable one-night stands—just as his obsession with death and repentance [...] confirmed that he knew the price he was paying both in this life and, unless he was careful, likewise the next. Williams referred to himself as "ole Hank" both on the air and in private.[1]

Audiences were by no means amused by or even tolerant of his most drunken performances, especially when he failed to remember lyrics (see Williams 1981, p. 180). His increasingly debilitating alcoholism culminated in his being thrown off the Grand Ole Opry in 1952 (ibid., pp. 172–73, 191, 196–98); his trips to sanitariums for drying out 'became almost routine' (ibid., p. 194). Nevertheless, audiences 'loved Hank partly because of his problems', according to Frank Page, associated with Shreveport's KWKH Louisiana Hayride (ibid., p. 198).[2] For those who saw his live performances, drunk or sober, his physical vulnerability was both obvious and affecting. In body he confounded the model of the self-reliant, self-contained in-shape and battle-tested post-war male ("He'd come slopping and slouching out on stage, limp as a dishrag" [ibid., p. 140, quoting Montgomery Advertiser columnist Allen Rankin]). [...]

Minnie Pearl was struck by his stage presence from the first time she encountered it: "He had a real animal magnetism. He destroyed the women in the audience" (ibid., p. 144).[3] He knew how to use his body; hunching forward into the mike, "He'd close his eyes and swing one of those big long legs, and the place would go wild" (ibid., p. 145, quoting Don Helms).[4] He played on a sexuality that was exciting precisely because of the contradictions it contained. Minnie Pearl suggests that Williams appealed to women's maternal instincts. Others suggest a far more sensual dimension, though both reflected his true character—a womaniser nevertheless dominated by his strong mother. This contradiction engenders an ambiguity of a simultaneously exciting but politically dangerous sort. It constitutes a partially masked refusal to adhere to standards of propriety established for a post-war culture of re-domestication, a culture built on self-contradictory and increasingly complex erotic economies of controlled role-playing. Williams—like Elvis soon after him—marked with his bodily gestures a language of difference and demand, just as one might expect (or hope for) in the young—thereby accounting for the insistence then, as now, that youth be tightly controlled, especially physically. Yet his speaking and singing voices also referenced acoustics culturally characteristic of middle age and beyond, just as his love songs consistently dealt with the failures of middle age, and his gospel tunes with death. In sound and sight alike, he encompassed the experiences of life's full range of contradictions, hopes and failures for a society which unquestionably recognized in him both what they loved and hated of themselves.

NOTES

1 See the examples quoted by Williams's second wife Billy [Billie] Jean in Horstman 1975, p. 194.

2 His chronic back problem, for example, was explained on a pre-recorded-for-broadcast apology that Williams produced from his hospital bed when he had to miss a December 1951 appearance in Baltimore. It is reproduced as the final cut on *Hank Williams: I Won't Be Home No More (June 1952–September 1952)*, Polydor 833 752–1 Y-2, volume 8, and the last, of Polydor's comprehensive, retrospective series of Williams's recordings.

3 On Williams's securing of women following show dates, see Williams 1981, p. 164. Nor was his stage presence effective only on women: "He quickly became the favorite act on a military entertainment entourage to Europe in 1951. [Moreover, o]n a celebrity-studded touring show known as the Hadacol Caravan he upstaged such luminaries as Jack Benny, Milton Berle, and Bob Hope, and eventually took over the closing spot" (Blaser 1985, p. 17, n. 18). For details of the Caravan tour, see Williams 1981, pp. 150–55; Koon 1983, pp. 36, 38.

4 Cf. Frank Page: "He was just electrifying on stage.... He had the people in the palm of his hands from the moment he walked out there" (Williams 1981, p. 74). See also Koon 1983, p. 28.

REFERENCES

Blaser, K. 1985. "'Pictures from Life's Other Side': Hank Williams, Country Music, and Popular Culture in America." *South Atlantic Quarterly* 84 (1), pp. 12–26.

Horstman, D. 1975. *Sing Your Heart Out, Country Boy* (New York).

Koon, G. 1983. *Hank Williams: A Bio-Bibliography* (Westport, CT).

Williams, R. M. 1970. *Sing a Sad Song: The Life of Hank Williams*. 2nd ed. (Urbana, IL).

| 46 |

Jett Williams (with Pamela Thomas): Excerpt from *Ain't Nothin' as Sweet as My Baby: The Story of Hank Williams' Lost Daughter*

Despite the tabloids' allegations of prescription drug abuse, drunken escapades, and sexual depravity, perhaps the most startling posthumous revelation about Hank Williams came in 1985, when Alabama newspapers broke the story that a thirty-two-year-old woman claimed to be his daughter. Rumors had long circulated about the existence of a mysterious illegitimate child, but none had ever been substantiated—until Cathy (Deupree) Mayer, now known as Jett Williams, came forward.

Christened Antha Belle Jett, Jett Williams was born in Montgomery, Alabama, on January 6, 1953, five days after Hank Williams's death. Her mother, Bobbie Webb Jett (1922–1974), a Nashville secretary and professional dancer, had been involved in an intimate relationship with the country singer during the months between his separation from Audrey in January 1952 and his marriage to Billie Jean the following October. Jett became pregnant sometime that spring, and, in an October 1952 agreement, she relinquished custody of their unborn child to Williams. After Antha Belle's birth, Williams's mother, Lillie Stone, cared for the infant and, in December 1954, legally adopted her and renamed her Cathy Yvone Stone. When Mrs. Stone died two months later, custody of the toddler fell to Williams's sister, Irene Williams Smith. Determined to protect her late brother's memory from a potentially damaging scandal of an out-of-wedlock child, Smith surrendered guardianship of Cathy Stone and, later, filed a successful court motion to strip her of any claim to Williams's estate. Declared a ward of the state, the little girl was adopted by the Deupree family of Mobile, Alabama, in 1959, and became Cathy Louise Deupree.

In 1974, upon turning twenty-one, Deupree received a two-thousand dollar inheritance from Lillie Stone's estate, prompting Deupree's adoptive mother to reveal to her that she might be Hank Williams's daughter. But since the Alabama courts had declared his estate a closed matter years

---

SOURCE   Jett Williams, with Pamela Thomas, *Ain't Nothin' as Sweet as My Baby: The Story of Hank Williams' Lost Daughter* (New York: Harcourt Brace Jovanovich, 1990), 249–50, 251–53, 262–63. Copyright © 1990 by Cathy D. Adkinson (Jett Williams) and Fletcher Keith Adkinson. Used by permission.

before, her mother told her that any attempt to prove paternity would be pointless. The Deuprees eventually had a change of heart, however, and, in the early 1980s, encouraged Cathy, who was now married, to seek the truth and to claim any birthright to which she was entitled. Her ultimately successful seven-year legal odyssey to gain a share of Hank Williams's estate, including his songwriting royalties, met initial opposition from her half-brother, Hank Williams, Jr., In recent years, however, the two have resolved their differences and, on occasion, have even become business partners, supervising, for example, the release of Hank Williams's "Mother's Best" recordings. A singer and songwriter herself, Jett Williams tours with an ensemble of musicians called the Drifting Cowboys, named after her father's famous backing band. In this poignant excerpt from her autobiography, she pieces together the details of Hank Williams's and Bobbie Jett's relationship, while attempting to understand the birth parents she never knew.

As far as I can make out, Bobbie met Hank Williams in late 1951 or early 1952. She liked to socialize, and possibly through friends or through [her uncle] Willard, who was well known around Nashville, she met many people from the [Grand Ole] Opry, who of course were the most glamorous folks in town. According to an entry in my adoption files, [Williams's mother] Mrs. Stone said that she first met Bobbie in early 1952, which would indicate that she would have known Hank for at least a while prior to that if they were friendly enough for her to visit him at his mother's home. [. . .]

By the time Hank moved into the Natchez Trace house [in Nashville around mid-January 1952, during his separation from Audrey], he had been recuperating from his serious back operation for only four weeks. Several people, including Mrs. Stone, allude to the fact that Bobbie was his "nurse" at some point. Although I have no record that she had any formal nursing training, her own mother, Pauline, was a trained nurse, and Bobbie had spent the preceding two or three years nursing her grandmother, Ocie Belle. Bobbie was working full-time during these years for the Selective Service, but it is not inconceivable that she offered to help look after Hank while he was laid up. She lived a few short blocks away from the Natchez Trace house, so "looking in" on him would have been "neighborly."

In any case, it is easy to see how they could be attracted to one another. Hank was the biggest star in Nashville, and Bobbie liked "stars." Bobbie was, of course, a very attractive woman, and according to her friends was fun-loving and easygoing. Also, Hank seemed to gravitate toward women with children. Audrey had had another child before she met Hank; Billie Jean Eshliman, whom Hank would marry the following October, had a child by an early marriage; and Bobbie had Jo.* The fact that Bobbie had a child, I suspect, had a powerful effect on him.

By April 1952, Bobbie was pregnant. Apparently Bobbie was not a person who readily confided in other people. Her friends of later years in California knew nothing of me or her relationship to Hank Williams, and even most of her Nashville friends during that time were unaware of her pregnancy. I can only imagine how painful and frightening the months of May, June, and July 1952 were for Bobbie. She already had one child, Jo, and now she was pregnant with another—by Hank Williams, no less.

Those months were no less painful for Hank. He was drinking heavily, showing up drunk for performances, and, in some cases, missing performances completely. Ray Price† found living with Hank in the Natchez Trace house impossible, and he moved out. Also, according to many sources, Hank seemed to be taking drugs. [...]

Hank was at Lake Martin [northeast of Montgomery] with Bobbie on August 15, was arrested for being drunk and disorderly on August 17 in Alexander City, [Alabama] and appeared on the Louisiana Hayride on September 20, 1952. On September 23, he did a Nashville recording—his last—which included "Your Cheatin' Heart," "Kaw-Liga," and "Take These Chains From My Heart." He would be dead in a little over three months, but at the last session, he recorded some remarkable songs.

To complicate his already complicated life, sometime in the spring or summer of 1952, Hank met another woman, Billie Jean Jones Eshliman. Billie Jean was a nineteen-year-old divorcée,‡ and "so pretty you couldn't look at her," as one man described her. She was a sexy redhead from Bossier City, Louisiana, who first showed up in Nashville as the girlfriend of another Opry newcomer, Faron Young. Again, Hank's and Billie Jean's first meeting is the stuff of legend. Some say he went out for a drink with Faron and Billie Jean, took Young aside, pulled a gun on him, and said he wanted Billie Jean for himself. [...]

---

* Bobbie Jett's oldest daughter (b. ca. 1948).

† A Texas-born singer (b. 1926), who was a protégé of Williams and a follow cast member of the *Grand Ole Opry*.

‡ At the time she met Williams, Billie Jean had just turned twenty and was still married to her estranged husband, Harrison Eshliman.

In late August 1952, just after Hank was let go [from the Grand Ole Opry], he and Bobbie Jett left for Alabama, and in late August, they spent two weeks at Kowaliga [Bay, on Lake Martin]. I have tried to analyze Bobbie and Hank's relationship a million times, turning it around and around in my head, looking at it from every angle I can think of, playing it out in every possible way. Did he love her? Did she love him? Did they consider marriage?

By August, Bobbie was almost five months pregnant and undoubtedly disturbed about her situation. I think it is fairly obvious that Hank Williams was a "marrying" kind of man. He got married for the first time when he was only twenty-one; he would get married again in October 1952, less than six months after his final divorce from Audrey. Bobbie, on the other hand, evidently hadn't married Jo's father and was still unmarried as she approached her thirtieth birthday. Many of her friends have described her as a "one-man woman"—that is, when she was "with" a man, she didn't run around on him—nevertheless, unlike Hank, she apparently wasn't the "marrying" kind.

Did they consider marriage? Possibly, but the fact is they didn't do it. On October 15, 1952, they signed a contract where Bobbie agreed to give up custody of her baby—me—to Hank. As painful as this is to me, I can only conclude that she did not want to be tied down with a second child—and very possibly didn't want a husband either. The contract states clearly that Hank very much wanted the baby for himself.

Three days after signing his agreement with Bobbie, Hank married Billie Jean Eshliman, not once, but three times.⁵ Did Hank think that Billie Jean would "mother" me? Apparently not, since the contract states clearly that Mrs. Stone would care for me for the first two years of my life. Nevertheless, in a crazy kind of way, Hank seemed to be trying to establish a family life for himself.

Did Hank and Bobbie love each other? Perhaps, but they must not have been "in love," although I find it odd that a man who was supposedly madly in love with another woman (Billie Jean) would spend two weeks in a secluded cabin with a beautiful woman—who happened to be carrying his child. I think they must have genuinely cared for each other. During the months they were together, they were both in states of extreme agitation and confusion. Yet, they managed to consider each other and the situation—that is, me—to the extent that they contracted for my care. They struck an agreement requiring that they be in constant contact with one another for the rest of their lives, rather like an amicable divorce where the partners share custody and visitation rights of their child.

---

⁵ The first of these weddings, a private ceremony, took place in Minden, Louisiana, on October 18, 1952, while the other two, public affairs at the New Orleans Municipal Auditorium before paying audiences, occurred the following day.

Even after Hank married Billie Jean, Bobbie continued to live with Mrs. Stone at the McDonough Street house [in Montgomery]. Granted, it would have been difficult for her to return to Nashville while she was so obviously pregnant, but if she felt "jilted" by Hank, she certainly could have gone to either Nashville or California—where Hank had agreed to send her. In any case, I don't think Bobbie behaved like a "woman scorned." [...]

Hank ended his life physically wasted and emotionally distraught, and yet, ironically—and apparently true to form—the last months of his life were not only prolific and productive, but most of the songs he wrote were happy, upbeat works, particularly "Jambalaya," "Kaw-Liga," and "I'll Never Get Out of This World Alive." Even "Your Cheatin' Heart," written during those last weary months, while not a happy song, is a straightforward, honest, and, in a sense, resigned expression of emotion. And what's more, it turned out to be one of the most successful songs he ever wrote.

I'd like to think that "my comin'" made my daddy happy. I suspect it did, since he wrote a happy song about "Sweet Yvonne" and our "kinfolk comin' by the dozen" to see me.¶ But it didn't work out that way, which, surely, would have made him sad. But as Hank might have said, given all the contradictions, this is "just one of those things that happens that you can't get by."

~~~~~~

| 47 |

Nolan Porterfield: The Day Hank Williams Died: Cultural Collisions in Country Music

Two of the scholars who wrote about Hank Williams during the 1990s went beyond standard academic analyses to offer personal reflections about his influence on their lives. In a 1992 article, noted country music historian Bill C. Malone presented his poignant memories of the day the singer died and the "deep personal loss" he felt upon hearing the news as an East Texas teenager.* Another future country music scholar and native Texan deeply affected by Williams's death was Nolan Porterfield, then a high school sophomore. Porterfield

---

SOURCE   Nolan Porterfield, "The Day Hank Williams Died: Cultural Collisions in Country Music," in *America's Musical Pulse: Popular Music in Twentieth-Century Society*, ed. Kenneth J. Bindas (Westport, Conn.: Greenwood Press, 1992), 175–79, 182. Copyright © 1992 by Kenneth J. Bindas. Reproduced with permission of ABC-CLIO, LLC.

¶ A reference to ˜Jambalaya (On the Bayou).˜

* Bill C. Malone, "Hank Williams: Stardom Beyond the Sunset," *Journal of the American Academy for the Preservation of Old-Time Country Music* 2 (February 1992): 9–11.

(b. 1936), who grew up on the West Texas plains, taught courses in American literature and creative writing at Southeast Missouri State University between 1964 and 1995, and has written several award-winning studies of American music and culture, including a highly acclaimed 1979 biography of Jimmie Rodgers. In the coming-of-age reminiscence excerpted below, Porterfield recounts the deep emotional impact that Hank Williams's death had on him and his classmates, while also recalling his youthful ambivalence about country music and what it seemed to represent in the early 1950s for the residents of his small rural town.

January 1, 1953, was a cold, blustery Thursday on the plains of West Texas. A blue norther howled down out of the Panhandle, and the sky was thick with gusting sand. New Year's Day, coming in the middle of the week, was just another slow workday in my dad's crossroads grocery store and gas station, ten miles from nowhere and about twice that far from the junky little town where I went to high school. In the early hours of that sandstorm morning, while I slept my zombie adolescent sleep and dreamed (if I dreamed at all) of misty English countrysides, flashy cars, and Nanabeth Cox, Hank Williams died in the back seat of his '52 Cadillac, somewhere in the wilds of eastern Tennessee.

I do not remember how I learned of Hank Williams's death, a realization that I now find strange and rather puzzling. But I was a strange and puzzled kid, square as a bear, and I missed a lot of what was going on. I was equally unaware of another great passing that very week—that of Fletcher Henderson, the musical genius who was largely responsible for the swing revolution that Benny Goodman got most of the credit for. But I had no reason to know about Henderson; after all, he was black and several cultural removes from the West Texas world of a decidedly unhip, muddle-headed white boy. Hank Williams, on the other hand, was one of us, as close to blood as blood gets, and I probably would not remember anything about his death if it were not for what happened four days later, when I went back to school, on a still sand-blown Monday morning, after the Christmas holidays.

It took a while to figure out what was taking place. Country kids in my day tended to be cold-eyed realists, too simple to be sentimental, and we desperately avoided public displays of emotion. But something was going around, quietly, awkwardly, out of a need too great to contain, in the first whispered communications that morning, eerily everywhere: "Hey. You hear Hank Williams died?" Even more unsettling was the invariable response: a solemn nod of the head, a troubled sigh, even now and then (but only from girls, of course) a tear or two. All that morning, kids gathered in small clumps in out-of-the-way corners and vacant classrooms, talking in hushed tones, sharing the news.

It was at once comforting and disturbing; I had never seen my schoolmates behave this way, and before that morning it had never occurred to me that anyone else paid much attention to Hank Williams, not the way I had. I am sure I did not realize then the full implications of what was happening—that I would remember it and someday recall it in such detail, in such awe and extravagance—but I knew that it was a turning point. It was like being a lone member of the Resistance, afraid your identity will be betrayed to the barbarian Nazis all around, then suddenly discovering, through the exchange of a secret sign, that you are safe among fellow conspirators.

For me the crucial point came just after lunch, when I went up to the second-floor nook, just off the tiny auditorium balcony, where Peggy McKee and I worked on the yearbook. Peggy was the solidest rock I knew, a senior, two years older than me, bright, long of limb, funny as hell—a girl with lots of sand, as Huck said of Mary Jane.[†] Because she was older and naturally protective, I chose to think of her as the big sister I never had. My fraternal attitude may also have been influenced by the fact that she was already dating a tall, hardrock cowboy whose daddy owned half the county.

I had never seen her without a smile and a ready toss of the head. But when I got to the yearbook room that day, she stood up from her desk, without a word, chin quivering, and came up to me and put her arms around me and began to cry. I confess to having had occasional fantasies about hugging Peggy McKee but not this way, in this circumstance. I was much embarrassed, worried that someone would see us. Hugging, even in grief, between opposite sexes on school property was not considered acceptable behavior in 1953. But I stifled my worser, nerdier self and comforted her as best I could.

What I could not do in front of her was cry too. When she seemed better, I went downstairs behind the stage and let go—for Hank, for Peggy, for me, for that whole sad, sand-blown, inexplicable West Texas day. In later times, in other places, and among other people, there would be quite a lot of this going on—fashionably, in the wake of Janis [Joplin] and Jimi [Hendrix], Elvis and John Lennon. But in 1953, for the young, innocent, straight-arrow fans of just one more redneck troubadour (and one whose career was, after all, in serious decline), it was bizarre and rather baffling behavior. To understand even vaguely the impact and meaning of that day, it is necessary to understand something about the character back then of country music and its audience.

[†] A reference to a passage in Mark Twain's celebrated 1885 novel, *Adventures of Huckleberry Finn*.

I am annoyed as much as puzzled that I do not remember the moment I learned of Hank William's death. But I think that the very fact that I do not remember is an essential part of the story. More than likely, I heard about it from the cheap little Wards Airline radio that played incessantly in my father's store, a static hodgepodge of swing bandstand, western roundup, time-news-temperature, Patti Page singing "How Much Is That Doggie in the Window," Les Paul's "Lady of Spain." It is possible that I read about Williams's death in the back pages of the next day's edition of the *Lubbock Morning Avalanche*—"Hill-Billy Song King Found Dead in Automobile by Chauffeur"—along with late bulletins from the Korean War, warnings that our schools and colleges were filled with communists, and, on a note of social progress, the news that, for the first time in decades, no one had been lynched in the United States during the previous year. Eisenhower was about to take office, Stalin still reigned, our schools were segregated, Elvis was a wimpy senior at Humes High, the whole world was dark and windy.

In 1953 nobody paid much attention to country music, at least not publicly. If you had any pretensions at all to culture and sophistication—if you just wanted to be "normal" and have nice people like you—you ignored country music wherever possible. If you could not ignore it, you made fun of it. Historians of country music like to think of the 1940s and 1950s as "The Golden Age," but in those days everybody called it "hillbilly music," and practically no one took it seriously.

What we mostly did was take it for granted. After all, country music was everywhere around us, as common and inevitable as the dust in the air we breathed. The twenty-four-hour all-country radio station had not yet been invented (that happened a year or so later, right in our very midst, when Dave Stone put KDAV on the air from a cotton field just south of Lubbock), but every 250-watter for miles around programmed three or four hours of pickin' and singin' daily— usually an early morning wakeup show beamed at the farmers ("Sunrise Frolics"), an hour or so of mid-morning jamboree for the housewives, and an all-afternoon "western request roundup" that kept the cards and letters coming in. I spent a lot of time listening, more or less mindlessly, to High Pockets' "Country Tune Corral" from KSEL in Lubbock while I stocked shelves and pumped gas. When anyone else was around, I made a point of tuning to "The 950 Club" (950 kilocycles, not "hertz," on the dial), where a Peter Jennings sound-alike named Wayne Allen played Artie Shaw, Benny Goodman, and Stan Kenton.

There were no bars in Baptist-dry West Texas in those days, but every café and gathering place had a jukebox. There was even one in my dad's country grocery, a decrepit old Wurlitzer that held only ten records. For several months one fall, nine of the ten slots held Hank Williams's "Lovesick Blues," because the distributor got tired of changing worn-out records. (The tenth record, I clearly remember, was Teresa Brewer's "Music, Music, Music," obligatory for every jukebox in those days: "Put another nickel in, in the nickelodeon…"). After Nanabeth Cox broke my heart in the eighth grade, my pal Bobby Kitchen and I spent a lot of time hanging out at Jackson's Drive-In, consoling ourselves with hamburger steaks and hillbilly music from the jukebox. Bobby, who looked like James Dean and had a mildly tough reputation, broke the hearts of more girls than I ever said hello to, but he always seemed to be between romances and as much in need of a cheatin' song as I was. Hank's "Cold, Cold Heart" and "I'm So Lonesome I Could Cry" seemed to fill the bill—equal parts of she-done-me-wrong, Lord-how-it-hurts, and somehow-I'll-live.

Because we were not allowed to dance at school and there were no other places to do it, often on Saturday nights several couples would drive miles out of town to some point where two deserted dirt roads crossed, park their cars facing the intersection with headlights on, tune all the radios to the same station, and dance in the center, waltzing and two-stepping and hug-dancing in the dusty light to string-band strains from "The Big D Jamboree" or "Louisiana Hayride." We claimed to hanker for the uptown rhythms of city orchestras, but ballroom dancing, even if we had known how, seemed out of place.

These rustic orgies left no permanent marks. We scarcely ever stooped so low as "The Grand Ole Opry" (too corny and hayseed, even when Hank was on it). Afterward we went right back to Patti Page and Frankie Laine and Joni James and Eddie Fisher (rock 'n' roll was yet unknown, still little more than a gleam in Chuck Berry's eye). We spoke intensely of "classical music"—our notions of classical tending in the direction of Mantovani or something by Sigmund Romberg—"Stouthearted Men," perhaps. I yearned for what I thought of as normalcy, "good taste," "respectability." In matters of popular culture, my idol had always been Jack Armstrong‡—"The All-American Boy," for those too young to remember—and I wanted nothing so much as to root-hog out of my country roots, get as far as I could from all the "howdys" and "you-alls," and sandstorms and hard-scrabble hickness that seemed to plague me everywhere I turned.

---

‡ Globetrotting title character of *Jack Armstrong, The All-American Boy,* a popular radio adventure serial that aired between 1933 and 1951.

I never quite made it—and lived to be grateful I had not. But I went on suffering from the symptoms of hypertoxic cultural dysfunction for some time. In the early 1960s, eight or nine years after Hank Williams died, when country music was still in the slump brought on by rock 'n' roll, and Hank was pretty much a fading memory, even in West Texas, one of my friends went to California to visit at UCLA one summer. He came back telling a wondrous tale of having lunched at the student center, where on grand terraces beneath huge spreading trees in which hung a network of loudspeakers, crowds of upscale, sophisticated children of the sun sat munching their avocados and alfalfa sprouts and listening reverently to the music of—you got it—Hank Williams, one record after another. I realized later that they were proto-hippies, although the term was not yet current. In my mind's eye, they were simply California preppies—clean-cut, rich, and respectable. After I got over my initial disbelief, there was a moment or two while I rejoiced that Hank and I were vindicated, his genius recognized in the real world beyond the arid intellectual climes of West Texas. Then I got mad. Where did they get off, liking Hank Williams at this late date? They were too young, and too affluent, and too citified; they had not earned the right, as I had— had not danced in dusty crossroads, scrounged for jukebox nickels, or suffered through the greasy meatloaf at Jackson's Drive-In. It was all quite irrational, but it illustrates the kinds of cultural mysteries inherent in country music. [...]

For some years after Hank Williams died, country music was no more and no less to me than it had always been—an ordinary fact of a dull life I hoped to change. Then in the 1960s, about the time Nashville was rebounding into the national consciousness, increasingly fashionable if not yet respectable, I fell in with a rowdy crowd of Texas poets, anarchists, and musicians who treasured country music and knew a lot more about it, historically and philosophically, than I ever had. Through them I learned, with some mild shock, that educated folks with academic titles were writing high-powered, footnoted tracts and even entire books on the likes of the Carter Family, Fiddlin' John Carson, Bob Wills, and Johnny Cash. In time, I too wrote such a book,[5] still absorbed by the cultural confusions that had begun to surface in my life the week Hank Williams died.

―――

[5] A reference to the author's biography, *Jimmie Rodgers: The Life and Times of America's Blue Yodeler* (1979).

| 48 |

Douglas McPherson: Sex, Drugs and Country Music: A Profile of Hank Williams, America's Darkest Legend

Although Hank Williams died a year or so before the birth of rock 'n' roll, he has been seen by many, at least since the 1970s, as a seminal figure in the development of that musical genre. By the mid-1980s, as a result of the writings of such new rock critics as Dave Marsh and John Morthland (no. 43), Williams's status as a proto-rocker was firmly established, and it was formally recognized in 1987, when he was elected to the Rock and Roll Hall of Fame in its Early Influence category. In this article, which originally appeared in the British fan magazine *Country Music People*, London-born entertainment writer Douglas McPherson (b. 1965) lays out what he sees as the hillbilly singer's impressive credentials as a godfather of rock 'n' roll.

While many would have you believe otherwise, rock 'n' roll was not an intrinsically black music that was stolen and dressed up anew by the white folk.

Rock 'n' roll—at its purest, dirtiest and most visceral—was born of a violent, drunken marriage of blues and hillbilly amid the poverty, prostitution, gambling, degradation and pride of depression era America; as much of the white trash in the honky tonk as the black in the juke joint.

It is impossible to say exactly where country, or blues, became rock 'n' roll but one thing is certain. When Elvis Presley walked into Sam Phillips' small recording studio in Memphis he was following a musical path that had been trod half a decade earlier by Hank Williams.

Listen to Elvis's *Blue Moon Of Kentucky*; then play Williams' *Hey Good Lookin'*.

More revealingly, compare *My Bucket's Got A Hole In It* with Gene Vincent's *Be Bop A-Lula*.

The casual shuffle of the slapping back beat is the same, as are the simple spartan guitar licks, the hard, raw voice with its trailed off whine and the off-hand sexual suggestion of the lyrics. With the legacy of aching standards that he left, Williams may be the King of Country Music but, on classics like *I'm So Lonesome I Could Cry*, he really was singing the white man's blues in its purest

SOURCE Douglas McPherson, "Sex, Drugs and Country Music: A Profile of Hank Williams, America's Darkest Legend," *Country Music People* 23 (December 1992): 48–50. Reprinted by permission of Douglas McPherson.

form; replace the steel guitar with a dollop of mike echo, and Hank Williams was singing rock 'n' roll.

Had he lived, Hank Williams may well have followed the path to becoming a full blown rock 'n' roller, and it is no coincidence that Jerry Lee Lewis would come to cite Williams, along with Jimmie Rodgers, as one of his very few musical heroes. Like Rodgers before him, Williams certainly appreciated and understood rhythm 'n' blues having taken much of his early musical tutoring from a black street musician called Tee-Tot, and he is long rumoured to have recorded an r 'n' b session that has since been suppressed by the Nashville establishment.

Williams, despite his gangling and, later, booze raddled frame, was also an undoubted sex symbol who knew how to whet the, er, appetites of his female fans with a knee jerking, crotch thrusting performance that Elvis and Tom Jones would later take to its logical extreme. Most of all there is little doubt that at the time of his death, on New Year's night [sic] in the back of his baby blue Cadillac, that Williams owed little allegiance to the Nashville establishment that had come to despise and ostracise him in the way that it would later condemn anyone (even country stalwart Johnny Cash) who had any connection, even by association (as with Cash who had recorded for Sun), with rock 'n' roll.

Williams' legacy to rock 'n' roll goes deeper than just the sound and style of his music. Williams had a rock 'n' roll attitude. He did what he pleased and to hell with the consequences. He may have written of pained hearts and broken minds but the soul of his songs came from the gut and, more often than not, the loins. Moreover, in both the knife edge existence of his life and the untimeliness of his death, Williams' life story is the ultimate tale of sex, drugs and rock 'n' roll, a virtual blueprint for every rock 'n' roll suicide that has left its blood, whisky and vomit stains on the pages of musical history.

Forty years since Williams' death somewhere in the lonely hours between December 31st 1952 and 1st January 1953 (as with the death of Jim Morrison the exact details of that last journey to Canton, Ohio, may never be known), and almost seventy years since his birth in Mount Olive, Alabama, in 1923, it is easy to forget that the largest legend in country music is built on a tragically brief period of living stardom.

From his first major exposure on the hallowed stage of the Grand Ole Opry one hot midsummer night in 1949—the ecstatic crowd forced him to encore *Lovesick Blues* six times and the record went on to spend forty two weeks on the charts—to his death, drunk, drugged, outcast and alone, was a career that spanned just three years.

In that time, Williams had major hits with classic recordings such as *Long Gone Lonesome Blues* and *Cold, Cold Heart* and wrote and recorded some of the biggest, best and most covered standards in both country and pop history.

He also found time, between penning timeless jewels like *Jambalaya* and *Your Cheatin' Heart*, to divorce his first wife, marry and alienate his second (and he married her no less than three times including twice before a sold-out theatre audience), and get so heavily into whisky and morphine that, by the end, he was missing performances, forgetting his lyrics and falling off stages as often as he stood on them. In just three years he rose from backwoods obscurity to depose Roy Acuff as the biggest star in country music only to be run out of Nashville as its most hated (by the establishment) figure.

If ever there was a man who lived up to the rock 'n' roll ideal of live fast, die young and leave a pretty corpse it was Hank Williams.

Not that Williams died soon enough to leave a pretty corpse.

Photographs of the twenty nine year old singer, taken in jail just months before his death, show the emaciated, wraith-like frame of a wizened old man, his deeply disturbed eyes staring with anguish from a gaunt and pain racked face.

It took an undertaker's skills to pretty Williams up for the gaudy, glitzy carnival of the open casket funeral that would cause stampeding and mass hysteria among the twenty thousand mourners who flocked to the Municipal Auditorium in Montgomery. The makeup, like the vocal tributes by Ernest Tubb, Red Foley, Roy Acuff and Little Jimmy Dickins [Dickens], was the first of many lies that, with shameless hypocrisy, would turn a shunned and heartbroken drunk into the most revered figure in country music.

His life snatched away, like Buddy Holly's, while he was still at the height of his artistic powers—before he had time to age into obscurity, mediocrity and self-parody—was a tragic end but one which, conversely, assured his immortality and his place as one of the industry's biggest earners.

Like his Hollywood equivalents, James Dean and Marilyn Monroe, whose legends were built on similarly short careers and who were treated just as ignobly during their lifetimes, Hank Williams would become a bigger star in death than he would ever have been in life, the human tragedy of the man behind the legend lost, ignored and conveniently forgotten beneath the din of ringing cash registers.

Like the many who would follow him down the flaming road of self destruction—Elvis, Jim [Jimi] Hendrix, Janis Joplin—the pain of Hank Williams' music was a direct print out of the pain in his life. It was not a clever man who wrote *I'm So Lonesome I Could Cry*. It was a tortured one. And when Williams wrings and tears those anguished, wailing notes from his throat—and they always sound as if they are being wrenched free with an almighty effort, his voice seldom flowing freely or softly—it is impossible, even through the medium of forty year old recordings, not to hear the pain of a man exposing his very soul in the name of entertainment.

The pain was rooted in Williams' childhood, poor, fatherless and little educated, and continued throughout a troubled adolescence when, by fifteen he was already an alcoholic. Even during his brief spell at the top there is little evidence that Williams found much lasting happiness beyond the dark and empty kind that he found between the thighs of throwaway groupies or the fleeting glee that could be gained from putting a bullet through an innocent hotel television.

The hard grind of life on the road merely deepened the problems of his combative marriage while fuelling his insecurity and the jealousy of his wife's real or suspected infidelities. The deluge of easy cash merely allowed Williams to buy in ever greater quantities the beer and whisky that he craved and, later, the painkillers and knockout drugs that he would become addicted to. [...]

How many stars, musically gifted and emotionally articulate on stage, have, offstage, been barely able to string a sentence together or plan their day beyond the next beer? How many of music's biggest money spinners have been ripped off not merely financially but artistically, spiritually and emotionally, their lives built up to God-like heights only to be sacrificed on the blood and vomit splattered altar of rock 'n' roll?

Elvis Presley didn't want to be king when he walked into Sam Phillips' studio to cut a song for his mother. It took the genius, ambition and greed of Colonel Parker to take him to those heights and, once he was there, to factory farm him until every scrap of talent, glory, dignity and commercial possibility had been exploited and, valuable only as a packaged memory, he was finally allowed to sink into the abyss of his own excess.

Hank Williams' Colonel Parker was his first wife, Audrey Mae Sheppard Guy, whom he married in a gas station after meeting at one of his shows and, at a time when such things were shocking, co-habiting for two years.

Having formed the Drifting Cowboys at the age of fourteen, Williams was already an accomplished musician but, by all accounts, an unambitious one. Miss Audrey was no great singer (although like the wives of Johnny Cash, James Brown and many others she would find her way on to her husband's shows) but what she lacked in talent she more than made up for with sheer ambition.

It was Audrey who, like Lady MacBeth, nagged Williams into his first songwriting contract with Acuff-Rose, his recording deals with Sterling and MGM, his appearances on the Louisiana Hayride and from there to the Opry, his first big hits and superstardom. It was Audrey who inspired him to write hurting songs like *You Win Again* and, undoubtedly, it was his divorce from Audrey, followed within months by his unceremonious firing from the Grand Ole Opry, that pushed Williams into his final slide into death.

Characteristically, when Williams finally died, and his popularity surged, Audrey was the first to capitalize on his name. Finally in the spotlight, she dedicated the rest of her life to sustaining her image as the one true Mrs. Hank Williams—and her claim to the largest share of his royalties which, after twenty years of legal bitterness, she finally lost to wife number two* just a month before her death, depressed, drugged, alone and possibly close to insanity in 1975.

Before Hank was cold in his grave, Audrey launched herself on a solo singing career as Audrey (Mrs. Hank) Williams and, for the next decade, continued to ride the Williams gravy train recycling her husband's hits with the Drifting Cowgirls. In direct competition, Williams' second wife of just two months, a nineteen-year-old [sic] divorcee, Billie Jean Jones Eshlimar [Eshliman], also went on tour as Mrs. Hank Williams before marrying Johnny Horton just eight months after Hank's funeral and, eventually, after Horton's death and another marriage, coming in from the cold to claim her rightful share of Williams' estate.

Poor Hank. He really knew how to pick 'em.

The final words on Hank Williams have to be the self penned phrase that adorns his tombstone: "Praise the Lord—I saw the light."

For a man who lived so long in the shadow of his own death, *I Saw The Light* stands as one of the most poignant gospel songs ever written; not a pious song but the ultimate prayer of thanks and repentance from a sinner who finally found the way.

The lyrics are unmistakably autobiographical:

"I wandered so aimless, life filled with sin...Now like a blind man who God gave back his sight, Praise the Lord, I saw the light!"

Whether Williams really saw the light on that last fateful journey to the New Year's concert that he never made will perhaps never be known but it would be nice to think that, somewhere in the ether, the Prodigal Son finally found his way home.

Perhaps he is looking down with that wry, gaunt smile at the cleaned up multi-million-dollar industry that was built almost entirely on his own dark legend. Perhaps his ghost is there in the smoke and whisky fumes as some unknown singer shoots up, drinks up and, carrying his guitar in trembling hands, walks into the blinding spotlight that will bring him stardom or destruction. Or perhaps he is somewhere else, far from it all, trading guitar licks and perhaps one last beer with Gene Vincent, Sid Vicious and Elvis Presley.

---

* On October 22, 1975, a U.S. District Court ruled that Hank Williams's second wife, now known as Billie Jean Berlin, was entitled to a share of his copyright renewals

| 49 |

Lee Smith: Review of Don Cusic, *Hank Williams: The Complete Lyrics*

As humanities scholars came to question inherited notions about the divisions between "high" and "low" culture, writers began to make claims about Hank Williams's importance beyond the narrow bounds of country music. In 1993, Don Cusic (b. 1948), a journalist-turned-academic then teaching at Middle Tennessee State University, published *Hank Williams: The Complete Lyrics*. In its introduction, titled "Hear That Lonesome Whippoorwill: Hank Williams as Poet," Cusic asserts that Williams's "Hillbilly Shakespeare" moniker constitutes "more than an empty tribute," and he finds significant similarities to Shakespeare in Williams's ability to connect with the masses by expressing universal emotions. Williams, Cusic argues, also stands as the musical forefather of contemporary singer-songwriters such as Bob Dylan, Kris Kristofferson, and Joni Mitchell, whom he considers the most important poets of their day. Cusic claims that their lyrics, like Williams's own, can profitably be read as poetry, separated from both melody and performance. In the following review of Cusic's book, however, acclaimed southern novelist and short-story writer Lee Smith (b. 1944) expresses her reservations about the notion that Hank Williams was truly a poet.

Never mind that he's been dead for over forty years, or that his career didn't even span a decade. Hank Williams's songs are still the pure heart of country music, just as Hank himself remains the prototype of the "country artist as tortured genius...a light and a darkness, a dream and a nightmare, a shining example and a shame," in the eloquent words of country music scholar Don Cusic, who has gathered and assembled this first (and definitive) collection of all the Williams lyrics known to exist—more than 130 of them, starting with a fragment of "W.P.A. Blues" which Hank composed and sang at amateur night at the Montgomery Empire Theater in Montgomery, Alabama, when he was only 13 years old, winning first prize. Though Cusic gives us a short introductory essay that puts Williams's work in the context of his life, the concentration here is upon the songs themselves—or the words to the songs themselves—and this sharp focus brings us some surprises.

SOURCE   Lee Smith, review of Don Cusic, *Hank Williams: The Complete Lyrics*, in *Journal of Country Music* 16 (1993): 58–59. Used by permission.

It is Cusic's contention that Hank Williams really was the "hillbilly Shakespeare," which he was often called; Cusic reminds us that "Shakespeare reached the masses with his words, his plays, and especially his sonnets, articulating the emotion of every man and woman. Hank Williams achieved the same thing." It's true that as poetry has become a little-known and increasingly academic art, songwriters have become our popular poets. We have relied on Bob Dylan, Bruce Springsteen, Merle Haggard, Woody Guthrie, Kris Kristofferson, Loretta Lynn, the Beatles, Paul Simon, Joni Mitchell, Willie Nelson, and others to tell us who we are and how we feel and what we hope for. We have relied on Hank Williams. And surely there is nobody better at capturing those essential moments of the human spirit: the anguish of lost love, the frustrations of love gone wrong, the hell of loneliness, the complexity of our feelings, the fragility of our relationships, our fear of death and belief in a life hereafter. Hank Williams was especially effective when he wrote about the joy of high spirits and feeling good—stepping out and cutting up.

But—poetry? I can't agree with Cusic here. To insist upon poetry seems to limit the scope of song. For me, listening to Hank Williams's songs is a lot better than reading their lyrics. I think Hank Williams was a great songwriter, but I don't think he was a great poet. A set of rhymes is not a poem. Poetry depends upon metaphor. The poet must connect the unconnected, see relationships to which most of us are blind—find a fresh image for a familiar feeling.

"I'm So Lonesome I Could Cry" (1949) is, for instance, a very fine poem. Here Williams gives us a whole set of indelible images for being lonesome: a whippoorwill "too blue to fly," the low whine of the "midnight train," time "crawling" by, the personified moon who has disappeared "behind a cloud to hide its face and cry," the weeping robin who has "lost the will to live," the "silence of a falling star" as it "lights up a purple sky." These wonderful images speak to all our senses—we can hear, see, and feel loneliness in many new ways. This poem is both specific and universal.

But look at the lyrics of "I Can't Help It (If I'm Still In Love With You)," written about the same time (1951). And (key point) pretend you don't know the tune:

Today I passed you on the street
And my heart fell at your feet
I can't help it if I'm still in love with you
Somebody else stood by your side
And he looked so satisfied
I can't help it if I'm still in love with you.

Do the same thing with the first verse of 'Your Cheatin' Heart," surely one of the greatest songs ever written.

Your cheatin' heart
Will make you weep
You'll cry and cry
And try to sleep
But sleep won't come
The whole night through
Your cheatin' heart
Will tell on you.

Here we have no metaphor at all, just bald statement of raw emotional fact, given to us in sing-song doggerel verse. So let's face it: a great song is not necessarily a great poem. For a great song brings us also the gift of music, the tune, which renders its words and its images (no matter how trite they may be) totally unique, totally memorable. We listen to it again and again. We connect its words to events and situations and emotions in our own lives. Even later when we are stuck in traffic or shopping in the supermarket or having a fight with our spouse, we hear that song running through our minds. It thus becomes ours, totally personal, though its language may be trite and its theme is usually universal.

With all the lyrics collected before us, it's interesting to look at Williams's themes. Out of the legacy of the more than 130 songs he left us, over half deal with love lost or love gone wrong. That's a lot. And many of them are his best songs ("You Win Again," "Cold, Cold Heart," "There'll Be No More [sic] Teardrops Tonight," for example), the very songs we know him by.

Some of these sad songs are awfully deep and dark indeed, crossing over into that kind of existential loneliness that lies at the heart of the human condition. "I'm So Lonesome I Could Cry" fits this category; so does "Somebody's Lonesome," "I'm So Tired of It All," and "A Stranger in the Night," which includes this verse:

Like a lonely dove that flies from pine to pine
My heart can't be gay and light
Like sightless eyes that will never see the sun
I'm lost like a stranger in the night.

Pretty good poem, pretty sad stuff.

Twenty or so songs present—in strikingly realistic fashion—the torments of a tortured relationship:

I just don't like this kind of livin'
I'm tired of doin' all the givin'
I give my all and sit and yearn
And get no lovin' in return
And I just don't like this kind of livin'

Why do we stay together
We always fuss and fight
You ain't never known to be wrong
And I ain't never been right.

(from "I Just Don't Like This Kind of Livin'")

Though these songs obviously derive from Hank's unhappy marriage to Audrey, they are universal in their depiction of a couple who can't live with each other and can't live without each other. It is in his deft handling of this kind of ambivalence that Williams seems so modern, so contemporary. Often he does this by combining a sad lyric with a catchy upbeat tune, as in "Wearin' Out Your Walkin' Shoes," "Long Gone Daddy," and my particular favorite, "Why Don't You Love Me," which contains the tragicomic lines "My hair's still curly and my eyes are still blue, Why don't you love me like you used to do?"

Williams's irony and humor often leavened his essentially dark view of life. He captured for all time the sheer goofy exuberance of falling in love with songs like "Hey Good Lookin'," "Baby We're Really in Love," "Howlin' at the Moon," or "There's Nothing as Sweet as My Baby":

I like candy, I like cake
I like jam but goodness sake
There's nothing as sweet as my baby.

—or the joys of going out on the town in his honky-tonking tunes. Seeing the lyrics on the page makes us appreciate the intricate rhythm and witty wordplay in a lot of these light-hearted songs, such as the famous "Jambalaya":

Goodbye Joe, me gotta go, me oh my oh
Me gotta go pole the pirogue down the bayou
My Yvonne, the sweetest one, me oh my oh
Son of a gun, we'll have big fun on the bayou.

Cusic reminds us that those who knew Williams well remembered him as a fun-loving, witty person—which belies the tragic image we have of him now. [...]

All in all, it is an amazing body of work, a "national treasure," as Cusic rightly proclaims. My only quibble comes from my own greed to know more than I am given in these pages, where the lyrics are simply presented as poems, arranged in alphabetical order. I'd love to know (without flipping constantly to the back of the book) the date of each song and the co-author, if any. I'd also like to know everything else that's known about each song—where he wrote it, and under what circumstances, and where he sang it, and when, and who else recorded it, because these aren't poems, they're songs; and I can't really separate them in my mind from the doomed and valiant man who wrote and sang them, who added the magic of music and voice to these simple words which tell again and again the truth of the human heart.

| 50 |

Colin Escott (with George Merritt and William MacEwen): Excerpt from *Hank Williams: The Biography*

Colin Escott (b. 1949), a self-described American roots music fan originally from Canterbury, England, has done more than any other individual to document Hank Williams's life and music. Among his most significant contributions are the liner notes accompanying the boxed sets, *Hank Williams: The Original Singles Collection...Plus* (1990) and *The Complete Hank Williams* (1998); the coffee-table book of photographs and documents, *Hank Williams: Snapshots from the Lost Highway* (2001, with Kira Florita); the PBS American Masters documentary film, *Hank Williams: Honky Tonk Blues* (2004, co-written with director Morgan Neville); and the liner notes to two recent collections, *Hank Williams: The Complete Mother's Best Recordings...Plus!* (2010), a landmark fifteen-CD boxed set, and *Hank Williams: The Legend Begins* (2011), a three-CD collection that includes Williams's earliest known recordings.

But of all his works on the now-legendary singer-songwriter, Escott probably reached his largest audience with *Hank Williams: The Biography*, originally published in 1994 and issued in a revised paperback edition in 2004. Written in collaboration with George Merritt and William MacEwen, Escott's book has earned general acceptance by historians, journalists, and fans alike as the most authoritative and certainly the most popular account of Williams's life. Escott

---

SOURCE Colin Escott, with George Merritt and William MacEwen, *Hank Williams: The Biography* (Boston: Little, Brown, 1994), 256–59. Copyright © 1994, 1995 by Colin Escott. Used by permission of Little, Brown and Company. All Rights Reserved.

avoids mythologizing Williams, finding the reality of the man to be somewhere between the "sainted Hank Williams who presided beatifically over country music" and the drunken, drugged-up "icon of bubba defiance." Unlike the social historians and cultural studies scholars writing during this period who sought to understand Williams in terms of his broader cultural significance for 1950s America, Escott defines him in much narrower terms, as a commercial artist who attained unprecedented popularity in the competitive postwar entertainment industry. In the excerpt below, Escott addresses a perennial question that has invited all manner of speculation over the decades: How would Hank Williams, who died so young and at the height of his powers, have fared had he lived longer?

Anyone who dies as young as Hank invites endless "What if…?" speculation. It has been an item of faith in country music circles that Hank would have had a rosy future if only he had lived. The reality might have been a little different. It's doubtful that he could have saved himself even if he had rested up in Shreveport or Montgomery, concentrated on songwriting, and made just short tours as he had once intended. Too many of his self-destructive behaviors were hard-wired. The spinal pain was irremediable, and the physical damage already done to his heart and perhaps his liver and other organs was irreversible. "He didn't have a chance," concluded Oscar Davis,[*] who had seen the contrast between the Hank Williams of early 1949 and the Hank Williams of late 1952, "[but] I think he died happy [because] he proved to the world he was somebody." Whether that was as much a consolation to Hank at the last as Davis thought is far from certain.

Before two years were up, Hank would have encountered at least one major hurdle—the loss of his quality-control department. Fred Rose[†] died on December 1, 1954. He had clearly been suffering from heart disease for several months, and had once suffered a heart attack in the recording studio, but his Christian Science beliefs prevented him from seeing a doctor. After Fred's death, [his son] Wesley Rose assumed total control and began to fancy himself a music man, but he could never have sat with Hank, as Fred had done, helping him polish those diamonds in the rough.

Even less could Wesley have helped Hank weather the upset triggered by rock 'n' roll. Seven months after Fred Rose died, an Elvis Presley record nudged

---

[*] Prominent Nashville music promoter (1902–1975), who served as Williams's manager at the early stage of his stardom, between 1949 and 1950, and then again between October 1952 and Williams's death two months later.

[†] Williams's song publisher and songwriting mentor (1898–1954).

its way into the country charts, signaling a wind of change in which the hard and fast borders between pop, country, and rhythm 'n' blues began to dissolve a little, and a new music aimed specifically at teenagers sprouted. In perhaps the most ludicrous statement he ever made, Wesley Rose said, "[If Hank had lived], I don't think we could have had a rock era." His contention was that rock 'n' roll filled the void left by Hank's death.

No one person could have arrested the social, economic, and musical elements that made rock 'n' roll. If a hypothetical question is to be asked, it is: How would Hank Williams have fared? If the fate of his contemporaries is any guide, the answer is: poorly. Webb Pierce, Hank Snow, Carl Smith, Faron Young, Red Foley, and Eddy Arnold all saw their careers take a precipitous downturn in the mid- to late '50s. One listen to Webb Pierce's *vocal* version of "Raunchy" is enough to appreciate the desperation that afflicted them. Hank's music, like that of his contemporaries was adult in content; rock 'n' roll was teenage music. The exaggeration and overstatement of rock 'n' roll were alien to the fundamental values of Hank's music, and the sledgehammer beat was the opposite of The Drifting Cowboys' sweet, mellow swing.

It's doubtful that there would have been a place for Hank Williams, with his thinning hair, his incorrigibly rural ways, and his "Pitchers from Life's Other Side," in the era of the Nashville Sound. He didn't have the ability to cross over that those who followed him, such as Marty Robbins and Johnny Cash, had. Hank's music had always needed to be carefully combed through and then re-interpreted for the mass audience. The market would not have changed to accommodate him. If he had tried to change to accommodate it, he would have lost the essence of his music in the process.

Some of Hank's records, like "Hey, Good Lookin'" and "Settin' the Woods on Fire," prefigured rock 'n' roll to some extent, but that was no guarantee that he could have weathered the storm any better than his contemporaries. Rhythm 'n' Blues singer Wynonie Harris had much of what became the rock 'n' roll swagger on his later '40s and early '50s hits, like "Good Rockin' Tonight," but that didn't help him score one hit after rock 'n' roll broke. He was too old and too black. Hank was probably too old and too hillbilly, but by dying prematurely, he avoided the indignity of trying to answer the question of what he would have done. He also left the tantalizing promise of what might have been as well as a blank screen upon which vested interests could project all manner of fantasies. For its part, MGM tried to imagine the sound by grafting drums, electric guitar, and piano solos onto his records and bathing the results in echo, beginning a long, sorry history of reinventing Hank's music according to the season.

Hank would have had an even tougher time in today's Nashville, the city founded upon reverence for him. In April 1972, the German record company Polydor, which later amalgamated with the record division of the Dutch electrical giant Philips to form Polygram, bought the repertoire of MGM Records.‡ In March 1985, Acuff-Rose was sold to Gaylord Broadcasting of Oklahoma City, the company that had bought *The Grand Ole Opry* from National Life and resituated it in Opryland, and later launched the Nashville Network. Today, Polygram's corporate monolith and the Acuff-Rose/Opryland Music monolith face off across Music Row, symbolizing the new, business-minded face of country music. Would the ol' Drifting Cowboy have made easy conversation with the MBAs who now walk the corridors of power?

What Hank Williams would have thought of the cookie-cutter country stars who now invoke his name is even harder to determine. The only certainty is this: the circumstances that combined to make him the most powerfully iconic figure in country music will never come again. No one will cut three or four classics in an afternoon session again; no one will redefine the vocabulary of the music in the way that he did. No one will be allowed to mess up in the way that he did, either. The stakes are too high, and professional help would have been foisted upon him. The specialness in Hank Williams would then have ebbed away, because the compelling nature of his records stemmed in great measure from the fact that he was a pressure cooker, holding altogether too much inside.

It was a unique combination of circumstances that brought Hank Williams to the fore and allowed him to accomplish what he did when he did. If he had started his career a few years earlier, he would have lived and died in almost total obscurity because the social and market conditions that brought about the wider acceptance of hillbilly music weren't in place, and the country was mired deep in the Depression. If he had lived a few years longer, he would have become an embarrassment to the changing face of country music—too hillbilly by half. But in arriving when he did and dying when and how he did he became a prophet with honor.

The final paradox is this: Hank Williams left no journals, almost no letters, and no extended interviews, and the people who knew him best have to admit that on some level they didn't know him at all; yet, for all the ambiguity and unknowableness, Hank Williams appears almost desperately

---

‡ According to *Billboard*, it was actually the PolyGram Corporation, a U.S. subsidiary of the PolyGram Group (formed in January 1972), that acquired MGM Records' catalog in April of that year.

real through his music. He escaped the obloquy of seeing his drunks and his dalliances splashed over the tabloids, but he left a life diarized in verses sung with such riveting conviction that we feel as though we know him well. At his best, he froze a moment or a feeling in terms simple enough to understand quickly, yet meaningful enough to listen to forever. That's still the essential challenge of the popular song.

Cover of *Weekly World News*, February 14, 1995. Courtesy of *Weekly World News*.

Part VII

~~~~~~

Our Hank Williams

Becoming an American Icon (1995–2013)

At the time of its publication in 1994, Colin Escott's *Hank Williams: The Biography* (no. 50) seemed destined to stand as the definitive account of the country star's life for the foreseeable future. But rather than closing off the need for additional interpretations, Escott's book appears to have accelerated the flow of writing about Williams. So, too, did a series of posthumous accolades, awards, and retrospective projects, all of which helped secure his undisputed status as an American cultural icon. During the period spanning 1995 to 2013, for example, he served as the subject of a two-day 1999 Smithsonian Institution symposium titled "A Tribute to Hank Williams"; a 2004 PBS American Masters series documentary, *Hank Williams: Honky Tonk Blues* (co-written and produced by Escott); and an enormously popular multiyear exhibit (2008–2011) at the Country Music Hall of Fame and Museum, *Family Tradition: The Williams Family Legacy*. Equally important, the singer's recordings also continued to receive reverent attention, and ensuing releases, many of which contained rare and previously unissued material, provided fans and scholars with a more comprehensive overview of his recorded legacy than ever before imaginable. In 1998, Mercury Records released *The Complete Hank Williams*, a lavish ten-CD boxed set that was favorably reviewed by many major publications in the United States and beyond. Time Life Entertainment's *Hank Williams: The Complete Mother's Best Recordings...Plus!* (2010) likewise garnered extensive media coverage. Containing transcriptions of seventy-three carefully restored 1951 radio shows, this fifteen-CD collection has been widely praised for offering a fresh perspective of Williams at the peak of his career.

In 2010, in a gesture that symbolized Williams's enshrinement in the nation's cultural pantheon, the Pulitzer Prize Board honored him with a posthumous Special Citation, the first ever awarded to a country artist, which recognized "his craftsmanship as a songwriter who expressed universal feelings with poignant simplicity," and credited him with playing "a pivotal role in transforming country music into a major musical and cultural force in American life." Hank Williams now occupies a rarified position as an emblematic—if perpetually enigmatic— artist to whom writers routinely turn when considering questions of American identity and culture.

Perhaps not surprisingly, the voluminous writing about him that has appeared over the past twenty years defies easy categorization or summary. Some authors have continued efforts to portray the "real" Hank Williams, like former Drifting Cowboy guitarist Joe "Penny" Pennington, who, in a selection from his memoir below, matter-of-factly recalled Williams as an aspiring singer and band leader in 1947–1948, just prior to his rise to stardom. Or John Gilmore, a chronicler of Hollywood's dark underside, who presented a harrowing glimpse of Williams at the other end of his career, during a 1952 encounter outside the famous Riverside Rancho dance hall near Los Angeles. Other writers have concentrated on debunking what they saw as myths that tenaciously cling to Williams. In *Creating Country Music: Fabricating Authenticity* (1997) (an excerpt from which is not included below), sociologist Richard A. Peterson iconoclastically depicted him as a rather unoriginal performer whose chief importance lies in the ways his image was manipulated and exploited by the Nashville music industry after his death. Likewise, in a 2007 journal article, American Studies scholar John R. George flatly dismissed the notion that Williams was, in any sense, a racial progressive, after analyzing the relationship between the teenaged Williams and his middle-aged African American mentor, Rufus "Tee-Tot" Payne.

Meanwhile, an ever-lengthening list of writers have paid tribute to Williams as an important influence on, or a source of inspiration for, their own lives and work. In his foreword to Colin Escott's and Kira Florita's *Hank Williams: Snapshots from the Lost Highway* (2001), Pulitzer Prize–winning journalist and memoirist Rick Bragg explained that Williams's songs provided a rich source of meaning and solace for multiple generations of his white southern family. In his memoir *Chronicles, Volume One* (2004), Bob Dylan recalled that, as a teenager in a small northern Minnesota town, he learned the basic tenets of songwriting by studiously listening to Williams's 78-rpm records. And Native American literary theorist Craig Womack recounted, in a 1997 autobiographical essay, how he drew strength from Williams's music during his adolescent struggle to resolve his conflicted personal identity.

Journalists and novelists during this period frequently were drawn to the more mysterious elements of the Hank Williams saga. In his 2003 travel account, "Retracing a Ghostly Night Ride," noted Nashville music journalist Peter Cooper described replicating the country star's fateful December 31, 1952–January 1,

1953, drive from Knoxville, Tennessee, to Oak Hill, West Virginia, in what he admitted was an ultimately fruitless attempt to bring clarity to now-unknowable events. Some fiction writers infused elements of Williams's biography with the supernatural or macabre in order to produce new and creative interpretations of his legacy. In *The Haunted Hillbilly* (2004), Toronto-based novelist Derek McCormack imagined Nudie Cohn, the famed western-wear costume designer, as a vampire responsible for Williams's early musical success and androgynous flamboyance on the *Grand Ole Opry*. Renowned alt-country singer Steve Earle, in his debut novel, *I'll Never Get Out of This World Alive* (2011), envisioned a fictional heroin addict nicknamed "Doc" (based on Toby Marshall) haunted by Williams's ghost, who, poignantly and pathetically, refuses to admit that he is dead. And just such a possibility was raised, characteristically enough, by the supermarket tabloid *Weekly World News*, which published a 1995 cover story alleging that the singer was actually alive, remarried, and happily living out his golden years in Paris, France. Ironically, this fantastical story inadvertently touches upon a version of the truth, for with the release of an ever-expanding body of recordings, documentary films, and writings, Hank Williams remains very much a living cultural presence in the early twenty-first century.

| 51 |

Christopher Metress: Sing Me a Song about Ramblin' Man: Visions and Revisions of Hank Williams in Country Music

No modern historical figure has inspired more tribute songs than Hank Williams. Commercial recordings of at least twenty such songs were released in 1953 alone, and in succeeding decades, that number has multiplied exponentially, with one recent estimate citing more than 1,300 songs honoring or mentioning him. Christopher Metress (b. 1963), a scholar of southern literature who now teaches at Samford University in Birmingham, Alabama, examines a few dozen of them in the following selection, which originally appeared in a 1995 special country music issue of *South Atlantic Quarterly*. By analyzing these songs, Metress demonstrates how Hank Williams's image has changed over the decades, a reflection of the shifting cultural perspectives, changing tastes, and, above all, evolving desires of songwriters and their audiences.

Oakwood Cemetery Annex is tucked away in a modest section of [Montgomery, Alabama], only a few blocks from the state capitol building. When you get there it's not hard to find his grave, for it's marked by an upright slab nearly twice the size of a man. Made of Vermont granite, it shines like marble in the afternoon sun. At the top of the slab you find the opening notes of "I Saw the Light." Below this and to the left, a bronze plaque shows him smiling and playing his guitar, and beside it, etched into the granite, sunshine pours through a thicket

SOURCE Christopher Metress, "Sing Me a Song about Ramblin' Man: Visions and Revisions of Hank Williams in Country Music," in *Readin' Country Music: Steel Guitars, Opry Stars, and Honky Tonk Bars*, ed. Cecelia Tichi, special issue of *South Atlantic Quarterly* 94 (Winter 1995): 7–14, 15–16, 19–23, 24–27. © 1995, Duke University Press. All rights reserved. Used by permission of the publisher.

of layered clouds. A little further down, just above eye level, the name "Hank Williams" is cut deep and thick and clean into the memorial stone.[1]

Resting at the base of this slab is an exact replica of Hank's hat, surrounded by small granite squares where someone has chiseled the front-page sheet music to some of Hank's greatest songs. A few feet in front of all this lies a flat slab that marks the grave itself. The whole area is framed by a rectangular border of stone, and inside this frame stand two urns for decoration and two benches for rest. The grave is not busy at this time of day. A few wrappers and cigarette butts on the artificial turf around the plot let you know that others were here not long ago, but in the quiet of this particular afternoon you rest awhile on one of the benches and spend a few moments listening to the clouds move soundless as smoke overhead.

When it's time to go you might decide to walk out the way you came in. But you shouldn't. If you do, if you leave the grave the same way you approached it, you will miss something very important. So, instead of retracing your steps, you get off the bench and walk straight toward the upright slab. Take it in one last time—the deep cut of his name, his sharp face molded in bronze, the clouds and sunshine etched into the granite like some fragile but palpable hope. Now move past the slab. Here, standing in the shadows at the back of the slender marker, you will find a poem entitled "Thank You, Darling." Unlike the lyrics and notes carved into the front of the stone, these words will be unfamiliar:

> Thank you for all the love you gave me
> There could be one no stronger
> Thank you for the many beautiful songs
> They will live long and longer
> Thank you for being a wonderful father to Lycrecia
> She loves you more than you knew
> Thank you for our precious son
> And thank God he looks so much like you
> And now I can say:
> There are no words in the dictionary
> That can express my love for you
> Someday beyond the blue

The poem is signed "Audrey Williams."

At first, what is happening on the backside of Hank Williams's gravestone seems quite clear: Audrey Williams, the grieving widow, is paying her final tribute to her husband. But something makes you uncomfortable. Is it the disjunction between the simple lyrics chiseled on the front of the slab and the discordant poetry cut into its back? Perhaps, yet there is something so touching in what you've just read: the widow fighting through her pain to write a final song for her songwriting husband. Still, something bothers you. It's only after you've listened a little longer to the silence overhead that you remember Audrey Williams wasn't Hank's widow.

Now you begin to understand what's really happening here on the shadowy side of Hank's grave. Everything about the gravesite centers on Hank, or so it first appears. The marker has his name on it, those are his lyrics etched in stone, that's his image cast in bronze. They've let his name, his face, and his words speak for themselves. When you look behind the grave, however, you see that Hank hasn't had the final say. Hank's a legend, after all, and legends become legends because we don't let them have the last word. Rather, after they are gone we continue to speak for them, creating them, if not in our own image, then at least in an image that serves our own purposes. And that's what's happening here in Montgomery. Miz Audrey is staking her claim, making Hank Williams *her* Hank Williams because she knows that another Williams, Billie Jean, is out there trying to stake *her* own claim. When Miz Audrey writes, "Thank you for our precious son / And thank God he looks so much like you," you can almost hear the satisfaction, the legacy and the claims of inheritance that are asserted in those lines. The Hank Williams buried here isn't just any Hank Williams but *her* Hank Williams.

In 1975 Moe Bandy released a song by Paul Kraft entitled "Hank Williams You Wrote My Life." As true as these words are to many country music fans, they may blind us to another important fact: just as Hank Williams wrote our lives, we have written his. Audrey Williams's poem at the gravesite in Montgomery was not the first attempt to take hold of Hank's life and inscribe it in a certain way. And it definitely wasn't the last. For instance, in 1953, the year Hank Williams died, every major recording studio in Nashville released a song about him, sixteen tributes* in all.[2] The first to be released was Jack Cardwell's

---

* According to hankwilliamslistings.com, at least four additional recordings of such tribute songs, not included in Metress's total, were released in 1953: Jimmie Lodgson's cover version of Jack Cardwell's "The Death of Hank Williams" (released under the pseudonym "Jimmie Lloyd"); another of the same song by Delbert Barker; and two versions of Marvin Rainwater's "Heart's Hall of Fame," one by the songwriter himself and the other by the group the Bailey Brothers and Happy Valley Boys. The website also lists another tribute song, "When Hank Williams Met Jimmie Rodgers," written and recorded, in November 1953, by Riley Crabtree. It, however, was apparently not released until the following year.

"Death of Hank Williams." A Montgomery disc jockey and singer for King Records, Cardwell knew Hank in his pre-*Opry* days. When he heard of Hank's death on New Year's Eve, he wrote a song about it that very night. A week later, on 8 January, King Records released "The Death of Hank Williams." It went as high as #2 on the charts, kept out of the top spot by one of Hank's own songs, "Your Cheatin' Heart." With more than 107,000 singles sold, "The Death of Hank Williams" may have been the most successful of all these tribute records, but it really wasn't that much different from the rest. Beginning with a peaceful image of Hank lying in the back of his car, "in a deep and dreamless sleep" from which he never awakens, Cardwell's song tries to reassure us that Hank Williams has "gone to a better land."

When listened to one after another, the sixteen tribute songs of 1953 construct a highly specific image of Hank Williams. A little more than a year before his death, remember, Hank had left Nashville in disgrace.† In the tribute songs, however, there is little, if any, mention of the Hank Williams who got himself fired from the *Opry* for repeatedly embarrassing the Nashville establishment with his drunkenness and unreliability. Yes, Arthur Smith sings, in his "In Memory of Hank Williams," about how, "like all of us Hank had his faults," but those faults are not specified in any of the tributes. What we get, rather, is a kind of hagiography, a portrait of Hank Williams as a country music saint who has gone peacefully to his just reward.[3] [...]

Jimmie Skinner's "Singing Teacher in Heaven" and Johnny Ryon's "That Heaven Bound Train" each maintains this comforting portrait of a singer called home to "his Maker." Skinner assures us that Hank has "traveled on to a house of gold" where "the saints of God [abide]." For Ryon, Hank "is riding to glory on that Heaven bound train," where he will find angels to sing "the many songs that [he] will bring." Moreover, both Skinner and Ryon imagine moments when they will join Hank in some unbroken circle in the sky. Ryon sings of how "someday we all will be with him again" when we are called upon to ride "that Heaven bound train," while Skinner prays for a reunion with Hank on the day when he himself must "join the heavenly choir."

In "Hank, It Will Never Be the Same Without You," Williams's good friend Ernest Tubb sings of how, from the start, Hank's life was full of "misery." But that misery doesn't matter now because, in his death, Hank has finally achieved that goal he struggled "so bravely for" in life: "eternal happiness." A similar sentiment is found in Jimmie Logsdon's "Hank Williams Sings the Blues No More," in which we are assured that Hank has now found "a new singing place

---

† Williams left Nashville for Montgomery, Alabama, shortly after being fired from the *Grand Ole Opry* on August 11, 1952, some four-and-a-half months before his death.

/ Where the sun shines on his face." In "The Last Letter," Jimmy Swan offers the most explicit assurance that the Ramblin' Man has indeed achieved eternal peace when he sings of how he dreamed one night of meeting Hank Williams in heaven. Swan's dream centers on an image of Hank holding tightly to a "little white Bible."

Many of these first tribute songs were written by artists who knew Hank well, so we certainly can't fault them for being sentimental portraits of a good friend. But as Hank Williams, Jr., said on one of his early albums: "In January of 1953, my father stopped being a man and became a legend."[4] These tribute songs initiated the construction of that legend. The man who died alone in the back-seat of a car because his heart finally failed him after so many years of heavy drinking had now simply passed away in a "deep and dreamless sleep." This long night's sleep, more of a summons from heaven than an actual death, had finally allowed the Ramblin' Man to gain his rightful rest. Moreover, the man who had been fired from the *Opry* two years before [*sic*] no longer existed. Instead, Hank now sings forever with the angels in some kind of *Grand Ole Opry* in the sky, and we too will sing with him "someday beyond the blue." Hindsight has allowed Hank Jr. to understand exactly what was going on in 1953. In *Living Proof*, his 1979 autobiography, he wrote: "While [Daddy] was alive, he was despised and envied; after he died, he was some kind of saint. And that's exactly how Nashville decided to treat Daddy—country music's first authentic saint."[5]

Nashville may have needed a saint, but Miz Audrey simply needed a husband. If the tribute songs served to smooth over the divorce between Hank and Nashville, Miz Audrey's songs served to smooth over her divorce from him. In a series of records released during the first two years after his death, Audrey Williams had her chance to write Hank's life the way she wanted it to be read. Fighting for custody of his memory as well as his estate, she was not only billing herself as "The One and Only Audrey (Mrs. Hank) Williams," she was singing about herself that way as well. On one of her early records, she tapped into the heaven imagery of the tribute songs, and just as the Nashville musicians imagined a reunion with Hank in the great beyond, Miz Audrey imagined a heavenly reprise of her wedded bliss with Hank on earth. "Are you writing songs for me up in Heaven?" she asks Hank. "So when I meet you beyond the blue, / You'll say 'Come here and listen to me,' / Then I'll smile and listen just as we used to do." In another song, entitled "My Life with You," she sings of how she and Hank first met and of how, when they were later married, she wept with happiness. She notes, however, that their "happiness didn't last long" because people started "wagging their tongues," and in the next stanza, she describes their divorce in a way that, well, makes it seem like they never got divorced:

Along about then, everything went wrong,
Little did we know it wouldn't be long
'Til you'd be in Heaven no more to be blue,
It's hard to go on without my life with you. [...]

As much as Miz Audrey was rewriting in song her husband's problematic past, she was also writing in life her son's promising future. Whereas other artists could only pen or perform tributes to Hank, Audrey Williams could turn her son into a living, singing tribute. And this she did. Although it was to a son named Randall Hank Williams that Audrey gave birth on 26 May 1949, she raised him as "Hank Williams, Jr." The boy's renaming was only the beginning. In his autobiography, Hank Jr. recalled those early years of careful refashioning: "Mother used to coach me in things Daddy said and then I'd go on stage and the audience would go crazy. They'd say I sounded just like ole Hank, and I guess I did."[6]

By age eleven, young Hank sounded enough like "ole Hank" to take the *Opry* stage and sing a few of his father's songs. Four years later, in 1964, he appeared on the *Ed Sullivan Show* and sang "Long Gone Lonesome Blues," a cover of his father's #1 hit from 1950. Peaking at #5, the song gave fifteen-year-old Hank Jr. his first chart record. When he tried to follow up later in the year with two singles of his own songs, he reached no higher than #42 on the charts. To the young Hank Williams, the message couldn't have been clearer: "There'd be the people [at my concerts] who came looking for my daddy, who wanted to hear nothing but 'I'm So Lonesome I Could Cry' and 'Jambalaya and a crawfish pie-a and a me-o-my-o,' and would be bitterly disappointed when they found only me."[7]

Hank Jr. didn't break into the top ten with one of his own songs until "Standing in the Shadows" was released in 1966. While this wasn't a cover of one of his father's earlier hits, it was nevertheless a song about his father. In "Standing in the Shadows," Hank Jr. maintains that he's "just doin' the best [he] can," but that "it's hard" when you have to stand in the shadow "of a very great man." He recognizes the burden of his father's legacy, but he also makes it quite clear that he's happy to bear that burden because it allows his father's music to "live on and on and on." [...] The success of "Long Gone Lonesome Blues" and "Standing in the Shadows," coupled with the failure of every other song [he wrote] up to that point, made something else quite clear to Hank Jr.: if he sang his father's songs, or sang about how willing he was to carry on his father's legacy, he'd be accepted; if not, he'd flounder at the bottom of the charts. It's no wonder, then, that early in his career he released such albums as *Hank Williams, Jr. Sings the Songs of Hank Williams* and *Songs My Father Left Me: The Poems of Hank Williams Set to Music and Sung by Hank Williams, Jr.*

In the late 1960s and early 1970s, Hank Jr. the performer remained faithful to the country-music-saint image of his father created by the tribute records and by his mother. [...] He knew [...] that he himself was "the chosen one," designated to walk in the shadow of that saint.[8] In his teens and twenties, Hank Jr. played the role perfectly, practicing the patter and giving back to Nashville the ghost it wanted to see and hear. But when he started popping pills and drinking booze and running around all over town, Nashville turned on him, and it did so by using his father against him. Music City had Hank Jr. in a double bind: On the one hand, he was expected to be the model son of the "Singing Teacher in Heaven." Then, when he proved to be no son of a saint, Nashville sighed with resignation: What else could they expect from a (Hank) Williams? The first one had let them down, and the second one was sinking even lower. Whichever vision of Hank Sr. they held up before him—country music saint or irredeemable sinner—Hank Jr. couldn't win. He was shadowed by a myth that the *Opry,* not the Son of Ramblin' Man, controlled. [...]

Before 1975, Hank Jr. had let everyone else tell him who his father was and what his father's life meant. As long as he listened to others' stories, he was stuck with the role of either the son of a saint or the son of a cheatin', boozin', no-account failure. But after 1975, Hank Jr. hung up the two-hat legend of Hank Sr. that Nashville had fashioned and started writing his own version of his father's life. What he linked up with was a third myth of Hank Williams—not the saint, not the sinful failure, but "the most wanted outlaw in the land."

In a steady series of revisionist songs, including "Feelin' Better," "Family Tradition," and "The Conversation," Hank Jr. took his lead from singer-songwriters like Kris Kristofferson and Waylon Jennings.[9] The Outlaw movement that began in the late 1960s and peaked in the mid-1970s had created an anti-establishment Hank Williams long before his son ever embraced that vision. While Hank Jr. was still trying to sort through all the things that "they" kept saying about his father, Kris Kristofferson began to tell Nashville that Hank Williams was an Outlaw, and, if "they" didn't like this image of Hank, well, "they" could kiss his ass. At the same time, Waylon Jennings was proudly proclaiming, "I'm a Ramblin' Man," thus offering himself up as the Second Coming of the original Outlaw. Moreover, Jennings had surveyed the Nashville music scene and wondered aloud, "Are You Sure Hank Done It This Way?" Seeing nothing in Nashville but "rhinestone suits and new shiny cars," Waylon concluded that country music needed to change. The change, of course, would come from the Outlaws themselves—as the ones who were out there speeding their young lives away, they were the rightful heirs to the Hank Williams legacy. In the early 1970s, the Outlaws were trying to tell Nashville that it no longer understood what country music was all about, and the best way to accomplish this was to show Nashville that it had never really understood what Hank Williams was all about. [...]

[Hank Jr.] could sing his own stuff now, a kind of Southern country rock less suited to Nashville than to "Macon and Muscle Shoals."‡ But in this new stage of his career, he was not just singing his own music; he was also writing his own version of his father's life. Nowhere was this done more forcefully, or more skillfully, than in two songs from 1979: the Top 10 hit "Family Tradition" and the Waylon Jennings duet "The Conversation."

In "Family Tradition," Hank Jr. admits that he's changed direction in the last few years, and that in doing so he has broken with the Nashville tradition. But then he asks Nashville to think about his "unique position." If he drinks, smokes dope, lives a hard and tragic honky-tonk life that runs counter to the Nashville tradition, well, that's just his "family tradition" after all. With this song, then, Hank Jr. was able to turn the tables on Nashville and the dictates of its tortuous logic: be like who we say your father was (the country music saint), but not too much like who we say your father also was (the irresponsible failure)—or we'll run you out of town for not being the living proof of your father that we want, and need, you to be. In "Family Tradition," Hank Jr. created his own kind of tortuous logic and then turned it on Nashville: Yes, he admitted, there's a Nashville family tradition. Fine. But there's also a Williams family tradition. And his family tradition isn't like their family tradition, and he's the one named Williams here. So, if "you stop and think it over," the Nashville tradition and the Williams tradition are nothing alike. In 1952, Music City may have kicked Hank Williams out of the family, but, in 1979, his son was returning the boot.

In the opening stanza of "Family Tradition," Hank Jr. sings about how, lately, some of his Nashville "kinfolk have disowned a few others and me." Then, teaming up in "The Conversation" with one of those disowned others—Waylon Jennings—Hank Jr. took back the family inheritance. In fact, what Hank Jr. and Waylon did in this song was akin to what Audrey Williams had done in Oakwood Cemetery Annex back in the 1950s—staking a claim to Hank Williams. First, these two disowned Outlaws set out to take control over what was said about Hank Williams. At the beginning of the song, they agree not to "talk about the habits / Just the music and the man." Next, having set the agenda,

---

‡ A reference to Macon, Georgia, home of Capricorn Records (founded 1969), a label for whom several southern rock bands recorded (including the Allman Brothers Band and the Marshall Tucker Band), and Muscle Shoals, Alabama, site of the celebrated Muscle Shoals Sound Studio (also established in 1969) at which many prominent rock acts recorded (among them the Rolling Stones and Lynyrd Skynyrd).

they set about exposing the hypocrisy of those who have staked false claims to Hank's memory. In their refrain, they both sing:

> Back then they called him crazy,
> Nowadays they call him a saint.
> Now the ones that called him crazy then
> Are still ridin' on his name.

The final revisionary step, of course, is to stake their own claim to Hank, to "write"—and thus "ride"—on his name. So when Waylon asks Hank Jr. whether his father would approve of the Outlaws if he were alive today, Hank assures Waylon that the original Ramblin' Man would be "right here by our side." The early tribute singers placed themselves beside Hank Williams in heaven; Miz Audrey claimed the same place with him "beyond the blue," where she would join Hank and he'd "say 'Come here and listen to me.'" Now, here were Hank Jr. and Outlaw Waylon claiming that the Ramblin' Man would "be the first one on [their] bus and ready to ride." "The Conversation," which begins with Waylon's invitation, "Hank, let's talk about your daddy," drives straight toward its calculated, revisionist conclusion, in which both voices are joined in proclaiming, "You know when we get right down to it, / He's still the most wanted outlaw in the land!"

Hank Jr., Waylon, and others continued to promote this outlaw image of Hank Williams well into the next decade. [...] In the 1980s and 1990s, however, yet another image of Hank Williams emerged, one that is best illustrated by two Top 10 songs: David Allan Coe's "The Ride" (1983) and Alan Jackson's "Midnight in Montgomery" (1992). In neither song is Hank portrayed as a saint or an outlaw, nor is he put on a heaven-bound train or the Outlaws' bus. Instead, the Ramblin' Man has become a weary ghost who cannot ride with either gang.[10]

"The Ride" (written by J. B. Detterline and Gary Gentry) sets out to revise every tribute song ever written about Hank by turning the "Singing Teacher in Heaven" into the tormented ghost of I-65. As Coe's recording of the song opens, he is making the same trek to Nashville that Hank made twenty years [sic] before. Thumbing his way north from Montgomery, he is offered a ride by a stranger in an "antique Cadillac." The Hank who had appeared to Jimmy Swan in a dream, holding a "little white Bible" in heaven, now appears as a "ghost white pale," "half drunk and hollow-eyed" stranger. No longer harmonizing with the angels in heaven, Hank is back on earth dispensing hard and bitter truths. In the song's haunting refrain, Hank warns the singer, "If you're big star bound, let me tell you it's a long hard ride." In the final stanza, Hank stops the car just south of

Nashville and begins to cry: his passenger must get out here because Hank is going back to Alabama. We're not told why Hank Williams won't drive on into Music City. In an Outlaw song, he would probably be rejecting Nashville. Hank's tears in "The Ride," however, suggest not a defiance of Nashville, but a longing for home and, perhaps, acceptance. Envisioned in this song as a lonesome exile, Hank is doomed to ride the highway between Montgomery and Nashville, never finding rest, never gaining peace, never getting home. [...]

At the beginning of "Midnight in Montgomery," Alan Jackson is headed in the opposite direction from Coe—or so it first appears. Riding south on I-65, Jackson is not "big star bound," he's already a big star (witness the Silver Eagle). On his way from Nashville to Mobile for a "big New Year's Eve show," Jackson stops for just a moment in Montgomery to pay homage to Hank Williams. He is surprised when a "drunk man in a cowboy hat," with "haunted, haunted eyes," appears. This ghostly Hank has little to say to Jackson except to thank him for caring enough to visit. When Hank quickly disappears, Jackson wonders whether he was "ever really there." Still uncertain, Jackson reboards his bus, leaving Hank behind. If the implication of "The Ride" is that Hank must drive eternally up and down I-65, then Jackson's song implies that Hank can't ever get on I-65, or any other road, for that matter, neither heading for Provo on the Outlaws' bus nor bound for glory on a celestial train. [...]

The developing visions of Hank Williams that I have mapped out here, from heavenly saint to defiant Outlaw to lonely ghost, should by no means suggest that every country artist has accepted this development, that Hank Williams's presence is now only that of a haunted, and haunting, apparition in country music. In "Me & Hank & Jumpin' Jack Flash," a song released in 1992, the same year as "Midnight in Montgomery," Marty Stuart dreams of a visit with Hank Williams in "hillbilly heaven." Stuart's Hank is still putting on concerts and giving his blessing to the truly authentic country singers (like Stuart himself). In fact, Stuart adds his own little twist to the narrative I've been tracing here when he implies that his entire album, *This One's Gonna Hurt You*, is actually a revelation from Hank himself—that Hank, not Marty, wrote all the songs.[11] Hank seems, to Marty Stuart at least, to still be the great "singing teacher in heaven."

In his biography of Hank Williams, however, Chet Flippo argues that this great singing teacher

> never really got it straight in his mind whether he was writing for Saturday night...or whether he was writing for Sunday morning.... He kept writing both kinds of songs and could never get it entirely straight in his own mind just where he belonged. He wanted to have Saturday night, drink it up and have a good time, but then he'd start to feel guilty and want to go back to Sunday morning and the sunlight and the white church and innocence.[12]

I think that much the same can be said for us. Just as Hank Williams struggled to figure out "where he belonged," we too have struggled to figure out what place he holds in country music. As soon as we have chiseled one version of Hank Williams's life we feel guilty, knowing that our song tells us more about ourselves than about the man. So we chisel another version. And then another. And yet another. Our own restlessness and uncertainty keep us on the road, on a constant journey between Nashville and Montgomery, between Music City and Hank's city, in search of an answer. But perhaps in the end there is no answer except this one: Hiram "Hank" Williams died on 1 January 1953, and, whether we want to admit it or not, we've all been writing on his back ever since.[13]

NOTES

1 Those who have been to the grave in recent years will be aware of how, in the spirit of this essay, I have revised the scene. [...] My apologies to Miz Audrey.

2 Here is a complete list of those 1953 songs [...]: "The Death of Hank Williams" (Jack Cardwell); "Hank, It Will Never Be the Same Without You" (Ernest Tubb); "Hank's Song" (Ferlin Husky); "Hank Williams Meets Jimmie Rodgers" (The Virginia Rounders); "Hank Williams Sings the Blues No More" (Jimmie Logsdon); "Hank Williams Will Live Forever" (Johnny [Johnnie] and Jack); "(I Would Have Liked to Have Been) Hank's Little Flower Girl" (Little Barbara); "In Memory of Hank Williams" (Arthur Smith); "The Last Letter" (Jimmy Swan); "The Life of Hank Williams" (Hawkshaw Hawkins); "Singing Teacher in Heaven" (Jimmie Skinner); "That Heaven Bound Train" (Johnny Ryon; Cal Shrum); "There's a New Star in Hillbilly Heaven" (The Virginia Rounders); "Tribute to Hank Williams" (Joe Rumore); "A Tribute to Hank Williams, My Buddy" (Luke McDaniel).

3 The one exception is Ferlin Husky's "Hank's Song."

4 See Hank Williams, Jr., *Insights Into Hank Williams* (MGM Records, 1974).

5 Hank Williams, Jr. (with Michael Bane), *Living Proof: An Autobiography* (New York, 1979), 64.

6 Ibid., 37.

7 Ibid., 17.

8 Ibid., 24.

9 These three songs, of course, do not represent a complete list of Hank Jr.'s revisionist songs, for example, "The Ballad of Hank Williams" or "A Whole Lotta Hank." [...] Note as well that Hank Sr. often appears in songs that are not devoted entirely to him. On *The New South*, for instance, several songs (e.g., "Montgomery in the Rain" and "The Blues Man") make reference to Hank Sr.

10 For another song that manifests this third vision, see Robin and Linda Williams's "Rollin' and Ramblin' (The Death of Hank Williams)," on their 1988 album, *All Broken Hearts Are the Same* (see also Emmylou Harris's version of this song on her 1990 album, *Brand New Dance*).

11 The opening song on the album, "Me & Hank & Jumpin' Jack Flash," ends with the suggestion that the next song was sung by Hank Williams during Stuart's dream. The third cut no longer plays with this suggestion—or so it appears. But the last song on side two is followed by fifteen seconds of silence, after which Stuart is heard to say, "And that's when I woke up," thus suggesting that the entire album was sung by Hank during Stuart's dream.

12 Chet Flippo, *Your Cheatin' Heart: A Biography of Hank Williams* (New York, 1981), 49.

13 Considerations of space and thesis have precluded discussion of every song ever written about Hank Williams. The following list, by no means definitive, covers songs not mentioned elsewhere in this essay and is intended to aid other scholars [...]: "The Car Hank Died In" (The Austin Lounge Lizards); "From Hank to Hendrix" (Neil Young); "The Ghost of Hank Williams" (The Kentucky HeadHunters); "Hank" (Jerry Bergonzi; Treat Her Right); "Hank Drank" (Bobby Lee Springfield); "Hank and George, Lefty and Me" (Tommy Cash); "Hank and Lefty Raised My Country Soul" (Stoney Edwards); "Hank, You Still Make Me Cry" (Boxcar Willie); "Hank Williams from His Grave" (Paleface); "Hank Williams Led a Happy Life" (The Geezinslaw Brothers); "Hank Williams's Guitar" (Freddy Hart); "Has Anybody Here Seen Hank?" (The Waterboys); "I Feel Like Hank Williams Tonight" (Jerry Jeff Walker); "I Remember Hank" (Lenny Breau); "I Think I Been Talkin' to Hank" (Mark Chestnutt); "The Night Hank Williams Came to Town" (Johnny Cash); "Wailin' with Hank" (Art Farmer Quintet); "When He Was Young, He Was Billed as the Next Hank Williams" (Jerry Farden).

| 52 |

Teddy Gerald: Hank Williams Sr. Is Alive!

Although Hank Williams's ghost has been a recurring figure in the literature, accounts of actual sightings of the long-presumed-dead star have been

SOURCE Teddy Gerald, "Hank Williams Sr. Is Alive!," *Weekly World News*, February 14, 1995. Reprinted by permission of *Weekly World News*.

comparatively rare. The following "strange-but-true" cover story, "Hank Williams Sr. Is Alive!," appeared in the *Weekly World News*, a supermarket tabloid known for its outlandish stories of supernatural phenomena. The issue's cover featured what was purported to be a photograph of the heavily wrinkled, seventy-one-year-old Williams wearing his familiar cowboy hat, along with the caption, "King of country music faked his death in 1953!," and a quotation, reportedly from the singer himself, explaining, "I just had to get out of that rat race." In the accompanying article, readers learn that he was, in fact, residing happily in a quiet neighborhood in Paris, France. Hank Williams thereby joined a lengthy procession of "alive-after-all" entertainment celebrities and historical figures—including Elvis, John F. Kennedy, Marilyn Monroe, Princess Diana, and Adolf Hitler, to name only a handful—whom the editors of the *Weekly World News* assumed would generate sales in the nation's grocery store check-out lanes.

PARIS—A frantic Hank Williams Sr. faked his own death in 1953 and is alive today—still picking and singing the heart-tugging honky-tonk songs that made him a country music superstar!

That's the conclusion of hundreds of flabbergasted fans who've reported seeing the country crooner strolling the streets of this French capital within blocks of the world-famous Eiffel Tower.

"He's much older now, of course—a little balder and a little paunchier—but there is no doubt in my mind that it's him," said Nashville, Tenn., retiree Edith Detmon, 76.

"I saw him sitting on a little stool near the entranceway to an apartment building while my husband and I were exploring the streets of Paris in November. He was dressed in slacks, a sports shirt and a cowboy hat, playing that same old guitar he played when I saw him on the Grand Ole Opry so many times back in 1949 and '50."

"He was singing *Cold, Cold Heart* and his voice was just as clear and beautiful as ever."

"And I said to my husband, 'My God, that's Hank Williams. I'd know him anywhere.'"

Astonished Edith said she approached the guitar-picking oldster, now 71, and asked him if he really was the king of country and the father of modern-day superstar Hank Williams Jr.

"He looked at me with those same haunted eyes I'd seen so many times and he said, 'Yes, Ma'am, I am,'" the shaken lady recalled. "He seemed so open and friendly, we actually had coffee with him in a little café and spent an hour and a half talking to him—and before we left, he even let me take a few pictures."

"He told me he hated deceiving people by pretending to be dead all these years, but he just had to get out and start over. He begged us not to tell anybody exactly where he lived—because he said he didn't want everybody and his brother coming around looking for him. I'll tell you, the whole thing sent chills up my spine."

And the dumbfounded former hairdresser is just one of countless Americans who have reported recent encounters with the hard-boozing superstar who supposedly died 42 years ago.

"We've had literally hundreds of people tell us they've seen Hank on the streets of Paris in the past year—and some of them say they have even had conversations in which he's admitted who he was," said a skeptical record company executive. "These people come from all parts of the country and all walks of life, and they're very sincere about this. They believe they've seen Hank Williams alive, there's no doubt about that. But on the other hand, there is so much evidence that he's dead and buried that it's hard to believe he could still be living after all these years."

Police reports say the hard-living, hard-loving composer of hits like *Your Cheatin' Heart* and *Jambalaya* died in the backseat of his Cadillac on Jan. 1, 1953, as a friend drove him through the West Virginia countryside on his way to a concert. Thousands of heartbroken fans attended his funeral three days later.

"I was right there at the funeral with all the rest, but now I know the whole thing was just an elaborate hoax," elated Edith said.

"Hank told me he'd had some friends help him fake his death because the pressures of life as a star were so great he was drinking himself into the grave."

"So he 'died' and moved to Australia where nobody had really heard of him much, and he said he made a pretty good living teaching music and writing songs under a pen name."

"Then last year, he married a French woman and moved to Paris, and he said he planned to live out his years there, just taking it easy."

"Talking to him was kind of like talking to a ghost, you know, after all this time."

"But it was nice, too, because he said he'd really been happy these last 42 years—and if anyone ever deserved to be happy, it was good ol' Hank."

| 53 |

John Gilmore: Excerpt from *Laid Bare: A Memoir of Wrecked Lives and the Hollywood Death Trip*

As Hank Williams's posthumous stature steadily increased in the 1980s and 1990s, those who had known or been acquainted with him, however briefly, continued to record their experiences. Such was the case with John Gilmore, who vividly describes meeting the country star in his revealing 1997 book, *Laid Bare: A Memoir of Wrecked Lives and the Hollywood Death Trip*. Born in Los Angeles, California, Gilmore (b. 1935) worked as a television and film actor, in the process developing friendships with now-legendary Hollywood stars such as Marilyn Monroe and James Dean. Gilmore eventually concentrated his efforts on writing, publishing more than a dozen true-crime books and "hard-boiled" novels, including the acclaimed *Severed: The True Story of the Black Dahlia Murder* (1994).

In *Laid Bare*, Gilmore offers a first-hand chronicle of the celebrity lives he saw destroyed by fame, fortune, and personal demons. In the following selection he recounts a chance encounter he had with Hank Williams in mid-April 1952, outside the Riverside Rancho dance hall, located a few miles north of Hollywood. Williams's scheduled performance there was part of a troubled West Coast tour that saw him break down in the famous "There ain't no light" incident with Minnie Pearl (no. 41) and then, only days later, sabotage a movie contract through his rude behavior toward MGM Studios production chief Dore Schary. In this excerpt, Gilmore paints a haunting portrait of the singer during his final relentless tailspin.

His bladder was in rotten shape, and he was stewed, though the two cowboys with him said Hank hardly ever boozed a performance. It was around spring of '52, and Williams was going bald. His face looked like a dead man's.

I never figured out if the picture of Hank I'd given Janis [Joplin] had been taken before or after I met Hank in the Riverside Rancho parking lot. He'd been pretty wobbly before he started sharing the Johnny Walker Red with me and Barry Bowron—son of L.A.'s then-mayor Fletcher Bowron—and another pal, Mike Parey, a Hell's Angels biker with a fat-bob Harley that had caught Hank's eye.

SOURCE   John Gilmore, *Laid Bare: A Memoir of Wrecked Lives and the Hollywood Death Trip* (Los Angeles: Amok Books, 1997), 17–19, 20, 23–27, 28–29. © 1997 by John Gilmore. Used by permission.

I'd wrecked my hotrod Ford in the Mojave desert months before, but with a couple of radio and acting bits, I was soon driving a '50 Mercury. Like Hank's song, I had "two-dollar bills to boot" [sic] and "the place just over the hill" was the Riverside Rancho.

"King of Western Swing" Spade Cooley had made it big there during the war, with Tex Williams singing in his band. Cooley then moved to the Santa Monica Ballroom the year after V-J Day, and Tex (no relation to Hank) formed his own Western Caravan band at the Rancho. It wasn't long after they began broadcasting Spade's Jamborees from the ballroom that Cooley killed his own wife and went to prison.

"Smoke, Smoke, Smoke That Cigarette," Tex's big one, was known around the world. Tex was starring in movies and lived in Bel-Air off Sunset Boulevard. He was also friends with my father at the Hollywood Masonic Lodge and often sang Bob Nolan's Sons of The Pioneers songs at shows and festivities. Once I walked with Tex across Hollywood Boulevard for cigarettes. We looked at the footprints outside Grauman's Chinese Theater, and a few people asked Tex for his autograph. We were talking about Gene Autry because Autry was considering me for a run in a new series. His Flying A Studios were opposite Hollywood High, where I was going to school. My girlfriend Sherry's father was Autry's head cameraman and friends with Jack Mahoney, the lead in the new project. I was being slated as Mahoney's kid sidekick—an orphan he'd rescued from a bunch of Apaches.

Autry was filming in Bakersfield, and Tex said another boy he knew, Hank Williams, was in Bakersfield "or maybe down in San Diego on the road." Hank was going to be in L.A. long enough to play a weekend at the Rancho for Tex, who invited Barry Bowron and myself to catch Hank's performance.

Tex later told me Hank's appearance had been a spur-of-the-moment decision. He said, "Hank was coming to town about a movie deal, and we got to chewing the fat about the Rancho, and I said I sure wish he'd come over and play a Saturday night, and Hank said that's what he had in mind if it suited me. I said it suited me fine."

Marty, the owner of the Rancho, worried about booking Hank for fear he'd fill the ballroom then fail to show, too drunk to make it. According to Dallas, Tex's wife and also a singer, Marty put a lot of faith in Tex's judgment. "Marty knew that if something went wrong," she said, "Tex would right it in a matter of minutes. If Hank had some kind of problem, Tex would back Hank up."

"Hank's a funny bird," Tex said that night at Grauman's Chinese. "He's got a truckload of troubles hitched to himself. Cut off like he is from Nashville, he's a salmon in the desert. The damn guy's running headlong at disaster, but nobody can figure it out." He said he loved Hank even though he was having a hard time making it to dates. But Tex knew he'd show at the Rancho. "It's a certain way we have of saying something and setting it between us."

Tex and Dallas convinced Marty of Hank's sincerity about staying sober long enough to do the show. Hank had been jailed for shooting a revolver in a hotel, and I'd been told he hardly ate anymore and sometimes couldn't remember where he was or where he was going. "His problems are getting the best of him," Tex said. "But I'll take his word because on certain things he's as solid as gold. I hope this'll be one of those occasions where he shines through."

Phones were jumping at the Rancho, Dallas told me later, and by that afternoon they were taking reservations, "and the Rancho didn't have reservations," she said. "We would just fill the place until the fireman came around warning us to herd a bunch of the people back out into the parking lot until the next show."

As soon I learned about Hank's appearance, I called Barry Bowron. We'd talked about forming a group called the Tumbleweed Trio while we were students at the Marion Colbert School for Individual Instruction. I passed on the news and drove to Mike Parey's in Burbank. A little older than Barry or myself, Mike hung with a rowdy bunch of Valley Hell's Angels. His father had been a drummer for Spade Cooley, and Mike played the best non-professional boogie piano I'd ever heard. [...]

Barry and I were at the Rancho when Mike showed up in his leather jacket with the skull on the back. He wasn't wearing Hell's Angels' colors, so he looked just like any other cycle-hound. We met in the Rancho's coffee shop, which occupied the west end of the brown wooden building. The rest of the structure housed the dance floor and the bar upstairs. A long, narrow platform along a side wall made up the stage, backed by a big "Home on the Range" mural that was brown as resin from all the smoke.

Other writers have described the Rancho as a "ballroom," but that isn't accurate. A wooden honky-tonk down in a gully with a barn-like dance floor and a bar in the hayloft is closer to fact. You turned off Riverside Drive, which borders Griffith Park on the north of Hollywood, and drove down into a wide dirt parking lot. [...] At the top of the slope and along the road ran a railing of two-inch steel pipe fitted into concrete to keep cars from crashing down into the parking lot. [...]

The Rancho's big sign sticking up from the roof on stilts announced DANCING to the passing traffic. On nights when the fog crept low, the sign had a pale green look of peeled paint, but at other times it glowed brightly, all the reddish-pink lights blinking on and off. After a while, the bulbs started popping out and nobody replaced the dead ones.

We sat in a booth by the window, eating chili burgers and pushing the jukebox buttons—Hank's songs, Teresa Brewer, Tennessee Ernie Ford, Kay

Starr, Les Paul and Mary Ford's "How High the Moon," Hank Snow, or Frankie Laine's "Mule Train," while headlights from cars coming off Riverside angled up and down the driveway like searchlights. People were pouring in to see Hank, even though he'd just been on the Kate Smith Show. [...]

Mike had gone out to check when the show would be starting, while Barry and I listened to the music beating through the east wall of the building. It wasn't Hank's Drifting Cowboys, more like the swing beat of the Caravan. Mike quickly reappeared at the window and knocked on the glass, saying something I couldn't quite hear about "Hank Williams" and pointing to the parking lot. He hurried into the café, shouting, "Williams is pissing in the lot behind my bike!"

Barry and I followed him out and to his Harley, which stood against the embankment between a big Packard and a panel truck. The Packard's left rear door was open, and two men were standing between the car and Mike's bike—one tall and lean like a rake handle, wearing a white suit with black music notes all over it like splotches of paint in the near-dark. The Packard faced the slope, and another man was reaching into the back seat. The taller one was Hank. He wasn't pissing right then, but he didn't have his hat on and the lights reflected off his balding scalp. He was leaning with one arm on a high-rise grip of Mike's angel wing handlebars and holding a paper sack the size of a milk bottle. When he saw the three of us approaching, he bent into the car and came out with his hat.

Mike was the first to reach him, and he nodded to Hank, saying something I couldn't hear. Hank said, "I sure do thank you for saying that." Then he smiled and said, "You don't think I hurt your motor-*sackle* none?" Shaking his head almost apologetically, Mike told Hank he could ride the bike if he felt like it. Nobody could hurt a Harley Davidson, he said.

Hank said, "I was looking at this here doohickey, a-gettin' a fix on its purpose, and I see there's one of these what you call suicide gears—"

"—shifters," Mike said. "You're right. It's called a suicide clutch because you got to let go with one hand to shift while you're squeezing with the other. No brake, no gas."

"Sounds like a fella's got his job cut out," Hank said, winking to the other cowboy standing beside the car.

"You get used to it like anything else," Mike said. "I'm serious, if you want to ride it, just take it out." Mike said he'd be honored, but Hank waved his hand, shaking his head a little.

"I'm just killing time on solid ground," Hank said, "partakin' 'til they're ready for us inside..." He said the last time he was on a motor*sackle* it had tried to get out from under him. "Just like a lot of gals I know," he said, and Mike laughed. Hank said, "You bein' one of these Harley fellas, you know that notion of goin' over the side of the road." He reached up his hand and made a fish-tailing motion. "Creepin' away from the road," he said.

"Going to the high side," Mike said. "A bike'll do that on a winding road or a curve in the highway."

"You're right about that highway," Hank said. "I don't recollect the particular road, but seems to me there was some pitch in it like an old road, sunken down in the middle, and the hind end of the motor*sackle* was a-slidin' uphill of it."

"Goin' to the high side," Mike said again.

"That's just what she did," Hank continued. He moved the top of the sack away from the mouth of the bottle and drank from it, then looked at me and asked Mike, "This here your brother? You California fellas just all this naturally good-lookin'?" Hank switched hands with the paper sack and reached to shake my hand. He said, "I'm called Hank."

I remember his handshake as if it were yesterday. A lot of people have joked around, saying, "Let me shake the hand that shook Hank Williams'," but it was really a funny feeling. His hand felt like bones, long and sinewy, and hard as though made of something other than skin. And icy, as if he didn't have any blood in his veins. I was reminded of touching my dead grandmother, the first dead person I ever touched. I was in the slumber chamber with my mom, seeing my grandmother laid out, and we talked about how her skin felt, and what the undertakers had done to get her looking as good as she did, and what they'd done to Jean Harlow with some kind of rubber tube or siphon device.

After shaking my hand, Hank stepped back like he was about to fall, then leaned towards Mike's bike, grabbing the seat to balance himself. "You don't mind if I sit on your saddle?" he asked Mike. Hiking a leg up and over, he eased onto the bike, his knees jutting out to the sides like a wishbone. Mike monkeyed with the headlight and ignition, saying he'd kick it over if Hank wanted to rev it a little, which seemed like a good idea. In a second the ignition was on. Mike turned down the pedal on the kick starter, then pushed down hard with his boot and the engine fired up. Hank laughed, nodding, but looked scared, and his teeth were very yellow. Mike twisted the grip a couple of times, stirring up some backfires, then killed it because Hank seemed too nervous and the other cowboy looked about ready to shut it off himself. "Bet she'll rip," Hank said. "Is she fast?"

Mike grinned. "Drives the cops nuts...But like I said, on the open road it can get a little spooky."

"Like knocking some gal up," Hank said. He glanced at the cowboy and said something, and the cowboy said he didn't know for sure if Hank had done it, and Hank said, "Oh, like shit it wasn't!" He'd handed the sack to Mike and was straddling the bike with both hands on the grips. "This boy's right," he said.

"This goin' to the high side's the way of puttin' it that makes it understandable." He said to Mike, "Talkin' about headin' for trouble..."

He gestured to pass the bottle along, and I took a gulp. It was Johnny Walker Red and I gasped. When Hank tipped it back, he seemed to just pour it down into himself as if swallowing water. Then he got off the bike, tilted closer to the car fender and said the cowboy was "Roy Rogers—here to make a motion picture movie about the pitiful side of life."

The cowboy said, "I'm not Roy Rogers, but if the law comes through here they're gonna be doin' some Roy Rodger'n with us lickerin' up juveniles."

Hank feigned a shocked look. "Are y'all juveniles?" he asked. We shook our heads, and Hank said, "Better finish what we're doin' before the law does get here." Then he asked, "What time *do* they get here?"

"The bewitchin' hour," the cowboy said, shaking his head. Hank offered the sack to Mike, who said no thanks and passed the bottle back to me. I drank as Hank watched me with a curious smile. He said I had a "yearnin' look" and looked like I was "goin' through life sideways...like seein' what he's maybe leavin' behind..." Barry wanted to take some pictures and Hank said he didn't mind, so Barry snapped off some shots with his new flashbulb attachment. I handed the bottle back to Hank, who shook it and said it felt like "half a pint," and then drank it straight down. There was a trickling sound, and I thought the liquor was leaking out of the sack. But it was Hank pissing in his pants as he drank. The urine trickled through his trouser leg to form a puddle around his double-eagle boots. Hank apparently didn't notice it, though he straightened up from the fender. When he saw the puddle at his feet, he said, "Well, son-ova*bitch!*" and spat down at the ground. The cowboy brought a small suitcase from the car and said something to Hank about changing his pants. Then Hank started to laugh. It was a hee-hawing sound like a donkey, and he rubbed his forehead hard with the fingers of both hands. He looked like a zombie.

Two other men had come out of the Rancho, one I recognized from the Caravan band. They looked at Hank disgustedly and at us, and one said they were set up inside. The Roy Rogers one said, "He doesn't do this as a rule, you understand..."

"It ain't their fault," Hank said. "Go on in and I'm comin' in." The men turned back to the Rancho as Hank climbed into the Packard to change his pants. "Now I 'spose I'm ready," he said, and as he climbed out and came forward he put his hand on my shoulder. We walked to the side of the Rancho with his hand placed there as though on a stick or a rudder. When we got to the door, he said, "You boys come in with us and enjoy the show." Then he said something like, "Any man that's been sharin' don't need a breach in companions..." He turned his head to Mike, who was right behind us. Hank's neck looked skinny, the collar sticking away from his skin when he moved his head. Caught between the dark of the parking lot and the bright lights of the ballroom, he looked very tall and wide, like a cut-out figure or a flat cowboy suit with wide padded shoulders hung out on a stiff clothes hanger. He said to Mike, "Some time, son, we're gonna take one of those rides."

"I'll ride you up the grapevine," Mike said eagerly. "A person can have a swell time heading up the mountains. Hell, it'll haul ass to Vegas quicker'n a car."

Hank asked the cowboy, "We been to Nevada?" but before he was answered, he said to Mike, "It's dark here as I reckon it gets there...They all run into one another, even for a natural-born traveling man I'd be all busted up come down on the side of night."

We followed Hank and the cowboy through the side door into a sort of atrium and past a stone wishing well and fireplace. Straight ahead through the big doors was the dance floor, the ballroom and the stairs to the second-floor bar.

Up on the Rancho's small stage, Hank and the Drifting Cowboys punched right into the music. It was the first time I'd heard "I'll Never Get Out of This World Alive," and Hank sang it twice. Where he sang "No matter how I struggle and strive," on the last part of "strive," his upper teeth and lower lip pulled the word out. The last sound to it, the "v-e," sort of caught and hung vibrating even while he'd gone on with "I'll never get out of this world alive."

Less than eight months later he'd be dead, keeled over in the back seat of his Cadillac convertible on the way to a big show in Canton. [...]

Hank had been dead about three years when I ran into Tex Williams eating pancakes in the Mayflower Coffee Shop on Hollywood Boulevard. I'd seen him a couple of times at Republic Studios when I'd been on movie interviews, but he'd never had time to talk about Hank. Tex asked me to join him in the Mayflower, and after some talk about my father and the Hollywood Masonic Lodge, I brought up Hank's aborted movie career. He had signed a contract to make pictures, then just turned his back on it. Slim Whitman once told me, "Oh, Hank forgot about it. He couldn't remember he'd done it, because he wasn't sober when he'd signed for all that money."

Hank's movie stardom was tossed out before it began. Tex said, "It could've taken place, by god—not like John Wayne or Tex Ritter, but he could've done better than Bob Wills, who wanted to be a movie star more than anything. Like Gene Autry did. Bob thinks of himself that way, and he's told me as much. Hank never said a thing about movies, because he didn't care about 'em."

Tex pointed to a sign on the coffee-shop wall, the Optimist's Creed: "As you ramble on through life brother / whatever be your goal / keep your eye upon the doughnut / and not upon the hole." For Hank, "Life was the hole," Tex said.

"He lived in life's hole and never got out. Even though he had fame by the tail and could've pulled himself through like you'd use a rope to get out of any hole, he couldn't hold it. He took fame down in the hole with him." Tex said that Hank had liked him, that they'd appreciated one another. "But we never did have a close affiliation outside of music. I don't know if anybody did or could have, because Hank was all alone. He had a streak like one of those characters chasing a carrot that's hung on a stick attached to his head. Spade Cooley was no different, except for his ability to trick people, and he was crazy to be top man on the hill so he never got stuck in a hole. Spade was chasing carrots front *and* hind end, and that divides a person." Hank didn't want to settle for a good-sized hunk of the doughnut, as Tex had done. "Hank was a divided fellow," Tex said, "and lacked Spade's sense of trickery. Couldn't play both ends." Spade wanted the whole doughnut, Tex told me, while Hank saw only the hole. It was Hank's outstanding talent as an artist that kept him alive as long as he lasted. "There was nothing," Tex said, "to be improved upon. The boy's life burned up fast."

Tex looked at me across the table and, almost mysteriously, said, "Hank's existence was misery and sadness. He lives on in people's insides, a real disturbance in other people's souls..."

~~~~~~

| 54 |

Craig Womack: Howling at the Moon: The Queer But True Story of My Life as a Hank Williams Song

As a singer and a songwriter, Hank Williams articulated the personal experiences and innermost feelings of his audiences to a degree that few American musicians have achieved, and decades after his death, his recordings continue to resonate with new generations of listeners. Craig Womack, a leading writer and theorist in Native American literary studies, celebrates the enduring emotional power and universality of one Williams classic in this excerpt from his coming-of-age essay, which originally appeared in the 1997 edited scholarly collection *As We Are Now: Mixblood Essays on Race and Identity.* Of mixed Creek and

SOURCE Craig Womack, "Howling at the Moon: The Queer But True Story of My Life as a Hank Williams Song," in *As We Are Now: Mixblood Essays on Race and Identity,* ed. William S. Penn (Berkeley: University of California Press, 1997), 37–38. © 1997, the Regents of the University of California. Used by permission of the University of California Press.

Cherokee ancestry, Womack (b. 1960) grew up in Martinez, California, among transplanted Okies, listening to the music of his Oklahoma-born father's favorite singer, Hank Williams. As this passage indicates, Williams, the Alabama "poor white" who made good, was an artist capable of speaking to the hurt and alienation felt by others who were similarly marginalized by mainstream American society, even those who might otherwise seem to have little else in common with him. In this case, Hank Williams's music helped the teenaged Womack bring together his divided identities as a Native American and a gay man.

My dad taught me to play the guitar, which I took up at age sixteen. My dad loves Hank Williams songs, and his dad used to tell me stories about the hobos and the freight trains, having hopped boxcars himself from Eufaula [Oklahoma,] out to the San Joaquin Valley [in California], starting at age fourteen, to work in the fields and orchards, then going back and forth to Oklahoma. We are a coming-and-going bunch. So grandpa, Lester Womack, liked all those Jimmie Rogers [Rodgers] songs. Hobo Bill's Last Ride. All around the water tower, waiting for a train. I'm going to California, where they sleep out every night. An Oklahoma Indian friend of mine, one night when we were sitting smoking and drinking coffee in Norman, told me, "In high school I used to go with my friends in Lawton to get somebody to buy beer for us. We'd get six packs of Little Kings and listen to Hank Williams, parked at the cemetery north of town." This was a small miracle; I had been listening to Hank Williams all my life. I told my friend how my dad sang Hank's songs incessantly; I may have been the only kid my age in Martinez, California, who knew that Hank started out doing talking blues and calling himself Luke the Drifter,* singing sad songs, one that I particularly remembered about the town slut who gets killed saving a little boy from a car wreck, the community realizing only too late that they had misjudged her. The name of the song is "Be Careful of Stones that You Throw."

I said to my buddy, "Yeah, I remember really clearly the day I first I heard 'I'm So Lonesome I Could Cry.' That was the purest, rawest, most emotional thing I'd ever listened to. I thought, good God, this isn't an expression of pain, this is pain, the stuff of which pain is made."

Sometime later, one beautiful Oklahoma summer evening, he and I and a couple of friends were driving back from the movies in Oklahoma City. I had stuck "Hank Williams' Greatest Hits" in my coat pocket and surreptitiously

---

* Williams did not record his first sides released under this pseudonym until January 10, 1950, a full three years into his commercial recording career; among the four Luke the Drifter titles he cut at this session was his first talking blues, "Everything's Okay."

slipped it in the tape player when our two white compatriots weren't looking (one of them referred to my Hank Williams collection as incestuous hillbilly warbling). My friend and I rolled down the windows and let in the humid summer air while we belted out "Howling at the Moon" in true coyote abandon, and this was minus the Little Kings. After the chorus, "You got me chasing rabbits, scratching fleas, and howling at the moon," we turned our faces up toward the black sky and wailed. Our friends looked aghast, and there was something about those Hank Williams songs that he and I shared that the other people in the car did not. I don't know quite how to put my finger on it, but it has to do with alienation, loneliness, a shitload of pain, and not being able to speak to the one you love, remaining hidden and silent in the shadows for a lifetime. The songs have everything to do with being queer; the songs have everything to do with being Indian, and me and my buddy were the only two people that night who knew the beauty and terror of both identities.

| 55 |

Sarah Vowell and Brian Alcorn: Two Reviews of *The Complete Hank Williams*

In 1998, to coincide with what would have been Hank Williams's seventy-fifth birthday, Mercury Records released *The Complete Hank Williams*, a ten-CD boxed set containing 225 studio and live recordings, demos, home recordings, and radio spots. Although not literally complete (the WSM "Mother's Best" radio transcriptions are missing, for example), this Grammy Award–winning collection represented a monumental compilation of his work, and its release inspired a number of eloquent and insightful reviews, two of which are reproduced below. The first is by Sarah Vowell (b. 1969), a National Public Radio personality, author, humorist, critic, and voiceover actress. She chiefly addresses a question originally raised by Greil Marcus in his ground-breaking 1975 book, *Mystery Train: Images of America in Rock 'n' Roll Music* (no. 36), namely, did Hank Williams represent the last gasp of an older, conservative southern tradition, or was he a proto-rocker who antici-pated the energy and spirit of the modern Sunbelt South? In the second piece, San Francisco music journalist Brian Alcorn (b. 1966) stresses what he sees as the profound contradictions in Williams's life, and credits him with bestowing "dignity to so-called 'hillbilly music'" and to the masses of ordinary Americans who listened to it.

SARAH VOWELL, "AIN'T NO LIGHT," *VILLAGE VOICE*,
SEPTEMBER 29, 1998[*]

One of the packaging perks of the new 10-CD box set *The Complete Hank Williams* is a series of postcard reproductions of recent art about Hank. A more useful inclusion might have been a refrigerator magnet with a toll-free number for Alcoholics Anonymous. Sure, there are jokes and novelties and "Hey Good Lookin'" among the 225 cuts, but the feeling you come away with is the essence of bleak. You can write it off as art, but by the second or third hour of that voice weeping 'round your living room it doesn't feel like anything as comforting as art; it feels like every reason you ever wanted to shut your lungs down and call it a life.

You can hear it in the defeated "You Win Again," famously recorded the day after Hank's divorce from his first wife was final.[†] You can hear it on the previously unissued hymn "Drifting Too Far From the Shore." And you can hear it in the final, pitiful track—Hank's prerecorded apology to an audience in Washington in 1951. (He'd had back surgery, but he had to reassure the paying customers that he hadn't flaked out, drunk.) But most of all, you can hear the death wish in a two-minute abyss lurking in the seventh disc, "Alone and Forsaken," a 20th-century landmark that isn't so much country music as French lit: *No Exit, L'Etranger*.[‡]

When country musicians and country fans talk about Hank Williams, they invariably call him "the real thing." As in, "I have a hard time separating the songs from Hank because he was the real thing." That's Kris Kristofferson: a testimonial decorating the booklet of *The Complete Hank Williams*. Of course, "real thing" in today's Nashville probably just means "not Canadian," but still, Williams is the original all-time all-star of musical authenticity. Just spend an hour or so with one of those Hank's greatest hits records every country music fan has owned, chocked full and weighted down with "Cold, Cold Heart" and "Lovesick Blues" and "I'm So Lonesome I Could Cry" (where even the damn moon has to hide behind a cloud in tears). All that anguish coming through, that catch of the voice so caught and so close. Those songs, and the way he performed them, have the stateliness of sorrow: anyone who shoves you that far into the depths is going to get your respect. And he had the biography to match: born poor in Alabama to a stifling mother and an absent father, married

---

[*] Used by permission of Sarah Vowell.

[†] The couple's divorce was granted on May 29, 1952, but Williams did not record "You Win Again" until six weeks later, on July 11.

[‡] A reference to two classic works of French existentialism: Jean-Paul Sartre's 1944 one-act play, *Huis Clos* (*No Exit*, in English), and Albert Camus's 1942 novel, *L'Étranger* (*The Stranger*).

to the bottle and a bitch, suffering from back pain, and dead at 29 in the backseat of a Cadillac on the first day of 1953. [...]

Colin Escott, author of the definitive biography *Hank Williams* and one of the box's producers, has scrupulously and coherently set forth this massive posthumous set list with an almost shocking truthfulness. This is a celebration of Hank Williams without being an ad for him. Coming clean right away, Escott notes: "Hank's first recordings didn't set a new agenda the way that Elvis Presley's did." Listen to Presley's "That's All Right" next to Williams's so-so gospel debut, "Calling You," and it takes two seconds to figure out which one's the end and which one's the new beginning.

Williams is frequently mentioned as a proto-Elvis—same race, class, region. Same basic gospel and blues influences. Same rise to stardom via *The Louisiana Hayride*. But when I think of Hank Williams I don't think of Elvis Presley. I think of Elvis Presley's dad. Elvis was fun and sex and cars and girls. Elvis's father Vernon was prison and debt and no-luck-at-all. When Elvis performed "I'm So Lonesome I Could Cry" in Hawaii, he called it "the saddest song I've ever heard." Vernon probably heard it as a rundown of every other night of his life, and he and his kind were Hank's true audience.

One of the many beauties of Elvis, who made his first Sun recordings only a year after Hank died, is that he was defiantly postwar. Except for some radio performances in the early '40s, Hank's recordings take place between 1946 and 1952, not that you'd know it. You can't hear the new American world of shiny gadgets and cute little houses and gold lamé pants. The war's over, but Hank might as well be stuck in Europe eating rations and walking through bomb rubble.

You could argue that the redemption in the Williams oeuvre is of the godly sort—that he included gospel numbers in all his shows, that he's the author of "I Saw the Light" with its "no more in [sic] darkness" refrain. I don't believe this for a second. If Hank Williams bought into Christian crap like "I'll Have a New Body (I'll Have a New Life)," his faith faded the second the song went off the air. At his worst, he might have been a false witness, preaching things he wanted to believe but didn't. In an epigraph from Minnie Pearl in the booklet, she describes once driving to a show with Hank, who just so happened to be sloshed. She remembered, "And I started singing his number 'I Saw the Light.' He started out, and all of us were singing 'I Saw the Light.' Then he stopped and said, 'Quit! Hush! I don't want to hear that. I don't want to hear it, 'cause there ain't no light.'" [...]

Hank Williams represents an extreme. It's not like he invented hopelessness, but he perfected it. These are very moving records, and I'll keep coming back to them. I can bear them in 1998, but I don't know that I could have in

1952. Because in 1998, I know what comes next. In 1998, I can trust myself with "Alone and Forsaken" because I'm vaccinated with awopbopaloobops and mmmbops and all the giddiness in between. More than anything, *The Complete Hank Williams* is an argument for rock 'n' roll.

BRIAN ALCORN, "WHISKEY-BENT AND HELL-BOUND,"
SF WEEKLY, SEPTEMBER 30, 1998[§]

Hank Williams was a drunk, a mean drunk who died at 29 in the back seat of a Cadillac. He was a semiliterate plagiarist, a whoremonger, a brawler, and an egomaniac. He was a stingy manager of top-flight musicians and a notoriously unreliable employee who somehow managed to get canned from the *Grand Ole Opry* at the height of his own popularity. And Hank Williams was one of the greatest popular songwriters in American history. In his brief recording career, from 1947 [*sic*] to 1952, he cut 66 songs in his own name, about 50 of which he wrote whole or in part. Thirty-six of those were Top 10 country hits.[**] He was a sensitive, deeply religious man and a doting father. He loved western movies and comic books, suffered from a degenerative spinal disease, and spent his entire life under the influence of domineering, grasping women.

Such are the contradictions of country music's most troubled legend, contradictions encoded in country music itself. From the very beginning, from the Carter Family and Jimmie Rodgers' Bristol Sessions, country music has had two souls. One is pure, pious, and sentimental; the other, "whiskey-bent and hell-bound." The best country artists—Merle Haggard, Patsy Cline, George Jones—have a little of each. But no single artist has encompassed both halves of this spirit like Hank Williams. He loved Jesus, women, and the bottle about equally. It's hard to say which passion caused him the most grief. [...]

Williams has often been called "the hillbilly Shakespeare," and even if the moniker is an insult to both writers, they do have much in common. Their influence is so pervasive, so much a part of our culture, that their contributions are almost invisible. Williams' lines—"Hey good lookin' / Whatcha got cookin'?"—are common parlance, just like "All the world's a stage." Trainspotters claim that neither man wrote his entire catalog. And Williams is now a specialty taste even more so than Shakespeare, while legions of imitators—including Williams' own son and grandson—have enriched themselves on his genius.

---

§ © 1998 by Brian Alcorn. Used by permission.

** Williams has had thirty-seven Top Ten hits, if one counts his 1989 electronically enhanced duet with Hank Williams, Jr., "There's a Tear in My Beer," which peaked at No. 7 on the charts.

And yet of all the American musical icons of this century—Elvis, Dylan, Sinatra, Armstrong, Ellington, Bernstein, Gershwin—Hank Williams is fading fastest from our national memory. His songs are no longer aired, even on so-called country radio. That's why *The Complete Hank Williams*, released to coincide with what would have been his 75th birthday, is as stunning to its genre as *The Complete Works of William Shakespeare* is to literature. The Hank Williams set locates the artist behind the legend and, without sentimentality, without hero-worship, without varnishing over his many faults, restores him to vibrant life. [...]

Each volume of the 10-CD box set shows that Williams' music, for all its traditionalism, was very much the work of a young man. The lows are bottom-of-the-bottle low. The highs are giddy, lick-the-world high. Every song, in every hue, is utterly self-centered. No fewer than 28 songs contain the word "I" in the title. "Like a piece of driftwood on the sea / May you never be alone like me," he sang in "May You Never Be Alone," and though the song is as bleak as anything Williams ever recorded, it's hard not to laugh when it's followed up by "I Won't Be Home No More," "I'll Never Get Out of This World Alive," "I've Been Down That Road Before," and so on. Unlike other masters of this confessional style, such as Merle Haggard, Williams wasn't personalizing universal sorrows. He was singing about Hank Williams.

It's also striking how well Williams avoided the classic country clichés. He rarely sang about prisons, getting drunk, or his mama (although he did love a good train song). And even though he sang about the poverty of the South, he didn't waste sentiment on the simple joys of hillbilly life or the virtue of a hard day's work, or any of the other patronizing, family-values themes that dominate country music today. As the comprehensive liner notes in the Mercury set point out, whatever clichés we now hear in Hank Williams songs are clichés because of his songs.

The best of his work captures the torture of heartbreak, but it's not of the morose, my-baby-done-left-me variety. The breakup in songs like "Cold, Cold Heart" and "You're Gonna Change (or I'm Gonna Leave)" is always just around the corner, and the pain and immediacy of life at the edge of disaster make his music at once intimate and intuitive. This feeling came from hard experience: Audrey scrapped with Williams—verbally and physically—until the last year of his life, when she threw him out after he allegedly shot at her. [...]

An astonishing number of his songs, including "Your Cheatin' Heart," "I'm So Lonesome I Could Cry," "Hey, Good Lookin'," "Cold, Cold Heart," "I Saw the Light," "Move It on Over," and "Jambalaya (on the Bayou)," distill the pain and joy of life in a way that no songwriter, not even Dylan, has been able to surpass. This is Hank Williams' lasting legacy. He was the greatest proponent of the idea that, to some people, popular music meant more than a bouncy melody and "moon / June" sentimentality. To them it was literature, a way by which they understood themselves and the world around them. "A song ain't nothin' in the world but a story just wrote with music to it," he once said.

Of all the many contradictions that made up his turbulent career, the ultimate contradiction is that somehow, throughout an undignified life, Hank Williams brought dignity to so-called "hillbilly music." It is a dignity that has been conferred on his fans, the farm boys and girls who, like him, left their homes out on the rural route and found nothing but a lost highway.

It's almost impossible to look at the hard men in fading postwar family photographs, the coal miners, the shipbuilders, the lumber-mill workers, the drifters, and the honky-tonkers, without a measure of respect. Hank Williams spoke to them, and now he speaks for them. His words are their lives.

~~~~~~

| 56 |

Joe "Penny" Pennington: Excerpt from *Lookin' Back on Hank: Some Things You Never Knew about the Legendary Hank Williams*

Hank Williams formed the first version of the Drifting Cowboys around 1937, and at the time of his death in 1953, his band, although by then comprised of an assortment of pick-up players, still went under this same name. During those fifteen or so years, according to Colin Escott, "literally hundreds" of musicians played, at one point or another, in Williams's band. Among them was lead guitarist Joe "Penny" Pennington, one of the band's last surviving members. Born in Plant City, Florida, Pennington (b. 1928) joined the Drifting Cowboys in the late summer or fall of 1947, and performed with Williams on his Montgomery, Alabama, radio program and at stage shows throughout the state. But he and his fellow band members severed their ties with Williams in April 1948, after a drunken bender landed the singer in a sanitarium. Pennington later worked as a solo artist and as a sideman for several other country stars, including Little Jimmy Dickens and a then-unknown Lefty Frizzell.

SOURCE   Joe "Penny" Pennington, *Lookin' Back on Hank: Some Things You Never Knew about the Legendary Hank Williams* (n.p.: privately published, 1999), 5–6, 7, 8–11, 12, 17–18, 20–21, 23–25. © 1999 Joe "Penny" Pennington. Used by permission.

Pennington's self-published memoir captures Hank Williams during a critical early phase of his career, after he had met Nashville music publisher Fred Rose and begun recording for MGM, but before he had joined KWKH-Shreveport's *Louisiana Hayride*. Other members of the Drifting Cowboys, such as Jerry Rivers and Don Helms, published memoirs that are relatively deferential to Williams. Pennington, a seasoned musician nearly the same age as Williams, was less impressed with his employer. But Pennington makes clear that he found Williams to be a business-minded professional who, despite the occasional drinking binge, was very much a man in control of his career, even at this early stage.

Chris* called Hank and told him he thought he had him a good guitar man who wanted to come up and play with him. I got on the phone with Hank and he said, "Chris tells me you play a pretty good guitar. Do you want to come up and try it with us a little while?" I said, "Ain't there no good guitar players up there around Montgomery?" Hank said, "Well, none I'd want to hire." Well, much later I found out that he'd hired just about all the good ones around there and fired most of them, too! That left the field wide open. I told him it would take me about a week to tie up loose ends around here and get on up that way because I didn't have a car. Hank told me to come on up and meet him at Mom's Rooming House† and gave me the address. I began checking the local papers and found a couple driving all the way up to Birmingham in a 1940 Model Fraser [Frazer], I believe. In a few days I was ready to make the trip. I rode all the way up with my luggage, my guitar and my amplifier.

I was dropped off at Mom's Rooming House which was just one block from the radio station. Within an hour or so I met the rest of the Band which were Lum York on bass, Red Todd on rhythm guitar and R. D. Norred on steel guitar. [...] I bunked in with Red and Lum, R. D. usually went back home on Sunday and maybe Monday or Tuesday, whatever, until it was time for the next job. He lived in Sylacauga. Everybody else stayed at Ma Williams' House and met up with Hank for the five-day-a-week broadcast there in the afternoon on WSFA. They invited me to come on down to the station a little early because they did a little broadcast there about four o'clock in the afternoon with Hank and sometimes Audrey. Sounded ok to me, the boys all seemed friendly enough. I went on down with them. We opened up the instruments, hooked up and tuned up.

---

* Clyde "Chris" Chriswell (1929–1971), Williams's former guitarist in the Drifting Cowboys.
† The boardinghouse run by Williams's mother, Lillie Stone, although no evidence exists that it operated under this name.

Seemed like everything was going pretty well. We played a couple of steel [guitar] tunes and I joined right in. [...] We worked up two or three things before the program was ready. Audrey and Hank came in and introduced themselves around. He seemed a likeable kind of guy. Hank wanted to hear how we did on a few of his tunes so we started in. I knew I wouldn't be playing near as much guitar as Chris had but I told Hank not to expect me to play as well, but that I would do my best. Hank seemed pleased with what I did. [...]

Before long we settled into the regular routine of being ready to go down to the broadcast about three to three thirty. Go on the air at four o'clock. Leave out at four thirty and load up and be on the road by five or six, however long it took to get to where we were going, what school house, dance hall or show we were going to play in some other little town, somewhere around Montgomery. It turned out to be the regular thing for quite a while without much incident. The boys had warned me that Ma Williams wasn't the friendliest type in the world because she had been hardened by life, mostly by musicians that worked for Hank, who a lot of times didn't pay their bills without encouragement. So, she wasn't all that friendly with new ones, either. [...]

Audrey didn't make a lot of shows with us but she came into the radio station frequently and did the programs with us. She and Hank would sing a number together or maybe attempt to try a number on her own. That was rather trying on us pickers because she didn't have a good sense of timing and the pitch of her voice lacked stability. I recall one instance, we were rehearsing before the broadcast and she wanted to try a number that Hank really did not want her to sing. Audrey couldn't get it right, couldn't get the timing right, or the pitch or something. I don't remember what it was but Hank told her in disgust, "Audrey, you just can't sing! Period!" One of the band members (not me!) piped up and said, "Well, Hank, you ain't so doggone hot yourself!" It was fortunate for us, I guess, that she didn't try to sing any more often than she did. Even though later she appeared on the [Grand Ole] Opry with Hank and they did duets and even recordings together. They didn't sound too bad, but I am sure there was a lot of rehearsing went on before that ever took place. [...]

It seemed like Hank was fairly nice and friendly, but at that time he just seemed like another regular ol' hillbilly boy with the band. No big deal. As far as I was concerned it was just like playing in another band that I'd played in a dozen or so times before. I had been paid somewhat better in some of the bands that I'd worked in, or one or two of my own. But I figured things weren't all that good in Alabama. I found out later that we only made union scale for Montgomery. If we didn't have a show booked, we didn't get paid. Sometimes that was fair and sometimes that wasn't so fair, but I was there, so I stuck it out. I began to feel like maybe that was another reason Chris had left this job to get back to Tampa where he could make even better money. Some of the places we'd played around South Alabama were what I'd consider plain old juke joints but in those days if you had a job to play during the week, you were glad to get it. Since Hank didn't have to pay any of us any more for one night than he did another, he kept the remaining amount of money so he came out a little better than most of us. I guess the boss is supposed to get a little more. I found [this out] in later times when I decided that I deserved a little more because I did the booking, the phone calls, scouting for the jobs and sometimes provided the transportation for some of the guys.

The juke joints [...] in Alabama, they were called Bloody Buckets, [because] the amount of blood that sometimes spilled on any given night made you feel like there was going to be a bucket full before it was over. I recall one particular night, I don't remember the town, we were playing, probably in our second hour, when the usual redneck crowd started getting pretty happy and some boys had decided to pick a fight outside. It wasn't anything unusual to find that some of those boys carried Saturday Night Specials or other side arms. We heard them crack one or two outside. It sounded pretty close but the boys in the band were accustomed enough to that kind of carrying on, that they started heading for cover. Well, I thought it wise to do the same thing because of what they were doing. I noticed Hank put down his guitar and reach into his inside pocket and darned if he didn't have one too! He came prepared. Anyway, that particular night the closest place for Lum and his big stand up bass was the ladies restroom, so he headed for that. Got inside all right. Seemed like a couple of us got behind the piano. There was an old upright piano there, we didn't have one in our band at the time but it was sitting up there in case somebody wanted to play it, I guess. There was a little yelling going on and every now and then you'd hear a shot fired. [...] Took about thirty minutes for them to all calm down and by then the Sheriff got there and kind of settled out everything. This place was one of those that had chicken wire stretched accrossed [sic] the band stand to keep flying beer bottles from hitting the band members. We did finally encourage Lum to get out of the ladies restroom and come back up to play. We finished out the rest of the night without too much of an incident but I thought that was really something. [...]

There was always little experiences and interesting things happening. Most of the time we rode in Hank's momma's new Oldsmobile, I think it was a 1946 or 1947 Olds. Hank had a 1945 or 1946 Chevy Sedan about the same size, but he preferred to show up in a brand new looking car, so he always borrowed hers. He'd drive it down to all of the show dates, just about. I don't remember very many times that he didn't want to drive momma's new car instead of his old Chevy. But anyway, we were used to packing the instruments, amps and the old big bass in the car. That was how just about all the bands used to travel in those days. It was no big thing. The fact that we were the Hank William's Band didn't matter because all the other bands were traveling the same way, at that time. [...]

Somewhere around November of 1947, the same year I joined the band, [a] little loan was extended by Hank to all the boys in the band. He loaned each of us $30 towards new western outfits. We were kind of proud of those outfits because all Hank's bands before us just wore western clothes or anything they felt like wearing. In the pictures of the earlier bands I saw they all wore different outfits. He and Audrey got together and told us we were going to get matching outfits, take some pictures and then cut some demo records to send up to Fred Rose. He was trying to get us a spot on one of the Nashville stations. They thought if we got on a live show we could then book out of there and really get on this thing. All totaled for the shirt, a hat and a pair of western cut pants it was about $30. He ordered them, not from Nudie[5] as you might expect. In those days Nudie outfits were big among the stars but these came from Miller Stockman out in Denver where I had ordered several pieces of western clothing previously. I thought that was pretty nice. Those were the outfits that we wore on the posters of the band. We were the first band [of Williams's] that ever had matching outfits but it wasn't because we could afford anything nicer or better. It just happened that was all we could afford at the time and we felt it would make us look like a regular band, at least for the time being. So we signed a note, which I still have the original copy of the paid off note that Hank's signature is on and my signature, for $30. We all paid that off in $10 installments a month until we had him paid back. He wasn't about to get himself into debt for $120 on outfits then have some of us run off without repaying him. I guess it was just good business. [...]

Days went into weeks and weeks into months and 1948 came. One of our biggest dates I ever played during the year I was with Hank came along after we got our new outfits. He booked the Temple Theater in Birmingham for two days of shows. One of the old vaudeville type theaters that had a movie and then a stage show, then a movie and back to the stage show. I think we played three or four little shows a day. Our part was probably only twenty five to thirty minutes long. Then Friday and Saturday we got our hotel paid. One of the few times I ever crossed swords, so to speak, with Hank, was around that time because we got the feeling we knew him pretty well by

---

[5] Nudie Cohn (born Nuta Kotlyarenko) (1902–1984), famed North Hollywood, California, designer of flamboyant, rhinestone-studded western wear, popularly known as "Nudie suits"; he later designed some of Williams's most recognizable stage costumes.

then. I was about nineteen years of age, had a little experience being with the band and was feeling like maybe we were supposed to get a little more money than we got. I was kind of talking to the boys about it before we went to Birmingham. We were union men and Hank was a recording artist and a member of the Montgomery local, which was a weak union. He had a contract on this job in Birmingham Union territory and we were Montgomery, so he had to file a contract with that local. He told us, we'd get paid for a room and fifteen dollars a day for shows. Well, fifteen dollars doesn't sound like much nowadays, but back then it was pretty good money. I was talking with the boys wondering if that was all we were supposed to get, or were we supposed to get more. I mean going to Birmingham, we ought to get some pretty good money. That got their curiosity aroused and they encouraged me to call the union and ask them what the scale was in Birmingham. I went to the café and called the local secretary and told him who it was. (I should have asked if my call was confidential.) Not really thinking he would turn right around and call Hank to tell him we had called to check up on him. That was the scale and everybody was satisfied, until that afternoon at program time, three o'clock. Hank came in and he looked like he was ready to bite a nail in two, seemed to me. He called the boys out onto the front porch of Ms. Lily's [sic] [boardinghouse]. We came out there and he asked, "Who was the bright boy that called the union local to find out how much we were supposed to make at the Birmingham theater?" Well, I knew no one else was going to own up to it, so I told him it was me. I figured it was going to hit the fan now. Hank asked what was I was trying to do. I told him, "I was just trying to make sure that I was getting what was coming to me." He said, "Friend, you going to get what's coming to you, alright!" He turned and walked away. He never said much more about that but I have a feeling that it took Hank a little while to get over someone not trusting him. [...]

The season came along that we weren't doing too many school shows so Hank booked a night club out on South 31 called the 31 Club. It was one of those places that a lot of folks like to go. Hank could draw a pretty good crowd out there, so he decided to book there for a few weeks until the schools and other places got better. He was still on the wagon all the way through the time I was with him. He never touched the stuff, that I knew of. Until one night, when the Opry Show came to town. The city auditorium had Cowboy Copas and some folks from California booked in on the same package including Johnny Bond and Rufe Davis. Hank was invited, as he usually was by then, because he had become rather popular and a lot of the folks from the Opry knew him. They knew of his first big hit "Move It On Over." Hank was invited to host the show by opening up and introducing the other acts.

He told us to go ahead and play the night club and he would be back about mid-evening. He said he would bring some of the stars back to sit in and we could back them up. Along about ten o'clock or so we noticed some of the boys coming in from the show and I recognized Johnny Bond and Rufe Davis. We introduced them over the microphone and told the folks that they were in the big show downtown and that Hank would be along in a bit. We wanted to get them to do a number or two. Rufe got up and did a little comedy and then Johnny Bond and some other guys got up to sing two or three of their songs. We asked one of the boys from the other show where Hank was. I don't recall who, but he said, "The last time he saw Hank, he and Copas was backstage with two gals and a bottle." R. D. piped up, "Well, you won't see him no more for a few days." He had memories of the times when Hank would get into one of his drinking spells and knew it would take him awhile to get over it. Sure enough, we didn't see anything of Hank for several days. We kept on playing the club because we figured we could do the singing. We had a drummer when we played the night club. Towards the end of the week Audrey came out and paid us off. We didn't hear much about Hank, what happened or anything and we didn't want to stir up anything, just as long as we could keep playing our job. The owner, who was also one of the bartenders, told us he didn't think Hank would be doing much for awhile and asked us if we wanted to continue to play for the same pay. We agreed, [as] we had no other job to go to. We got together later and decided one of us needed to go and tell Hank. We found out he was in a sanitarium, drying out. That's the way they did it in those days. Monday of the next week, Red and I were chosen to break the bad news to Hank. We went up, Audrey was sitting beside the bed and Hank was sitting up in bed. We had casual greetings and then told Hank the boss was getting another band and that he offered us the job. He acted kind of surly, but he said it was alright. We wished him well and left.

We played out there a couple of weeks or so after we quit playin' for Hank. By then Red, Lum and I felt it necessary to move from Ms. Lily's. We got another room upstairs just caddy-corner from another rooming house that Ms. Lily just happened to buy. It was really strange the way it worked out. One time I was looking out the window onto McDonough Street and saw Hank just sitting in the swing. Dressed in his usual suit and hat just sitting there in the afternoon, whiling away the time, which he seemed to have a lot of about then. That is the last time I remember seeing him before leaving Montgomery.

| 57 |

Rick Bragg: Foreword to *Hank Williams: Snapshots from the Lost Highway*

The son of an abusive, alcoholic father and an overwhelmed but resolute mother, Rick Bragg (b. 1959) grew up in impoverished circumstances in the northeastern Alabama community of Possum Trot. Eventually he became a journalist, working for a series of newspapers before joining the *New York Times*, where his work earned him a Pulitzer Prize in 1996 for what judges termed his "elegantly written stories on contemporary America." In his first and most acclaimed book, the harrowing memoir *All Over but the Shoutin'* (1999), Bragg writes with pride and compassion about his parents and the hardscrabble people he grew up among. Hank Williams was a heroic figure to these men and women, as Bragg explains in the following foreword that he penned for *Hank Williams: Snapshots from the Lost Highway*, a 2001 book of photographs and documents. Bragg stresses two principal themes. One is his profound dissatisfaction with contemporary country music and what he sees as the genre's ever-increasing distance from its working-class origins. The other is also the overarching theme of this anthology—the transfiguration of Hank Williams from a mere "hillbilly" singer at the time of his death to one of the essential icons of American culture half a century later.

When he died on the way to a show on New Year's Day 1953, the Yankee newspapers called him a "hillbilly star."

He was declared dead in Oak Hill, West Virginia, but everyone knows he died in the back seat of a big sedan as it rushed along the blacktop, so there is no way to tell, really, where he died, on which mile of asphalt, in which zip code. How long did his spiritless body ride, before the car's driver shook him, to see if he was okay?

It's just one more little thing about him we will never know. We only know he was 29, which is not much life at all, and that he suffered from a back misery so intense that it left him bone white under the stage lights, and that he died in a car somewhere between a snowed-in airport [*sic*] in Knoxville and a coroner's inquest in Oak Hill, and that the greatest country music singer who ever was and probably ever will be passed into history.

SOURCE   Rick Bragg, Foreword to *Hank Williams: Snapshots from the Lost Highway*, by Colin Escott and Kira Florita (Cambridge, Mass.: Da Capo Press, 2001), 13–14. © 2001 Colin Escott. Reprinted by permission of Da Capo Press, a member of the Perseus Books Group.

A hillbilly star.

It might have been the fact he sang under a cowboy hat, or that he was from Alabama, or it might have been his spelling and pronunciation, that made them call him that. He spelled things the way they sounded, like hillbillies do, and punctuated them with sorrow, love, and regret. Like this song, which he wrote for his wife Audrey after she left him:

We met we lived and dear we loved
Then came that fatal day
The love that we felt so dear
Fade far away
To night we both are alone
And heres all that I can say
I love you still and all ways will
But thats the price we have to pay [*sic*]*

It was almost like the words poured straight out of his heart and bypassed his head, and for the people in the auditoriums that smelled of floor wax and popcorn, it was like they swirled from the microphone straight through their ears and down, down, deep into their own hearts. Heads didn't have much to do with it. Hillbillies are funny that way.

Now, almost a half-century later, he is brilliant, the music experts say. It's the same music, but the hillbilly star is now pure genius. He is a pioneer, an innovator. I guess there are just a lot more hillbillies now, in high places.

Some people like to go stand by his grave, but I never wanted to do that. That would be admitting that he is finished, that he is gone.

He is not. Hank Williams is merely dead, and that is not at all the same thing.

I am not like those Elvis fans—good people, a lot of them—who won't admit that the King is dead. I wonder, sometimes, if what they really see, when they see him at the Waffle House, the Wal-Mart or the Shriner's Pancake Breakfast, is their own heart. They wish him alive, so strongly.

It's not that way with me and Hank, with a lot of people and Hank. Hank is dead, his body is dust and bones, and he will never again walk up to a microphone, so thin and elegant in his Nashville-tailored Western suits, and sing his heart out. He is dead, free from the whiskey that wobbled him, free from the pain

---

* The scribbled song fragment, almost certainly the last Williams ever wrote, which was found on the rear floorboard of the Cadillac in which he died.

in his spine and soul, free from the demons that flogged him, free to sleep in ever-lasting peace—unless you believe in the heaven he sometimes sang about.

But gone?

Not as long as there is electricity, or dusty radios, or pawnshop guitars, or people who believe that music is a story, a story about people like them.

Like most people who sing something so true that it makes us cry, or at least makes us smile and tap our toes, he left tracks in the red dirt and black bottomland and Gulf Coast sand, and left pieces of himself in photos and scrawled-out song lyrics and faded posters of shows he performed and some he never showed up to at all. But people still don't know him, really. They have seen only specks and glimmers and slivers, maybe because his life was so short, but more likely because that is about all he lets us see. Even the very old, the ones who were alive when he sang his music at country fairs, who filled auditoriums in Montgomery and Bossier City, know little more than those of us who know his music from hearing our mommas sing his words over dish pans. And we, in turn, know only a little more than the ones who came after us, who heard his words for the first time on gleaming compact discs that have had the scratches magically lifted away.

So we are hungry for the details, for insights, maybe even for answers to why he was able to bend us the way he did, and why he did not last. We want to know little things as much as monumental things. I guess we just want to know, period. [...]

Smart people can talk about his impact on American music as a whole, and it seems like every day some guitar slinger with pink-tipped hair is saying how he feels some of his best words were influenced by Hank Williams, dude. I know he has been borrowed from just as he borrowed himself—from the bluegrass and the buck dancers and the white and black men who sang to their mules as they worked themselves half to death and sometimes all the way.

But there seems, to me, precious little of him that actually shines through in the music of the young, and that may very well be why those of us who love his music will never move on from it, and why he seems to find new fans every day among people who think music should be more than reverb and pierced belly buttons and pounding monotony.

Even among country musicians, he is as different as a rattlesnake is from a coiled garden hose. There seems no real country in it, except the hats. The women wear Versace, and sing about affairs in the summer before their boyfriend left for college. The men? All hat and no cow, most of them. One even sings about his girlfriend leaving him in a goddamned Suzuki.

I will never forget sitting in a music hall in St. Petersburg and listening as a man in a big hat, a warm-up act for Allison Krauss, took the stage and sang clichés. And then—I am not making this up—he referred to himself as *moi*.

Moi.

College.

Suzuki.

I guess some people would say it is country for the new world, the new age, but it is not country at all—it is pop music in snap pearl buttons, and it should be more than that.

It should be Hank—or at least Merle [Haggard] or Johnny Horton or Johnny Cash or Patsy Cline or George Jones or, more lately, Steve Earle. But much of what is good, today and forever, you can see Hank in it. We have to look back, all the way back to Hank, because that is where the words and the music and the talent converge for more than just mere sound—forgettable sound.

His fans, now, range from Harvard professors to New York book editors to concrete finishers and laid-off cotton mill workers. College students study his language; dropout guitar pickers, somewhere at this very moment, are picking through "I Can't Help It (If I'm Still In Love With You)" or "Lost Highway," and singing it in accents that would have made Hank smile.

I guess we can share him with them. I have no claim on him, really. He was dead before I was born. His live voice belongs to my kin, who heard him on the radio, singing and selling tonic, who paid one dollar and twenty cents to hear him sing sacred songs and pretended not to like the other ones, but they did. He belongs to my grandmother, Ava, who sang him to me, and to my momma, and to every old drunk man who ever tried to tune a guitar on the front porches of my life.

Once, marooned by an ice storm in Atlanta with a tall, redheaded woman, I played her some Hank Williams. She was from Staten Island, and I did not think it would take.

Before the ice had melted, she was singing "I'm So Lonesome I Could Cry."

| 58 |

Peter Cooper: Retracing a Ghostly Night Ride

Since the first newswire reports announced that Hank Williams had died en route to a New Year's Day 1953 show, fascination with the circumstances of his

SOURCE Peter Cooper, "Retracing a Ghostly Night Ride," *Nashville Tennessean*, January 1, 2003. © 2003, *The Tennessean*. Reprinted with permission.

death has only intensified. Exactly when and where did he pass away? Was he already dead on the night of December 31, when his apparently lifeless body was carried from his Knoxville, Tennessee, hotel room to his waiting Cadillac, or did he quietly perish in the early morning hours of January 1 somewhere on the road? What was the actual cause of his death? Where did he and his driver, eighteen-year-old Auburn University freshman Charles Carr, stop and whom did they encounter along the way, before the journey came to a tragic and abrupt end in Oak Hill, West Virginia?

In this 2003 article commemorating the fiftieth anniversary of Williams's death, *Nashville Tennessean* music correspondent Peter Cooper (b. 1970) retraces the route the two men traveled on that night. In recreating that now-mythic drive, Cooper combines Carr's account with the recollections of those who claim to have encountered the country star along the way, while noting the few buildings and landmarks still remaining half a century later. Although he manages to piece together a relatively detailed timeline of Hank Williams's last hours, at the end of his eerie pilgrimage Cooper concludes that the country star's death remains "shrouded in questions that are likely unanswerable."

Look for the ghost of Hank Williams at Edd's Grocery in Corryton, Tenn., and all you'll find is yo-yo wax, cigarettes and panty hose boxes from the disco era. Might as well comb the nearest beachfront for hockey pucks.

But the well-scuffed little store is a landmark of sorts. It's a U.S. Highway 11W slow-down point, a 66-year-old relic that's positioned just to the Knoxville side of what used to be the Skyway Drive-In Theater.

Fifty years ago, a pale blue Cadillac carrying a similarly hued, 29-year-old Hiram "Hank" Williams sped north from Knoxville, right past Edd's.

The Skyway—now intimated by a rusted sign in a weed-happy field where locals toss garbage—marks the place where a patrol officer stopped Williams' driver, a 17-year-old Auburn University freshman named Charles Carr.* The officer, Swan H. Kitts, ticketed Carr for speeding and driving recklessly. To this day, Carr denies the charges.

Either way, the man now viewed as country music's single greatest, most important and most legendary performer lay motionless through the hubbub. As Dec. 31, 1952, passed silently into the new year, Williams may have already passed, as well.

Hank Williams died in Knoxville or Bristol or Mount Hope, W. Va., or any number of other places. Maybe it was within a couple of miles from where the

---

* Charles Harold Carr (1934–2013) was actually eighteen years old at the time.

Daddy Owes Pool Hall now stands in Bean Station, Tenn., or right around where you'll see Hillbilly Auto Sales in Ghent, W. Va.

The only place he surely didn't die along twisted 11W or desolate 19 North is the place listed on his death certificate: the West Virginia town of Oak Hill.

"What difference does it make?" snaps Dr. Stuart McGehee, a historian at Bluefield, W. Va.'s Eastern Regional Coal Archives. "What does it possibly matter, other than to satisfy the obsessive people who want to know exactly where did he draw his last breath?"

Maybe the death spot doesn't matter, but the route does. Jan. 1 signifies a new year and commemorates an old, never-to-be-healed wounding.

And while Williams' native Alabama boasts its own Hank Williams Memorial Lost Highway, there is no more sorrow-bound succession than Knoxville to Blaine to Bristol to Bluefield to Princeton to Mount Hope to Oak Hill, with only *The Complete Hank Williams* boxed set for company.

"It's a tough drive, I promise you that," said Carr, who only drove it once, when he had Hank Williams for cargo if not for company. "If I had known what was going to happen, I would not have made the trip."

Stop to snap a photo of the old Skyway sign, step through brush and over a toppled toilet to get back to the car and listen to Hank sing Leon Payne's words: "*And now I'm lost / Too late to pray.*"

It's a spooky deal for sure, and not at all like a trip to Graceland.

I JUST DON'T LIKE THIS KIND OF LIVIN'

The latter part of 1952 was a strange and not altogether pleasant time to be Hank Williams.

The expiring year had brought divorce from first wife Audrey; an affair with a woman named Bobbie Jett, who became pregnant with a girl who became singer Jett Williams; the recordings of now-classics including *Jambalaya, You Win Again, Kaw-Liga* and *Your Cheatin' Heart*; his firing from the *Grand Ole Opry*; a marriage to the former Billie Jean Jones Eshliman; a continuation of physical frailties including persistent and sometimes debilitating back pain; more than enough pills and booze to derail stronger, stouter men; and a health-related leave of absence from the *Louisiana Hayride* radio show.

Williams ended the year as country music's best-selling artist, but he hoped 1953 would bring comparative peace and calm. He had moved from stressful Nashville in August, first returning home to Montgomery, Ala., then taking an apartment in Shreveport, La., and relocating again to Montgomery.

With a Dec. 31 show booked in Charleston, W. Va., and a gig the next day in Canton, Ohio, Williams stopped on Dec. 29 to see old friend Daniel Pitts Carr at Carr's Lee Street Taxi Co. It was a place of comfort and familiarity, and Hank liked to drink there.

"I had known Hank most of my life," said Charles Carr, now a 67-year-old Montgomery, Ala., businessman. "My dad looked after him before he became a star, and Hank never forgot that."

Charles agreed to chauffeur Williams to the concerts in exchange for money that would help with the next semester's tuition. On Dec. 30, after Williams took a shot of morphine to ease his back pain, the young man and the country superstar drove off in Hank's conspicuous 1952 Cadillac.

Also because of his back pain, Williams was carrying chloral hydrate, a drug intended to induce sleep. Chloral hydrate can slow the heartbeat, and things can get weird when the drug is combined with alcohol. In the movies, when a bad guy puts someone to sleep by "slipping him a Mickey," chloral hydrate is what the villain has placed in the victim's drink.

"A mixture of chloral hydrate, morphine and alcohol will more than likely bring about psychosis," said Brian Turpen, a Bedford, Ind., police captain who has conducted exhaustive research into Williams' death. "That combination is sometimes used to euthanize critically ill patients."

The two travelers made it to Birmingham that night, and the next morning they reached Knoxville.

Planning to fly to Charleston, they boarded a 3:30 p.m. plane, but poor weather conditions necessitated a boomerang flight. The fellows were back in Knoxville by 6 p.m., knowing that Williams wouldn't make his scheduled performance and figuring there was a long drive involved in making the Canton show.

(Contrary to many reports, the problem with the Charleston airport was fog, not snow. Many—even most—published accounts have Carr and Williams driving through a perilous mix of snow and ice, but Dec. 31, Jan. 1 and Jan. 2 newspapers in Knoxville, Bluefield and Charleston reported no such precipitation.)

In Knoxville, Carr checked his man into the elegant Andrew Johnson Hotel, owned by Mrs. R. J. Reynolds and known for its showy lobby and old-money clientele. By then, a reasonably normal afternoon had become a lousy evening as Hank was back to drinking. Convulsive hiccups necessitated a call to a doctor, and more morphine (two shots, along with some vitamin B-12) soon surged through Williams' blood. At some point, Hank fell to the hotel room floor.

Carr and Williams left the Andrew Johnson before 11 p.m., with the singer's cognizance in question.

"Hank Williams stayed here after a performance, and it is rumored that he died here in 1953," reads a passage in a notebook kept by the public affairs office of the Knox County school system, now located in the old hotel. That rumor stems from porters' reports that an otherwise somnambulant Williams emitted two "coughing" sounds while being carried to his Cadillac. Dead men sometimes make such sounds when being picked up.

But Carr is adamant that he spoke to Williams on a couple of occasions after Knoxville, and the Oak Hill, W. Va., mortician who handled Williams' body says the singer was neither cold nor stiff enough to have died in East Tennessee.

With no complaints from his rider, Carr pressed northward. Pulling out to pass—right past Edd's, next to the Skyway Drive-In sign, and quite near the dividing line between Knox and Grainger counties—he drew the notice of Officer Swan Kitts.

The officer pulled the Cadillac to the roadside. And for a half-century, Kitts has told people that he noticed the zonked-out Williams in the back seat, asked Carr whether the singer was dead and received assurance that Hank was under sedation, had been drinking and was certainly alive.

Kitts later came to believe that Hank had indeed died before the stop, an opinion that still angers Carr.

"Hank was asleep," Carr said. "If he was dead, what was this officer doing letting a 17-year-old [sic] ride around with a corpse?"

The Cadillac followed Kitts to the house of a justice of the peace in Blaine, where Carr says he answered "$75" when asked how much money he was carrying.

"You want to know what the fine was?" he said. "You guessed it: $75. In the police report, it said I was fined $25. I wonder what happened with that extra $50?"

All parties were made aware that Williams—the celebrated hillbilly performer—was in the back of the Caddy. Yet neither Kitts nor anyone else checked for a pulse.

BRISTOL TO BUTCHER SHOP

Ask around in the border city of Bristol, and someone will point you to the Burger Bar and tell you that's where Hank Williams ate his last meal.

But Williams' last meal was a few bites of steak at the Andrew Johnson Hotel, and he and Carr never stopped at the Burger Bar. There *was* no Burger Bar: In the early 1950s, the building housed a dry cleaners.

Carr did stop, however, at the corner of Moore and Sycamore streets, where he says he spoke briefly with a groggy Williams, bought some gas and bought a sandwich at Trayer's Restaurant, a few blocks from the spot where Jimmie Rodgers and The Carter Family recorded the 1927 "Bristol Sessions" that helped give rise to the commercial country music industry.

In Bristol, Williams might have taken a couple of the chloral hydrate pills that he had stashed for the trip and washed them down with Falstaff beer: Bottles were later found on the Cadillac's floorboard.

Some historians believe Carr obtained a relief driver, Donald Surface, in Bristol. But Carr recalls that pickup as having occurred several hours up the road, in Bluefield, W. Va. Surface hailed from Bluefield and worked at the Bluefield Cab Co., so Bristol would seem an odd embarkation spot.

Between Bristol and Bluefield, 11W falls away in favor of 19 North, and curves begin to sharpen as the elevation increases. Even when the road is clear, filthy snow hugs the winter shoulders. Pop Williams' songs into a car stereo CD player, and his sorghum-and-razor-blades voice is poorly matched to the area's ice and stone.

If Williams was still alive after Bristol, his body was under internal attack. He needed a doctor, and not for another morphine shot. Instead, he got as smooth a ride as could be had over that terrain, as the Cadillac rolled on through the dark early morning.

Bluefield was then a bustling coal town, and the Dough Boy Lunch was open all night. Carr remembers getting a sandwich and a Coke at what was likely the Dough Boy, then speaking to a cab company dispatcher who offered Donald Surface's services.

In today's Bluefield, the Dough Boy has been razed, as has the Cab Co. building. One other potential landmark, the Bluefield Sanitarium, has been torn down as well: At least one published report has Carr seeking a doctor in Bluefield at the sanitarium, trying unsuccessfully to get yet another shot for Hank.

Today, Carr says Williams was awake in Bluefield but that there was no sanitarium excursion.

"The only doctor he saw was at the hotel in Knoxville," he said.

Williams' death is regarded as one of country music's defining moments, yet the Bluefield newspaper—like many others—didn't find the news terribly important. On Jan. 2's front page, a story headlined "Voluntary Health Insurance for Aged and Ill is Urged" was played higher and bolder than was "Hank Williams, 29, Dies."

Just up the road in Princeton, the blue Caddy stopped again, probably at the Courthouse Lunch at 101 Alvis St. (it's now a bank). Carr could have let Surface off here or Surface might have continued on the doomed journey, as Carr is simply not sure what happened to the "relief driver." Surface himself died before the matter was resolved to anyone's satisfaction.

The Cadillac wound higher north, over the Bluestone River, past farms and goats and white birches that reached out as if to ensnare. The Bluestone's overpass at Spanishburg, W. Va., is now called the Hank Williams Sr. Memorial Bridge, and the Valley General Store next to it sells coffee for 35 cents.

Asked whether folks in Spanishburg ever talk of Hank Williams' last ride, Valley patron Drema Hall said: "Very seldom. But if you want a story, I'll give you a story: There's an *all-girl* butcher shop just up the road. It's just women that work there."

I'LL NEVER GET OUT OF THIS WORLD ALIVE

Algisa Bonifacio was, by her account, a silly teenager when Hank Williams' Cadillac entered Mount Hope, W. Va. Bonifacio remains in the same place she says she was that late-dawning morning: Behind the counter at Bon Bon's, a store along Mount Hope's main drag, on what used to be Highway 19.

She insists that the Caddy stopped right across the street from her, that a young driver came into Bon Bon's, and that she fixed him a lemon sour because he said: a) He had Hank Williams in the car, b) Hank wasn't feeling well, and c) Hank needed a drink. She knows that Williams was pronounced dead a few miles down the road.

"Here's one for you," she said, passing a Styrofoam cup filled with the sweet blend. "OK, don't die."

When passing through Mount Hope, Carr was monumentally exhausted and probably quite worried about the well-being of his famous passenger, but today he is certain he didn't stop at Bon Bon's.

Carr remembers continuing on toward Oak Hill, a town in which Hank had never performed, never stayed and possibly never heard of, yet which would become forever intertwined with the Hank Williams legend.

Somewhere between Mount Hope and Oak Hill, Carr says, he noticed that Williams' blanket had slid off his frame.

The driver reached back and found Williams' hand cold and stiff. Carr says this happened six miles from Oak Hill, at the side of the road. Investigating officer Howard Janney reported that it happened in the Skyline Drive-In restaurant's parking lot and that Carr talked to an employee at the Skyline. Researcher Turpen thinks it may have been at one of several gas stations closer to the heart of Mount Hope.

Wherever it was that Carr discovered Hank Williams had died, the teenager soon checked with an attendant at what he describes as "a cut-rate service station."

"There was a big heater across the glass front," Carr said. "A man at the service station came out with me and looked in the back seat and said, 'I think you've got a problem.' He was very kind, and said Oak Hill General Hospital was six miles on my left."

Here, oral remembrance and accepted history diverge again. Numerous reports have Carr driving to Oak Hill and pulling into Pete Burdette's Pure Oil station, less than a quarter-mile from the hospital. Deputy Sheriff Janney recently told a reporter with *Goldenseal* magazine that he and another officer (Orris Stamey, now dead) came to Burdette's and saw the lifeless Williams and that Janney then escorted the car down the street to the hospital.

"No, I drove straight to the hospital," Carr said. "Burdette's had nothing to do with it. I went into the back of the hospital and two interns looked at Hank and said, 'He's dead.' I said, 'Is there anything you can do for him?' They said, 'No, he's dead.' They took him, and they didn't use a stretcher. They put him on an examining table."

"I called my dad and told him what happened, and then Hank's mother called me at the hospital," Carr said. "One of the parting things she said was: 'Don't let anything happen to the car.'"

"So I gave the car keys to a law enforcement officer, and he pulled the car across the street to the funeral home. After that, Burdette allowed us to put the Cadillac in one of his bays at the Pure Oil station, so no one would mess with it."

61–6, or *THE ALABAMA WALTZ*

Enter Oak Hill today, and signs proclaim the town as the home of Marian McQuade, the lady who founded National Grandparents' Day.

But the town's only true claim to fame is its permanent place in the Hank Williams time line: "Born Sept. 17, 1923, Mt. Olive, Ala. Died Jan. 1, 1953, Oak Hill, W. Va."

In December 2002, the former Burdette's Pure Oil features a Santa's Workshop scene. Pete Burdette is gone, having killed himself out back of the place, years after taking Williams' cowboy hat from the car.

The hospital is still there, though it's undergone a makeover. And across from Santa's Workshop is the old mortuary, though undertaker Joe Tyree has long since moved his operation to another spot in town. But from the street, passers-by can glimpse the window to the upstairs room where an autopsy was performed on Williams and where Hank was prepared for his Alabama homecoming. The official cause of death was heart failure.

"I don't think he died here in Oak Hill, or in this county," Tyree said. "But he hadn't been dead for more than a couple of hours. I feel like he was alive in Bluefield."

Tyree said he never saw relief driver Donald Surface, who was mentioned in police reports as being present in Oak Hill.

Awaiting the arrivals of his father and Hank's mother, Carr was alone in a very strange place at a very bad time. He remains grateful to Tyree for comforting him.

"We tried to help Charles Carr, because he was in a peculiar situation," Tyree said. "Charles was a nice young boy. We took him to an apartment at the funeral home, and he stayed with our sons."

Tyree remembers that Carr watched New Year's Day football games at that apartment, though Carr thinks he watched at an Oak Hill city council member's home. One of those games was the Orange Bowl, in which Alabama defeated Syracuse, 61–6.

Across Alabama, folks cheered for the Crimson Tide. Many of the Tide backers didn't yet know that one of the state's favorite sons lay still in West Virginia.

"Have you seen the pictures of him at the funeral?" Tyree said. "We put that outfit on him, and we put him in that casket."

Leaving Oak Hill, a modern-day, Nashville-bound car can take one more snaky two-lane highway out of town, then hop on the interstate and make it to big-city Charleston within an hour. Then it's on to Huntington and down to Olive Hill [Kentucky], where a country music fan can start considering the bucolic birthplace of Tom T. Hall and try to stop dwelling on the hopeless final hours of Hank Williams.

Hank's death is shrouded in questions that are likely unanswerable, and the ride from Knoxville to Oak Hill consequently spurs depth of feeling, not breadth of knowledge.

Highway 11W to Highway 19 North was a pathetic, sad-sack end, but Williams' legacy is as enduring as his life was transitory. Fifty years after he exited that Cadillac, it seems likely that *Cold, Cold Heart, Hey, Good Lookin', Jambalaya* and *I'm So Lonesome I Could Cry* will be around, will be enjoyed, will be *alive* even after Bean Station, Corryton and Mount Olive crumble to history.

Curse that road. Bless this music.

~~~~~~

| 59 |

Derek McCormack: Excerpt from *The Haunted Hillbilly*

Since the publication of Babs H. Deal's 1969 novel, *High Lonesome World: The Death and Life of a Country Music Singer*, several other writers have produced fictional works that feature either Hank Williams, or, more often, a

SOURCE Derek McCormack, *The Haunted Hillbilly* (Toronto, Ont.: ECW Press, 2003), 32–36, 37–42. © Derek McCormack, 2003, from *The Haunted Hillbilly*, published by ECW Press, ISBN: 978-1-55022-610-2.

figure he inspired, as a major character. One of the most imaginative treatments appears in the campy phantasmagorical novella, *The Haunted Hillbilly*, by Canadian writer Derek McCormack. Based in Toronto, McCormack (b. 1969) has made a name for himself with a series of indie-published short story collections and novels characterized by their sparse prose, black humor, and bizarre plots. *The Haunted Hillbilly* tells the story of the rise and premature demise of a country-and-western singer named Hank, as recounted by Nudie, his gay couturier-manager who also, it turns out, is a vampire. Nudie is loosely based on flamboyant clothing designer Nudie Cohn (born Nuta Kotlyarenko; 1902–1984), who tailored garish, rhinestone-studded western suits, known as "Nudie suits," for Hank Williams, Elvis Presley, Gram Parsons, Elton John, Liberace, and a galaxy of other music and film stars.

In the novella, the Svengali-like Nudie designs Hank's gaudy stage costumes and helps launch his career on the *Grand Ole Opry*, only to then destroy him. Also making appearances in the book are Hank's spiteful wife Audrey, his new girlfriend Bobbie, his jealous rival Ernest Tubb, and a host of other *Opry* stars, along with a colony of killer bats that Nudie controls. In the following excerpt, Nudie prepares Hank for his debut on the *Opry* and then, after the singer's show-stopping performance, promptly checks him into a hospital, where he is subjected to barbaric "medical treatments" for his alcoholism and to Nudie's unimpeded sexual advances.

I knock. No answer.

It's nearly noon. I press an ear to the door. From my pocket I pull a stitch ripper. Slip it in the keyhole. Click.

I slip in. The room's a shambles. The radio's on. Hank's on it. Bedding strewn like splatter sheets.

Hank is in the bathroom. Head in the toilet. American Standard. The bowl full of gin. Bathtub full of empties. He moans. Help me. Or maybe, Audrey.

"Audrey's gone. She doesn't love you." I pop pills in his mouth.

In a flash he's up. "I'm up, I'm up."

"Get undressed."

Off comes his undershirt. His underpants. His ass round as a food dome. Smooth as silver plate.

"Put this on." I unzip a garment bag.

"Whoa." He teeters like a paper doll. "What did you do?"

"I flashed it up." The blazer's ablaze. Sleeves studded with musical bars. Staffs are sequins. Notes are glass beads. A treble clef is scores of rhinestones.

"I feel dumb." Hank sinks into his seat. His suit tears the interior.

"Remember," I say. "You're flash. If you want to be a star, you've got to dress like a star. Now what do you want?"

I steer down the alley behind the Ryman Auditorium. The Ryman used to be a church. Hank climbs out. I park by Skull's Rainbow Room.

I tune the radio to WSM. Their needle towers over Nashville.

Their needle, I think, is no match for mine.

I laugh in block letters.

Auditorium, the door says.

Hank sees: Audreytorium. He steps inside. Clodhoppers everywhere.

He passes Stringbean. Stringbean's in jeans. Roy Acuff in an off-the-rack three-piece. Hank Snow in a string tie with Navaho slide. Minnie Pearl's Minnie Pearl.

Ernest Tubb comes up. His suit's Sears. "Hey, kid," he says. "How many batteries does your suit take?" He laughs till he coughs.

Hank reaches for his boot. A flask hidden.

The Opry throbs. Pews are packed. Standees in the nosebleeds.

"We've got a real nice treat for you tonight," says Judge Roy Hay. He's in black tie. "His first time on the Grand Ole Opry. Let's give him a big down-home hand!"

Hank steps out. A gasp goes up. His suit's starry. Spotlights bend off his blazer. He sings his song. The one on his suit. About being blue.

The place goes ape. Folks hoot. Folks holler. Folks sweat. Work pants reek of dung. House-dresses cling. One-note perfumes. Radio Girl. Vogue.

In the wings the Judge gestures. "Again!" he mouths.

Hank goes again. The crowd encores again.

Nine encores later. Even the curtain is ruffled.

Where's Nudie? Hank thinks.

"Little punk," Tubb says. He storms up the alley toward Skull's. The air's staticky. His suit staticky. The seat's shiny. "Nobody upstages Ernest Tubb!"

Thunder. Lilac sheets of lightning. The night engrossing ink.

A bat makes a moustache on the moon. [...]

Hank strides through a honky-tonk. Sawdust floors. Under each table a tray of kitty litter. To puke in.

He straddles a stool. Shining. He's still in his spangly suit. "Rum and Coke," he says.

He downs it. "To the Opry!"

He gets another. "To success!" He toasts till he's toasted. Couples reel on the dance floor. Wood planks laid over horsehair. Horsehair makes wood springy.

"In the shower!" Hank yells from the shower.

I move through his room. His scarf a Q on the carpet. His suit a glittering pile. Steeped in smoke. Cigarette scorch on a sleeve. "Did you have a good night?" I say.

"Quiet." Hank comes out. Steaming. He towels off. Clothes on his bed. A new suit. Sequinned with cattle brands. The running pitchfork. The sleeping coffin. Sundry slashes. "What's this for?"

"Interviews," I say. "Everyone wants the Opry's new star. *TIME. LIFE.* And another. *Hillbilly Fan,* I believe."

"That's my favourite!"

"Good. Here are your answers."

"What?" A typed sheet. He reads. "'I'll be taking a few days off. Going to Texas. For some serious R & R.'" He looks at me. "Am I really going to Texas?"

"No," I say.

Hank's strapped to a gurney.

"Gin?" the doctor says. He shuts Hank's nostrils with a clothespin. Puts a funnel in his mouth. Pours gin.

Hank gulps, then gulps air.

The doctor's old. He looks like Alfred. Batman's butler. He unsheathes a hypodermic, fills it. Something blue. He sticks it in Hank's arm.

Hank's eyes spin. He pukes. Gin. And what remains of a western. Sandwich. Hank blacks out.

The room's private. I'm by the dresser. "Sweet dreams?"

Hank shakes his head. Or vice-versa? Teeth chatter like novelty teeth. Lips, gown, hospital bracelet—hypothermia blue.

"I brought amenities." Slippers. Bathrobe. Both bespoke.

"Thanks." Syllables shiver. "For nothing."

"The Opry will fire you if they find out you drink. Not to mention what the newspapers will do. Is that what you want?"

"No."

"You're in good hands here," I say. "Dr. Wertham pioneered aversion therapy in middle Tennessee."

"How do you feel about vodka?" the doctor says.

"Hate it," Hank says, squirming. The restraints are leather.

Dr. Wertham pours. Injects. Hank bucks. Upchucks. Vodka. Gin. Blood. A Bloody Mary. Of sorts.

Hank blacks out.

"Ouch." Hank flips onto his stomach.

"Ouch." Hank flips onto his back.

He swings his legs around. Gets out of bed. Shuffles across the room. It's dark. Slippers slap.

He flips on the bathroom light. Pees. Elbows holey as needle books. His back hurts. Pain lines pour. And his ass. It feels like something's sliding out.

Why does my ass hurt? he thinks.

"Don't," Hank says. "Please."

"Little prick." Dr. Wertham sticks him with a hypo.

Hank pukes up beer. Then blood. Then air. Then blacks out.

I step from behind a curtain.

"He's vomiting sooner," Wertham says. He rolls Hank onto his side. Takes his pulse. Stethoscopes his chest. Shakes out a thermometer.

"Allow me." I stick it in Hank's rectum. Pull it out. Lick it.

"Is he hot?" the doctor says, smiling.

"You tell me." I roll Hank over so he's facedown.

"Breathtaking, isn't it?" the doctor says. "It's the Mount Rushmore of asses."

My face is in it.

~~~~~~

| 60 |

Mark Jacobson: Hank Williams

By the beginning of the twenty-first century, scholars and writers routinely ranked Hank Williams among the most celebrated giants of American arts and letters. A case in point can be found in *American Rebels*, an anthology published by Nation Books, an independent publisher affiliated with the left-liberal weekly magazine, the *Nation*. The collection contains specially commissioned essays celebrating prominent American historical figures who stood, accord-

SOURCE   Mark Jacobson, "Hank Williams," in *American Rebels*, ed. Jack Newfield (New York: Nation Books, 2003), 23–26, 27–28. © 2004 Jack Newfield. Reprinted by permission of Nation Books, a member of the Perseus Books Group.

ing to the book's editor, as "real rebels against conformity, commercialism, racism, oligarchy, the bogus, conventional wisdom, stacked decks, and sacred cows." Among the forty-five individuals profiled is an array of intellectuals, writers, activists, and musicians, ranging from Walt Whitman, Joe Louis, and Woody Guthrie to Rachel Carson, César Chavez, and Bob Dylan.

Also garnering a chapter is Hank Williams. While other writers had defined him primarily as a blues singer, *New York Magazine* contributing editor and acclaimed writer Mark Jacobson (b. 1948) gives this idea perhaps its fullest expression to date in his provocative essay below. Casting Williams as a rebel who challenged the racial barriers of American popular music and the conservative codes of Nashville's 1950s music establishment, Jacobson offers an updated literary spin on the "Original Outlaw" and "Rock 'n' Roll Pioneer" interpretations in his efforts to claim the country star as an icon for the American Left.

It is one of those myth moments people from America, a land too new to have a pantheon of Olympian gods or a Yahweh to call its own, are so adept at manufacturing: Hank Williams, the greatest country singer of all time, dead at twenty-nine in the back of a powder blue Cadillac outside the don't-blink-or-you'll-miss-it town of Oak Hill, West Virginia. On New Year's Eve [*sic*], to boot. First they said it was a heart attack, but the fans knew better, back in 1953 and today, too. They know Hank died not only from the drinking and the ingestion of pills prescribed by bogus doctors throughout the South. He succumbed to a surfeit of myth/art, and a special knowledge of the highest American form of that particular expression, which is the blues.

A man with an instinctive grasp of the American mythscape and his place within it (he formed "Hank Williams and His Drifting Cowboys" at age thirteen while growing up in Montgomery, Alabama, a place not exactly known for its cattle drives), Hank sang the blues like no one else, fusing Jimmie Rodgers' high-register hillbilly yodel with the low-moan syncopation of black sharecropper bards like his street-singing mentor, Rufus (Tee Top [*sic*]) Payne, and the great Charley Patton. What came of it was a music without which there could have been no Elvis, and probably no Chuck Berry, which would mean no rock and roll, at least in its earliest, wildest, most miscegenated form. As Berry, who thought of himself as a bluesman and loved white hillbilly music, pushed the envelope, Hank Williams pressured from the opposite end. He was a self-designated "peckerwood," growing up in the highly segregated environs of Montgomery, Alabama (where, at age fourteen he won $15 for singing "WPA Blues" and came to be called "The Hillbilly Shakespeare"). Yet, like Eminem and thousands more, he readily boasted that he learned how to sing on the "other" side of town, i.e., the black side.

Williams did present some rather conventional complaints/tropes of bluesiana. Troubled by a congenital spina bifida condition, his back always hurt him, which made him drink. His wife, the well-lampooned Audrey Mae, whom he married at a filling station in Andalusia, Alabama, ran around and gave him grief, which made him drink more. But there is always something about a Hank Williams record which goes deeper, beyond rationality and the exhaustive scholarship accorded early and mid-twentieth-century American music. Probably the greatest folk-based American songwriter outside of Bob Dylan (who has always rated Hank "my favorite"), a singer whose falsetto whine imbues the sort of heartbreak to rival Al Green, Sam Cooke and Billie Holiday, Williams transcended the twelve-bar blues form and the particular limits of his Deep South cracker roots. It is no great stretch to say that when considering the uppermost range of blues-based artists, people like Patton, Robert Johnson, Sonny Boy Williamson, and even Louis Armstrong, Hank Williams more than holds his own, which sets up the certain-to-be-contentious argument that the greatest American bluesman might actually be a white man. Except that, as anyone who ever heard tunes like "I'll Never Get Out of This World Alive," "Cold, Cold Heart," or the nonpareil "I'm So Lonesome I Could Cry" understands, his was an artistry that, for a blessed moment, made race irrelevant.

A good number of mid-century iconic American artists died young (Charlie Parker, James Dean, and Jimi Hendrix among them), and to be sure there is a built-in romance in the early exit, the glorious, short-lived Achilles comet snuffed out in mid-streak. Possibly because he talked with a drawl and wore the kind of goofy embroidered suits which disqualified him from liberal Woody Guthrie-style art-hero status in the minds of knee-jerk Peter, Paul, and Mary-loving civil rightists, Hank Williams is rarely included in the pop gallery of e-ternally frozen youth. Cynics might contend that it was just as well that Hank didn't live long enough to see his loudmouth, modestly talented, yet huge-selling son, Hank Williams Jr. (nicknamed by his father "Little Bocephus" after a popular Grand Ole Opry ventriloquist dummy), scream "are you ready for some football?" on a thousand *Monday Night Football* broadcasts. But with Hank, we don't think of time stolen, and the hundreds of great songs he might have written if he lived to be eighty-nine like Roy Acuff, his publisher and keeper,[*] who was still paying Williams $50 a month against royalties well into his hit-making days. In retrospect, Hank never seemed young, singing to the young, even

---

[*] The author has apparently confused Roy Acuff with Fred Rose (1897–1954), his business partner, who is generally regarded as the single most influential figure in Hank Williams's musical career.

on those scratchy 1941 demos when he billed himself as "The Singing Kid." He was always too knowing, too much in touch with [the] hurting side of life both personal and spiritual, too much the bluesman. By the time he joined the Louisiana Hayride in his middle twenties, his voice already had taken on the ring of eternal authority. [...]

Yet, despite all the success and subsequent lionization, there remains an outsideness to Hank Williams, as if the testimonials to his consummate artistry and down-home soul parroted endlessly by the corporate types at Country Music Association award shows signify nothing more than lip service to an unruly ghost everyone would just as soon stay dead and buried. It figures that the insurgent non-Nashville "alt. country" movement, noting the more than passing coincidences between Hank's story and the life later played out by Kurt Cobain, has adopted Williams as its patron, harrowed saint. The mainstream world has never known what to do with Hank Williams. The Hollywood dementos got George Hamilton to play him in *Your Cheating Heart—The Hank Williams Story* [sic] for chrissakes! It is a grievous cinematic mistake that, outside of the odd Rip Torn Hank-like portrayal in the long-forgotten *Payday*,[†] has not yet been corrected.

Dead half a century—it was fifty years to the moment last New Year's Eve [sic]—Hank still sells, but he has yet to be packaged in the manner of, say, Jim Morrison, one more American music icon who died young. While Morrison remains forever sexy in his callow way, still at home on the cover of *Rolling Stone,* the picture of Hank Williams which stands out is the hair-raising shot taken of him in 1952, as he left jail, where he had landed on a drunk-and-disorderedly charge.[‡] By far the biggest star in the history of a form which was already on its way to reconfiguring itself from raucous "hillbilly" to the often sterile Nashville "hat" music of the 1990s and today, Williams had been banned from the Grand Ole Opry and many other high-paying venues for showing up drunk or not at all. Hugely famous but flat broke, he landed back in Montgomery, living in the boardinghouse run by his mother, the formidable Lily [sic], the erstwhile organ player at the Mount Olive Church, who bought Hank his first guitar at Sears [sic] for $3.50 back when he was ten. Taken 19 weeks before his death, [the] greatest of honky-tonk heroes appears in the jailhouse photo shirtless, his rib cage visible in the manner of a concentration-camp survivor, skin pulled

---

[†] A 1973 film, in which Torn plays Maury Dann, a hell-raising country singer-songwriter who seems to be modeled on Hank Williams.

[‡] Although this well-known photograph has long been presumed to date from Williams's August 17, 1952, arrest in Alexander City, Alabama, Colin Escott suspects that it was "probably taken on the occasion of an earlier arrest" of the singer there, also for being drunk and disorderly.

tight across the angular features of his face. His eyes are tormented dots, his mouth, through which passed some of America's most sublime self-knowledge, including the chill of "I'll Never Get Out of This Life [*sic*] Alive," is a sickened, horrified gash. It is as if he has seen some awful apocalyptic vision and cannot free himself from it. Then again, maybe he sees another kind of Paradise, like the one described in "I Saw the Light": "No more darkness, no more night," Williams sings, "Now I'm so happy, no sorrow in sight." Perhaps that's the reason for the look of horror on Hank's face: in a world without pain, what would he write?

| 61 |

Bob Dylan: Excerpt from *Chronicles, Volume One*

Bob Dylan is universally acknowledged as one of the towering figures in the history of American popular music, a revered and massively influential singer, songwriter, and performer. Born Robert Allen Zimmerman in Duluth, Minnesota, and raised in nearby Hibbing, Dylan (b. 1941) dabbled in rock 'n' roll as a teenager before beginning his career as a folk singer while still a student at the University of Minnesota. He dropped out of college in 1961 and moved to New York City, where he visited his ailing idol, Woody Guthrie, played the Greenwich Village folk club circuit, and soon landed a recording contract with Columbia Records. During the 1960s, Dylan wrote and recorded such songs as "Blowin' in the Wind" and "The Times They Are A-Changin'," which became anthems for the decade's progressive-minded social movements. In the half century since, he has performed in a variety of styles—rock, country, and even Christian gospel—but throughout has remained a significant musical force. In 2008, he was honored with a Special Citation from the Pulitzer Prize Board in recognition of his "profound impact on popular music and American culture, marked by lyrical compositions of extraordinary poetic power."

Dylan has repeatedly cited Hank Williams as one of his earliest and strongest influences, and he remains dedicated to perpetuating the country star's legacy. In 2001, he performed "I Can't Get You Off of My Mind" on the Williams tribute album *Timeless*, and a decade later, he organized a group of singer-songwriters to record tracks for *The Lost Notebooks of Hank Williams*, a CD project (released in conjunction with his own Egyptian Records label) on which he and the other performers created melodies and additional lyrics for song fragments that Wil-

---

SOURCE   Bob Dylan, *Chronicles, Volume One* (New York: Simon and Schuster, 2004), 49, 95–97.
© 2004 by Bob Dylan. Reprinted with the permission of Simon and Schuster, Inc. All rights reserved.

liams left behind. In this excerpt from his acclaimed 2004 memoir, *Chronicles, Volume One*, Dylan explains how he initially encountered Hank Williams's songs and what they taught him about the songwriting craft.

The songs of Woody Guthrie ruled my universe, but before that, Hank Williams had been my favorite songwriter, though I thought of him as a singer, first. [...] The first time I heard Hank he was singing on the *Grand Ole Opry*, a Saturday night radio show broadcast out of Nashville. Roy Acuff, who MC'd the program, was referred to by the announcer as "The King of Country Music." Someone would always be introduced as "the next governor of Tennessee" and the show advertised dog food and sold plans for old-age pensions. Hank sang "Move It On Over," a song about living in the doghouse and it struck me really funny. He also sang spirituals like "When God Comes and Gathers His Jewels" and "Are You Walking and a-Talking for the Lord." The sound of his voice went through me like an electric rod, and I managed to get a hold of a few of his 78s—"Baby We're Really in Love" and "Honky Tonkin'" and "Lost Highway"—and I played them endlessly.

They called him a "hillbilly singer," but I didn't know what that was. Homer and Jethro were more like what I thought a hillbilly was. Hank was no burr head. There was nothing clownish about him. Even at a young age, I identified fully with him. I didn't have to experience anything that Hank did to know what he was singing about. I'd never seen a robin weep, but could imagine it and it made me sad. When he sang "the news is out all over town," I knew what news that was, even though I didn't know. The first chance I got, I was going to go to the dance and wear out my shoes, too. I'd learn later that Hank had died in the backseat of a car on New Year's Day, kept my fingers crossed, hoped it wasn't true. But it was true. It was like a great tree had fallen. Hearing about Hank's death caught me squarely on the shoulder. The silence of outer space never seemed so loud. Intuitively I knew, though, that his voice would never drop out of sight or fade away—a voice like a beautiful horn.

Much later, I'd discover that Hank had been in tremendous pain all his life, suffered from severe spinal problems—that the pain must have been torturous. In light of that, it's all the more astonishing to hear his records. It's almost like he defied the laws of gravity. The *Luke the Drifter* record, I just about wore out. That's the one where he sings and recites parables, like the Beatitudes. I could listen to the *Luke the Drifter* record all day and drift away myself, become totally convinced in the goodness of man. When I hear Hank sing, all movement ceases. The slightest whisper seems sacrilege.

In time, I became aware that in Hank's recorded songs were the archetype rules of poetic songwriting. The architectural forms are like marble pillars and they had to be there. Even his words—all of his syllables are divided up so they make perfect mathematical sense. You can learn a lot about the structure of songwriting by listening to his records, and I listened to them a lot and had them internalized. In a few years' time, Robert Shelton, the folk and jazz critic for the *New York Times*, would review one of my performances and would say something like, "resembling a cross between a choirboy and a beatnik...he breaks all the rules in songwriting, except that of having something to say." The rules, whether Shelton knew it or not, were Hank's rules, but it wasn't like I ever meant to break them. It's just that what I was trying to express was beyond the circle.

| 62 |

John R. George: Imagining Tee-Tot: Blues, Race, and the Legend of Hank Williams

One welcome development of the increased historical interest in Hank Williams during the past two decades is the attention that scholars have begun to pay to his musical mentor, the African American musician Rufus "Tee-Tot" Payne (ca. 1884–1939), of Greenville, Alabama. Until the 2000s, biographers, relying on the memories of Williams's relatives, depicted Payne as an elderly, hunchbacked street singer who deferred to the younger Williams, while teaching him the rudiments of guitar playing and the rhythms of the blues.

In the 1990s, acting on a newfound fascination with the relationship between his father and the street singer, Hank Williams, Jr. decided to erect a monument to Payne and hired Alice K. Harp, an Alabama librarian and researcher, to locate his burial site. She not only tracked down the few public documents that mentioned Payne, but also managed to find and interview his only son, Henderson. Harp never found Payne's exact resting place, because, as she discovered, he had been buried in an unmarked grave in Montgomery's segregated Lincoln Cemetery (although the cemetery now commemorates him with both a state historical marker and a nine-foot-tall marble monument that Hank Jr. had erected). But, based upon her interviews and research, Harp offered a bold revision of Payne's life, asserting that he had lived in New Orleans during his youth, was much more refined in both his physical appearance and musical ability than previously believed, and, in fact, had commanded the respect of Greenville's white residents.

SOURCE John R. George, "Imagining Tee-Tot: Blues, Race, and the Legend of Hank Williams," *Southern Studies* 14 (Spring/Summer 2007): 33–35, 36–37, 38–45. Reprinted by permission of the Southern Studies Institute, Northwestern State University, Natchitoches, Louisiana. All rights reserved.

More important, Harp claimed that Payne, an African American man, and Williams, a white youth, had forged an "inseparable" bond akin to a father-son relationship that in many ways violated Alabama's Jim Crow conventions.

In a 2007 article published in the academic journal *Southern Studies*, John R. George addressed Harp's radical new assertions. George (b. 1965), who wrote this piece while completing his master's degree in American Studies at the University of Alabama, challenges any claim that the relationship between Williams and Payne somehow flouted contemporary racial norms. To view the much older black musician as his young white pupil's intimate friend, George concludes, represents merely another version of the "Uncle Remus" stereotype, and to consider Hank Williams as racially enlightened constitutes a myth-making exercise that seeks to burnish the country star's legend to fit modern social mores.

Legends seldom have much to do with the reality of the figure at their core; rather, they are images created and revised to suit changing times and attitudes. These images validate the legendary figure in the present-day, or the creator by association. An excellent example of this process can be seen in the mythologies of Hank Williams, one of the leading recording artists of post–World War II America. Within days of his alcohol and drug-induced death on New Year's Day, 1953, Hank Williams the Man was replaced by Hank Williams the Legend. The country music establishment forgave the personal sins for which they had admonished him in life. In death, a revised Hank Williams quickly became a gifted (if slightly troubled) "Hillbilly Shakespeare," the desired personification of country music.[1]

Hank Williams died right at the cusp of a major societal and cultural transformation; less than two years after his death, the America he had known was changing fast. *Brown v. Board* and the Montgomery Bus Boycott made institutional segregation increasingly untenable, and an emerging youth culture adopted blues-based rock 'n' roll, which quickly supplanted other forms of music in popularity. The country music industry and its freshly minted icon suffered together. The adult-themed songs of country artists, and the "hillbilly" image (with bigotry attached) were neither particularly relevant nor appealing in the new world of emerging racial awareness and rock 'n' roll. S. E. Hinton makes this evident in her classic of young adult fiction *The Outsiders* (1967), when she writes of the bucktoothed cowboy Buck Merril: "He was out of it. He dug Hank Williams—how gross can you get?"[2]

Curiously, two decades after Hinton dismissed a "corn-poney" Hank Williams, the country music legend was inducted into the Rock and Roll Hall of Fame. There had been a revision of Hank Williams in the intervening years; somehow the "Irving Berlin of the straw stack" had come to be associated with the music of the youth culture. His 1987 induction as an "early influence" (alongside bluesman Aaron "T-Bone" Walker and "jump blues" great Louis Jordan) might seem out of place; however, Elvis Presley and Bob Dylan were among the rock icons that had recorded Williams's material, and progressive country-rock artists idolized him. Willie Nelson pointed to the apparent connection between Williams's music and rock 'n' roll: "The blues. You can't miss it." And Williams's connection to the blues has *always* been cited as Rufus "Tee-Tot" Payne, an African American musician and Williams's boyhood mentor.[3]

Among Hank Williams's fans, Rufus Payne has evolved into a legend in his own right. The tale is compelling—a black man who nurtured a young white boy's musical ambition in a time and place where racial boundaries were supposedly not to be crossed. The common telling has a young Williams, enamored of Payne's music, incessantly following the street singer from corner to corner trying to learn to play the guitar. Payne eventually gave lessons to Williams, and in time the two began busking around their hometown of Greenville, Alabama—the auspicious launch of Williams's career in music.

Rufus Payne has been a persistent presence within the Hank Williams narrative from the beginning. Williams acknowledged Payne in interviews and was said to have often mentioned him on stage. The earliest sketch of Williams's life, written by his mother and Montgomery newspaper columnist Allen Rankin, credited "Tee-Tot [for] the only music lessons he ever had" and a band member wrote that Williams learned "the basic tune and lyrics of 'Lovesick Blues' [his first hit] from an old Negro named 'Tee-Tot.'" While these early biographies established Payne's place within the legend of Hank Williams, they offered no factual record of the man. For instance, the MGM biopic, *Your Cheatin' Heart* (1964) presented Payne and Williams as something of a latter-day version of Huck and Jim and began with a vividly inaccurate portrayal of Williams singing "Jesus Loves Me" as Tee-Tot dies in his arms.[4]

Roger M. Williams's *Sing a Sad Song* (1970), the first full-length critical biography of Hank Williams, marked the first published attempt at discovering who "Tee-Tot" was, including the first mention of his proper name rather than his sobriquet (even if that took the informal form of "Rufe"). Later biographers have relied very heavily on *Sing a Sad Song*, and thus it provides the foundation for much of the Tee-Tot legend. Roger Williams recounted Rufus Payne as an old, more or less itinerant, hobo that "just played and sang on the sidewalk...[for] a nickel or dime at best, in his battered hat." But Roger Williams's research on Payne was limited to white respondents, members of Hank Williams's family and other local residents who claimed to have "known" Tee-Tot. Their memories say more about the racial attitudes of that time than they do about Payne. Hank Williams's cousin, J. C. McNeil, recalled Payne as "just a good old common nigger. His hands were so long they came to his knees. All niggers got some kind of rhythm and good timin', and he sure had it." This image of an impoverished "Uncle Remus" has persisted, although more recent research offers a different picture.[5] [...]

There can be little doubt that Rufus Payne was important to Hank Williams's musical formation. Williams's own comments, as well as those [of people] close to him, bear this out—there would have been no inclination to acknowledge Payne otherwise. [...] [But] [t]here is a presumption within the Tee-Tot legend, a classic semiotic equation: rural black man plus guitar equals blues. This presumption disregards both the strong African American string band tradition and the realities of making a living through music. Black musicians had a tremendous influence on string band music, which was becoming increasingly associated with white musicians. During the early days of commercial recording, black string bands were ignored in favor of blues, a better sell for the "race" market, leaving the impression that blues was the only popular musical form among rural blacks. Though certainly declining in regard among young people, black string bands were still common in the early 1930s. Payne's age, and the make-up of his busking combo, could easily place him within that waning tradition or in the vanguard of blues and jazz. Payne was probably adept at many styles, as success as a busker required playing whatever song an audience would pay to hear. In particular, African American musicians would often craft their repertoire to appeal to white audiences, Rufus Payne certainly did: his son recalled, "My daddy [could] play blues, but he didn't like to play blues. He always wanted to make money, so he played hillbilly music. That's what he called it." J. C. McNeil, who also took lessons from Payne, remembered that he and Williams "sang and played what [Payne] did. We didn't know many songs of our own." It seems likely that what Williams learned from Payne was "hillbilly" songs, but with a strong rhythm. McNeil noted, "the main thing [that Payne pointed out to the youngsters] was keeping time." Payne is always credited with the bluesy feel of Williams's music. But the supposition that Payne was strictly a bluesman takes both him and Williams out of the context of that musically dynamic era.[6]

The nature of the relationship between Payne and Williams has also been taken out of the social context of the time and place in which they lived. Payne has appeared in all of the various media forms (film, stage, song, and especially written biography) in which Williams's story has been told. The scant documentation, lack of recordings, and absence of even a single photograph of Payne has forced biographers to rely on their own imaginations. The way that these filmmakers, playwrights, singers, and authors have imagined Payne and Williams is revealing. The earliest biographies characterized the relationship as simply that of teacher and pupil; over time, the association has been increasingly represented as much deeper, even familial.

Jay Caress, in his *Hank Williams: Country Music's Tragic King* (1979), imagined Tee-Tot as "a little gray-haired, good-natured, black man." Payne and Williams are described as "soul brothers," a trendy term from the 1960s usually implying a commonality between black men. [...] For Payne researcher Alice Harp, Tee-Tot is imagined as being "more like a father figure" for the young Williams, whose own father was absent throughout most of his childhood. She maintains that the friendship "[was a] wonderful, overlooked story of the South...they saw each other as human beings and as friends." She insists that, in spite of the segregationist customs of the period, when Payne played in the homes of whites that he went in the front door, and "it was Hank that had to use the backdoor when he went to the fancy homes, not Tee-Tot."[7]

Given what we know about the realities of race relations in the segregated South of the 1930s, there seems to be a disconnect between how those relations actually were as opposed to how biographers wish they had been. [...] Payne's son pointed out that while Payne and Williams were busking, "They would travel around to the houses, and Hank would knock on the doors since he was white, you know." It does seem very unlikely indeed that Payne would have stepped through a front door on which he could not knock. The only published quote of Payne (and that in dialect) demonstrated that he knew his "place" in segregated custom. Young Hank followed Payne around so persistently that he was worried people would think he was leading the boy astray: "Little white boss...these here white folks won't like me takin' so much keer a-you." Payne certainly was aware that any "impertinence" with whites, real or perceived, could potentially have serious consequences for a black man in the segregated South. Defining thirteen-year-old Hank and a fiftyish Tee-Tot as soul brothers denies Payne the maturity and experience of an adult. That he and a child would be on equal terms suggests the stereotype of immaturity so often applied to black males. Deeper still, this imagining of Rufus Payne makes him a one-dimensional player in the life of Hank Williams, without fullness of life. The troubles that would litter the adult Hank Williams's path to self-destruction—alcohol abuse, marital infidelity, and separation from his beloved young son—were paralleled in Payne's own life. Payne's son, who was raised in the home of his maternal grandmother, recalled that his father was unwelcome there: "My grandmother thought he and the music were just evil. It was devil's music. And they wouldn't let me play that music myself. They didn't like old Tee-Tot's drinking either." Rufus Payne was every bit as complex a person as Hank Williams, and to deny him that complexity robs him of his humanity.[8]

Hank Williams could not understand the crushing reality of being black in a white-dominated society, though he could at least empathize on some level with part of that experience—he certainly understood the mind-numbing frustration of poverty and the stinging contempt of the haves for the have-nots. But there was an essential difference, as music historian Tony Russell has succinctly pointed out, "...there was a parity in the living conditions of black and white southerners; they ate the same food, spoke substantially the same language, endured the same poverty and found relief from it in similar ways,...[but] count up the troubles of the white man and then those of the black, and the second list will always be longer by one entry."[9]

Chet Flippo's *Your Cheatin' Heart* (1981) has been the most controversial work on Hank Williams's life, with criticism centered on fictional conversations between characters—a method seen as susceptible to taking liberties with the facts. But Flippo's creative license apparently allowed more for interpretation rather than intentional fabrication; and his interpretation, more so than that of any other biographer, has put the relationship between Hank Williams and Rufus Payne within the social context of the segregated South.[10]

Two of Flippo's imagined exchanges invoke the realities of Jim Crow. The first recounts the beginning of the tutelage: "Even though [Hank] with his shoe-shine kit was lower than Tee-Tot on the economic scale, he was still a white man, even if he was only twelve years old. So he demanded that Tee-Tot teach him guitar." In the second, Flippo's Tee-Tot explains the frustration of a demanding audience that felt as though they owned the performer. "'They be making you so mad you want to take and kill 'em,' Tee-Tot had told Hank when he was just a kid and Hank had laughed: Tee-Tot was a nigger. Of course white folks would tell him what to do." The scenes demonstrate the unequal balance of power within the segregationist system—the requirement that blacks acquiesce to the demands of whites. Regardless of their own low place in a stratified economic order, the privilege of race allowed poor whites to occupy a position of authority over blacks with the expectation that their authority would be respected. Though Flippo successfully invokes the tenor of the times, his account of the beginning of the relationship isn't accurate according to Williams's recollection. In a 1952 interview, Williams said that he followed after Tee-Tot "to get him to teach me to play the git-tar. I'd give him 15¢ or whatever I could get a hold of for a lesson." Though Flippo imagined the relationship in such a way to emphasize the realities of southern society in the 1930s, relationships between blacks and poor whites were more complicated.[11]

Williams's own attitude towards African Americans reflects the complicated relationship between poor whites and poor blacks. Though there are no published direct quotations of Williams's thoughts on race, his own culturally born

biases and paradoxes can be ascertained in comments he made to one inter-
viewer, as well as [on] one of his recordings. Williams always acknowledged the
role Payne played in his musical education, at a time when that was not the
norm. He rather proudly stated that all of the musical training he ever had was
from Rufus Payne: "an old colored man in Montgomery," and nostalgically recalled "shinin' shoes, sellin' newspapers, and following this old Nigrah around."
His memory of Payne reveals a sense of admiration and affection for his mentor—but he also betrays a segregated sense of difference and separation. Payne
is, after all, not just an old musician, or just an old man; he is an "old Nigrah."
One of Williams's recitations recorded under the pseudonym "Luke the Drifter"
is told from the point of view of a white visitor at the funeral service for a black
child. "The Funeral" was adapted from a nineteenth-century poem, intended
for recitation in dialect. Part of Williams's version includes references to the
child's "curly hair" and "protudin' lips," and this description of the minister:

Rose a sad old colored preacher
From his little wooden desk
With a manner sort of awkward
And a countenance grotesque
The simplicity and shrewdness
In his Ethiopian face
Showed the wisdom and ignorance
Of a crushed, undying race

Those present when "The Funeral" was recorded recalled that at the finish
of the recitation Williams had tears in his eyes. While Williams showed some
awareness in choosing not to use dialect, and was obviously moved by the work,
he nonetheless could not—or would not—see past the cultural bias of that time
and recognize that the language itself was demeaning and racist.[12]

This is not to say that Williams was a racist in the worst sense of the word.
There is no indication that he harbored hatred toward blacks, and there is no
reason to doubt that his friendship toward Rufus Payne was not genuine. However, that friendship, like all friendships between black and white in that era,
was complicated by perceived essential difference and white superiority. Any
attempt to portray Williams as being a "visionary" on race is not conducive to
a true understanding of him or his relationship with Rufus Payne. Simply put,
Hank Williams was born, raised, and buried in the era of segregation—he was
a man of his time, not ours.

Hank Williams the Legend is, of course, of our time and not his. His induction into the Rock and Roll Hall of Fame validated him in the present; his fans

are no longer so far "out of it." Rufus Payne the (unknown) Man has emerged as Tee-Tot the Legend—secondary to that of his famous pupil—for the sole purpose of keeping Hank Williams relevant in a culture very different from the one in which he lived. Payne's tutelage and friendship provides Williams with a link to the blues (the progenitor of rock 'n' roll), and places him firmly on the right side of race, even if these connections require some imagination.

NOTES

1 See Christopher Metress, "Sing Me a Song about Ramblin' Man: Visions and Revisions of Hank Williams in Country Music," *South Atlantic Quarterly* 94 (Winter 1995): 7–27; also Richard A. Peterson, *Creating Country Music: Fabricating Authenticity* (Chicago: University of Chicago Press, 1997), 173–185.

2 S. E. Hinton, *The Outsiders* (New York: Viking Press, 1967), 66.

3 Ibid, 74; see Inductees, *Rock and Roll Hall of Fame and Museum*, <http://www.rockhall.com/hof/inductee.asp?id=142> (October 2005); Rufus Jarman, "Country Music Goes to Town," *Nation's Business* 41 (February 1953): 45; Geoff Boucher, "Before He Was Hank," *Los Angeles Times*, 3 January 2003, sec. E, p. 1.

4 Boucher, 1; Lillian S. [*sic*] Stone with Allen Rankin, *Life Story of Our Hank Williams: "The Drifting Cowboy"* [*sic*] (Montgomery: Philbert Publications, 1953), no pagination; Jerry Rivers, *Hank Williams: From Life To Legend* (Denver: Heather Enterprises, 1967), 13; *Your Cheatin' Heart*. Produced by Sam Katzman, directed by Gene Nelson. 99 min. MGM, 1964. DVD.

5 Roger M. Williams, *Sing A Sad Song: The Life of Hank Williams* (Garden City, New York: Doubleday, 1970), 25–26. Roger Williams is not related to Hank Williams.

6 See William R. Ferris, Jr., "Racial Repertoires Among Blues Performers," *Ethnomusicology* 14 (September 1970): 439; Douglas Fulmer, "String Band Traditions," *American Visions* 10 (April/May 1995): 46; Henderson Payne, in *Hank Williams: Honky Tonk Blues*. Produced by Colin Escott and Morgan Neville. 60 min. Educational Broadcasting Corporation and Nashville Public Televisions, 2004. DVD; R. Williams, 28.

7 Jay Caress, *Hank Williams: Country Music's Tragic King* (New York: Stein and Day, 1979), 22; [...] Boucher, 1; Alice K. Harp interview by author, 15 August 2005, Tuscaloosa, Alabama.

8 Boucher, 1.

9 Ibid.; R. Williams, 31; Tony Russell, *Blacks, Whites and Blues* (New York: Stein and Day, 1970), 102.

10 See George W. [Bill] Koon, *Hank Williams, So Lonesome* (Jackson: University Press of Mississippi, 2001), 130.

11 Chet Flippo, *Your Cheatin' Heart: A Biography of Hank Williams* (New York: St. Martin's Press, 1981), 24, 100; Ralph J. Gleason, "Hank Williams, Roy Acuff, and Then God!!" *Rolling Stone*, 28 June 1969, 32.

12 Gleason, 32. See Steve Goodson, "Hillbilly Humanist: Hank Williams and the Southern White Working Class," *Alabama Review* 46 (April 1993): 126–127; Colin Escott, with George Merritt and William MacEwen, *Hank Williams: The Biography* (Boston: Little, Brown, 1994), 126; Thomas L. Wilmeth, "Pictures From Life's Other Side: Southern Regionalism in Hank Williams's Luke the Drifter Recordings," in *Language Variety in the South Revisited*, edited by Cyntia [Cynthia] Bernstein, Thomas Nunnally, and Robin Sabino (Tuscaloosa: University of Alabama Press, 1997), 250–255. Goodson refers to Williams's "condescending" use of "dialect" in his recording of "The Funeral," while Wilmeth rather convincingly demonstrates that the recitation was performed in Williams's own natural vernacular.

| 63 |

Steve Earle: Excerpt from *I'll Never Get Out of This World Alive*

Grammy Award-winning alt-country singer-songwriter Steve Earle (b. 1955) rose to fame with the 1986 release of his debut album, the rockabilly-inflected million-seller *Guitar Town*, which won both critical and popular acclaim and reached No. 1 on *Billboard's* Top Country Album charts. His third album, the hard-rocking *Copperhead Road* (1988), was also a best seller. But despite his commercial success, Earle struggled with heroin and cocaine addiction, and in 1994, after being sentenced to a year in jail for drug possession, he opted instead to serve his time in a drug treatment center. Since his release, the rehabilitated Earle has devoted much of his career to documenting, through music and writing, his former self-destructive habits and his wholesale embrace of the romantic myth of the suffering, hard-living artist, one of whose archetypal figures is Hank Williams. Since the publication of his 2001 collection of semiautobiographical

---

SOURCE Steve Earle, *I'll Never Get Out of This World Alive* (Boston: Houghton Mifflin Harcourt, 2011), 20–25. (©) 2011 by Steve Earle. Reprinted by permission of Houghton Mifflin Harcourt Publishing Company. All rights reserved.

short stories, *Doghouse Roses: Stories*, Earle has also garnered a following as a fiction writer and essayist.

Earle's debut novel, *I'll Never Get Out of This World Alive*, takes its title from the Hank Williams song that was on the *Billboard* country-and-western charts at the time of Williams's death. Set in early 1960s San Antonio, Texas, where Earle grew up, the book tells the story of Joseph A. "Doc" Ebersole III, a compassionate but washed-up New Orleans-born physician in his mid-fifties. Stripped of his license to practice medicine and addicted to heroin, he now resides in a skid row boardinghouse and supports his drug habit by performing abortions for prostitutes, Mexican immigrants, and other social outcasts who inhabit the "shadow world" of the South Presa Strip. Loosely based on the medical charlatan Toby Marshall, "Doc," like his real-life counterpart, once served as Williams's personal physician. Doc was travelling with the country star in his Cadillac when he died of a drug overdose, and it was he who gave the singer the fatal shot of morphine. (For more on Marshall, see no. 21.)

Doc is now haunted by Hank Williams's surly, embittered ghost, a major character in the novel who materializes whenever Doc shoots heroin. In the following excerpt, which reveals glimpses of their dysfunctional, codependent relationship, the two bicker about the possibility that Williams is actually still alive. Like all the passages in which the ghost appears, this one is rendered in italics. Visions of Hank Williams's ghost constitute a recurring minor theme in the writings about him, but Earle gives the singer's phantom its most prominent and articulate voice to date.

Most junkies had to settle for homemade contraptions contrived from eyedroppers and rubber bands, but not Doc. His rig was a family heirloom, part of a fine old set of German-made instruments that his grandfather had given his father when he graduated from medical school. Dr. Ebersole the second had kept them unused in a glass case in his office until the proud day they were handed down to Doc. Only the syringe had survived, and at times he'd been tempted to toss it into the nearest trash can, but the truth was that Doc hadn't carried it around all these years for sentimental reasons.

In a half cc of water (the capacity of the average rig on the street), three bags of Mexican brown cooked down to the consistency of a good milk shake. Granddaddy's giant-size German behemoth held three times that amount, so Doc could load up without fear of a clogged needle and a wasted thirty-dollar shot.

Yeah, Doc liked the big shots, the kind that would kill most junkies, the kind that rattled his teeth and made him sweat and drool as he rocked back and forth on the edge of his chair. But he never fell out. He always came back at the last possible instant, blinking and sighing in resignation as he found himself back in his shit-hole room. And the ghost was always there watching him.

"You got to help me, Doc, I'm in pretty rough shape."

Doc always tries to tell himself that it's just the dope talking but that never stops him from talking back.

"I can't do nothin' for you, Hank. I told you. I'm not a doctor anymore."

"Now, Doc," the ghost admonishes in a stage whisper too thin to conceal his contempt, "we both know you weren't no doctor when I first laid eyes on you. Just another snake-oil salesman hangin' around after the show as far I knew. But I took all them potions and powders you was hawkin'. And you took my cash money, make no mistake there. But let's forget all that. That's business. Why, we're old fishin' buddies, you and me!"

Doc opens his eyes and finds the apparition perched on the edge of the spare chair in the corner, narrow shoulders hunched over as if he were racked by pain or cold. Impossibly thin, Hank is, and the straw-colored western-cut suit he's wearing hangs flat and limp on his frame as if there is nothing substantial inside to fill it out, and there's not. His silverbelly Stetson hat casts a diagonal shadow across his face, which is as pale and drawn as it was in life, and his one visible eye is hungry, expectant, one of a pair of frightened-animal eyes frozen in a perpetual, silent scream, and Doc knows better than to allow himself to look in there. He focuses his gaze a little lower and shudders as he realizes that he can easily read the house rules posted on the door through the visitor's transparent torso. There are some things about being haunted that Doc will never get used to.

"The way I remember it, Hank, you called me whenever your back hurt, you or your mama, God rest her, and I came running. Maybe I got a line wet at some point in the process but that was small consolation when it was all said and done!"

"You were always paid for the shots, Doc. In advance. Hell, I've shelled out a small fortune to quacks like you for one remedy or another. Some helped. Some didn't. You said it yourself, Doc, that you never in all your life seen nobody walkin' around with such a bad case of the spinal-whatever-it-was you called that bump on my back."

"Spina bifida, Hank. It's Latin. Means 'divided spine.' And I have no doubt that it hurt like hell when you were alive—"

"That's another thing!" the ghost hisses. "I've been thinkin', Doc. Maybe I ain't dead!"

"Oh, you're dead all right."

"Well, what if you got it wrong? I mean, I'm sittin' here talkin' to you, ain't I? Maybe this is all just a bad dream and any minute now I'm gonna wake up—"

Doc's patience collapses.

"Well, wake the fuck up then, Hank! It's about goddamn time, being that it's the summer of nineteen-sixty-fucking-three. That's ten years! Ten fucking years and God only knows how many miles and it would appear that you have, indeed, expired somewhere along the way, amigo, seeing as how you've taken to walking through

walls and exhibiting all manner of other unnatural fucking behavior. Actually, it is my own personal belief as well as my professional opinion that you are merely a figment of my fucking imagination but that hasn't deterred you from dogging my every step from Louisiana to hell and back to here, now, has it? But you're dead all right, Hank! That is, if you are who you say you are and I must say that if you ain't Hank Williams then you're his spittin' image and one thing I know for certain is that Hank Williams is dead. Deader than the proverbial doornail, don't you know, and if you're him then there ain't no fucking way that you're in any kind of physical pain, not anymore, anyway, and even if you were I'm still not sure I could bring myself to feel sorry for you. Hell, to tell you the truth there are times that I wish I had the luxury of an incurable, chronic infirmity to cry about every time I get a hankering for a shot of dope!"

The ghost stands up or maybe he simply grows like the afternoon shadow of a ramshackle church spreading across a graveyard until he looms over Doc, wagging a skeletal finger in his face.

"Now, you just hold your horses there, Doc! Maybe I'm dead and maybe I ain't, but one thing for goddamn certain is I ain't no hophead. I never took nothin' that a doctor didn't order. Never give myself a shot neither, and I always took mine in the pants pocket, not straight in the mainline like a goddamn nigger!"

Suddenly conscious of the tourniquet that still encircles his upper arm, Doc unwinds it and puts it away. As he rolls down his sleeve he rests his hand palm-down on one quivering knee, shielding tiny telltale flecks of dried blood from the phantom's view... or maybe not. If Doc can see through Hank, maybe Hank can see through him as well. He stands up and pulls on his coat.

"How many of those other doctors told you to stop drinking, Hank?"

"Oh, here we go..."

"How many times did I tell you the same goddamn thing? You weren't listening to them back then. And you're not listening to me now."

"Okay, so I drink."

"No. Actually, Hank, you don't," Doc parries.

"Maybe, sometimes I drink a lot. It ain't like I got nothin' goin' on in my life that wouldn't drive a man to drink, Doc."

"You can't drink, Hank. And you've got no life because you're dead, goddamn it!"

Hank continues to whine. "People buzzin' all around like skeeters on a hog!"

Doc sidesteps to the dresser, uncaps the bottle of pure grain alcohol there, pours two fingers into a dusty tumbler, and slams it down on the table next to Hank.

"Here you go, Hank."

The spirit begins to quiver, or maybe shimmer is a better word. Doc persists.

"What you waitin' for?"

The ghost recoils into the corner, flattening into two dimensions, twisting and writhing like a ribbon in the wind.

"Go on, Hank, have a goddamn drink!" Doc barks, and he empties the contents of the glass in the phantasm's face, but both the alcohol and the ghost instantly vaporize, leaving a sickly-sweet fume hanging in the air. [...]

"Asshole." Doc exhaled.

Epilogue

"Certainly no country hero has inspired as much contemplation of the meaning of his life and art and, yes, death, as has Hank Williams," observes Daniel Cooper in an essay accompanying the 1998 ten-CD boxed set, *The Complete Hank Williams*. So where, after more than sixty years of such contemplation and writing, does this leave the field of Hank Williams literature? We have reached a point at which Williams is now almost universally celebrated as one of the giants of twentieth-century American music. Thanks to a wealth of newspaper and magazine articles, biographies, reviews, album liner notes, tribute songs, novels, poems, Hollywood films and documentaries, scholarly studies, memoirs, television and musical tributes, and Web-shrines and blogs, we know more about him, his work, and his influence than ever before. There remains, however, significant disagreement regarding the essence of the man and his music, his place in American history and culture, and his ultimate significance. In the final summation, Williams has become an infinitely malleable figure, serving, Colin Escott has remarked, as "a blank screen onto which people projected their vision of him."

As this anthology has shown, Hank Williams has inspired a remarkably diverse and talented array of writers. Only time will tell, as we move ever further from his heyday of the early 1950s, if this fascination will persist and what paths it might take. The year 2011 alone saw the release of creative works such as director Harry Thomason's film *The Last Ride* (starring Henry Thomas as the Williams character "Hank Wells"); Steve Earle's novel *I'll Never Get Out of This World Alive*; Stephen Mertz's *Hank & Muddy: A Novel*; Don Carmichael's *The Night Hank Williams Died (A Tale of Hillbilly Redemption)*; and a German-language edition of Søren Glosimodt Mosdal's 2010 Danish graphic novel, *Lost Highway*.

Perhaps the biggest flurry of media coverage that year occurred when Columbia Records, in conjunction with Bob Dylan's Egyptian label, released *The Lost*

Notebooks of Hank Williams, a CD compilation of twelve songs that Williams left behind as lyrical fragments. The songs were completed and recorded by Dylan, Merle Haggard, Lucinda Williams, Alan Jackson, and other singer-songwriters who claim a musical kinship with the legendary country star. The album ignited a minor controversy, however, as some questioned the legitimacy of finishing Williams's work ("If you were a painter," asked Chet Flippo, "and were asked to execute a painting based on a very rudimentary fragment of sketches by Picasso, would you do that?"), while others criticized the project's line-up of artists (Williams's grandson Hank Williams III, for example, was not invited to participate).

In attracting attention and spurring debate, *The Lost Notebooks* underscores the yet-unfolding nature of Williams's story six decades after his death and suggests the manner in which future albums, exhibits, anniversaries, and controversies will likely spark additional writing about him. Expanding access to the Internet, already the site of a great deal of Hank Williams-related material, will no doubt allow countless individuals to share their interpretations of the country music star and his enduring legacy. If the contents of this anthology are any indication, Hank Williams promises to intrigue, captivate, illuminate, befuddle, and inspire indefinitely.

Acknowledgments

Our idea for *The Hank Williams Reader* originated at the 2006 International Country Music Conference, held on the campus of Belmont University, in Nashville, Tennessee. In writing and compiling this anthology over the past seven years, we benefited from the knowledge, generosity, and assistance of dozens of individuals and institutions. Unfortunately, it is impossible to thank everyone, but we wish to acknowledge the following people for their critical support: the late Keith Adkinson, James E. Akenson, Brian Alcorn, Jim Arp, Michael Bane, Wayne Bledsoe, Stephen Bock, Joey Brackner, Jay Caress, David Caron, Robin Collier, Don Cusic, Joan Dew, Colin Escott, the late Chet Flippo, Martin Gostanian, Kevin Fontenot, Margaret Gaston, John R. George, John Gilmore, Larry Gragg, the late Archie Green, Bill Koon, Jon Langford, Richard Leppert, George Lipsitz, Bill C. Malone, Greil Marcus, Barry Mazor, Neil McGinness, Douglas McPherson, Christopher Metress, John Morthland, Alanna Nash, Frankie Pennington, Joe "Penny" Pennington, Charles Pellegrin, Donald C. Polaski, Nolan Porterfield, Larry Powell, Gregory Rockwell, Arnold Rogers, Stuart Swezey, Stephen R. Tucker, Sarah Vowell, Dudley West, Ardala Wigman, Jett Williams, Tom Wilmeth, the late Charles K. Wolfe, Craig Womack, and the two anonymous manuscript reviewers for Oxford University Press. We are particularly grateful to Diane Pecknold for her invaluable comments and suggestions that significantly improved the manuscript, and to George Merritt and Brian Turpen for their generosity in sharing rare materials from their private collections. We also extend special thanks to Martha Goodson for compiling the book's index. At Oxford University Press, we had the pleasure of working with Norm Hirschy, an extraordinarily patient and thoughtful editor, and his first-rate staff, particularly Lisbeth Redfield and Joellyn M. Ausanka. Thank you for believing in us and in this project.

We are also grateful for the generous financial support of several institutions. At Missouri University of Science and Technology in Rolla, Robert W. Schwartz, vice provost for Academic Affairs, and Larry Gragg, chair of the Department of History and Political Science, graciously supported this project with subventions to help underwrite the costs of permissions. In addition, a Fall 2012 development leave that Patrick Huber received from his department helped accelerate the revision of the manuscript. At Louisiana Tech University in Ruston, Stephen Webre, chair of the History Department, supported and provided guidance for this project from the beginning, as did Ed Jacobs, now-retired dean of the Liberal Arts College. We are especially thankful to the McGinty Trust at Louisiana Tech for its financial support of this project.

We also benefited from the expertise and assistance of the staffs of the following libraries, archives, and institutions: the Country Music Hall of Fame and Museum in Nashville, Tennessee, particularly John Rumble, Michael Gray, Tina Wright, Emily Hester, and the late Bob Pinson; the Southern Folklife Collection at the University of North Carolina at Chapel Hill, particularly Steve Weiss; the Alabama Department of Archives and History in Montgomery; the Alabama Tourism Department, also in Montgomery; the Hank Williams Boyhood Home and Museum in Georgiana, Alabama; the Nashville Public Library in Nashville, Tennessee, particularly Ronnie Pugh; the Oklahoma State Archives in Oklahoma City; the Tennessee State Library and Archives in Nashville; the Margaret Herrick Library at the Academy of Motion Pictures Arts and Sciences in Beverly Hills, California; the Special Collections Department of Prescott Memorial Library at Louisiana Tech University, particularly Peggy Carter and Joyce Chandler; and the Music Library and Sound Recordings Archives at Bowling Green State University in Bowling Green, Ohio, particularly Susannah Cleveland. We are especially indebted to the librarians at Missouri S&T's Curtis Laws Wilson Library; Louisiana Tech's Prescott Memorial Library, particularly Regina Foster; and the University of West Georgia's Irvine Sullivan Ingram Library for their cheerful assistance in securing interlibrary loan materials for us.

Finally, we owe our deepest appreciation to our loved ones and family members who sustained and encouraged us through the long slog that it took to produce this anthology. Patrick Huber wishes to thank his wife, Kate Drowne, his children, Genevieve and William, and his late parents, Paul A. Huber and Mary "Midge" Huber, for their unconditional love and support during the course of this project and all his endeavors. In addition, Kate edited several drafts of this manuscript, and this book is a far superior work because of her careful eye and superb writing skills. Steve Goodson wishes to thank his unfailingly supportive wife, Martha Goodson, his inspiring son, Sam, his knowledgeable brother, Gary, and his understanding mother, Gloria. He would also like to express gratitude to his late father, Howard Goodson, the late Julia Goodson, and Barbara Goodson.

Thanks as well to his colleagues in the History Department at the University of West Georgia, and to his friend Shelly Elman. David M. Anderson wishes to thank Lesley Young for her encouragement, and Marko Maunula for his friendship, his parents, M. H. "Andy" Anderson and the late Dawn Anderson, for their love and support, and especially, Jay Coughtry, who taught him, among many other things, that the history of popular music is a serious business.

Selected Bibliography

The following bibliography is divided into historical periods that correspond to the parts of this anthology. An asterisk before a citation indicates that the item, or an excerpt from it, is reprinted herein.

PART I. "KING OF THE HILLBILLIES" (1947–1953)

"Bouncin' the Pop Bayou: 'Jambalaya' Man Makes It Again on Big-Time Charts." *Billboard*, August 30, 1952, p. 20.

*Cleghorn, William E. "Hank Williams Rides on Down Trail of National Popularity on Air Records." *Montgomery Examiner*, August 21, 1947.

*"Famous Song Composer Is Arrested Here." *Shreveport Times*, December 12, 1952.

Gleason, Ralph J. "The Rhythm Section: 'A Song Ain't Nothin' But a Story Just Wrote with Music to It.'" *San Francisco Chronicle*, June 1, 1952.

*"Gold in Them Hillbillies." Unidentified newspaper, March 10, 1951.

*"Golden Oatunes: H. Williams Clefs 22 Hillbilly Toppers." *Billboard*, October 27, 1951, p. 15.

*"Hank Has a Method: Williams Tells How and Why His Disks Click." *Billboard*, November 24, 1951, p. 22.

"Hank Williams Sued by Wife." *Nashville Tennessean*, January 11, 1952.

*"Jarman, Rufus. "Country Music Goes to Town." *Nation's Business*, February 1953, pp. 44–46, 48, 51.

*Lindeman, Edith. "Hank Williams Hillbilly Show Is Different." *Richmond (Va.) Times-Dispatch*, January 30, 1952.

*Rankin, Allen. "Rankin File: 'Cause Hank Is Moving In, Move It Over, Big Time." *Montgomery Advertiser-Alabama Journal*, April 4, 1948.

*Roe, Gene L. "Got 'Lovesick Blues'? No Sir, Not Hank Williams." *National Hillbilly News*, January–February 1950, pp. 51–52.

Soanes, Wood. "Hillbilly Hits the Jackpot after Lean Years in Youth." *Oakland (Calif.) Tribune*, July 10, 1950.

*Turnipseed, Rev. A. S. "Pulpit Echoes." *Montgomery Examiner*, December 11, 1947.

Williams, Hank, and Jimmy Rule. *Hank Williams Tells How to Write Folk and Western Music to Sell*. Nashville, Tenn.: Harpeth, 1951.

"Witness Box, The: Hank Williams." *Country Song Roundup*, June 1952, p. 7.

"WSM Drops Contract for Hank Williams." *Nashville Tennessean*, August 15, 1952.

PART II. "HANK, IT WILL NEVER BE THE SAME WITHOUT YOU"
(JANUARY–FEBRUARY 1953)

*Azbell, Joe. "Hank's Funeral Is Far Largest in All Montgomery's History." *Montgomery Advertiser*, January 5, 1953.

"E-T Officer Suspected Williams Wasn't Alive." *Knoxville News-Sentinel*, January 2, 1953.

Gehman, Nev. "Williams: Fans Clamor for Disks of Late Singer." *Billboard*, January 17, 1953, pp. 1, 25.

"Hank Williams, Folk Tune Star, Dies Suddenly." *Billboard*, January 10, 1953, pp. 13, 19.

"Heart Condition Killed Hank, Coroner's Jury Says in Report." *Montgomery Advertiser*, January 11, 1953.

"Hillbilly Star, Song Writer, Dies in Auto." *Nashville Banner*, January 1, 1953.

"In-Pouring of Tributes to Williams Continues." *Billboard*, January 31, 1953, p. 15.

Jones, Eddie. "Thousands at Rites for Hank Williams." *Nashville Banner*, January 5, 1953.

"'King of Hillbillies' Dies in Sleep in Auto." *New York Times*, January 2, 1953.

Letters to the editor. *Montgomery Advertiser*, January 7, *January 11, January 13, January 14, January 15, and *February 24, 1953.

*"Mystery Shrouds Death of Singer Hank Williams." *Knoxville Journal*, January 2, 1953.

*Rankin, Allen. "Rankin File: So Long, Hank. Hear You Later." *Montgomery Advertiser-Alabama Journal*, January 4, 1953.

Rankin, Allen. "Rankin File: The Hank Williams Tidal Wave." *Alabama Journal* (Montgomery), February 4, 1953.

"Sadly the Troubadour." *Newsweek*, January 19, 1953, p. 55.

Stone, Mrs. W. W., as told to the *Montgomery Advertiser*. "I Remember Hank as a Little Boy." *Montgomery Advertiser–Alabama Journal*, January 11, 1953.

*Teeter, H. B. "Hank Williams Had Premonition of Death." *Nashville Tennessean*, January 2, 1953.

Turnipseed, Rev. A. S. "Pulpit Echoes: Hank Williams' Appeal to Southern Masses." *Montgomery Examiner*, January 8, 1953.

PART III. "HANK WILLIAMS WON'T DIE" (1953–1964)

Ackerman, Paul. "Hank Williams Made Lasting Contribution to World Music." *Billboard*, November 7, 1964, p. 14.

Azbell, Joe. "60,000 Friends, Fans of Hank See Memorial Parade." *Montgomery Advertiser*, September 22, 1954.

Brown, Ricardo. "Court Fight Is Indicated over Estate of Williams." *Alabama Journal* (Montgomery), January 7, 1953.

Brown, Ricardo. "Widow Denies Audrey's Claim." *Alabama Journal* (Montgomery), January 10, 1953.

Brown, Ricardo, and Martha Garrett. "Hank Planned to Remarry Her in February, Former Wife Says." *Alabama Journal* (Montgomery), January 9, 1953.

"'Cold, Cold Heart' Changeover into Cold, Cold Cash." *Montgomery Advertiser*, January 5, 1955.

Churchill, Allen. "Hank Williams: The Fabulous Career of America's Saddest Troubadour." *Bold*, May 1956, pp. 46–53.

Doherty, John Stephen. "Hank Williams Won't Die." *Climax*, May 1959, pp. 8–11, 83–91.

"Fred Rose Meets Hank Williams: Wesley Recalls the Memorable Event." *Billboard*, "World of Country Music" Special Issue, November 2, 1963, pp. 31–32.

"Hank's Widow Illegally Wed." *Alabama Journal* (Montgomery), January 15, 1953.

"Hank Williams Day." *Billboard*, October 2, 1954, pp. 41–42.

"Hank Williams Died 'Poor Man.'" *Nashville Tennessean*, January 8, 1953.

"Hank Williams Immortal to Cornball Fans." *Variety*, April 29, 1953, pp. 1, 52.

"Hank Williams Tribute." *Hoedown*, January 1954, pp. 18–25.

Hentoff, Nat. Liner Notes to Hank Williams, *I'm Blue Inside*. MGM Records SE-3926. 1961.

Hutsell, James K. "Minnie Pearl Describes Hank Williams as She Knew Him in Opry." *Montgomery Advertiser*, September 5, 1954.

Kaye, Jay. "They're Still Hankerin' for Hank." *Pageant*, March 1958, pp. 94–97.

*Lamb, Charlie. Liner Notes to *Hank Williams' Greatest Hits*. MGM Records E3918. 1961.

*Linn, Ed. "The Short Life of Hank Williams." *Saga*, January 1957, pp. 8–11, 86–91.

*Mabrie, Sanford. "The Strange Life and Death of Hank Williams." *Behind the Scene*, September 1955, pp. 28–29, 47–48.

Mackey, Wayne. "Singer Given Leopard Drug." *Oklahoma City Times*, March 11, 1953.

McKee, Don. "First Wife out of Hank's Plans, Widow Declares." *Montgomery Advertiser*, January 10, 1953.

*Smith, Irene Williams. "Hank's Corner." *Country Song Roundup*, March 1955– March 1959.

"Special Hank Williams Memorial Issue." *Country Song Roundup*, June 1953, pp. 5–17.

*Stone, Mrs. W. W., with Allen Rankin. *Our Hank Williams, "The Drifting Cowboy," as Told by His Mother to Allen Rankin.* Montgomery, Ala.: Philbert Publications, 1953.

Sullivan, Phil. "Williams' Estate Left in 3-Way Tangle." *Nashville Tennessean,* January 9, 1953.

Swietnicki, Ed. "Hank Williams Legend Grows." *Montgomery Advertiser,* June 23, 1957.

*Waldron, Eli. "Country Music I.: The Death of Hank Williams." *Reporter,* May 19, 1955, pp. 35–37.

Waldron, Eli. "The Life and Death of a Country Singer." *Coronet,* January 1956, pp. 40–44.

*"Was Singer a Suicide?" *Oklahoma City Times,* March 18, 1953.

*Williams, Audrey, as told to the *Montgomery Advertiser.* "Hank's First Wife Tells Up and Downs of Marriage." *Montgomery Advertiser,* January 13, 1953.

PART IV. BRINGING THE LEGEND TO LIFE (1965–1974)

*Azbell, Joe. "No Direction Signs Exist." *Montgomery Independent,* September 12, 1968.

"Cinema: Hillbilly Shakespeare." *Time,* June 4, 1965, p. 67.

Deal, Babs H. *High Lonesome World: The Death and Life of a Country Music Singer.* New York: Doubleday, 1969.

Dodson, Lou. "A Conversation with Audrey Williams." *Country Music World,* January–February 1974, pp. 28–31, 47.

*Gleason, Ralph J. "Perspectives: Hank Williams, Roy Acuff and Then God!!" *Rolling Stone,* June 28, 1969, p. 32.

*Halberstam, David. "Hank Williams Remembered." *Look,* July 13, 1971, p. 42.

Harford, Margaret. "'Cheatin' Heart' Survives Clichés." *Los Angeles Times,* April 2, 1965.

*Malone, Bill C. *Country Music, U.S.A.: A Fifty-Year History.* Austin: University of Texas Press, 1968. 3rd rev. ed., as Bill C. Malone and Jocelyn R. Neal, *Country Music, U.S.A.* Austin: University of Texas Press, 2010.

*Moore, Thurston, ed. *Hank Williams, The Legend.* Denver, Colo.: Heather Enterprises, 1972.

Odom, Mr. and Mrs. Burton. *The Hank Williams Story.* Greenville, Ala.: Butler County Historical Association, 1974.

*Pleasants, Henry. *The Great American Popular Singers.* New York: Simon and Schuster, 1974.

Rivers, Jerry. *Hank Williams: From Life to Legend.* Denver, Colo.: Heather Enterprises, 1967. 2nd ed., n.p.: privately published, 1980.

*Rockwell, Harry E. *Beneath the Applause (A Story about Country & Western Music and Its Stars—Written by a Fan).* Chambersburg, Pa.: privately published, 1973.

Shestack, Melvin. "'The World's Not Yet Lonesome for Me.'" *Country Music,* January 1973, pp. 38–46.

*Smith, Irene Williams. "My Treasured Life with a Beloved Brother." In *Hank Williams, The Legend,* edited by Thurston Moore, 5–7. Denver, Colo.: Heather Enterprises, 1972.

*Williams, Roger M. *Sing a Sad Song: The Life of Hank Williams.* New York: Doubleday, 1970. 2nd ed., with discography by Bob Pinson. Urbana: University of Illinois Press, 1981.

PART V. SCENES FROM THE LOST HIGHWAY (1975–1984)

Arp, Jim. *The First Outlaw: Hank Williams.* Kings Mountain, N.C.: A & B Enterprises, 1979.

Ayers, Tom. "Hank Williams: The First Renegade." *Country Rambler,* September 23, 1976, pp. 21–23.

*Bane, Michael. *The Outlaws: Revolution in Country Music.* New York: Country Music Magazine Press, 1978.

*Bock, Al. *I Saw the Light: The Gospel Life of Hank Williams.* Nashville, Tenn.: Green Valley Record Store, 1977.

Campbell, Roy. "Little Skeeter's Gotta Learn." *Hustler,* March 1978, pp. 68–70, 78–80, 88–90.

Caress, Jay. *Hank Williams: Country Music's Tragic King.* New York: Stein and Day, 1979.

Chase, Jeremy. "If Hank Williams Had Lived." *Country Rhythms,* April 1982, pp. 32–33.

*Flippo, Chet. *Your Cheatin' Heart: A Biography of Hank Williams.* New York: Simon and Schuster, 1981.

Hank as We Knew Him: Memories of the Early Life of Hank Williams as Recalled by Some of Those Who Knew Him. Georgiana and Chapman, Ala.: Three Arts Club of Georgiana and Chapman, 1982.

Hickey, Dave. "Hank: The Music: 'Hank Asked the Questions and Now We Have to Live with Them.'" *Country Music,* Hank Williams Special Issue, March 1975, pp. 32–33.

Horstman, Dorothy, [comp.]. *Sing Your Heart Out, Country Boy.* New York: E. P. Dutton, 1975. 3rd rev. and expd. ed., as *Sing Your Heart Out, Country Boy: Classic Country Songs and Their Inside Stories, by the Men and Women Who Wrote Them.* Nashville, Tenn.: Vanderbilt University Press and Country Music Foundation Press, 1995.

*Horton, Billie Jean. "Fear and Loathing at Hank's Funeral." *Texas Music,* June 1976, pp. 45–47.

Hurst, John. "Ole Hank Is Still in Their Hearts." *Los Angeles Times,* November 13, 1983.

King, Larry L. "The 'Hillbilly Shakespeare' Left 'Em Sobbing in Their Beer." *TV Guide*, March 5, 1983, pp. 42–45.

Koon, George William. *Hank Williams: A Bio-Bibliography*. Westport, Conn.: Greenwood Press, 1983. Rpt. in abr. form as Bill Koon, *Hank Williams, So Lonesome*. Jackson: University Press of Mississippi, 2001.

Krishef, Robert K. *Hank Williams*. Minneapolis: Lerner, 1978.

*Marcus, Greil. *Mystery Train: Images of America in Rock 'n' Roll Music*. New York: E. P. Dutton, 1975.

Moon, Buck. "Tribute to a White Trash Saint." *Rocky Mountain Musical Express*, March 1977, p. 20.

Morris, Doug. "Hank Williams' Death Still Issue." *Knoxville Journal*, December 15, 1982.

*Pearl, Minnie, with Joan Dew. *Minnie Pearl: An Autobiography*. New York: Simon and Schuster, 1980.

Powell, Larry. "Hank Williams: Loneliness and Psychological Alienation." *Journal of Country Music* 6 (Fall 1975): 130–35.

Rumble, John W. "Fred Rose and the Development of the Nashville Music Industry, 1942–1954." Ph.D. dissertation, Vanderbilt University, 1980.

Schrader, Paul. "Eight Scenes from the Life of Hank Williams." Unproduced screenplay, 1978. The Weekly Script. http://www.weeklyscript.com/. Acc.: December 8, 2010.

*Williams, Jr., Hank, with Michael Bane. *Living Proof: An Autobiography*. New York: G. P. Putnam's Sons, 1979.

Williams, Roger M. "Hank Williams." In *Stars of Country Music: Uncle Dave Macon to Johnny Rodriguez*, edited by Bill C. Malone and Judith McCulloh, 237–54. Urbana: University of Illinois Press, 1975.

PART VI. "GONE BUT NOT FORGOTTEN BLUES" (1985–1994)

*Blaser, Kent. "'Pictures from Life's Other Side': Hank Williams, Country Music, and Popular Culture in America." *South Atlantic Quarterly* 84 (Winter 1985): 12–26.

Bolton, Joe. "Lines for Hank Williams." In *The Last Nostalgia: Poems, 1982–1990*, edited by Donald Justice, 139. Fayetteville: University of Arkansas Press, 1999.

Clendinen, Dudley. "Daughter Seeks Hank Williams's Songs and Name." *New York Times*, September 6, 1985.

Cusic, Don. *Hank Williams: The Complete Lyrics*. New York: St. Martin's Press, 1993.

Escott, Colin. Booklet Notes to *Hank Williams: The Original Singles Collection…Plus*. Three-CD boxed set. Polydor Records 847 194-2. 1990.

*Escott, Colin, with George Merritt and William MacEwen. *Hank Williams: The Biography*. Boston: Little, Brown, 1994. Rev. ed. Boston: Little, Brown, 2004.

Friedman, Kinky. *A Case of Lone Star*. New York: William Morrow, 1987.

Goodson, Steve. "Hillbilly Humanist: Hank Williams and the Southern White Working Class." *Alabama Review* 46 (April 1993): 104–36.

Graves, Kay Williams. "A Piece of Hank." *Atlanta Journal-Constitution*, September 13, 1992.

Green, Ann. "Hank's Grave." *Alabama Journal* (Montgomery), December 1, 1987.

Greenhaw, Wayne. *King of Country: A Novel*. Montgomery, Ala.: Black Belt Press, 1994.

Hilburn, Robert. "The 'Hillbilly Shakespeare' Gets His Due." *Los Angeles Times*, January 5, 1991.

*Leppert, Richard, and George Lipsitz. "'Everybody's Lonesome for Somebody': Age, the Body and Experience in the Music of Hank Williams." *Popular Music* 9 (October 1990): 259–74.

Malone, Bill C. "Hank Williams: Stardom Beyond the Sunset." *Journal of the American Academy for the Preservation of Old-Time Country Music* 2 (February 1992): 9–11.

*McPherson, Douglas. "Sex, Drugs and Country Music: A Profile of Hank Williams, America's Darkest Legend." *Country Music People*, December 1992, pp. 48–50.

Moffeit, Tony. *The Spider Who Walked Underground*. Erie, Penn.: Kangaroo Court, 1985.

Moses, Mark. "Randy, Reba, and Hank." *New Yorker*, May 9, 1988, pp. 110–15.

Palmer, Robert. "The Pop Life: The Artistry of Early Hank Williams." *New York Times*, September 17, 1986.

*Porterfield, Nolan. "The Day Hank Williams Died: Cultural Collisions in Country Music." In *America's Musical Pulse: Popular Music in Twentieth-Century Society*, edited by Kenneth J. Bindas, 175–83. Westport, Conn.: Greenwood Press, 1992.

Rogers, Arnold, and Bruce Gidoll. *The Life and Times of Hank Williams*. Nashville, Tenn.: Haney-Jones Books, 1993.

Smith, Irene Williams. "The Day Hank Williams Lived." *Washington Post*, December 27, 1992.

*Smith, Lee. Review of Don Cusic, *Hank Williams: The Complete Lyrics*. In *Journal of Country Music* 16 (1993): 58–59.

Sutton, Juanealya McCormick. *The Man Behind the Scenes: Neal (Pappy) McCormick and Hank Williams*. DeFuniak Spring, Fla.: privately published, 1987.

Tosches, Nick. "Ernest Tubb, Hank Williams, and the Bartender's Muse." In *Country: The Music and the Musicians*, edited by Paul Kingsbury and Alan Axelrod, 222–55. New York: Abbeville Press, 1988.

*Williams, Jett, with Pamela Thomas. *Ain't Nothin' as Sweet as My Baby: The Story of Hank Williams' Lost Daughter.* New York: Harcourt Brace Jovanovich, 1990. Rpt. Jett Williams, with Keith Adkinson and Pamela Thomas, *Lost & Found: The Story of Hank Williams' Daughter.* Hartsville, Tenn.: Adjett Productions, 2009.

Williams, Lycrecia, with Dale Vinicur. *Still in Love with You: The Story of Hank and Audrey Williams.* Nashville, Tenn.: Rutledge Hill Press, 1989.

Wilson, Charles Reagan. "The Death of Southern Heroes: Historic Funerals of the South." *Southern Cultures* 1 (Fall 1994): 3–22.

PART VII. OUR HANK WILLIAMS (1995–2013)

Anderson, David, and Patrick Huber. "'The Log Train': Hank Williams's Last Recorded Song." *Tributaries: Journal of the Alabama Folklife Association* 2 (Spring 1999): 9–39.

Applewhite, James. "Hank Williams Dream." *Southern Review* 38 (Spring 2002): 219–20.

Beck. "74: Hank Williams." In "The Immortals: The 100 Greatest Artists of All Time." *Rolling Stone,* April 21, 2005, p. 82.

Boucher, Geoff. "Before He Was Hank." *Los Angeles Times,* January 3, 2003.

Boucher, Geoff. "Honky-Tonk Poet." *Smithsonian,* January 2003, pp. 96–103.

Brackett, David. *Interpreting Popular Music.* Cambridge: Cambridge University Press, 1995.

*Bragg, Rick. Foreword to *Hank Williams: Snapshots from the Lost Highway,* by Colin Escott and Kira Florita, 13–14. Cambridge, Mass.: Da Capo Press, 2001.

Bragg, Rick. "I Thought He Lived in Our House." Introduction to Liner Notes to *Hank Williams: Live at the Grand Ole Opry.* Two-CD boxed set. Mercury Records 314-546 466-2. 1999.

Brumback, Kate. "Rediscover Country Music along Alabama's Hank Williams Trail." *USA Today,* October 23, 2006.

Carmichael, Don. *The Night Hank Williams Died (A Tale of Hillbilly Redemption).* N.p.: privately published, 2011.

Chase, Jefferson. "Lonesome Whistle." *Boston Sunday Globe,* December 29, 2002.

Ching, Barbara. *Wrong's What I Do Best: Hard Country and Contemporary Culture.* New York: Oxford University Press, 2001.

Cooper, Daniel. "No More Darkness, No More Night." In *The Stories: The Complete Hank Williams.* Book notes to *The Complete Hank Williams.* Ten-CD boxed set. Mercury Records 314 536 077-2. 1998.

*Cooper, Peter. "Retracing a Ghostly Night Ride." *Nashville Tennessean,* January 1, 2003.

Derbyshire, John. "The Old Weird America: Appreciating Hank Williams." *National Review Online*, January 29, 2003. http://www.nationalreview.com/articles/205685/old-weird-america/john-derbyshire. Acc.: October 30, 2010.

Diehl, Matt. "Hank Williams, Country's Unknowable Heart." *Washington Post*, September 25, 1999.

*Dylan, Bob. *Chronicles, Volume One*. New York: Simon and Schuster, 2004.

*Earle, Steve. *I'll Never Get Out of This World Alive*. Boston: Houghton Mifflin Harcourt, 2011.

Egan, Peter. "Hank's Last Drive." *Road & Track*, April 2008, pp. 94–96, 98, 100, and May 2008, pp. 92–94, 96, 99–100.

Escott, Colin. "Notes on the Music." In *The Stories: The Complete Hank Williams*. Book notes to *The Complete Hank Williams*. Ten-CD boxed set. Mercury Records 314 536 077-2. 1998.

*Escott, Colin, and Kira Florita. *Hank Williams: Snapshots from the Lost Highway*. Cambridge, Mass.: Da Capo Press, 2001.

Fahey, John. *How Bluegrass Destroyed My Life*. Chicago: Drag City, 2000.

Fillingim, David. "All I Need to Know I Learned from Hank Williams: Ethics Lessons from Country Music." *Sojourners*, March–April 2000, p. 14.

Friedman, Kinky. *Roadkill*. New York: Simon and Schuster, 1997.

Friedman, Kinky. *'Scuse Me While I Whip This Out*. New York: William Morrow, 2004.

Friskics-Warren, Bill. "Family Tradition." *New York Times*, October 30, 2008.

Fu, Yun-Cheng. "The Musical Style of Hank Williams (1923–1953)." Ph.D. dissertation, University of Memphis, 2004.

*George, John R. "Imagining Tee-Tot: Blues, Race, and the Legend of Hank Williams." *Southern Studies* 14 (Spring–Summer 2007): 33–45.

*Gerald, Teddy. "Hank Williams Sr. Is Alive!" *Weekly World News*, February 14, 1995.

*Gilmore, John. *Laid Bare: A Memoir of Wrecked Lives and the Hollywood Death Trip*. Los Angeles: Amok Books, 1997.

Harp, Alice K. "Rufus Payne: Teacher/Mentor/Friend to Hank Williams, the Child." *Hank Williams Fanzine*, September 2000, pp. 40–43.

Helms, Don, as told to Dale Vinicur. *Settin' the Wood on Fire (Confessions of Hank's Steel Guitar Player)*. Nashville, Tenn.: Audrey's Dream, 2005.

Hemphill, Paul. *Lovesick Blues: The Life of Hank Williams*. New York: Viking, 2005.

Hoover, Lycrecia Williams, and Dale Vinicur, eds. *"Dear Mama Williams": Sympathy Cards and Letters to the Hank Williams Family*. Nashville, Tenn.: Audrey's Dream, 2004.

Horn, Elizabeth A. "Poetic Organization and Poetic License in the Lyrics of

Hank Williams, Sr. and Snoop Dogg." Ph.D. dissertation, University of Texas at Austin, 2010.

Humphrey, Mark A. "Hillbilly Heaven." *Guitar World Acoustic* 29 (1998): 27–28, 30, 32, 34, 88–89.

*Jacobson, Mark. "Hank Williams." In *American Rebels*, edited by Jack Newfield, 23–28. New York: Nation Books, 2003.

Johnson, Rheta Grimsley. *Hank Hung the Moon...and Warmed Our Cold, Cold Hearts*. Montgomery, Ala.: NewSouth Books, 2012.

Jones, Tim, with Harold McAlindon and Richard Courtney. *The Essential Hank Williams: A Special Book, about a Very Special Man, Written for His Special Fans*. Nashville, Tenn.: Eggman, 1996.

Keillor, Garrison. "Long Gone Daddy." *New York Times*, September 25, 2005.

Kistler, Maura. "'I Won't Be Home No More': The Death of Hank Williams." *Goldenseal* 28 (Winter 2002): 54–63.

Lewis, Randy. "'Lost Notebooks of Hank Williams' Finds Good Company in Bob Dylan." *Los Angeles Times*, October 2, 2011.

Light, Alan. "Stars Add New Tunes to Country King's Lyrics." *New York Times*, September 23, 2011.

Logan, Horace, with Bill Sloan. *Elvis, Hank, and Me: Making Musical History on the Louisiana Hayride*. New York: St. Martin's Press, 1998. Rpt. as *Louisiana Hayride Years: Making Musical History in Country's Golden Age*. New York: St. Martin's Press, 1999.

MacPhail, Paul. *Hank Williams: From the Cradle to the Grave*. Stratford, Prince Edward Island, Can.: privately published, 2011.

Masino, Susan. *Family Tradition: Three Generations of Hank Williams*. Montclair, N.J.: Backbeat Books, 2011.

Maze, Steve A. *Hank Williams and His Drifting Cowboys*. Arab, Ala.: privately published, 2004.

Maze, Steve A. *Hankin' Around*. Arab, Ala. Yesterday's Memories Magazine, 2006.

*McCormack, Derek. *The Haunted Hillbilly*. Toronto, Ont.: ECW Press, 2003.

*Metress, Christopher. "Sing Me a Song about Ramblin' Man: Visions and Revisions of Hank Williams in Country Music." In *Readin' Country Music: Steel Guitars, Opry Stars, and Honky Tonk Bars*, edited by Cecelia Tichi, 7–27. Special Issue of *South Atlantic Quarterly* 94 (Winter 1995): 7–27.

Moore, Ralph. *The Death of Hank Williams: The Mystery of His Final Journey*. Rev. ed. N.p.: privately published, 2003.

Myler, Randal, and Mark Harelik. *Hank Williams: Lost Highway*. New York: Dramatists Play Service, 2004.

O'Quinn, Beecher, Jr. *The Story Behind the Hank Williams Commemorative Stamp*. Wautauga, Tenn: McKinnis Books, 2005.

Papanikolas, Zeese. *American Silence*. Lincoln: University of Nebraska Press, 2007.

*Pennington, Joe "Penny." *Lookin' Back on Hank: Some Things You Never Knew about the Legendary Hank Williams*. N.p.: privately published, 1999.

Peterson, Richard A. *Creating Country Music: Fabricating Authenticity*. Chicago: University of Chicago Press, 1997.

Piazza, Tom. "Still Standing Tall Over Country." *New York Times*, November 8, 1998.

Russell, Rusty. "American Songcraft: Hank Williams—Lessons from the Lost Highway." *Guitar Player*, November 1996, pp. 47–50, 52, 54.

Turpen, Brian. *Ramblin' Man: Short Stories from the Life of Hank Williams*. Many, La.: Old Paths, New Dreams, 2007.

Turpen, Brian, and Robert Gentry. *Hank Williams & Billie Jean Jones: A Country Music Wedding Extravaganza*. Many, La.: Old Paths, New Dreams, 2010.

Underwood, Ryan. "A Not-So-Lonesome Hank Revealed." *Nashville Tennessean*, October 5, 2006.

Vandermeer, Philip R. "Religious Ideals, Musical Style, and Cultural Meaning in the Gospel Songs of Hank Williams." Ph.D. dissertation, University of Maryland, 1999.

"Was Hank's Death a Homicide?" *Club Jett Newsletter* (Jett Williams Fan Club), January 2012, pp. 6–9. http://www.jettwilliams.com/club-jett/. Acc.: January 23, 2012.

Waugh, John. *A Hank Williams Journal* (blog). http://ahankwilliamsjournal. wordpress.com/. Acc.: October 30, 2011.

Wilmeth, Thomas L. " 'Pictures from Life's Other Side': Southern Regionalism in Hank Williams's Luke the Drifter Recordings." In *Language Variety in the South Revisited*, edited by Cynthia Bernstein, Thomas Nunnally, and Robin Sabino, 250–55. Tuscaloosa: University of Alabama Press, 1997.

Wilmeth, Thomas L. "Textual Problems within the Canon of Hank Williams." *Papers of the Bibliographical Society of America* 93 (September 1999): 379–406.

*Womack, Craig. "Howling at the Moon: The Queer But True Story of My Life as a Hank Williams Song." In *As We Are Now: Mixblood Essays on Race and Identity*, edited by William S. Penn, 28–49. Berkeley: University of California Press, 1997.

Woodroof, Martha. "Sharing Demons with Hank Williams." *New York Times Sunday Magazine*, August 15, 2010, p. MM50.

Index

782.421642 WILLIAMS

**The Hank Williams
reader**

SOF

R4002321444

SOUTH FULTON BRANCH
Atlanta-Fulton Public Library